Necessary Theater

Six Plays About
the Chicano Experience

Compiled by and with introductions and
commentaries

by

Jorge Huerta

Arte Publico Press
Houston

Necessary Theatre. Six Plays about the Chicano Experience is made possible through support from the Ford Foundation and the National Endowment for the Arts.

Arte Publico Press
University of Houston
Houston, Texas 77204-2090

Necessary Theatre: Six Plays about the Chicano Experience /
edited by Jorge Huerta.
p. cm.
ISBN 0-934770-95-6 :
1. Mexican Americans—Drama. 2. American drama—Mexican
American authors. 3. American drama—20th century. I.
Huerta, Jorge A.
PS628.M4N4 1989   89-283
812'.54'080352036872073—dc19   CIP

Each individual play is copyrighted by its author.

The paper used in this publication meets the minimum
requirements of the American National Standard for
Permanence of Paper for Printed Library Materials Z39.48-1984.

Copyright © 1989 Arte Publico Press

Printed in the United States of America

Contents

Introduction   5

Soldierboy
  by Judith and Severo Pérez   18

Latina
  by Milcha Sánchez-Scott and Jeremy Blahnik   76

The Shrunken Head of Pancho Villa
  by Luis Valdez   142

Guadalupe
  by El Teatro de la Esperanza   208

Money
  by Arthur Girón   258

La víctima
  by El Teatro de la Esperanza   316

Bibliography   366

Introduction

Art, it is said, is essential in a civilized society. If art is essential, then Chicano theater has been more than essential, it has been a vital proclamation of the Chicanos' identity, their very existence, within the broader context of North American society. Since the inception of what can be termed the Chicano theater movement, initiated by Luis Valdez and the Teatro Campesino in 1965, Chicano theater has been a necessary theater. Brought forth out of the farmworker's struggle, Valdez's troupe defined the initial direction of the movement that was to follow: a network of grassroots teatros that educated their audiences by dramatizing the politics of survival.

If Chicano theater was necessary in its early stages as an educational tool, it is equally important today, as evidenced in the six plays published here. Through a variety of styles, spanning a period of twenty-four years, these plays serve as historical documents and living examples of a necessary theater; they are expressions of the Chicanos' continuing struggle for cultural, linguistic, economic, spiritual and political survival. Every one of these plays is just as valid today as when it was first produced.

All theater should be necessary; otherwise, why bother to produce it? Like the theater of ancient Greece, the dramatic expressions of the Mesoamerican cultures were born out of ritual—ceremonies that were essential to the well-being of the communities from which they emerged. Sometimes the ritual combined human sacrifice in a cosmic drama that embodied in action what Christianity has taught us to re-enact in symbolism. In either case, whether symbolic ritual or actual sacrifice, the rite has always seemed a necessary part of the daily struggle for survival, both spiritual and earthly.[1]

Anthropologists tell us that indigenous peoples have always needed ritual, and contemporary urban Chicanos, though no longer tied to the earth, are no different. Certainly, the Chicano/Mexicano farmworkers who attempted to break-out of a long history of oppression in 1965 understood the ritual of the seasons and what each represented in terms of sustenance. Like their indigenous ancestors, campesinos know the course of the sun. Perhaps this understanding of the power of the elements brings farmworkers closer to their ancient ancestors. Farmworkers also know about the strength of the spirit and it was no coincidence that César Chávez's followers marched (and continue to march) behind the banner of the Virgen de Guadalupe, the Brown Virgin, national symbol of the Mexicanos' indigenous identity.

5

For generations prior to 1965, Chicano theatrical expression varied from the spiritual to the secular; it was produced in churches and community centers, as well as in legitimate theaters and union halls.[2] Performed mainly in Spanish, for barrio audiences, these plays instilled a sense of pride and history in the participants and the observers. The events were infused with the ritual of theater and a vital sense of cultural identity crucial to any immigrant group.[3]

During the 1930's, anthropologists and theater historians discovered Spanish religious folk theater in the Southwest and recognized the importance of the plays to the people who participated in them as audience and actor.[4] The sense of spiritual necessity permeated those early pageants, informed more by spirit than "art." Like the ancient ritual-dramas that had preceeded them, these plays brought the community together, spiritually, culturally and linguistically. Everyone in the audience could feel the joy of Christ's birth at Christmas-time, and all could weep at the re-enactment of the Passion of the Savior in the spring. They still do.[5]

But when César Chávez gave impetus and meaning to the farmworker struggle and Luis Valdez joined forces with this effort and created a vital theater years later, observers were moved by the fact that these people were not actors, but real farmworkers involved in a struggle for their lives. Further, these were Mexicans and Chicanos, representatives of an "invisible minority" that was no longer satisfied with second-class status. The spiritual necessity of the early theater was supplanted by the socio-political urgency of the 1960's. Because they have been second-class citizens since the beginning of Anglo domination, Chicanos have had to struggle with a variety of issues, thus creating an air of urgency that has also defined their theater.

When Luis Valdez decided to form a farmworker's theater, there were no anthologies of Chicano plays for him to read, no histories of Mexican-American theater that he could study. There were the above cited articles about Spanish religious folk theatre hidden away in libraries, but little or nothing about other types of theatrical expression could be found beyond articles published in Spanish-language newspapers prior to the 1930's.[6] Those newspapers were scattered in archives throughout the Southwest and not readily available. But finding and reading those articles and reviews would not have helped Valdez in 1965, for his need was immediate and necessary, based on a continuing crisis. Thus he and his troupe collectively created what he termed "actos," brief sketches designed to educate and entertain, exposing issues and offering possible solutions.

Following the Teatro Campesino's example, other Chicano theater troupes began to emerge, mostly student-based, that had been influenced by the extremely effective actos. Many of these incipient teatros began by emulating the Teatro Campesino's actos. The farm labor struggle remained an important issue, but the Teatro Campesino and the emerging groups began to explore other themes relevant to their audiences, such as the war in Vietnam and the war at home: the battle against inadequate schooling, violence, drugs, poverty and police brutality in the barrios. Mainly creating collectively, the teatros began to demonstrate a world beyond the agricultural fields of California.[7]

From community-based troupes to student theaters, the different Chicano theater companies reflected the diversity of their audiences. Themes varied according to the circumstances, but a relative constant was the overriding sense of "us against them": Chicanos in some sort of struggle against societal forces, usually represented by unsympathetic Mexican-American or Anglo bosses, teachers, police or judges. The threat to the family as workers or students, young or old, remained a constant.

For many of the Chicanos politically active in the 1970's, it was a period of Mexican nationalism and a symbolic negation of U.S. citizenship—a time when Chicanos said, "This is not my country, I am not responsible for the carnage in Vietnam or Yankee imperialism in the Third World." In effect, many Chicanos became self-marginalized, seeking their cultural alliance with Mexico rather than the country of their birth. And many teatros expressed these sentiments through their productions. The plays and actos became declarations of independence from a system that had excluded them, anyway.

During this period, the vitality of the actos and the urgency of the situation negated the kind of critical assessment due most theater companies. Indeed, the majority of teatros were totally uninterested in what theater critics had to say (if they said anything at all), for their purpose was not determined by box office revenue. There was no attempt to be classified as "professional" by any of the teatros for several years during which politics came before economics. Also, because many of the actos were collectively created, there were few individuals on which to focus aside from Luis Valdez, who remained the most visible playwright/director.

But when Valdez made the decision to write and direct *Zoot Suit*, he introduced a new era of professionalism for himself and other Chicano theater artists. *Zoot Suit* employed more Chicanos and Chicanas in a professional theater than any other production before it in contemporary times. By calling *Zoot Suit* "an American play," Valdez was initiating an attempt to enter the mainstream; it meant an end to the idea that the United States was not the Chicanos' country too.[8] Valdez said it best when he repudiated the "wetback" theory by writing, "We did not, in fact, come to the United States at all. The United States came to us."[9] Valdez and others began to reevaluate their marginalization and to see themselves as necessary infiltrators, getting into the system in order to exploit it for their own artistic and political ends.

Today, there is a move towards more professionalism as Chicano actors, directors, designers, dramaturgs, technicians and playwrights attempt to earn a living in the theater. Community-based teatros still exist, independently or connected to cultural or political organizations, and they serve a continuing need in their respective communities. However, the majority of the people involved in these groups have other jobs outside of theater and these commitments usually hinder their growth as artists. Other individuals wishing to make a different statement have studied theater formally and are working with professional Chicano/Hispanic theaters as well as regional theaters with Hispanic projects.[10]

The move towards a more professional form of Chicano theater was inevitable. Some of the artists involved in the movement realized that their teatros were performing only for the initiated—a noble cause, but one limited in its outreach. For some, this awareness precipitated a serious attempt to raise their artistic principles; it recognized that their audiences deserved a higher standard of performance. Surrounding this evolution, however, was a period of political apathy.

The political climate had changed drastically during the Reagan years, leaving teatros with no broad political cause on which to attach themselves, despite the fact that conditions were not getting better for large segments of the Chicano community. Perhaps inevitably, the political organizations had become hopelessly factionalized and the sense of a national "movement" no longer prevailed. However, this political confusion did not deter some teatros and playwrights from continuing to create theater that would have lasting value. The plays in this collection are proof that even as their creators worked towards a more professional theater, their commitment to a necessary theater did not wane.

The arenas in which one finds Chicano theater today are quite different from the early venues of fields, streets and community halls, but they are no less important. The urgency that informed the farmworker actos is still there, but the conditions have changed. A few groups have had to court the growing middle-class Hispanic population in order to survive economically, following in the footsteps of the regional theater movement.[11]

By moving towards a more affluent community, the professionally-oriented theater groups are changing their relationship to their public in order to ensure that they will have a place in which to work in the future. After years of calling for economic survival for other Chicanos, these same artists are fighting for their survival as artists. All of the plays in this collection have provided some income, however modest, for the artists involved in their production.[12]

This is not the first anthology of Chicano plays to be published.[13] What distinguishes this collection from the others, however, is that each of the plays in this volume has been successfully produced by a professional company. Further, with the exception of the first play, none of the works have previously been available in print.[14] These plays have reached a variety of audiences in a broad spectrum of settings, including universities, community theaters and professional houses. And although two of the authors represented are not specifically of Mexican heritage, their plays deal with the Chicano experience, a necessary criteria for inclusion in this volume.[15]

Certainly, each of these scripts can be seen as dramatic literature, but because they represent a necessary theater, they must be imagined in a live performance before the audience for whom the playwrights have written. These plays have effectively reached non-Chicano audiences, but when performed within a Chicano context, the relationship between the audience and the performer is different: it is based on grateful acceptance.

Too often ignored by theaters and the media, Chicanos are proud of their people on stage and listen attentively when the characters reflect their reality with honesty and sincerity. It is this special relationship that creates a necessary theater, a dramatic event that means something to its audience beyond mere entertainment. Chicanos in the audience know that other people share the same desires, confusions and problems. But it is important to note that these plays are also entertaining and retain their effectiveness as they challenge the creative team; they are not easy to perform.

In terms of organization, each play in this collection is preceeded by a brief biography of the author, followed by the text of the script. The script is then followed by a production history and commentary on the play. Ultimately, although the plays address a different theme or themes, they each investigate the question of survival. Luis Valdez's *The Shrunken Head of Pancho Villa* appropriately begins this collection, not only because it was the first Chicano play to be produced in this generation, but because it asserts a search for identity so prevalent in other Chicano plays that followed. Valdez's first play is about survival of the family and, concurrently, economic, political and cultural survival as well.

El Teatro de la Esperanza's first docu-drama, *Guadalupe*, also addresses survival; but beyond the issues of economics, family and culture, the protagonists are workers, fighting for their lives. Based on actual events, *Guadalupe* impressed non-believers, but it also served to educate the people on whom the docu-drama was based. This play gave an entire community the will to continue in its struggle.

Arthur Girón's *Money* was not written for a Hispanic theater, per se; it was, however, created as a response to a system that affects Chicanos and non-Hispanics alike: the corporate foundation world. Written by a man who was working in the corporate foundation world when he wrote it, this play takes an insider's critical look at that structure. *Money* is relevant to the Chicano experience because the two central characters are Chicanos and its theme continues the exploration of cultural and economic survival.

Teatro de la Esperanza's second major documentary, *La víctima*, complements its predecessor, *Guadalupe*, by expanding the documentary form to include a mixture of fact and fiction. Once again, the central question is how to maintain a cultural identity. However, in this case the protagonist works for a federal agency that challenges the very nature of Chicano/Mexicano relations: the Immigration and Naturalization Service. Economic survival clashes head-on with cultural survival in this Brechtian account of one man's inner struggle.

Milcha Sánchez-Scott's play, *Latina*, contrasts the economic survival of Latinas employed as maids with the Chicana protagonist's identity crisis. Told simply and humorously, this play, based on the playwright's own experiences, explores the prevailing theme through pathos and comedy, farce and satire, to achieve its goals. It is one woman's struggle, but it represents the plight of all Chicanos in search of their place in this society.

Finally, Judith and Severo Pérez's *Soldierboy* employs a mixture of melodrama and expressionism to recreate real life events in Mr. Pérez's youth during World War II. Centered around a 1940's Chicano/Mexicano family, *Soldierboy* concludes this collection with another family in crisis. This family, however, will survive. Given the proper productions, these plays, too, will survive beyond these pages as living testaments to a generation of Chicanos and Chicanas dedicated to dramatizing a people's condition.

[1]For more on the Mesoamerican theater and ritual, see: José, J. Arrom, "Raíces indígenas del teatro americano," *Selected Papers of the XXIXth International Congress of Americanists* (Chicago: University of Chicago Press, 1952):

299–305; Willard C. Booth, "Dramatic Aspects of Aztec Rituals," *Educational Theatre Journal*, 18 (December 1966): 421–28; Maxine Klein, "Theatre of the Ancient Maya," *Educational Theatre Journal*, 23 (October, 1971): 269–76; and Carlos Mérida, "Pre-Hispanic Dance and Drama," *Theatre Arts Monthly* (August 1938): 559–68.

[2]For more information about the early professional Spanish-language theater in the United States, see: John Brokaw, "A Mexican-American Acting Company, 1849–1924," *Educational Theatre Journal*, 17 (March 1975): 23–35 and Nicolás Kanellos (ed.), *Mexican-American Theatre: Then and Now* (Houston: Arte Publico Press, 1983).

[3]For an informative account of other immigrant theater movements in the U.S., see Maxine Schwartz Seller, *Ethnic Theater in the United States* (Westport: Greenwood Press, 1983).

[4]Major scholars writing during the 1930's about the Spanish-language theater were: Mary Austin, "Folkplays of the Southwest," *Theatre Arts Monthly* (August, 1933): 599–606; A. L. Campa, *Spanish Religious Folk Theatre of the Southwest* (Albuquerque: University of New Mexico, 1934); A. L. Campa, "Religious Spanish Folk-Drama in New Mexico," *New Mexico Quarterly* 1 (February 1931): 3–13; Winifred Johnson, "Early Theatre in the Spanish Borderlands," *Mid-America*, 13 (October 1930): 121–131 and Edwin B. Place, "A Group of Mystery Plays Found in a Spanish-Speaking Region of Southern Colorado," *The University of Colorado Studies, Series A; General Studies*, 18 (1930): 1–9. For a more complete bibliography of books, plays, articles and dissertations on Chicano theater before 1965, see Jorge A. Huerta, *Chicano Theatre: Themes and Forms* (Tempe: Bilingual Press, 1982): 245–248.

[5]As noted in footnote 1, above, much attention was given to the Spanish religious folk drama in the 1930's. But though there is not much written about today's religious plays, they do exist. One of the most notable examples is the Teatro Campesino's alternating productions of *Las pastorelas* (The Shepherds) and *La Virgen del Tepeyac* (The Virgin of Tepeyac) performed in the Mission of San Juan Bautista, California, each Christmas since the early 1970's.

[6]For articles about early Mexican-American theater, see: John Brokaw, "A Mexican-American Acting Company, 1849–1924," *Educational Theatre Journal*, 17 (March 1975): 23–39; Brokaw, "The Repertory of a Mexican-American Theatrical Troupe: 1849–1924," *Latin American Theatre Review*, 8 (Fall 1974): 25–35; An excellent compilation of articles revealing the wealth of secular Spanish-language theater prior to 1965 can be found in Nicolá Kanellos, *Mexican American Theater: Legacy and Reality*, (Pittsburgh: Latin American Literary Review Press): 63–126.

[7]For an analysis and evaluation of the Chicano theater movement from 1965 to 1980, see Jorge A. Huerta, *Chicano Theater: Themes and Forms* (Tempe: Bilingual Press, 1982).

[8]Mr. Valdez and I were walking around Washington, D.C. one night in the late 1970's and as we both marvelled at the beauty of the nation's capital, I said, "You know, Luis, this is our country, too," and he responded, "That's what I've

been trying to say, Jorge."

[9]Stan Steiner and Luis Valdez, (eds.), *Aztlan* (New York, Vintage Books, 1972): xxxiii.

[10]The programs referred to include the Los Angeles Theater Center's "Latino Unit," the Old Globe's Teatro Meta Project, in San Diego, California and the South Coast Repertory Theatre's "Hispanic Playwright's Project" in Orange County, California. These projects are designed to mainstream Hispanic theater artists, bringing different voices to these non-Hispanic theaters. Chicano theater companies that are able to pay their artists include the Teatro Campesino, Teatro de la Esperanza and the Biligual Foundation for the Arts in California. San Antonio's Guadalupe Cultural Arts Center produced *Soldierboy* with a core of professional actors supported by a strong company of community performers.

[11]For a brief but very informative and complete overview of Hispanic-American theater today, see Joanne Pottlitzer, *Hispanic Theater in the United States and Puerto Rico* (New York: The Ford Foundation, 1988).

[12]The reader is reminded that few theater artists in the United States earn a decent living in the theater, much less in Chicano theater. Professionally produced versions of the plays included here provided the artists with some recompense, allowing them to focus on the production in question for the period of rehearsal and performance.

[13]Luis Valdez and the Teatro Campesino published the first anthology of Chicano plays, appropriately titled *Actos*, in 1971. Valdez's collection was followed by other anthologies over the years, each one dedicated to the exposure of the work for both performers and readers. The bibliography lists other Chicano anthologies and individual plays that are also available in print.

[14]Luis Valdez's *The Shrunken Head of Pancho Villa* has been published, but it is included here because it is integral to this collection of plays about the Chicano experience.

[15]As indicated in the biographies preceeding their plays, Arthur Girón's parents were Guatemalan and Milcha Sánchez-Scott's mother is Indonesian, Chinese and Dutch while her father is Colombian. Further, because of the criteria listed above, two pioneering Chicano playwrights could not be included in this volume: Carlos Morton and Estela Portillo Trambley. Plays by these two important authors that might have been included in this volume have either already been published or have not been produced professionally.

Soldierboy

Soldierboy was first produced by El Teatro Campesino, under the direction of Luis Valdez in the Teatro's rustic playhouse in San Juan Bautista, California, in 1982. The fact that the Teatro's theater is a converted agricultural packing shed added a certain sense of irony to this play about a produce merchant; it was a touch that gave the production a wonderful sense of immediacy. That first version of the play was a work-in-progress with a professional artistic and technical staff. Carlo Allen played Frank, Tony Genaro created the role of his father and Danny de la Paz was a sympathetic Willie. These fine actors were complemented by Socorro Valdez as Petra and Yolanda Márquez as Esther.

Like other premiere productions, the play needed some re-writing, but it generally moved the critics to praise the effort. Steve Hauk observed, "On the plus side, it is vital, the characters are alive and full-blooded, and one senses a good play struggling to get out."[1] Steven Winn wrote, "Like the play's ambitions, the cast is large, and largely successful. But there are superfluous characters—an extra cousin, an extra great aunt—as well as themes that could profitably be pared away."[2]

Fortunately, the authors listened to constructive criticism, and began to improve the play, trimming text and cutting characters that were, indeed, superfluous.[3] The newly-revised play was produced in 1987 by the Division of Drama at the University of Southern California, under the direction of Romulus Zamora. This production culminated months of rehearsals with a generally inexperienced cast of student actors from a variety of Los Angeles colleges. The production was highlighted by the presence of Alma Rosa Martínez, a professional actress whose powerful portrayal of Petra enhanced the young actors' performances.[4]

In 1988 the play was produced by the Guadalupe Cultural Arts Center in San Antonio, Texas, under the direction of José Manuel Galván, a Mexican director who has been involved in the Chicano theater movement since the early 1970's.[5] The local company was complemented by two professional guest actors from Los Angeles: Danny de la Paz, re-creating the role of Willie and Enrique Castillo playing Frank. Petra was played by Ruby Nelda Pérez, a moving force behind the Guadalupe Cultural Arts Center's theater program, as well as a consummate actress and veteran of several important teatros.[6] Hailed by one reviewer as "One of San Antonio's best actors," Pete Sánchez played Beto.[7]

Soldierboy in effect "came home" to San Antonio and the community embraced this play as an homage to one of its own. One enthusiastic reviewer began his commentary with the following statement: " 'Soldier-boy' marks nothing less than a watershed in the history of San Antonio theater. It tells the previously untold story of the birth of the Mexican-American middle class."[8] Another emotional reviewer observed, "For the majority of those present, 'Soldierboy' brought memories so close to home that one could almost feel the entire audience holding its collective breath."[9]

Because *Soldierboy* takes place in 1945, it is a play that places its Chicano family in a familiar, yet historical context. The musical context is also historical, framed by Mexican rancheras as well as Glenn Miller and "White Christmas." However, unlike Luis Valdez's earlier historical play, *Zoot Suit*, this piece is not based on a public event. Rather, the play revolves around a hardworking Mexican-Chicano family in a southwestern setting, welcoming its war hero home while also adjusting to a new life after the war. This is a memory play, based on Mr. Pérez's actual family, and as such it is a delicate slice of the Chicano reality worth savoring and thinking about.

The central figures of Frank and Willie are juxtaposed within the familial setting as each tries to relate to a society changing around them. Frank is a wonderful mixture of sensitive male and valiant warrior whose nightmares are revealed through the flashbacks. His war buddy, Watts, and Watts' mother, Eugena, are the only non-Hispanic characters in the play and they add a strong counterpoint to the Mexican/Chicano family structure; each family has its sense of loyalties and each is connected to the other through the young soldiers.

Willie's character keeps our attention as the play progresses and we observe the sibling rivalry that the two young men assert. We like Willie and want to see him succeed. His love of Frank's son, Junior, reveals his warm humanity, but the rivalry between the two brothers is heightened by Junior's preference for his uncle rather than his father. Junior is a poignant blend of innocence and bewilderment in the face of conditions he cannot understand. Frank's wife, Esther, confronts her situation and her husband with a sense of love, concern and strength, although she is unable to understand what is happening to her husband. The father and mother round-out the family unit, bringing a proud reality to the proceedings. Petra has a fine sense of humor as well as a loving concern for her brood. Beto typifies the dominant father, proud of his own accomplishments as a small businessman and eager to include his first-born son in the family business.

Soldierboy is a play in the tradition of Elmer Rice or Clifford Odets, it is a domestic drama that engages us because of the common bond we may feel with the characters onstage. These are people from a barrio reality familiar to most Hispanics of the period portrayed. The conflicts in the play range from Frank's readjustment to civilian life, his search for a decent job, his brother's rivalry and his wife's wish for a home of their own. Family problems, yes, but problems nonetheless. There is no earth-shattering obstacle to overcome, yet the story engages us as it unfolds. It keeps our attention as it reveals Frank's war experience in Europe and the too-familiar war at home: finding a job or a house in racist America. The racial conflict is underplayed, but it is there, sharply contrasted with the comradeship between the Anglo and the Chicano soldiers, as revealed in the several flashback scenes.

In the 1987 production of this play at the University of Southern California, the audience was enthralled with the characters and their situation. In his review of this production, Jorge Luis Rodríguez observed, ". . . el superobjetivo es el mismo: elevar a una dimensión universal las pequeñas vidas cotidianas, la multitud expresada mediante la riqueza del individuo."[10] Arturo Ramírez observed, "Although the play verges on melodrama, there are several saving graces. One is the vitality of the characters, the breath of life they have been infused with, which produces Chicano characters with universal human dimensions in an engrossing play peopled with characters an audience can identify with, and relate to."[11]

Emotions flowed freely during the USC production when the characters demonstrated their common humanity. When Frank told Mrs. Watts that her son was dead, thus finally releasing the poor mother's pent-up tears, the audience members cried with her and for all the mothers who have lost their sons in combat. And if we wanted the two characters to hug or at least touch, we knew that the director had judiciously kept them apart for this was, after all, Texas in the 1940's and Anglos and Chicanos could not share a common grief in most situations.

Because its audience is bilingual, the Guadalupe Cultural Arts Center chose to add much more Spanish to its production of *Soldierboy*, bringing the play and its characters closer to San Antonio's linguistic reality. As noted in the introduction to this volume, the question of language is always central to a play's veracity and to the producing company's credibility with its particular audience. The text as reproduced here indicates the idea that Petra does not speak English, although we have been listening to her speak both Spanish and English for most of the first act.

For those who might not understand that Petra is actually speaking Spanish, the playwrights point it out when Petra declines to go to the welcoming ceremony by saying, "Me siento incómoda allá con toda esa gente que habla inglés." Shortly after, Mrs. Watts appears at the door and Petra calls to her son, "¡Willie! ¡Habla inglés!" The remainder of the dialog is between Willie and Mrs. Watts and we realize that Petra has not understood what they have been discussing when she asks Willie who the woman was. In either case, employing more Spanish or less, the play retains its effectiveness, as evidenced in the positive responses to each of the three versions produced to date.

Soldierboy is one of the most recent plays in this collection and the authors can look forward to more productions as this script becomes available to a wider audience. Producers and directors will undoubtedly take note of the fact that the play reflects a Chicano family in crisis with sensitivity and good taste. The truth in the characters makes them not only acceptable to a Chicano audience, but to the broader society as well. The universality of war gives this play an enduring fascination, and the simplicity of its central conflict adds a common denominator to the whole.

[1]Steve Hauk, "El Teatro Campesino: 'Soldierboy' Has World Premiere," *Monterey Herald*, 20 November 1982, n.p.

[2]Steven Winn, "Two South Bay Theaters Tackle Families With Problems," *San Francisco Chronicle*, 30 November 1982, p. 44.

[3]For other reviews of the Teatro Campesino production of *Soldierboy*, see: Glenn Lovell, " 'Soldierboy' Speaks from the Heart," *San Jose Mercury*, 22 November 1982 p. C-1; Roberto Robledo, " 'Soldierboy' Features Strong Acting, Technical Effects," *Salinas Californian*, 20 November 1982, p. 34; Carol Sellers, "Teatro's 'Soldierboy' Has Heart, and Soul," *Evening Free Lance*, 26 November 1982, p. 24; Marybeth Varcados, "Valdez Returns to 'Teatro' with Powerful 'Soldierboy,' " *Watsonville* (Calif.), 26 November 1982.

[4]Directed by Romulus Zamora, Stop Gap Theater, University of Southern California, January 22–24, 29–31, 1987. For reviews of this production, see: Arturo Ramírez, " 'Soldierboy,' una muestra de la eficacia del teatro chicano de hoy," *La Opinion*, 24 May 1987, pp. 12–13; and Jorge Luis Rodríguez, *La Opinion*, January, 1987, n.d., n.p.

[5]Mr. Galván was a founding member of the Mascarones, a Mexico City-based troupe of young actors under the direction of Mariano Leyva. Most recently, Mr. Galván has been a member of the Grupo Zero, a collective troupe based in Cuernavaca, Mexico, which had split-off from the Mascarones in the late 1970's.

[6]The Chicano theater movement produced several very capable professional actors, some of whom continue to work with professional Chicano theaters. Two such talented people who participated in this production of *Soldierboy* were Enrique Castillo, formerly with the Teatro Campesino and Ruby Nelda Pérez, formerly with the Teatro Bilingue of Kingsville, Texas, and the Teatro de la

Esperanza.

[7]Jasmina Wellinghoff, " 'Soldierboy' Tells Powerful Truths," *San Antonio Light*, 5 March 1988, p. H–3.

[8]Ed Conroy, " 'Soldierboy' a Dramatic Chronicle of Mexican-American Life," *Express-News* (San Antonio), 5 March 1988, p. 3–F.

[9]Jasmina Wellinghoff, op. cit.

[10]Jorge Luis Rodríguez, *La Opinión*, January, 1987, n.d., n.p.

[11]From an English translation by Arturo Ramírez of his above-cited article in *La Opinión*, p. 13.

Judith and Severo Pérez

Soldierboy was co-written by Judith Schiffer Pérez and her husband, Severo. Severo was born in San Antonio, Texas, in 1941; Judith was born in New York City in 1945. The two met while studying at the Unversity of Texas at Austin. While at Austin, Mr. Pérez completed a degree in History while the future Mrs. Perez graduated in Anthropology. The Pérez's married ten years later and now reside in Los Angeles, California, with their two children, Rafael and Rachel. *Soldierboy* is the Pérez's first play.

Mrs. Pérez completed her M.S. in Education at the University of Southern California and is a master teacher, writer and curriculum consultant. Most recently, Mrs. Pérez completed a historical novel for young adults, titled *El pueblo*. Seen through the eyes of eight-year old Maria Villavicencio, one of the city's original settlers, the story deals with the founding of the city of Los Angeles in a multi-cultural context. *El pueblo* was published by the Los Angeles Unified School District and has been distributed throughout the District, reaching hundreds of thousands of young people.

Mr. Pérez is an independent filmmaker who has been writing since he was thirteen years old. He has produced over one hundred films, most notably, *Seguin*, for American Playhouse. Not coincidentally, the first draft of *Soldierboy* was a screenplay and Mr. and Mrs. Pérez completed the play during a nine-month residency with the Teatro Campesino in San Juan Bautista, California in 1982. Mr. Pérez was playwright-in-residence, working closely with Luis Valdez and members of the Teatro to prepare the script for production.

Most recently, Mr. Pérez wrote, produced and directed a one-half hour documentary, "Los piñateros," a film about the craft and life of piñata makers. Another recent film written, directed and edited by Mr. Pérez was "Yolanda/de nuevo," a one-half hour drama for American Spanish-language television starring Kamela López. Los Angeles' leading Spanish-language newspaper gave this drama a glowing review, while also taking the opportunity to criticize that city's Spanish-speaking television stations: " . . . bajo la excelente dirección de Severo Pérez . . . 'Yolanda/de nuevo' se constituye en un buen ejemplo de lo que hasta el momento no han podido hacer los canales 34 y 52 . . . producir programas de televisión acordes a nuestra realidad."[1]

Whether writing for film or the stage, Judith and Severo Pérez still have much to say about the Chicano/Mexicano experience in this country. Hopefully, they will collaborate on more plays like *Soldierboy*, domestic

18

dramas that speak truthfully to their audiences, with characters that are based on real life rather than stereotyped images of what the Chicano and Mexican are supposed to be.

[1]Juan Rodrigues Flores, " 'Yolanda/de nuevo' ofrece otras perspectivas a la television hispana," *La Opinión*, Panorama Dominical, 12 junio 1988, p. 3

Soldierboy

By Judith and Severo Pérez

Dedicated to
four generations of the Pérez Family
and to the memory of
Guillermo (Willie) Pérez

It is August, 1945. The de la Cruz home is a two-story frame struc-
ture in westside San Antonio, Texas. The house is pleasant, roomier than
most. In the kitchen the stove is crowded with pots containing a homecom-
ing dinner.

In Willie's room newspaper clippings are spread across the bed
along with an open scrapbook. An ancient 22 caliber rifle hangs above the
chest of drawers.

In one corner of the living room, Petra has made an altar to the
Virgen de Guadalupe.

The dresser, the bed, and a cedar chest in Esther's bedroom are her
cherished personal possessions in the home of her husband's parents.

Littered throughout the house are children's toys: a broom horse, a
castle made of strawberry boxes, a multi-colored ball.

If we could stand on the porch beyond the audience's line of sight,
we would see an oddly rural-urban setting. When built fifty years before,
the houses were spaced to accommodate growth--more white frame houses
with wide porches overlooking the dirt road to Helotes. But the road to
Helotes was never finished, and the neighborhood withered during the
Depression.

Most of the Scotch-Irish and German millhands moved to California. The rest just relocated to the north of town, away from the Mexicans taking over the neighborhood.

While a piece of gingerbread clinging here and there to roof trim betrays the Victorian pretentions of the previous owners; now in the summer of '45 there are few pretentions left. Urbanization has crept to the doorstep. Cinderblock warehouses have taken over the vacant lots intended for the white frame houses. Some of the houses have even given way to the sprawl. A row of commodes yawns in the front yard next door, unbashful tombstones.

Beto has built a fence to obscure the blight. There is a clean well-maintained driveway where the truck spends the day because the family is in the produce business and works nearly every night.

CHARACTERS

FRANK DE LA CRUZ, 25, is a decorated hero returning home from Europe after World War II. He is the oldest son of Beto and Petra de la Cruz. The war has changed Frank. Having survived four years of the worst fighting in Europe, he has a fierce and uncompromising determination to make his own way in the Anglo world. Although he is fluent in Spanish, he now speaks only English. He is not rejecting his culture, but challenging the barriers he believes have kept *Mexicanos* poor. Frank's wardrobe varies from the few conservative suits he had before the war to the shirts and ties Esther buys for him after his return.

ESTHER, 24, Frank's wife, is a high school graduate who values her independence. During the war, she found work sewing in a uniform factory and continues working there to make extra money to help buy a house. Her family came from Mexico to the United States during the Mexican Revolution, before she was born. In Mexico her family had owned land and a foundry; they now run a blacksmith shop in San Antonio. While none of the wealth or luxury of their former life remains, her family continues to value education and property. Esther wears clothes she has tailored herself in her favorite colors: lavender and marine blue.

WILLIE, 20, Frank's younger brother, was injured in an auto accident several years before. He uses a cane to assist his walking and becomes winded after any exertion. Willie enjoys a good joke, swing music and baseball. He dresses in work clothes, sturdy gray or brown trousers with a sport shirt. When he goes out, he wears a pullover sweater over his dress shirt and dark colored slacks.

JUNIOR, 5, Frank and Esther's son, is inquisitive and active. He is devoted to his uncle, Willie, who spends hours playing with him.

BETO, 60, married late, having supported his mother until her death. He was born on a small farm near Rio Grande, Texas, where much of his family remains. Although he didn't go to school, he has a rudimentary knowledge of reading and writing. He speaks English with a heavy accent, but feels more comfortable in Spanish. Beto has worked hard all of his life, since he was old enough to carry buckets of greenbeans in the fields. He has been an ice truck delivery helper, construction laborer and farmworker. For over fifteen years he has had a stand in the produce district, and makes deliveries early in the morning to long-established customers. He sits straight-backed, both feet on the ground, with his hands on his knees. He wears a traditional felt stetson.

PETRA, 45, was born in Pearsall, Texas, where her brothers run a small restaurant and gas station servicing Spanish-speaking travelers and truckers on the highway to San Antonio. Petra didn't go to school either, but was taught to read and write by her mother. She speaks only Spanish, but can understand some English. At home she wears an apron over a simple gray or tan dress with a discreet pattern which gives her clothes a hint of color. When she goes outside the house, she wears a dark gray or navy blue dress, black shoes with low heels and a hat. At Sunday Mass all the other women her age dress similarly.

WATTS, 26, Frank's war buddy, is a dirt-poor farmboy from Floresville, Texas. Until the war he'd never been to the "big city" of San Antonio, 30 miles away.

EUGENA WATTS, 50, Watts' mother, still lives with her husband on the farm near Floresville. She wears floral print cotton dresses, faded from numerous washings.

RADIO ANNOUNCER (taped)

Note* *The language spoken in this play in actuality should be a combination of English and Spanish. When Frank, Esther, Junior and Willie speak with one another, they would normally speak English. Petra and Beto would speak only Spanish, even when talking to the English-speaking members of the younger generation. In this version of the play Petra's dialogs have been written so an English speaking audience can understand her. But an effort should be made in the staging and characterization of Petra to convey to all audiences that she does not speak English.*

ACT ONE

It is evening. Stage lights to black.

SCENE ONE

In darkness, Esther, Petra, Frank and Watts take their positions on the stage: Esther on her bed sorting through a box of letters; Petra at the kitchen table, her back turned three-quarters from the audience; Frank and Watts, center stage.

Willie is out of sight, hidden behind the couch. Junior is on the porch behind the window, also out of sight. Beto is off-stage.

Still in darkness, a deep resonant echo rumbles from far away, transfiguring from a heartbeat, to a drum, to distant thunder. A strobe-like flash briefly illuminates the stage. Frank is slumped over, coughing, sputtering, vomiting. He is supported by Watts. The flash is followed by a profound "Kaboom."

A dim shimmering light comes up on Frank and Watts. Watts tries to keep Frank on his feet, but Frank's legs give out from under him, and he folds to his knees.

WATTS: Hell . . . Hell . . . Hell . . . Come on, buddy. Try to stand. Stand, goddammit!!! I got you back across. The river's behind us now. De la Cruz, are you alive? Sergeant! There's a hell on the other side . . . a whole fucking hell. Try to stand. You're going home a hero. Yeah, Sergeant, you went across with how many companies? F, C, H Companies. B Company, E Company.

FRANK: (*Frank speaks slowly, his voice slurred, as if he were drunk. He appears to be unaware of a wound to his chest. Coughs.*) Watts? Where's my wallet? My side arm? I lost my piece over there. M-my pack, it's gone. Where's my wallet? Shit! (*Frank sits, attempts to search for his wallet.*) There's no . . . no . . . wallet.

WATTS: You're lucky that's all you lost. Get on your feet, Sergeant.

FRANK: You ain't seen it, have you? The picture of my kid?

WATTS: Nah, I ain't seen nothing, nothing but fog, mud and the goddamn river. Can't see a living soul now. None of us could see where you was leading us. But we followed you—all the men did. They're all dead now. All of them.

FRANK: Watts, I put the picture here, so it wouldn't get lost. *A still image of a small boy dressed as a soldier appears on the screen door to the porch, center stage.* I got to cross the river and find my kid. He's right over there, on the other side.

WATTS: That's enough, Sergeant. We got to get the hell out of here!

FRANK: I can't leave him over there.

WATTS: You're crazy! You'll get yourself killed. We got to get you some help or you'll die here like the rest of them. You're my ticket out of here. I can't go back without you, de la Cruz. Come on. Frank, I gotta take you with me. (*Watts hoists Frank onto his shoulders in a fireman's carry and struggles with him off-stage. The shimmering blue light fades with Frank and Watts' exit. A train whistle calls in the distance as the stage lights return to evening.*)

SCENE TWO

It is 9:30 in the evening. Outside the sky is still streaked with an orange and inky hue. The photograph in the doorway comes to life. Frank, Jr., wearing a soldier's uniform complete with garrison cap, enters from the front porch.

JUNIOR: (*Whispering.*) Willie . . . (*Walks three steps.*) Willie . . . Willie! (JUNIOR *holds a silver cap-pistol in his hand. From behind the couch we hear* WILLIE *humming, imitating the soundtrack of an adventure film.*)

WILLIE: Ta Ta Tum . . . Ta Ta Tum . . . Tatatum . . . Tata *Tum*, Tum, Tum, . . .

JUNIOR: I see you Willie. You're over there behind the sofa.

WILLIE: (*In a falsetto.*) No, I'm not. Ta Ta Tum . . . (*Continues.*) I'm not over there, I'm behind you.

JUNIOR: No. You're not. (*Points gun at* WILLIE. *POW! POW!*) WILLIE *staggers out from behind the couch, falls over and plays dead. In the kitchen* PETRA *wipes a speck of dust off a plate, realigns a napkin.*

WILLIE: Ah, Ah, Ah . . . (WILLIE *lies motionless.* JUNIOR *approaches* WILLIE *cautiously, ready to spring away in an instant if* WILLIE *grabs for him. This is a game they've played before. After a moment,* WILLIE *still doesn't move.*)

JUNIOR: Willie?

WILLIE: (*Beat*.) Jesus, my aching back. Aren't you tired yet?

JUNIOR: No. Let's play again.

WILLIE: *Chinita*, Junior. Don't you ever get tired? (JUNIOR *shakes his head*.) I'm tired. Come on. I'll let you lie down on my bed, all right? (JUNIOR *shakes his head*.) Oh, come on. You said you'd go to bed right after we played.

JUNIOR: But I'm not tired. I'm hungry. (WILLIE *crawls on his hands and knees toward* JUNIOR.)

WILLIE: Again? Come here. I'll show you who's hungry. I'm going to eat you up. Bite. Bite. Bite. I'm going to bite your ears, then your nose and *then* your elbows. Yum, yum, yum, I love elbows. (JUNIOR *screams with delight and jumps on the couch to get away.* PETRA *enters*.)

PETRA: Willie! (PETRA *stands* JUNIOR *up on the floor and straightens up his soldier's uniform*.) Look at him! What kind of surprise is he going to be? Look at his knees.

WILLIE: I was putting him to bed.

PETRA: Is that the way you put him to bed?

JUNIOR: But I'm hungry. (PETRA *crosses to the kitchen*.)

PETRA: There's some leftover *guisado* on the stove. (WILLIE *reaches for a cane and pulls himself up with it*.)

WILLIE: What about some of that chicken *mole*?

PETRA: You can wait like everyone else.

WILLIE AND JUNIOR: No *mole*?

WILLIE: We've been waiting like everybody else. In fact, we are everybody else, *Chinita*.

PETRA: Don't use that language around here.

WILLIE: What did I say, *Chinita*? That's not a bad word. Is it, Junior? If I said *Chin* . . .

PETRA: Willie! That's enough. You're getting Junior all excited.

WILLIE: Are you excited? (JUNIOR *shrugs*.)

PETRA: You're worse than a kid yourself. Eat and be quiet, or stay out of my way.

WILLIE: Come on, Junior. We know where we're not wanted. (JUNIOR *and* WILLIE *exit toward* WILLIE*'s room*.)

JUNIOR: Is Grandma Petra mad at me?

WILLIE: Nah, she's just excited because your daddy's coming home from overseas. (JUNIOR *climbs onto* WILLIE*'s bed*.

JUNIOR: Why is my daddy coming home? (WILLIE *thinks a moment*.) Why?

WILLIE: I told you before. Did you forget already? (JUNIOR *nods his head, yes.*) The war is over, and he belongs here. He's gonna take care of you and your mama.

JUNIOR: But you and Grandma take care of me.

WILLIE: We love you. But it's your papa's job to take care of you. You know, he's a very special man. He's a real hero.

JUNIOR: You told me before. (WILLIE *moves* JUNIOR *and shows him a news clipping in the scrapbook.* WILLIE*'s excited. No one in the family has ever been in the newspaper.*)

WILLIE: Look at his picture. (*Reading.*) "Under heavy and continuous fire, Sergeant Frank de la Cruz wiped out two enemy machine gun nests and led his regiment in taking Salerno Beach. Sergeant de la Cruz has been awarded the Silver Star for Gallantry in action and a Purple Heart."

JUNIOR: What does it mean?

WILLIE: It means he could have been killed. And even though he got hurt, that didn't stop your papa. He kept on going until he killed all those Nazis. Pow! Tatatatata, Ka-boom! Five or six dead Nazis right there.

JUNIOR: Did he cry?

WILLIE: Grown men don't cry, Junior.

JUNIOR: Well, where's he gonna sleep?

WILLIE: With your mama.

JUNIOR: But where'll I sleep?

WILLIE: (*Laughs.*) Don't worry. We'll find a place for you. You and your daddy will play baseball. Maybe he'll even take you squirrel hunting.

JUNIOR: Will you come, too?

WILLIE: Nah. Just you and your papa.

JUNIOR: Please . . .

WILLIE: Junior, you know I'll always play with you. Come on, go to sleep. (WILLIE *puts a pillow under* JUNIOR*'s head, goes to the door and turns off the light. He continues downstairs.* BETO *enters carrying a basket of produce.*)

BETO: Where's Junior?

WILLIE: In bed. Poor little guy. He couldn't keep his eyes open anymore. (WILLIE *tunes the radio and leans back on the couch.* BETO *enters the kitchen.*)

PETRA: I thought you were going to call the station, *viejo.*

BETO: Frank will call us when he gets here. Don't worry. The *nogal* is so heavy with pecans, a few have fallen already. They're not ripe, but two more months and we'll have bushel baskets full.

PETRA: *¿Nueces?* Beto. Maybe something happened.

BETO: Nothing happened, Petra. It's late *nada más.*

PETRA: Nothing more. (*Gesturing toward the basket.*) What's that?

BETO: Just a few extra things I had on the truck.

PETRA: I don't have any place to put them.

BETO: So leave them in the basket.

PETRA: So where will I put it?

BETO: So leave it outside. (BETO *reaches for the basket.*)

PETRA: Now, where are you going with that?

BETO: You said you didn't have any room.

PETRA: I said no such thing.

BETO: I just heard you.

PETRA: What did I say?

BETO: Petra, Petra. Calm down. (*Puts his arm around her.*) *No hay nada que hacer sino esperar.*)

PETRA: *Yo sé. Yo sé.* I'm sorry. But my knees feel like springs. I can't stay sitting down. (ESTHER *closes the box of letters and returns it to the dresser. She touches up her lipstick, smoothes her hair. She puts on her shoes and joins* WILLIE.)

ESTHER: Are you going to stay home?

WILLIE: I'm beat. Maybe if he calls right now, I'll go.

ESTHER: You stay, Willie. I'll ask Papa to take me down.

PETRA: Esther, did you call your brothers? I told them you would call. We have plenty of food. María, *Prima* Cornelia, *Tía* Concha. Five extra—we have enough plates.

ESTHER: It's too late for company tonight, Mama.

BETO: It's nearly ten o'clock. Huh? He's only six hours late.

ESTHER: Maybe we should have stayed at the train station. I'm ready to go back and wait until his train gets in, even if I have to wait all night.

BETO: They told us to go home! There's no use taking up space.

WILLIE: They didn't want the produce truck in front of the train station.

BETO: Ah-h . . .

WILLIE: It was a loading zone, Papa.

BETO: I park in loading zones all the time. I'm not going to take a taxi, not when I have a truck.

WILLIE: A truck with "De la Cruz Produce" painted in red and white.

BETO: Ah? You're ashamed. That's what you are. You're ashamed of your work what puts food in your mouth. Eh?

PETRA: Beto . . .

ESTHER: (*Softly.*) Willie's not ashamed, Papa.

WILLIE: I'm not . . . (*Laughs.*) Whatever you say, Papa. You think I'm ashamed, huh? But that's not the point. Frank is coming home on a special train. He'll be welcomed by a brass band. A full colonel from Fort Sam is even gonna give a speech. So, maybe we could pay a taxi this time, and not ride with all six of us stuffed into the front seat of the truck like a bunch of Mexicans.

BETO: (*Dismissing* WILLIE.) Ah . . .

ESTHER: It won't make any difference to Frank. He just wants to come home. I want to go back to the station now and meet him. I can't stand this waiting around here anymore.

BETO: Maybe I could take you. I'd park the truck down the street.

PETRA: All those *borrachos* falling down drunk. Who's going to take care of the truck in that neighborhood?

BETO: We'll park at the market and walk. The market's only six blocks . . .

PETRA: So, you might as well take a taxi.

WILLIE: Just make up your mind, and I'll do it.

ESTHER: (*To* BETO.) You could just drop me off.

PETRA: *Sola* . . . at 10:00 at night? No. No. (*Frustrated,* WILLIE *exits to his room.*)

ESTHER: I'll be all right. There's at least fifty M.P.'s there.

PETRA: *¿Qué? De eso hablo, los M.P.s.* I saw those M.P.'s hanging around the wives. Eh! In front of everyone.

ESTHER: Mama! Nothing's going to happen to me. There's a lot of people there. Can we just go now, please. (*A taxi pulls up in front of the de la Cruz home.*)

BETO: It's a taxi! Did you call a taxi! (*Looks out the window.*) Hurry up! He's here.

ESTHER: Frank! (ESTHER, BETO *and* PETRA *exit the house.* FRANK *enters with his arm around* ESTHER. *They embrace.* PETRA *throws her arms around* FRANK *and holds him tightly.*)

BETO: Petra! What's the matter?

PETRA: Until . . . I couldn't believe we knew the truth. Two wounds . . . I don't know what I expected to see.

FRANK: Two small holes. They're all healed, nothing worse than when Papa cut his foot with the rake.

PETRA: Was that all? And the scars . . .

FRANK I'm fine, Mama. (PETRA *embraces* FRANK *again.* BETO *begins to cry.*)

PETRA: *¿Y tú, qué traes?*

BETO: I can't help it. (WILLIE *coaxes* JUNIOR *from sleep.*)

WILLIE: Hey, boy . . . boy . . . Wake up, boy. Wake up. It's your daddy. (*He holds* JUNIOR *closely for a moment before he carries him downstairs.*)

ESTHER: It's true, Frank? Nothing?

FRANK: All healed. (*He embraces* ESTHER.)

BETO: We were just leaving for the train station, Frank. We got there at 2:00 this afternoon. Shoot. We waited and waited. But Junior got tired. There was no place to sit down, and Petra's new shoes were tight and hurt her so bad, she said . . .

PETRA: (*Interrupting.*) Beto. You don't have to tell him that. He doesn't want to know. ¡*Qué vergüenza*!

WILLIE: Here's your son, Frank. (JUNIOR *is slumped sleepily over* WILLIE*'s shoulder.*)

ESTHER: He's tired, Frank. He waited up to see you.

FRANK: (*To* JUNIOR.) Did you wait up to see me? (JUNIOR *shakes his head, no. All laugh.*) How the hell are you, kid? (FRANK *gives* WILLIE *a bear hug, embracing both* JUNIOR *and* WILLIE *at the same time.*) You're as thin as a broom. Doesn't Mama feed you? (PETRA *reacts.*)

WILLIE: You know, same old Willie. Why didn't you call us from the station? I wanted to see all those G.I.s

BETO: Can you imagine? There we were with the mayor and the sheriff and the army band. Of course, the mayor only lasted until four o'clock, the sheriff until six and the army band . . . poor guys, until about eight.

PETRA: (*To* FRANK.) Come sit down, son. I've made some chicken *mole, calabacitas—estilo mío*!

BETO: Maybe he's not hungry. Why don't you ask him?

PETRA: Of course, he's hungry! Aren't you hungry? (*She takes* FRANK *by the arm and pulls him toward the kitchen. Everyone follows.*

WILLIE: The *mole*'s been ready for hours, and you think we got any?

FRANK: It should be delicious, Mama.

ESTHER: Frank, you look exhausted.

FRANK: I haven't slept for four days. The guys started drinking in New Jersey, and they're still drinking. Some shavetail lieutenant met us at the train station and told the G.I.s that the army brass wanted us to stay at Fort Sam overnight so we could show up in the morning— like we just arrived—and the mayor could officially welcome us home. God bless . . . (*Restrains a profanity.*) the army. You should have heard what the G.I.s told the lieutenant. I've been discharged. I don't have to go.

WILLIE: Aw, come on. Will the army band be there?

FRANK: I guess so. God bless. Willie. That's what made the train so late. There was a band playing at every whistle stop we came to (*Hums "Stars and Stripes Forever".*) Ta, Ta, Ta, Ta, Ta, Ta, Ta, Tum . . . (*Continues. Everybody laughs as* FRANK *leads an imaginary band with his spoon.* PETRA *places an enormous bowl of* mole *in front of* FRANK.)

BETO: Your mother made enough *mole* for all the soldiers on the trains . . . and the bands, too. (*Everybody laughs.*)

PETRA: The tortillas will be ready in just a moment.

BETO: There's rice and beans, *calabacita* . . . and . . .

FRANK: Isn't anyone else going to eat?

ESTHER: No, thanks. I can't eat anything.

WILLIE: (*Indicating* JUNIOR *and himself.*) Yeah, what about us?

PETRA: (*Laughing.*) Tonight, if you wait for maid service, you won't eat nothing. Help yourself. (PETRA *sits next to* FRANK.)

ESTHER: I'll get you some, Willie. Do you want some *mole*, Junior? (JUNIOR *shakes his head no.*)

PETRA: Everybody's been calling all day, *m'ijo*. My sister, Junior's *madrina*. Esther's brothers. (*Starts to get up.*) I better call them now.

FRANK: Not tonight, Mama, okay? It's been a long day for all of us.

ESTHER: It's Frank's first night home.

PETRA: You can't deny them. They're family. (ESTHER *hands* WILLIE *a dish of* mole.)

WILLIE: We're family.

ESTHER: Frank's tired.

FRANK: (*To* JUNIOR.) Come over here and sit by me.

WILLIE: Go ahead. (JUNIOR *shakes his head and looks down.*)

WILLIE: (*To* FRANK.) He hasn't slept all day.

FRANK: (*To* JUNIOR.) Maybe later . . . hum?

PETRA: (*To* WILLIE.) Let Frank see the uniform. Stand up, Junior. Where's your cap?

WILLIE: It's on my bed.

FRANK: Let me see, Junior. (WILLIE *stands* JUNIOR *up.*)

PETRA: It's not much of a surprise now. He's all wrinkled.

ESTHER: He looks just fine.

FRANK: Look, I'm wrinkled too. I've worn these clothes for four days. (*Everyone stares at* FRANK.)

WILLIE: Your company gave the Germans hell, huh, Frank?

FRANK: (*Eating a mouthful.*) Ah hummm. This is great, Mama.

PETRA: How are the tortillas? For breakfast I'll make whatever you want—*chorizo con huevos y . . .*

BETO: Breakfast, breakfast? We'll eat breakfast tomorrow. (JUNIOR *rests his head on* WILLIE's *shoulder.*)

ESTHER: Is he asleep?

WILLIE: I think so.

PETRA: I put some sheets on the sofa.

ESTHER: Thank you, Mama. (ESTHER *carries* JUNIOR *to the sofa and covers him with the sheet.*)

WILLIE: It must have been something marching into Berlin, huh, Frank? (FRANK *doesn't respond. He stares at the food.*)

PETRA: He can tell us about it tomorrow . . . (*To* FRANK.) You're not eating. (WILLIE *shrugs at* PETRA *in exasperation.*)

FRANK: Everything is so good, but I ate a sandwich on the train.

BETO: What a day, huh? It was like a game of donkey baseball, huh?

PETRA: And who are the donkeys?

BETO: *¡Pues!*

PETRA: *¡Y tú, viejo feo, cara de caballo!*

FRANK: (*Laughing.*) It's good to be home.

ESTHER: It's very late.

BETO: Shoot, look at the time. The last time we stayed up this long was the night of Willie's accident.

PETRA: What a terrible thing to say! (PETRA *breaks down, crying.*)

BETO: I didn't mean it like that . . .

PETRA: You didn't mean, you didn't mean . . . You don't think what you say.

WILLIE: Papa, why did you say that?

FRANK: It's okay, Mama.

WILLIE: I'm going to be . . . I'll see you tomorrow, Frank.

FRANK: Yeah, good-night, Willie.

WILLIE: We can talk some more then, okay?

FRANK: Yeah, sure. (*Stands and embraces* WILLIE.) I'm tired, too, Mama. (WILLIE *exits.*)

BETO: (*To* PETRA *who is still crying.*) What I meant was, look at the time, huh. I got to get up in two hours. (*To all.*) That's not what you're used to is it, Frank? Work all night, sleep all day? Ya gonna have to get used to that again. (BETO *hugs* FRANK *and exits.* PETRA *turns to clear the table.* FRANK *embraces her. She turns and manages a smile.*)

PETRA: You two go along to bed, *por favor.* I'll see you in the morning. *Buenas noches.*

FRANK: Goodnight, Mama. (PETRA *returns the embrace.*)

PETRA: In the morning, *m'ijo*. (FRANK *and* ESTHER *go to their room.* PETRA *exits and turns off the light in the kitchen. The living room is filled with moonlight.*)

ESTHER: You're home . . . You're finally home. (FRANK *touches her face.*)

FRANK: I can hardly believe it myself. I still feel like I'm riding on the train betwwen Waco and Waxahatchie with three-hundred miles to go.

JUNIOR: (*From the living room.*) Mommy, Mommy. (ESTHER *rolls her eyes. She goes to the door.*) I can't sleep.

ESTHER: Just close your eyes.

JUNIOR: I don't like it here. It's bumpy.

ESTHER: You have a good bed there. Now go to sleep. I'll see you in the morning.

JUNIOR: Can I have some water?

ESTHER: (*Whispering.*) Go to sleep. (*Goes to him.*) I'll rub your back. (*Rubs his back and hums half a verse of "Cuatro Milpas" as a lullaby.*) How's that? Now close your eyes. Go to sleep. (*Kisses him.* WILLIE *appears at the head of the stairs and signals for* ESTHER *to go to bed. She pauses to listen for a protest from JUNIOR. Hearing none, she returns to the bedroom.* FRANK *is asleep. She loosens his tie and takes off his shoes. She turns off the bedroom light and lies down beside him.* JUNIOR *tosses on the sofa and kicks off the sheet.* WILLIE, *with a sheet wrapped around him, descends the stairs, leaning heavily on his cane. He covers JUNIOR, then sits on the floor facing JUNIOR. A moment later he draws the sheet over himself and lies on his side.*)

SCENE THREE

The moonlight is replaced by a red glow. FRANK *sits up in bed, startled. He hears the rattling treads of a German tank.* WATTS *enters through the front door and kneels beside* WILLIE*'s form.* FRANK *crosses to the living room.*

WATTS: (*Whispering.*) He's real bad, Frank. Let's get the hell outa here before there aint' no way out.

FRANK: Wait. (*Touches* HERRERA.) Herrera . . . (HERRERA *groans.*)

Let's go. I'll carry you, man. (*Pulls* HERRERA.) C'mon. Give me a hand.

WATTS: Let's get the fuck out of here. They're gonna take this place anytime now.

FRANK: He's coming with us. Take his other arm, Watts!

WATTS: Let him be captured. Maybe then he'll have a chance. If we try to carry him, he won't make it. You know that, Frank.

FRANK: Herrera, Herrera. (*To* WATTS.) This is Manny. How the hell can I leave him here like this? God, he looks bad. (FRANK *opens the blanket. Now curled fetus-like, "Herrera" shivers.* Say something! Say something, man. His shirt's hot. It's burning hot. (*Looks at his hand.*) It's blood, all over me.

HERRERA: Don't leave me, please. Don't leave me alone. (*Sound of gunfire, half-tracks approaching.*)

WATTS: (*Panicked.*) Let's get out, Frank. Now! There ain't no more time.

FRANK: Herrera?

HERRERA: (*Whispering.*) Please, don't leave me. (FRANK *covers* HERRERA *with the sheet.* WATTS *pulls* FRANK *away.*)

FRANK: Herrera! (WATTS *backs out the front door, leaving* FRANK *behind. The red light is replaced by moonlight.* FRANK *walks toward the form on the floor and places his hand on it.* FRANK *reacts, surprised.*) Willie . . .

WILLIE: (*Waking.*) Hi. I came down to see if Junior was okay. Did I scare you?

FRANK: No.

WILLIE: Go back to bed. You must be beat. (WILLIE *goes upstairs.* FRANK *returns to his room, undresses, and slips into bed with* ESTHER.)

SCENE FOUR

Dawn. Morning light creeps into the house. PETRA *descends the stairs and enters the kitchen. She turns on the radio and does a few dance steps to "Stormy Weather." The song ends.*

RADIO ANNOUNCER: No stormy weather today, folks. It's clear and dry. And here's the 6:00 a.m. news. Our boys are home! Last night

33

the Southern Pacific-Katy Station saw the arrival of two 36th Division combat companies, heroes all. Among them was San Antonio's own Sgt. Frank de la Cruz, the G.I. with the longest continuous service with his company. Welcome home, boys . . . (*Music resumes. PETRA reacts. She's about to call out but restrains herself. JUNIOR stirs. He slips off the couch and puts on his pants and shirt. He tiptoes to his parents' bedroom and peeks in. BETO appears at the front door.*)

BETO: Hey, boy. (*Calling.*) Petra! Petra! (*To* JUNIOR.) Is your papa awake? (PETRA *motions to* BETO *to keep his voice down. She switches off the radio.*)

BETO: (*Lower.*) What's he going to do, sleep all day? (ESTHER *sits up in bed. She leans over to* FRANK; *he's still asleep. She puts on her bathrobe and exits the bedroom.*)

PETRA: No, Beto. It's only six o'clock.

BETO: It's the middle of the morning already.

PETRA: That's your morning, not the rest of the world's. (*Enter* ESTHER.)

ESTHER: Good morning, Mama, everybody. How'd you sleep, Junior? (*Kisses him.*)

PETRA: *Buenos* . . . He's fine. (*To* JUNIOR.) Aren't you? (JUNIOR *shrugs.*)

BETO: (*Opening the newspaper.*) Esther, take a look. This article about the 36th Division mentions Frank. It even gives our address. Look. The whole thing's right here in the paper. How about that?

PETRA: (*Nodding.*) Hm-m. It was on the radio, too!

BETO: *¡Qué va!* Everybody. Everybody at the market wants to see Frank. *El viejo*, Mr. Soloff, came by. Can you figure that? (*Enter* WILLIE, *yawning.*)

WILLIE: Can't expect to get any sleep around here.

BETO: If I let you, you'd sleep all day! Look at this. I got that little surprise for Frank in the truck, huh, Willie?

WILLIE: (*Looking at the paper.*) Yeah, well. I don't know if it's such a good idea, Papa. (JUNIOR *maneuvers himself onto* WILLIE*'s lap.*)

BETO: Of course, it's a good idea.

ESTHER: What's a good idea, Papa?

BETO: You'll see. You'll see. When's Frank getting up?

ESTHER: I thought I'd just let him sleep. It's still early.

BETO: (*Calling.*) Frank! Frank!

ESTHER: Papa!

PETRA: Beto! Leave him alone. *Déjalo en paz.* (FRANK *sits up in bed and holds his head in his hands for a moment. He goes upstairs to wash.*) The boy's tired! Four days on a train. *¿Qué estás pensando?* (JUNIOR *plays with his tortilla. He tears a hole in it and sticks his tongue through.*)

BETO: I'm thinking we got a lot to do today. There's the ceremony, gotta go back down to the market . . .

ESTHER: There'll be plenty of time for that. Junior, stop playing with your food. C'mon, eat your eggs.

BETO: Things are different now at the market.

WILLIE: Sure are. We got rid of that leaky old garden hose and bought a new Sears and Roebuck special. We've upgraded our maintenance department, too. We bought two new brooms: one for me and one for Frank!

BETO: That's not funny! You know we got lots more customers . . . like Siete Mares and Juanita's Cafe. And there's gonna be more . . . You'll see.

ESTHER: I know things are better, but Frank's not . . .

BETO: Shoot! You don't know what it was like ten years ago. We used to go door-to-door selling carrots four bunches a penny, huh, Willie? Now Juanita buys a whole crate for a dollar. With Frank home, we'll get more restaurants. We can get another truck. We can close down the stand and move into a little store. What do you think?

ESTHER: It's too soon, Papa. There's plenty of time to talk later. Frank and I haven't had any time together. He might want to take a trip with Junior and me.

BETO: What trip? He's home.

WILLIE: Yeah, he hasn't even been home one day. (ESTHER *pats* WILLIE*'s arm.*) Why don't you ask Frank what he wants to do? (*Enter* FRANK, *dressed in his military trousers.*)

FRANK: I want to sleep and take a hot bath and read the funnies . . . sleep some more . . . and eat . . . and be with my wife and my big boy . . . (*Kisses* ESTHER*'s check. To* JUNIOR.) Where's my big boy? Come on over here. Come on. (JUNIOR *huddles close to* WILLIE. WILLIE *signals "later" to* FRANK. FRANK, *disappointed, sits down.*)

BETO: You planning any trips?

FRANK: (*Still looking at* JUNIOR.) Not me.

PETRA: *¿Qué te pasa?* Do you miss the army breakfast already?

FRANK: No, Mama. What the army does to eggs is a sin. (*Sniffs.*) Is that what I think it is?

PETRA: I have whatever you want—*chorizo con huevos* . . . tongue . . . *rancheros . . . lo que quieras.*

BETO: Huh? What will it be? Your mother's already fed us.

FRANK: *Chorizo*, Mama, please. Tomorrow, *rancheros* . . . The day after . . .

BETO: (*Interrupting.*) *Chorizo*, and let's be quick. We got lots to do.

FRANK: Don't wait for me. Nothing's going to move me from here today. (*Picks up a tortilla.*) Tortillas. You know there aren't any tortillas in the army.

BETO: No? How do they eat their *huevos rancheros*?

PETRA: ¡*Pues, con los dedos*!

FRANK: This cook, Gómez—a guy from Harlingen—used to get me Italian sausages . . . and cook 'em with fresh eggs. He used to say, "Here, Sarge, I got these for you, special." That was the *last* time I ate something good.

WILLIE: How long ago was that?

FRANK: That was . . . that was . . . a year ago? God, I forget.

WILLIE: What happened to Gómez?

FRANK: He was shipped home in a box.

WILLIE: No. (FRANK *shrugs. He drags over his army duffle bag.*)

FRANK: I'm not going to miss hauling this thing around. (FRANK *pulls out a German army helmet. He tries to put it on* JUNIOR *who backs away. Instead, he places it on* WILLIE*'s head.*)

WILLIE: Look at that bag. That's something. Can I have your duffle bag?

FRANK: Sure . . . and you can keep this in it. (WILLIE *partly unfolds a large Nazi flag.*)

WILLIE: Whew! Look everybody. Where'd you get it?

FRANK: It was captured in the Alsace. (*He hands the flag to* WILLIE. *Something is inside—a bayonet.* WILLIE *holds up the flag for all to see.*)

PETRA: *Qué feo.* (*She gives* FRANK *his breakfast.*)

FRANK: Thank you, Mama. Smell that food . . . Mama, now I feel like I'm home.

JUNIOR: (*To* ESTHER.) Mommy, those are presents!

FRANK: (*To* JUNIOR.) There's something for you, too. (JUNIOR *tugs at* WILLIE*'s pocket.*)

JUNIOR: (*To* WILLIE.) Which one's for me?

WILLIE: Wait just a minute, Junior. (*To* FRANK.) The Alsace—isn't that where the Germans had the 36th surrounded, but you broke through? December 1944. Right?

FRANK: (*Surprised.*) Yeah, you know all that? (WILLIE *holds up the bayonet, feeling the weight of it.*)

WILLIE: I've been reading. God, this is heavy. Where does it come from?

FRANK: That's from a place called Ribeauville.

WILLIE: Ribeauville! I saw that place in the newsreel: "Tired by a tough campaign in the Vosges Mountains, the 36th burst into the Alsace Plain and seized Ribeauville . . . " (*Tickles* JUNIOR *on the ribs.*) And some other towns. I forgot which. I saw the newsreel twice. I kept hoping maybe you'd be in it, but I never saw you.

FRANK: The bunch of guys I was with was so ugly, the photographers thought our faces would break their cameras.

JUNIOR: Is a minute over yet? (FRANK *reaches into his duffle bag and brings out two more presents, a small box for* JUNIOR *and a thick envelope for* PETRA.)

FRANK: This is for Junior and Mama. (JUNIOR *looks at* ESTHER, *then eagerly opens it. Inside is a set of painted soldiers and a miniature German artillery piece. He kneels on the floor, inspects the soldiers in turn and stands them up in rows.* PETRA *carefully opens her envelope and takes out an Italian shawl.*)

PETRA: Frank . . . I've . . . never seen anything like it. So soft. Look at the tiny stitches. (*Shows* ESTHER.) It takes months to do work like this. Thank you, *m'ijo*. And smell. It's perfumed. (*Puts it over her shoulders.*)

WILLIE: Um . . . Hey, I can smell it way over here.

ESTHER: *Mamá, qué elegante. Como señora muy fina.*

WILLIE: Are you going to wear it to Mass?

PETRA: Not around here. *¡Qué casualidad!* You'll have to take me to church downtown—in a taxi.

WILLIE: (*To* FRANK.) Where'd you get it?

FRANK: Some town in Italy.

WILLIE: Was it a lot of money?

FRANK: Two packs of cigarettes.

BETO: That's all?

WILLIE: Didn't you get the Distinguished Service Cross in the Alsace, Frank? The citation said you captured fifty German soldiers . . .

FRANK: Yeah.

WILLIE: How did you do that?

BETO: Fifty German soldiers, huh? That's going to be a story.

WILLIE: How did you do that, huh, Frank? Did you have a machine gun?

FRANK: It was nothing. Really. My gun didn't even work.

WILLIE: No. How did you do it then?

FRANK: This guy, what was his name? Anyway, he says, "They're sending me up, de la Cruz, but my piece is jammed." So I gave him my
piece and he gave me his. The fighting was two or three kilometers
away. Then I hear these Germans shouting, "*Kamerad . . . Kame-*
rad . . . " And these sorry-looking Germans start coming out of
everywhere with their hands on top of their heads (*Demonstrating.*)
and there I am with that jammed M1. I didn't capture them. They
gave themselves up because they had no ammunition and they were
hungry. There I was marching back with 50 prisoners, with a gun
that didn't shoot.

BETO: ¡*Orale!*

WILLIE: Whew! And that's how you got the DSC.

FRANK: Nah, I think they gave it to me because I had to feed the bastards
for two days.

WILLIE: (*Covering* JUNIOR*'s ears.*) Whoops!

PETRA: (*Shocked.*) *Qué valiente.* (*Beat.*) You never learned how to cook.
(*Everyone laughs.* FRANK *produces two more boxes. He hands one
to* ESTHER *and one to* BETO. JUNIOR *is separating his cavalry-
men from his infantrymen.* WILLIE *joins him.*)

JUNIOR: Some have horses and others don't. (ESTHER *opens her
present. Inside are bottles of French perfume, all broken.*)

PETRA: Perfume! Better throw all that glass away right now. It's bad
luck . . . *muy mala suerte.*

BETO: It's not bad luck, Petra. Broken mirrors—that's bad luck, not
broken perfume bottles.

ESTHER: The bottles broke, that's all. It doesn't mean anything.

WILLIE: That's what smells so good.

BETO: Look at this. (*Holds up a beer stein.*) I'm gonna fill it with Lone
Star tonight, huh, Petra?

PETRA: It's just what you needed—an excuse.

FRANK: (*To* ESTHER *softly.*) I'll make it up to you, sweetheart. I'm
sorry.

ESTHER: It's okay, Frank. It is . . . even the broken bottles are beautiful
to me. But I wouldn't trade having you home for all the perfume in
France.

WILLIE: Tell us about the battle of the Rapido River, Frank.

FRANK: What about it?

WILLIE: There have been . . . maybe five or six newspaper articles
about the Rapido River. I clipped them for you . . . all the other
articles, too. (*He shows* FRANK *the scrapbook. Phone rings.* PE-
TRA *answers it.*)

PETRA: *Hola* . . . yes. Yes, tía.

WILLIE: Here, Frank, this is for you.

FRANK: Thank you, Willie. (*He leafs through the scrapbook.*)

PETRA: (*Into the phone.*) Everything is fine. But it was too late to call you. I know. But your lights were out. Yes. What time? (*Laughs.*) I'll ask him. Don't worry. That too. I won't forget. Bye, tía.

FRANK: Don't believe everything you read in the papers. (FRANK *puts the scrapbook aside.* WILLIE *opens it.* PETRA *hangs up, shaking her head.*

WILLIE: Look. It says, "The men fought valiantly at the Rapido River and died courageously."

FRANK: (*Angrily.*) No, Willie. They just died. That's all.

WILLIE: But you're a hero!

FRANK: Come on, Willie . . . soldiers aren't heroes; soldiers are survivors. (WILLIE *turns away, surprised by* FRANK*'s anger.*)

BETO: (*Breaking the tension.*) There's going to be a hero's welcome this morning . . . huh, Esther?

FRANK: I don't think so, Papa.

PETRA: That *Tía* Concha . . . She wants us to stop by later, after Mass.

BETO: She made many *novenas* for you, Frank. Your mother, too.

PETRA: Your father went to church—sometimes—not because he wanted to.

BETO: You know it's these bony knees. *¡Mis huesitos tiernos!* I can't kneel through all those "Holy Marys, Mothers of God." And they don't say it ten times—but 100 times!

PETRA: *Ya*, Beto . . .

BETO: It wasn't the prayers that brought him home . . .

PETRA: Beto!

FRANK: So Tía Concha is still getting around? How old is she now? Eighty-five, eighty-seven?

BETO: Nothing gets past that old owl.

PETRA: *Ya*, Beto. (*To* FRANK.) Tía asked if you still have that St. Christopher's Medal she gave you, the one she brought from Mexico? (FRANK *stands and goes to the door. He answers after a moment.*)

FRANK: No, I don't. I lost it.

BETO: Come on, Willie, help me with the . . . you know.

WILLIE: Big surprise . . . (BETO *and* WILLIE *exit.*)

PETRA: (*Still talking about the medal.*) We'll have to tell Tía Concha something, *m'ijo* . . .

ESTHER: He lost it. He's home safe. That's what counts. Concha will understand.

WILLIE: (*From outside*.) Hey, you didn't tell me it was going to be heavy. Junior, get the door. (JUNIOR *opens the door*. WILLIE *and* BETO *enter carying a 3' x 8' sign that reads: "De La Cruz and Sons Produce."*

BETO: Careful with that . . . you'll wreck the corners.

WILLIE: I've got to sit down . . . (*Coughs*.)

BETO: Eh? What do you think, soldierboy?

FRANK: (*Irritated*.) What am I supposed to say? (WILLIE *continues to cough*.)

FRANK: Willie, are you all right?

WILLIE: I'm fine. I just need to catch my breath.

ESTHER: I'll get you some water.

WILLIE: I'm fine. Don't bother. What do you think, soldierboy?

FRANK: Papa, I'm not ready . . .

BETO: Of course, of course. You rest a day or two . . . take off the whole week. We got plenty of time to make our plans. Remember old man Soloff? He came by this morning and asked about you. He said Barlow's old warehouse was for sale.

FRANK: What happened to Barlow?

BETO: Ever since his son was killed overseas, he let his business slide . . . shrewd old coyote like that. Who could figure it? He finally just stopped showing up about a month ago. Old man Soloff asked me if we wanted to take over Barlow's warehouse, now with you coming home and everything. Eh? A couple of months ago he wouldn't cross the street to say "hello." Now he calls me Mr. De la Cruz. Can you figure that?

FRANK: Sounds good, Papa. But I mean it. I'm not ready. You understand?

BETO: I put a little money aside—nothing much. You know? This is going to be a great year for pecans . . . two-hundred bucks, maybe. I think I can get a good deal on another truck . . . maybe a one and a half ton. When Barlow closed down, his truck had less than ten-thousand miles on it. It's still sitting there.

FRANK: Papa, let's not talk business today. All this is interesting, but . . .

BETO: (*Interrupting*.) If I talk to him right, I betcha I can talk him down. What do you say?

FRANK: Papa . . .

BETO: I know, I know. I remember when you were a young kid—Junior's age. Eh, Petra? You used to beg to come help me on the old wagon. Those were the days. We'd go out early to buy produce·off the farmers, then up and down the streets selling all morning. Remember, Petra? I'd carry him into the house asleep. (*To* FRANK.) You never liked being shut up in school . . . always wanted to be with me in the streets—learn the business. We saved every penny. Then when you were—how old?—thirteen?—we bought our first truck.

FRANK: Listen to me, Papa! I am not coming back to sell produce. Not in a day or two. Not ever!

BETO: Frank!

FRANK: (*Angry.*) I'm not going to unload trucks the rest of my life.

BETO: That's a hell of a thing to say. All those years . . . even in the Depression we never went hungry.

PETRA: Your Papa has worked hard for all this. This family has never been afraid of hard work.

FRANK: Mama, I'm not afraid of working hard. You know that. I helped Papa before school, after school . . . for years. Now I'm ready to do something else. I learned something about radio in the army.

BETO: What do you mean? Like one of them announcers on the radio?

FRANK: No, Papa, there's other things to do in radio. They told me a vet could get a job at Kelly Field, and that's what I want to do.

WILLIE: Kelly Field! Uy, yuy, yueey . . . high class.

FRANK: I'm going over there in a couple of days.

BETO: Radio . . . you have a family, son . . . think about them.

WILLIE: Papa, Frank has to make up his own mind.

BETO: You stay out of this.

ESTHER: These things take time . . .

FRANK: I've made up my mind. It's time *mexicanos* did something besides pick and sell produce.

PETRA: Frank!

WILLIE: (*Whispering.*) He's joking, Mama. *Oye,* Papa, I guess we should keep the old sign, huh?

BETO: . . . Nah, well. We'll see. If radio don't work out, you'll always have a job with us Mexicans, huh, Frank? It's a good business.

PETRA: *Pues, si* . . .

BETO: People have to eat.

PETRA: *Claro.*

BETO: (*Getting up.*) Come on, Frank . . . let's go downtown for the ceremony. Then to the market . . . not to talk business, just to visit. Everybody's been asking for you, son.

FRANK: Well . . .

BETO: Come on. It'll be like a party.

ESTHER: (*To* FRANK.) We could stay for just a little while.

FRANK: All right. (*Exit* ESTHER *and* JUNIOR *to her bedroom. She combs his hair, puts on his cap.* FRANK *and* BETO *get up.*)

BETO: Maybe the newspaper will want to take your picture.

FRANK: And I'll say, "Nope, I won't do it. But you can take a picture of my dad in front of his truck."

BETO: C'mon. We better get going. Willie, you go start the truck.

WILLIE: I'm going to stay here and rest.

BETO: Come on, son! (WILLIE *raises both arms indicating, "That's enough."*) Petra? Come on, let's go.

PETRA: *Me siento incómoda allá con toda esa gente que habla inglés.*

BETO: You understand English. Just don't wear your new shoes.

PETRA: Don't worry about me. I have too much to do here. You can tell me all about it when you get home.

FRANK: You sure, Mama?

PETRA: *Váyanse.* (*While* FRANK *goes to his bedroom to put on his coat,* WILLIE *helps* BETO *carry out the sign.* WILLIE *returns and fiddles with the radio dial until he finds music.* FRANK *exits with* ESTHER *and* JUNIOR. PETRA *stands at the door and watches them go.*) *Con Dios* (WILLIE *lies back on the couch.* PETRA *carries a basket of laundry from the other room and folds clothes.* WILLIE *coughs.* PETRA *pats his back and after a moment goes to the kitchen for water. There is a knock on the front door.* PETRA *hurries back in and sets down the water. Standing at the door is Eugena Watts, a severe-looking Anglo woman in a flowered dress, hat and gloves. She is clearly uncomfortable in this neighborhood.* PETRA *and the woman stare at each other for a moment.*)

EUGENA: Hello. Is this where Frank de la Cruz lives?

PETRA: (*Upset.*) Willie! *Habla inglés* . . . (WILLIE *pulls himself up and turns down the volume of the radio. Still coughing, he goes to the door.*)

WILLIE: May I help you?

EUGENA: Ah, yes. Is this where Frank de la Cruz lives?

WILLIE: Yes, ma'am.

EUGENA: Is he the Frank de la Cruz who was in the 36th Division, C Company?

WILLIE: Yes. He just got home yesterday.

EUGENA: I know. I have to talk to him.

WILLIE: He's not here right now. He went downtown for the ceremony and all.

EUGENA: Yes, of course. I just took a chance that he might be here . . . I'm sorry.

WILLIE: That's all right, ma'am. He's my brother, you know. Do you want to leave him a message?

EUGENA: No. No, thank you. Did your brother tell you about fighting in Italy?

WILLIE: Well, yes.

EUGENA: Did he talk about . . .

WILLIE: (*Coughs.*) Excuse me, ma'am.

EUGENA: Please, just tell him Mrs. Eugena Watts from Floresville wants to talk to him. He don't know me. We don't got no telephone. I'll come back another time. Thank you. (EUGENA *nods at* PETRA *and leaves.*)

PETRA: ¿*Quién es*, Willie?

WILLIE: I don't know, Mama. Some *americana* asking for Frank. (WILLIE *coughs.* PETRA *gives him the glass of water. He sits down and swallows a few gulps. He coughs again.* PETRA *goes with* WILLIE *to his bedroom and adjusts his pillow. He lies down.* PETRA *watches him for a moment and goes back downstairs. She turns off the radio, picks up her laundry and exits.* WILLIE *coughs once, then twice and is silent. His room darkens.*)

SCENE FIVE

Same day, evening. FRANK *and* ESTHER*'s bedroom:* FRANK *and* ESTHER *finally find themselves alone after a day of celebration.* FRANK *begins removing his uniform.* ESTHER *takes the jacket and admires it at arm's length.*

FRANK: As far as Papa is concerned, I should wear it forever. (*They look at one another and laugh.*)

ESTHER: You look good in uniform. But I'd rather see it in the closet. (FRANK *takes a suit out of the closet and tries on the jacket.*)

ESTHER: Sometimes I find myself still thinking that you're on the other side of the world. But here you are. Today's been . . . like a dream—the bands, the speeches, but I'm glad all that's over.

FRANK: Let's see this. Do you think it's still in style? What do you think? Hum? It feels a little tight.

ESTHER: It looks fine. Maybe if you leave it unbuttoned.

FRANK: I'll have to wear it to my interview at Kelly Field. I'm supposed to see a fellow named, uh, Kroger.

ESTHER: That's better. You look good.

FRANK: Has it been hard for you living here? I mean, sometimes—like today—I feel like a bug in a jar.

ESTHER: Your parents have been very generous, Frank. But I'm like a guest here. Your mother does lots of nice things for me. She remembers my birthday. She helps me so much with Junior. She even made me a dress. It was her style. It makes me look like I'm forty and had three grown kids. I know she keeps waiting for me to put it on. I don't know what to tell her. I don't want to hurt her feelings. I'm glad she hasn't asked. At least the color is nice. Your mother doesn't push me too much or question me. It's the little things. Everything has to be done her way. When you iron shirts, you have to do the shoulders first. When I decided to get a job, she was upset, but she didn't keep me from doing it. Most of all she wanted to make sure I came directly home right after work . . . and I did, too.

FRANK: (*Laughs.*) I know.

ESTHER: Sometimes I have to be careful how I say things to them. When I mentioned that we wanted to get our own place, I think their feelings were hurt. Beto made it clear I couldn't make a decision without you. (*She sits on the bed and touches* FRANK's *arm.*)

ESTHER: Are you tired?

FRANK: A little . . . I was thinking about today.

ESTHER: What?

FRANK: Today when we were down at the produce market, I saw Marcos . . . that wino who unloads trucks for Papa. It's hard to explain. At first I didn't recognize him. He looked so old. Then it hit me. I hadn't thought of him for a long time . . . all the time I was gone. I thought about the market, even old man Soloff . . . but not Marcos. It was like he didn't exist. And I've known him all my life. Do you understand?

ESTHER: I think so.

FRANK: Junior . . .

ESTHER: What about Junior?

FRANK: Junior won't come near me. Do you think he's scared of me?

ESTHER: He's not used to you yet. We talked about you all the time. He played like he was writing letters to you . . . like me.

FRANK: He just hangs on to Willie.

ESTHER: Willie spends a lot of time with Junior. I . . . hope you understand.

FRANK: What am I supposed to understand?

ESTHER: They're very close. When Willie was getting better after the accident, he had a lot of time to play with Junior.

FRANK: Like how?

ESTHER: They spent hours together. They played baseball; they listened to the radio. Willie read him the funnies. (*Silence.*) Did you miss me?

FRANK: What kind of a question is that? Of course, I did.

ESTHER: Then why haven't you touched me, Frank?

FRANK: We need time. That's all. (ESTHER *switches off the bedside lamp.*)

ESTHER: We have . . . all the time we want. (PETRA *appears in the hallway outside* WILLIE*'s room. She listens at his door, then enters.*)

PETRA: *Siéntate. Siéntate.* (WILLIE *is wheezing. He coughs.*) *Agácha-Aquí está la almohada. Ahora recárgate. Trata de respirar lentamente.* (WILLIE*'s coughing intensifies.* PETRA *goes to the kitchen and starts to heat water.* FRANK *turns from* ESTHER. *He goes to the door and sees* PETRA *in the kitchen.*)

FRANK: Mama, what's going on?

PETRA: It's Willie. He's having trouble breathing. The air is too dry. Go back to bed. Everything's fine.

FRANK: He sounds bad. What's wrong with him? Is it asthma or TB?

PETRA: No, no. Nothing like that. He just coughs. He's not as strong as he was before the accident. But he's getting better. He goes to work. (FRANK *goes to* WILLIE*'s room.*)

FRANK: How you doing?

WILLIE: (*Catching his breath.*) It's hard to breathe once I start coughing. (FRANK *picks up* WILLIE*'s cane.*)

FRANK: Why are you using a cane? Do you really need it?

WILLIE: My cane? It's part of my dance routine. I'm like Fred Astaire. (*Wide sweep with arm.*)

FRANK: That's not funny. (PETRA *enters with boiling water in a small metal tub.*)

WILLIE: I'm not going to need that. I'm better. Frank, turn off the light, okay?

FRANK: What is it, Willie? You wrote me you broke a couple ribs. How much more is there?

PETRA: Frank, your brother is fine. He goes to work . . .

FRANK: Are you sure, Willie?

WILLIE: I lost a lung. But the other one works great. (*Coughs.* FRANK

45

turns away. He returns to his bedroom.)

ESTHER: How is he? I tried to tell you, Frank. I wrote the letters and tore them up. I didn't know where you were, if I'd get a telegram from the War Department, or if I'd ever see you again. I didn't want to worry you. Maybe I made it sound too minor—like Willie only broke some ribs—but it was bad, Frank. Junior never left him all that time. And little by little Willie got better. You worrying wouldn't have helped him.

FRANK: Mama says he gets around. He goes to work. (FRANK *stands up and turns his back to her.*)

ESTHER: He's not the same as he was before the accident. (FRANK *leaves the room and exits the house.* ESTHER *calls after him.*) Frank? Frank? (*Lights down.*)

SCENE SIX

Dream sequence. Lights in the living room. WATTS *enters the front door and stands center-stage.*

WATTS: Hey, what do you think of this goddamn army? Ah, de la Cruz, just 'cause you're a sergeant and all . . . What is this shit? You think we was fighting the goddamn rocks and sticker-bushes. Two days in a row they drive us out to a hill and tell us to pound the shit out of it with mortars and rifle fire. We don't know if we're shooting at Jerrys, Italians, Pollack partisans, or a row of goddamn nuns. We don't see nobody, and nobody shoots back. What do you think, de la Cruz? Does the brass have their goddamn maps upside down, or was the Jerry's just watching us and laughing sideways? I felt like a goddamn fool out there, shooting at nothing. Like we was all doing a circle jerk behind the barn. But the pisser . . . my god, the real pisser has got to be old Jenkins. Old Jenkins. He shoots himself in the foot, and he's going to get a Purple Heart! You know, they got nothing but morons running this army. Had to be that fool, Jenkins. Wish to hell I'd thought of it myself.

(WATTS *turns and exits through the front door. Lights down.*)

SCENE SEVEN

A few days later. 11:00 am. FRANK enters, returning from his job interview. He picks up the mail from the floor, goes to the refrigerator and takes out a bottle of beer. He removes his jacket and sits at the kitchen table. A pink envelope from the stack of mail catches his attention. He sniffs it. It's perfumed.

FRANK: Mama! (*Waits.*) Esther! (*He is joined by* WILLIE.)

WILLIE: Hi, Frank. Having a beer? I'll have one with you. (*Opens the refrigerator.*) You got a phone call about 15 minutes ago.

FRANK: Me?

WILLIE: It was this woman, Mrs. Watts. I told you she came by the morning after you first got home. You know, when all the stuff was in the paper. She wants to talk to you about something. She said she'd be coming to town pretty soon.

FRANK: (*Irritated.*) Damn! Where is everybody?

WILLIE: I don't know. I just got home from work . . . when the phone was ringing. They're probably out getting some stuff for you. Mama and Esther took out some of your army clothes and were checking for sizes. (*Laughs.*) I could never keep a secret.

FRANK: How are you doing?

WILLIE: Me? I'm getting along pretty good. Sometimes the dry air gets me, and I can't breathe, you know?

FRANK: There's a letter for you. (*Waves the letter under* WILLIE's *nose.*)

WILLIE: Can't keep any secrets around here. Just one of my many sweethearts. (*Opens letter and reads it.*) Janie's inviting me to a college dance, Brown's Business College! Semi-formal . . . like a funeral.

FRANK: You going? (WILLIE *shrugs.* ESTHER, PETRA *and* JUNIOR *enter through the front door loaded down with packages.*)

ESTHER: (*Laughing.*) Oh, Frank. You're home already. We hurried so we'd get here before you. How'd it go?

PETRA: You were always hard to buy things for.

FRANK: I was going shopping myself. You shouldn't have bothered.

PETRA: You're not going to deny us this. We wanted to.

JUNIOR: Willie, I got new shoes, look.

WILLIE: Let me see. Wow. They're so shiny I can see my reflection. But you can't wear them for the big game. What's happening today?

JUNIOR: The Shreveport Oilers are playing the San Antonio Missions in the playoffs.

WILLIE: That's right. Change your new shoes and we'll play. I'll get the baseball and bat.

PETRA: Willie, don't tire youself out.

WILLIE: I'm fine, I'm fine. Don't worry about me. (WILLIE *takes the letter in the pink envelope, surreptitiously tears it up and throws it away. He helps* JUNIOR *with the shoes, and on their way out he grabs a large rubber ball and a broomstick.*)

ESTHER: (*Referring to* FRANK*'s interview.*) Well, how'd it go? What happened?

PETRA: We didn't get you much. And if you don't like the colors, they said you could exchange them.

ESTHER: He'd better like the colors. I chose them.

PETRA: Well, they're not the colors I would have picked. Black goes with everything. Why don't you try on the clothes. I have to change these shoes. (ESTHER *takes out several shirts, socks, and ties. She hands them proudly to* FRANK. FRANK *gives the clothes passing attention and places them on the kitchen table. Exit* PETRA.)

JUNIOR: (*OS*) Home run, home run, home run . . .

WILLIE: (*OS*) Just you wait. This is just the top of the seventh inning. I'll get even.

JUNIOR: (*OS*) Pitch the ball, Willie. Pitch the ball. (ESTHER *puts her arms around* FRANK, *but he is not responsive.*)

ESTHER: How'd it go? What happened? (FRANK *pushes past her.*) What about the job?

FRANK: I got a job.

ESTHER: Is it in radio? What is it?

FRANK: (*Frustrated.*) It's a job. I'm a warehouseman helper.

ESTHER: What's that?

FRANK: Sometimes I stack boxes, or move a lot of crates. It means I unload trucks.

ESTHER: Frank, you got a job at Kelly Field. That's what you said was important.

FRANK: The foreman told me in a few months, if I learn to drive a forklift and keep my nose clean, because of my outstanding war record I might have a chance to become a warehouseman.

ESTHER: You got in. Now you can . . . (*Confused by* FRANK*'s reaction.*) You, you have opportunities, Frank. The radio field's wide open. Isn't that what you told me?

FRANK: (*Angrily.*) I got in. What does that mean? Are you going to quit your job? Are you going to stay home now and take care of Junior, like a mother's supposed to?

ESTHER: No, I'm not going to do that. I took the day off so we could have some time together.

FRANK: There's no reason for you to work now . . . and you've always hated the job. You told me yourself. Your hair gets full of lint. Piecework, it's not for you.

ESTHER: Why are we arguing, Frank? Why?

FRANK: (*Sarcastically.*) Can't you figure it out? You're a high school graduate.

ESTHER: Frank, I don't know what you mean. Look, I make more money sewing than I would as a typist. And you know your mother. I couldn't be here all day.

FRANK: You don't have to work.

ESTHER: I know. But right now I want to work. Maybe I'll quit in a few months . . . when everything's settled down.

FRANK: Junior needs you with him, Esther. A mother should be home.

ESTHER: Are you ordering me to stay home, Frank?

FRANK: No.

WILLIE: (*OS*) Just wait! This is only the top of the ninth. The game isn't over yet. Becerra, winds up . . . looks at first base.

JUNIOR: (*OS*) Pitch it. Pitch it, Willie.

WILLIE: (*OS*) There you go.

JUNIOR: (*OS*) Home run, yay! Yay, yay!

ESTHER: Frank. I think Junior's doing just fine. If we're going to buy a house, we could use the extra money. When we live in our own house, Frank . . . then I'll want to stay home.

WILLIE: (*OS*) Yes, ladies and gentlemen. There'll always be next year for the San Antonio Missions. (FRANK *stares out the window at his brother and son.* ESTHER *exits.* FRANK *remains at the window as the light changes from dusk to night. He crosses to the kitchen table and begins to read from a textbook. The light changes again to dawn.*)

SCENE EIGHT

A Sunday morning in September. Kitchen and hall lighted up.

FRANK *is at the kitchen table studying.* BETO *enters and starts to prepare coffee.* PETRA, *in her robe, knocks on* WILLIE's *door. He is in bed.*

PETRA: Willie, Willie.

WILLIE: (*Sleepily.*) I don't want to get up. I don't have to get up. It's Sunday.

PETRA: We're all going to Mass.

WILLIE: *Ay qué la fregada.*

PETRA: (*Interrupting.*) Willie, shut your mouth.

WILLIE: It's Sunday, and I'm going to sleep in. You hear that, Jesus? I'm tired and I need some rest. You hear me, Mary? Mama, they know where I am if they need to find me. (BETO *pours two cups of coffee and sits down.*)

BETO: You like your new job?

FRANK: It's okay, Papa.

BETO: You can't trust them. I know them, huh.

FRANK: I think I know them, too. It isn't like the old days, Papa.

BETO: Don't fool yourself just because of the war. I know what I'm talking about. They'll do you just like they did Marcos. Big shot thought he was going to work at Kelly Field just like an *americano.* Huh, for what? He lasted over there two weeks. Nothing he did was good enough for them—sweeping the warehouse, digging a ditch. The *gringos* always found something wrong with it.

FRANK: Do you think I'm like Marcos?

BETO: Well. You know what I mean.

FRANK: The job's temporary until I can get into radio.

BETO: Radio, you think they'll let you in?

FRANK: I don't know, Papa. I don't know. Look, Papa, I'm trying to study.

BETO: I started going house to house on foot when your mother and I got married. I walked for miles, carrying those buckets of tomatoes until I thought my fingers would fall off. Rain or shine, sick, we had to eat. I made regular customers. Then twenty years ago I got me a mule and wagon. (*Sings.*) "FRESH FRUIT, VEGETABLES— PEACHES, PEARS, BANANAS, SWEET CORN." Why do you think I've broken my back all these years? I built something for this family. (WILLIE *covers his head with a pillow.*)

FRANK: Look, Papa, you got Willie. You don't need me.

BETO: Willie . . . Far as I can tell, your Kelly job ain't no different from working at the market, son, except over there you rub shoulders with a few *gringos*. You're making $5 a week less than you could get with me. At least at the market you'd be working for your own family.

FRANK: Papa, are you going to try to sell to some big buyers like the Santa Rosa Hospital? What about an army base like Fort Sam? That's the future for the business . . . not a nickle and dime produce stand. (ESTHER *enters, dressed for Mass. She is carrying the Sunday paper. Hearing the tone of the conversation, she stays in the living room.*)

BETO: The big buyers belong to the *gringos*. We do all right selling to our own people.

FRANK: I'm not going to work at the produce market. I told you before. You made me quit school when I was thirteen to work for you. You had me running in the street picking pecans off the ground. My friends were going to school, carrying their books. I looked at them, with my hands full of pecans, and I felt ashamed. To you school's not important. You think if you can read and write, that's enough. It's not enough, Papa . . . not anymore. I'm going to get into radio. If I had more school, I'd get in sooner. People with high school diplomas are accepted no questions asked. People like me—we have to take a test.

BETO: Tests? You and your books. That's not our way. That's their way. You've changed, but the *gringos* haven't. You'll see. (*Enter* PETRA.)

PETRA: Beto, that's enough. *Es todo.*

BETO: I'm just thinking about his own good.

FRANK: I'm no kid. I can take care of myself . . . and my family. (*Exit* BETO. FRANK *attempts to study, but is distracted by his argument with* BETO. ESTHER *enters the kitchen, puts the paper on the table. She takes* FRANK's *hand.*)

PETRA: I'm going to get ready for Mass. (PETRA *exits.* FRANK *withdraws his hand from* ESTHER's *and pretends to study.* ESTHER *pulls out the classified ads and starts reading. Simultaneously,* WILLIE *gets out of bed and puts on his bathrobe. He notices the German helmet and puts it on his head. He goosesteps to the mirror and salutes himself.* WILLIE *reaches into his dresser drawer and grabs a handful of bullets. Using his cane as a rifle, he shoots at imaginary snipers hiding in his room, tossing up a bullet with his thumb for each shot. He points it at an imaginary enemy and makes a "rat-ta-ta" with his tongue.*)

WILLIE: Rat-ta-ta-ta . . . Take that, you Nazi! Got him! Rat-ta-ta . . .

Ahh . . . (*Grabbing his shoulder.*) Got me in the arm, you bastard, but that won't stop me . . . (*Shooting with his other arm.*) Rat-ta-ta-tat . . . That'll show you! Blam-blam-blam! (*Tosses his cane aside.*) You got me . . . (*Falls back in bed.*)

ESTHER: (*Holding open the classifieds.*) Look, Frank. The house on Waverly is still listed.

FRANK: Do we have to talk about this now, Esther?

ESTHER: I thought you wanted to go house-hunting. We've been looking forward to this all week.

FRANK: Let's talk about it later, huh?

ESTHER: But we have to decide where we're going to look. (*Showing him the classifieds.*) There are a lot of places. I liked the German lady's house over on Poplar Street, the one with the big pecan tree in front.

FRANK: That old lady sure hemmed and hawed when she saw who we were. Aw, maybe she had already sold the house. Nah, all these ads are come-ons. They're putting together a sucker list of returning vets.

ESTHER: You think so?

FRANK: Who knows.

ESTHER: The fella over on Zarzamora was friendly.

FRANK: Sure, his house was falling down. Why wouldn't he be? (*Reaches for his book.*) You read all those classifieds . . . and mark the good ones. We'll go out later this afternoon . . . after I finish this studying. (*He goes back to his book. JUNIOR comes banging in the front door.*)

JUNIOR: Willie! Willie!

WILLIE: (*From his bedroom.*) In here. (WILLIE *begins gathering up the bullets. JUNIOR goes to* WILLIE*'s room. WILLIE puts the bullets in an ashtray on top of his dresser.*)

JUNIOR: Can you read me "Nancy"?

WILLIE: Sure. Go get the funnies. I'll meet you in the living room.

JUNIOR: (*Picking up the bullets.*) What's this?

WILLIE: Bullets.

JUNIOR: Bullets? What are they for?

WILLIE: They're for shooting squirrels. Watch! (*Palms them in his other hand and opens now-empty hand.*) They're gone. Where'd they go? (JUNIOR *looks around, confused.* WILLIE *produces the bullets again and shows them to* JUNIOR.) I don't want you ever touching these, okay?

JUNIOR: Okay.

WILLIE: Go get the funnies. (JUNIOR *exits* WILLIE*'s room and goes* *downstairs.* WILLIE *puts the bullets in his dresser drawer. He follows* JUNIOR. JUNIOR *enters the kitchen where* FRANK *is studying. He sorts through the newspapers piled on the table.*)

JUNIOR: Funnies, funnies, funnies . . .

FRANK: Quiet, Junior.

WILLIE: Comic Weekly Man. I'm the Comic Weekly Man. (*Together with* JUNIOR.) I've come to read the funnies to all you boys and honeys. (JUNIOR *continues rustling through the papers.*)

FRANK: Goddamn it! Why can't I get any goddamn peace in this house?! (*Enter* WILLIE.)

WILLIE: Hey, brother. We're just getting the comics. (FRANK *glares at the two of them.*)

FRANK: I got this test, you understand? I just need a little quiet around here. (WILLIE *picks up the comics and takes* JUNIOR *to the couch.*)

WILLIE: See that little bird? It thinks Nancy's hair is its nest, so that's why all its eggs are up there. So she can't move . . .

ESTHER: Frank? (*He looks at her.*) I know passing this exam means a lot to you. But Junior's only six. He doesn't understand these things, and . . .

FRANK: (*Yelling.*) No one in this goddamn house seems to understand a gooddamn thing!

ESTHER: Frank! (FRANK *gets up and goes to his bedroom.* ESTHER *follows him.*)

WILLIE: (*To* JUNIOR.) Look at this. (*Pointing to the paper.*) We can learn about radio, too. (*Reads.*) "Amazing radio, needs no electricity, only $1.98."(ESTHER *closes the door behind them. She glares at him.*)

ESTHER: Maybe if you explain to Papa that your warehouse job is temporary.

FRANK: (*Angry.*) That's a real smart idea. Willie could be doing more to help Papa. He knows the business as well as I do, better. (ESTHER *turns, crying.*) But Willie doesn't seem to give a damn. I'm not going back to the market, though. And I'm not going to unload trucks at Kelly for the next ten years either.

ESTHER: (*In tears.*) You're not going to unload trucks for the next ten years.

FRANK: (*Fighting back his anger.*) Who knows. Maybe I will. Who the hell knows? Maybe he's right.

ESTHER: I was just trying to help.

FRANK: You ought to know Papa by now.

ESTHER: I do.

FRANK: (*Sarcastically.*) Sometimes I wonder.

ESTHER: No matter how old you are, Beto's still your father. In his mind, you're deserting him. But he's concerned about you, too. Try to understand that.

FRANK: Why are you taking his side?

ESTHER: (*Angrily.*) I'm not! I can't say anything right to you. You hardly speak to me. Then when you do, you blow up. What do you want from me?

FRANK: I want you to understand how important this is to me.

ESTHER: What am I? Furniture? I'm your wife.

FRANK: Look, Esther, I'm sorry. It's not you. The way Junior hangs onto Willie . . . I'm his father, for godsakes. The kid is spoiled rotten.

ESTHER: Don't blame it on him. He's not spoiled rotten. Frank, I don't know how to talk to you, or when to leave you alone. You used to look at me. You used to want to hold me. Remember? I remember.

FRANK: We just need some privacy, you and me.

ESTHER: That's why we have to find a house, Frank. (ESTHER *grabs her hat and leaves the room.* FRANK *paces, stops, stares at the walls.* BETO *and* PETRA *are standing in the living room ready for Mass. They exit with* ESTHER *and* JUNIOR. WILLIE *goes to his room.* FRANK *lies on the bed. Lights go down.*)

SCENE NINE

Dream Sequence. A spray of gunshots hits a wall; the bullets "zing" about the room, ricocheting.

FRANK: Shit. The fucking house. (*Lights up dimly.* FRANK *is lying on the floor.*) Watts, (*Whispering.*) You all right? Did you see where it was coming from? (WATTS *enters.*)

WATTS: They're in those houses, one of those.

FRANK: Some of our guys are in a house up the road. Where the hell is B Company? They're hiding out there in the field until we take the town.

WATTS: Look what these guys left. This luger is a real beauty, clean, no nicks. Did you see something move? Over there. I'm going to try to get to the wall. Just don't let them shoot me. (WATTS *crawls along the ground until he makes the cover of a low wall. He takes out a hand grenade and pulls the pin. He rises to his knees, takes a beat to aim, throws the grenade and dives to the ground. The grenade bounces on a stone floor; terrified children scream in panic. The grenade blows up with a deafeningly loud explosion, accompanied by a bright flash and smoke. The screams stop.*

FRANK: Jesus, Watts. It was kids. (*Lights to black.*)

ACT TWO

SCENE ONE

A day in November, late afternoon. WILLIE*'s alarm clock rings. He wakes and silences the clock and falls back into bed. Downstairs in the kitchen* PETRA *and* JUNIOR *are playing "Lotería," a game similar to Bingo.*

PETRA: (*Calling out.*) *La golondrina, el gaitían, la muerte, el corazón, la mano.*

JUNIOR: I win!

PETRA: Not yet. You didn't fill the card, *la estrella.* See?

JUNIOR: You already said *la estrella.* I covered it and the bean fell off.

PETRA: You can't do that again. You tried that before and it worked. You won't do it again. *¡Mira qué cosa!*

JUNIOR: Look, there's the card.

PETRA: Oh, no. I did call it. You won.

JUNIOR: How many pennies did I win? Six, seven, eleven! (WILLIE *arises and dresses.* JUNIOR, *hearing* WILLIE *stir, runs upstairs to the room.* PETRA *shakes her head and puts away the game.*)

JUNIOR: Willie, guess what?

WILLIE: What, what?

JUNIOR: I beat Grandma at Mexican Bingo.

WILLIE: (*Loudly, for* PETRA *to hear.*) That's great. That is something. (*Whispers.*) Did you do the trick?

JUNIOR: Yes. (*Whispers.*) I got eleven pennies.

WILLIE: Where did you hide the cards, under the tablecloth? (JUNIOR *nods yes.*) Don't ever tell her I told you how to do it. Ever, ever, okay? She's been doing that to your grandpa for years.

JUNIOR: Okay. Will you buy me some baseball cards with the pennies?

WILLIE: You better give Grandma back her pennies, you know. It takes her a long time to get them away from Grandpa. She'll be upset.

JUNIOR: But I won them.

WILLIE: Did you have any pennies when you started?

JUNIOR: No. Can I have some bubble gum, anyway?

WILLIE: I think I can do that. (WILLIE *and* JUNIOR *go to the kitchen.* PETRA *has gone.*) Well, she's not here. What do you think? (JUNIOR *shrugs. Arriving at the front door is* EUGENA WATTS, *wearing a faded cotton print dress, white gloves and a hat. She is holding a newspaper.* WILLIE *answers the door.*) Hello.

EUGENA: Hello, I'm Eugena Watts. I called some time back to talk to Frank de la Cruz. (PETRA *re-enters.*)

PETRA: ¿Quién es?

WILLIE: (*To* PETRA.) Mamá, una americana. (*To* EUGENA.) Please come in. I remember you. You came here the day Frank came home. I'll get Frank. (*Shouting.*) Frank!!

EUGENA: (*To* PETRA.) Sorry to show up unannounced.

WILLIE: Frank! There's somebody here to see you. (*To* EUGENA.) He'll be right here. (*Enter* FRANK *and* ESTHER. FRANK *carries his radio books. He places then on the sofa.*) This is Frank.

FRANK: Hello. Can I help you?

EUGENA: I'm Eugena Watts, Mr. de la Cruz. (*She extends her hand to* FRANK.)

FRANK: I'm pleased to meet you, Mrs. Watts. Did you come alone?

EUGENA: No, I . . . my husband's out in the car.

FRANK: This is my wife, Esther. And you spoke with my brother.

EUGENA: Pleased to meet you, I'm sure.

ESTHER: It's very nice meeting you. This is Frank's mother, and our son.

EUGENA: Pleased to meet you, too, I'm sure. (PETRA *nods.*) What's your name, little boy? (JUNIOR *hides behind* ESTHER.)

ESTHER: He's Frank Junior.

EUGENA: What do you have in your hand? Let's see. Pennies? (*Opens her purse.*) Here, here's a dime. (JUNIOR *looks at* ESTHER.)

ESTHER: It's okay.

FRANK: My mother was on her way to visit a neighbor. Mama, go ahead. It's all right. (PETRA, *so animated a few moments before, pauses at the door to stare at* EUGENA, *then exits.*)

EUGENA: I don't want to take a lot of your time, but I come from Floresville, Mr. de la Cruz.

ESTHER: Does your husband want to come in?

EUGENA: No, he . . . just . . . (*To* FRANK.) I was hoping to talk with you alone, if I could.

WILLIE: Ah, sure, why don't we go upstairs, Junior.

ESTHER: Certainly, it's all right.

FRANK: We were on our way out, too.

ESTHER: We still have a little time.

EUGENA: (*To* ESTHER.) Thank you, Mrs. de la Cruz. I would like to talk to your husband about my son . . . and I'd like to do it alone, if you don't mind.

ESTHER: I understand. Frank, it's okay. (WILLIE, ESTHER *and* JUNIOR *exit*.)

EUGENA: I'm sorry to put you out, Mr. de la Cruz. That's what Ernest called you—de la Cruz. And you called him Watts.

FRANK: That's right. Many of the guys . . . I never knew their first names.

EUGENA: The 36th Division is going to have a convention soon. I saw in the paper some men are bringing up some sort of resolution there. They're real upset about what happened at the Rapido River . . . Isn't that were my son died, Mr. de la Cruz?

FRANK: I can't help you, Mrs. Watts.

EUGENE: I thought maybe you were going to the convention.

FRANK: No, I'm not.

EUGENE: Ernest was your friend. He said he knew you better than anyone he ever knew. He wrote me about you. You're like I pictured you.

FRANK: Mrs. WAtts, I really can't help.

EUGENA: I want to know what happened. The letter said he was missing in action at the battle of the Rapido River.

FRANK: Watts was a buddy. But things happen. You can't always keep track of each other.

EUGENA: You saw it all, didn't you? You were there, next to him.

FRANK: (*Annoyed*.) I said I can't help you.

EUGENA: I brought him into this world, Mr. de la Cruz, and I want to know how he left it. I cannot believe my son is dead. I don't have a body to put in the ground. I read his letters, and there's a letter from Ernest dated after the day he was supposed to have disappeared. He couldn't write a letter if he was dead. I don't have a tear for him until I know. If you could tell me, maybe I could believe once and for all.

FRANK: He's dead. He was like a brother.

EUGENA: Mr. de la Cruz, you say he was like a brother. My husband won't come in here because he wishes it was you that was missing, and Ernest the one that came home. I'm telling you this because it's the truth and I need to know exactly how it happened.

FRANK: He put the date on a letter for the day he thought he could mail it. He died clean, Mrs. Watts. He didn't know what hit him. He didn't say a word. It's God's honest truth.

EUGENA: Thank you, Mr. de la Cruz. I'll be going. It was kind of you to take the time. (*She extends her hand.*) Tell your wife goodbye for me. She's very pretty. You have a fine family.

FRANK: Look, I'm sorry about Ernest. But I'm not sorry about coming home.

EUGENA: I know. Goodbye, Mr. de la Cruz. (EUGENA *exits.* WILLIE *enters, crosses to the doorway and watches the car drive away.*)

WILLIE: What did she want to know about? (FRANK *is about to walk out when he meets* ESTHER *coming in.*) Huh, Frank? Did she say something about the newspaper? (FRANK *tries to walk around ES-THER, but she takes his arm and puts it around her.*)

ESTHER: Frank?

WILLIE: She mentioned the Rapido River. There was this article in the paper yesterday. I cut it out and put it in the book. You want to see it?

FRANK: No. I don't want to see it.

WILLIE: I made the book for you, Frank. Maybe you can save it for Junior.

FRANK: You keep the book, Willie. I'm not interested. (*Angrily.*) Leave me alone, will you? (*Enter* BETO *and* JUNIOR.)

WILLIE: Hey I don't mean to butt into your personal business, Big Bro. (FRANK *pulls away from* ESTHER.)

BETO: Get ready, Willie. We have to get going.

WILLIE: I'll get ready when I'm damned good and ready. Go ahead. Frank's not the only person who lives here, you know. (WILLIE *exits.*)

ESTHER: We better go, Frank.

FRANK: (*To* BETO.) Why do you let him get away with that?

ESTHER: Frank? (FRANK *pulls away from her again.*)

FRANK: What! Willie is walking all over Papa. He wouldn't have me pull that kind of stuff.

BETO: You got your job, Frank. You take care of it.

FRANK: I would like to, you know. But not in this house. Let's go.

JUNIOR: Where are we going?

FRANK: We're going to see about a house.

JUNIOR: I don't want to. I want to stay with Willie.

FRANK: (*Kneels.*) You're going to have your own room. You won't sleep on the sofa any more. You'll like that.

JUNIOR: I . . . won't. This is my house. (FRANK *stands.*)

FRANK: We're supposed to be there at 5:30. Let's go. (ESTHER *takes* JUNIOR *by the hand, all three exit. Lights down.*)

SCENE TWO

Dream Sequence. It is an overcast night lighted by strobing explosions of artillery only a few miles away.

FRANK: Watts! Watts! Where the hell are you?

WATTS: De la Cruz! Here! I'm over here! Look what I got! (*Holds up a bottle.*)

FRANK: Where'd you get that?

WATTS: From that farmhouse. They don't need it anymore.

FRANK: Jesus. That place was flattened. Where did you find it?

WATTS: Did you ever go fishing?

FRANK: Yeah . . . so?

WATTS: (*Laughs.*) Me and an axe handle went fishing in the latrine.

FRANK: Keep your voice down. You mean the farmhouse crapper?

WATTS: Yeah. It was all wrapped up like a birthday present and it ain't even my birthday. (*Laughs.* WATTS *drinks.*)

FRANK: You could have told me something else. Give it here.

WATTS: Speaking of fishing. My daddy used to take us fishing and tell us stories about Alligator Joe. This crazy guy used to keep an alligator on his farm in one of them stock tanks. One day he found his old lady in bed with a local shoe salesman. Anyway, the wife and the shoe salesman disappeared and the farmer started wearing alligator shoes. (*Laughs.*) It used to scare me and my brother. (*Cries.*) De la Cruz, it's one lousy war, isn't it?

FRANK: Yeah. Where would we be if it weren't for this war?

WATTS: We wouldn't be in this craphouse drinking a bottle of schnapps. I'd be a plumber's apprentice for my uncle in Lufkin.

FRANK: I'd probably be working all night moving produce for my old man.

WATTS: Hey, I got something for your kid. Found it complete, box and all. Only it's got this little burn on the box . . . it's toy soldiers.

FRANK: I don't know if we're gonna make it back, Watts, but I want you to have this. (FRANK *removes a chain with a gold medallion from around his neck and hands it to* WATTS.)

WATTS: It's made out of gold.

FRANK: So it won't turn your neck green. It's a St. Christopher's medal blessed by the Bishop of San Antonio. (WATTS *puts the chain around his neck.*)

WATTS: Give me that bottle, buddy. (*Sound effects of half-tracks approaching.*)

FRANK: Let's get the hell outta here. (*They exit. Lights down.*)

SCENE THREE

A Saturday afternoon, several weeks later. As the lights come up, PETRA *is at the stove singing "Cuatro Milpas." ESTHER joins her in the last four lines. WILLIE and JUNIOR are in WILLIE's room sitting on the bed. WILLIE cuts an article from the newspaper.*

PETRA: *Cuatro milpas tan sólo han quedado*
De aquel rancho que era mío.
Ai yai, ya yai.

De aquella casita tan blanca y bonita
Lo triste que está.
Los potreros están sin ganados.
Ya todito se acabó.
Ay yai, ya yai.

Ya no hay amapolas, ni hiedras, ni aromas,
ya todo murió.
Pero me prestarás tus ojos, morena,
Los llevo en el alma, que miren allá.

Los despojos de quella casita tan blanca y bonita
Lo triste que está. (ESTHER *applauds.*)

ESTHER: I'd like to learn more of your songs, Mama. Some of the women at the factory sing while they're sewing. I don't think I could do it.

PETRA: You don't have to work, Esther.

ESTHER: If I even let myself start thinking about something, I make too many mistakes, and I fall behind.

PETRA: Singing can help you keep from thinking. When we first came here from Rio Grande, Beto could only get day work. It was never enough. And I had to go to work shelling pecans. I had never worked like that before, twelve, sometimes sixteen hours. I thought I'd go crazy with my thinking. What was I doing in this cold packing shed? *Mis dedos hinchados*. I felt even my mind didn't belong to me anymore. So I soon understood why the women sang. It was the only thing that gave the miserable work a little humanity. Some of the foremen would say in English, "Stop singing. You're having too much fun!" But when we stopped singing, we didn't clean as many pecans. So they let us sing.

ESTHER: I always loved to sew, but piecework takes all the pleasure out of it. Mama . . . Frank and I saw another house this morning.

PETRA: Frank is late.

ESTHER: He went back to see the owner. (PETRA *turns her back to* ESTHER.)

PETRA: (*Calling.*) Willie, it's time to eat. (WILLIE *is sitting on his bed. He is pasting a clipping in the scrapbook.* JUNIOR *gets up and starts going through* WILLIE*'s dresser.*)

WILLIE: (*Replying.*) We'll be right down. (*To* JUNIOR.) I have to add three more pages . . . three more articles.

JUNIOR: What about?

WILLIE: You wouldn't be interested . . . just a convention, a lot of people talking. Junior, put those bullets away. You know you're not supposed to touch them.

JUNIOR: I want some bubble gum. (BETO*'s truck pulls into the driveway.*)

WILLIE: Come on, Junior. After we eat. Hey, there's your grandpa. Run down and meet him. I'll be right there. (JUNIOR *runs downstairs.* BETO *enters carrying a bushel basket of grapefruits.*)

JUNIOR: Hi, Grandpa!

BETO: Hey, Junior. Lookit what I got. (JUNIOR *takes a grapefruit, tosses it a couple of times and follows* BETO *into the kitchen.* BETO *hangs his coat over the back of a chair and puts his hat on the table.*

BETO: I used to pay the politicians off with five dollars in a handshake, you know. "Yes sir, Mr. Callahan, it was very good to see you again. (*Shaking hands with an imaginary person.*) Yes siree, Mr. Callahan." Now they call it taxes. And they still want the bushel basket of ruby red grapefruits. "My wife shore enjoyed that basket of ruby reds you sent, Mr. de la Cruz." Petra! Lookit! (BETO *sits.* WILLIE *takes his cane and the scrapbook. With difficulty he goes downstairs.*)

PETRA: Beto, *¿otra vez?* What am I going to do with all those grapefruits? (PETRA *removes* BETO*'s hat from the table and replaces it with a dish of "guisado."*

BETO: You could say, "Thank you."(*Rubbing his hands.*) It's getting cold out there. These are the last of the valley grapefruits for this year. We're going to have a norther. I can feel it down to my toes.

PETRA: I suppose Tía Concha could use the grapefruits for her digestion. *Ya, con las toronjas.* The *guisado* is going to get cold.

BETO: *Guisado* every Wednesday, *guisado.*

PETRA: *Mira, pues. Entonces, ¡no comas!* (PETRA *takes* BETO*'s plate.*)

BETO: No, no, no. I'm kidding! (*Takes plate back.*) I'll eat your *guisado* Wednesday, Thursday, any day. Hey, Junior, you want to go pick up some pecans with me tomorrow? If it freezes, they're going to fall tonight. (JUNIOR *nods.* WILLIE *joins the family in the kitchen.*)

WILLIE: Did you read the paper, Esther?

ESTHER: No, why?

WILLIE: Listen to this: "The 36th Division was outnumbered by well-entrenched German forces. In 40 hours of brutal combat at the Rapido River, three thousand brave Americans were reduced to a handful of survivors. The men of the 36th call for a congressional investigation into the Rapido River failure . . . "

BETO: Let me see that. What does it mean? (WILLIE *gives him the scrapbook.*)

WILLIE: It means the men of the 36th Division are asking for Congress to find out what went wrong in the Battle of the Rapido River. They're saying some general made a big mistake.

PETRA: Congress? *¿Qué es eso?*

BETO: They're not going to call Frank, are they?

ESTHER: He hasn't said anything about it.

PETRA: Beto, *¿qué es eso?*

BETO: Well, it's like when someone goes to trial, except the president is the judge. (WILLIE *laughs.*)

WILLIE: No, Papa. The president has nothing to do with it. This is Congress.

BETO: Isn't it the same thing? They're all politicians.

PETRA: *¿El congreso . . . los diputados?*

ESTHER: Yes, Mama. (FRANK *enters. He removes his jacket and hangs it by the door.*)

PETRA: Frank, you're late. *¿Quieres comer?*

FRANK: Sí, Mama. Hello, everybody. It's cold. (FRANK *sits.*)

WILLIE: There was this article in the paper. It said something about the congressional investigation into the Battle of the Rapido River.

FRANK: It's got nothing to do with me.

ESTHER: But it sounded serious.

FRANK: It's mostly some guys who are still in the Texas National Guard. I've been discharged.

BETO: Will you have to go away?

FRANK: I don't think so.

WILLIE: What's it all about? It's a congressional investigation.

FRANK: I don't want to talk about that now, Willie. Esther, I got news.

ESTHER: (*Excited.*) What did he say?

FRANK: (*Stands.*) I think we got the place. (*To everyone.*) It was between us and another couple. But their bank loan didn't come through, so the owner took my check for earnest money.

ESTHER: (*Stands and hugs* FRANK.) Since we left there this morning, I haven't let myself talk about the house. I was so afraid if I said something, I'd put a hex on it, and we wouldn't get it. (*Laughs.*)

FRANK: It goes into escrow Monday.

PETRA: So soon? What if there's something wrong with the house?

ESTHER: The house is small, but it has two bedrooms. In the kitchen there's an old-fashioned yellow stove that works—the kind with legs. But the best part is the yard. There's a path back to the alley and a good sunny place by the back door for *portulacas.*

FRANK: We didn't know what kind of guy the owner would be, you know—maybe a banker-type with tight shoes. But he turned out to be completely different.

ESTHER: He's lived alone in that house for years—since his sister died. But he keeps it so clean . . . for a single man. He's very polite. He owns the tailor shop near the Gunter Hotel. You know the one. I think he's Jewish. Right, Frank? (FRANK *nods.*) He served us hot tea and homemade sponge cake, like we were company. He told us about his sister, her cats and her roses. He wanted to make sure we'd take care of her rosebushes. He asked if we had children. Then he asked Frank if he'd been in Germany during the war. He wanted to know about a place called . . . what was it called, Frank?

FRANK: Landsberg.

ESTHER: A lot of his family died there.

WILLIE: Didn't I read about Landsberg? You were there, weren't you, Frank? What was it?

FRANK: I don't know . . . a kind of prison.

WILLIE: Yeah, it was a concentration camp!

FRANK: Hey, Junior, come over and sit by me. (JUNIOR *shakes his head, no.*) Come on, son. Come here. Look at what I got for you, a real baseball. Come on. (JUNIOIR *shakes his head again.*) You can throw away that other ball. Come on, catch it. A real baseball. Catch. (*Underhands ball to* JUNIOR. JUNIOR *tries to catch the ball but drops it. He hides behind* WILLIE.)

WILLIE: Whasa matter? Huh? Whasa matter? You afraid of your daddy? You shouldn't be afraid of your Daddy. (WILLIE *swings* JUNIOR *into the air like an airplane.*)

WILLIE: Zoom . . . Rat-tatatata . . . Ta . . . Flying Tiger. Rat-ta-ta-ta . . . EEEEEEE . . . MMMMMMMM . . . CRASH!

JUNIOR: Put me down, Willie. Put me down. (WILLIE *puts* JUNIOR *down.* JUNIOR *is giggling.*)

WILLIE: (*Winded, sits down.*) Wanna go again? (JUNIOR *shakes his head no.* JUNIOR *then grabs his coat and exits.* FRANK*'s eyes meet* WILLIE*'s.* WILLIE *climbs the stairs to his bedroom. He slumps on the bed.*)

ESTHER: What if we don't get the house?

FRANK: It looks good. The V.A.'s got to inspect it, but I don't think there's going to be any trouble.

FRANK: Mama . . . The money's safe.

PETRA: It took you a long time to save it.

BETO: Petra's right, son. Something can always go wrong.

FRANK: That's why they have escrow, Papa, to make sure nothing goes wrong. (*EXPLOSION*! FRANK *jumps to his feet.*) What the hell . . . that was a gun shot! (FRANK *exits.* WILLIE *hurriedly rejoins the family.*)

WILLIE: What was that? (*Calling.*) Junior? (FRANK *carries* JUNIOR *in.* JUNIOR *is crying and holding a bleeding hand.*)

ESTHER: What happened? (*She takes* JUNIOR *and sits him on her lap.* FRANK *exits.*) What happened? Let me see your hand.

PETRA: *Dios mío. ¿Qué te pasó? Abre la mano.*

WILLIE: Open your hand. Let us see your hand. (JUNIOR *allows his hand to be examined.*)

WILLIE: Let's see. That's a big boy.

ESTHER: I think it's just this cut. It's like a burn. It's bleeding, but I don't think it's so bad.

BETO: Nah, he's tough. Aren't you, Junior? (BETO *washes and bandages* JUNIOR*'s hand.* FRANK *returns with a smashed 22 shell.*)

FRANK: Where the hell did he get this bullet? It looks like he smashed it with a rock.

WILLIE: It must be one of mine.

FRANK: (*Furious.*) Are you stupid? How could you leave this where a kid could get ahold of it? Do you know what one of these things can do? Do you? Do you? Stupid fool! Goddamn stupid fool! (*He shoves* WILLIE, *then hits him several times.*)

WILLIE: I'm sorry . . . I . . . I'm sorry. They were put away. I'm sorry.

FRANK: He could have been killed! Goddamn fool. (BETO *steps between them, trying to keep* FRANK *away from* WILLIE.)

BETO: Stop it, Frank! (FRANK *shoves* WILLIE *to the floor.* JUNIOR *is crying from fear as much as from pain. He's never seen grownups behave this way before.*)

PETRA: ¡Deja! ¡Déjalo! Frank! Willie did a stupid thing! But you can't hit your brother! You'll hurt him. Control yourself, Frank. What's wrong with you?

FRANK: (*To* WILLIE, *shouting.*) I want you to leave Junior alone, do you understand? You're not his father.

WILLIE: You don't know how to be a father. You don't care about Junior. All you care about is getting into radio. Big man. You think you're too good for us.

BETO: That's enough, Willie.

FRANK: Willie, what do you mean, "too good"? What in hell are you talking about?

WILLIE: You come home with all your plans for the future. Everybody's tiptoeing around keeping quiet so you can study. The war's over, Frank, and you're not Sergeant de la Cruz to us.

FRANK: You want to go outside and talk about it some more?

WILLIE: No. Are you going to beat me up? Is that going to make you right?

ESTHER: Willie! Don't say anymore.

FRANK: (*To* WILLIE.) It might put some sense into your head.

ESTHER: Both of you, stop it! Can't you see you're scaring Junior? (WILLIE *stands and exits towards his room.* FRANK *catches up with him in the hall.*) Frank, please. Come back. Leave him alone.

FRANK: I'm tired of you, Willie. You know that? I don't want you to say anything about my life!

WILLIE: I'm not talking about your life. It's all going to come to you, Frank.

FRANK: Then what the hell you talking about?

WILLIE: I wanted to join the army. You knew that. I wanted to go, but I was 4F. I tried to join the Navy, Marines, even the Coast Guard. I wanted to go. But they turned me down because of my accident. And who gives a damn about me? Who's got to stay awake when real people sleep? Good ole Willie, that's who. Good ole Willie, do this, good ole Willie, open the store.

FRANK: You're feeling sorry for yourself. And we're all sick of it, Willie. What's the matter with you? All you do is lie around the house. You haven't been to the market for weeks. You used to have friends—girl friends. I can't figure you out . . . 20 years old, and you're like an old man. All you do is listen to music and play with Junior. Do you think I like the way you use him? I want you to leave him alone. Do you understand?

WILLIE: Anything you want, Frank. Anything you want. (WILLIE *goes to the front door, takes his jacket and exits.*)

PETRA: Willie, you can't go out. It's cold. Willie, you'll get sick.

FRANK: Stop treating him like a baby, Mama. Face the facts. He's a grown man.

PETRA: Willie has to be careful.

FRANK: What are you talking about? Willie's just lazy. Did you listen to what he was saying? He's lazy and jealous.

PETRA: Ah, nobody can talk to you now. You're not thinking. Why don't you look after your son? (PETRA *takes* BETO*'s arm and they exit.* FRANK *approaches* ESTHER *and* JUNIOR. *He kneels next to them and examines* JUNIOR*'s now bandaged hand.*)

ESTHER: Junior should lie down now. (*Leaving* FRANK *alone, she takes* JUNIOR *to her bedroom and puts him to bed.* FRANK *follows them to the door, but doesn't enter.*)

ESTHER: (*To* JUNIOR.) Where did you find the bullet?

JUNIOR: In Willie's drawer.

ESTHER: Why'd you take it?

JUNIOR: I wanted to see what was inside.

ESTHER: Sometimes it's not good to look inside things. You see what happened?

JUNIOR: I didn't mean to.

ESTHER: Sh-h. Rest, *m'ijo*, for a little while. (ESTHER *kisses* JUNIOR, *rises and joins* FRANK *at the doorway. They look at each other, then embrace.*)

FRANK: Where does Willie go?
ESTHER: Sometimes he goes out with his friends. But I don't know where.
FRANK: I'll be back. (FRANK *takes his coat and exits through the front door. Lights down.*)

SCENE FOUR

Living room, same night, about 1:00 a.m. A single light burns in the living room. FRANK and WILLIE arrive on foot. WILLIE throws up outside the front door. WILLIE, leaning heavily on his cane, has to be helped to the sofa.

WILLIE: You know, I couldn't keep my eyes off of her. Flesh—soft, smooth and cool, too; and hot and warm . . . and wet. She was as big around as this (*Miming.*) and smelled like carnations and sweat.
FRANK: This is the craziest thing I've ever seen you do, Willie.
WILLIE: It was heaven.
FRANK: Is that what you want?
WILLIE: Sure, isn't that all there is?
FRANK: You really do need to use that cane, don't you?
WILLIE: It's in style. People think I'm a veteran. All I have to do is wink and they see Gaudalcanal written all over me.
FRANK: I guess it works for you single guys.
WILLIE: Hell, it doesn't fool anyone. Who am I going to impress at the market? Marcos? Huh? Tonight it was a thirty-five year old woman with six kids. Sure, she was impressed. I had five bucks.
FRANK: She's not what I'd call your type. You know.
WILLIE: She's my type. You can count on that. My size, too. Extra large.
FRANK: What made you do it?
WILLIE: I had to see what it was like, just once. I thought a lot about it, you know. I figured it was better than the Butterfly Lounge. "Hey there, guy, it's the Butterfly!" Bed and bugs. (WILLIE *tries to get up.*)
FRANK: Do you need some help?
WILLIE: Do I look like I need help?

FRANK: You look like hell.

WILLIE: That's better than dead. 'Cause you're right, bro. I am an old man at 20. I'm wearing out. Nothing's working right anymore.

FRANK: You're full of shit, you know that?

WILLIE: You're so damn right all the time, aren't you.

FRANK: This isn't like you, Willie.

WILLIE: What do you know about me? You don't know a goddamn thing about me. (*He tries again to get up.* PETRA *appears at the steps.*)

PETRA: Frank, I'm going to take Willie to bed now.

WILLIE: Thanks for coming to the rescue. Maybe you shouldn't have wasted your time. They don't give Silver Stars for bringing home drunks. One thing, Frank. Please don't tell Junior. I don't want him to remember me as the uncle who got drunk, okay? It's something to watch a kid grow. I learned a little about that while you were away. You're a real lucky guy. (PETRA *helps* WILLIE *to his feet.* WIL-LIE *pulls away from her and continues alone to his bedroom.* ES-THER *appears at her bedroom door.*)

FRANK: (*To* PETRA.) How often does he do this?

PETRA: What? Get drunk? You gonna tell me you never got drunk?

FRANK: You know that's not what I'm talking about.

PETRA: Don't talk to me like that!

FRANK: Stop treating him like a baby, Mama. He made up his own mind to go out tonight.

PETRA: Willie has to take care of himself. He's not strong.

FRANK: Mama, he doesn't try.

PETRA: He does try. But he gets tired. He's much better than he was after the accident.

FRANK: You can't blame the accident for everything Willie does.

PETRA: You're wrong, Frank. I don't blame the accident for anything. Willie is here with us. What he does or doesn't do—it doesn't matter. The night of the accident I was here, worrying. Three, four in the morning. Willie didn't come home. He didn't show up for work. Then they called—the hospital. "Come now," they said. "He might not live until morning." Papa rushed home and took me there. We waited in a little white room, papa and me. The doctors wouldn't tell us nothing. Father Romero came and gave Willie the last rites, but he lived, *gracias a Dios.* Willie came home. You weren't here, Frank. I'm grateful to have Willie alive. (PETRA *exits.*)

FRANK: (*To* ESTHER.) You treat him like an invalid, he's going to act like an invalid.

ESTHER: I . . . (FRANK *crosses to the back porch.*)

FRANK: I'll be in soon. (*Lights dim.*)

SCENE FIVE

Dream sequence. FRANK *remains on the porch. Inside the house* WATTS *appears He takes a long drag off a cigarette and disappears. Lights down.*

SCENE SIX

Kitchen, early evening. WILLIE *sits at the table. He's wearing a plaid robe over flannel pajamas. He occasionally coughs into a well-used handkerchief. The parts of a crystal radio set are spread in front of him. Confused, he has redone the coil several times. The radio plays Christmas music in the background.* FRANK *enters the front door. He's just come home from work.*

FRANK: Esther! Junior?
WILLIE: Frank, can you help me with this?
FRANK: What have you got there?
WILLIE: A radio that doesn't need electricity. I got it in the mail. What do you think?
FRANK: All radios need electricity. Looks like you're having trouble with the coil.
WILLIE: Yeah. It's harder than it looks. The instructions say a child of ten can put it together.
FRANK: Ah . . . You almost have it. Look here. This goes like this.
WILLIE: Sure. (*Picks up headset.*) Why would people pay lots of money for a big radio when they can have one of these?
FRANK: Well, a crystal radio's limited, you know. (WILLIE *listens through the headset.*)
WILLIE: I think I can hear something. Not very loud, sounds like music. (*Laughs, disappointed.*) That's what you get for a dollar and ninety-eight cents. I was going to give the radio to Junior for Christmas.

Do you think it's worth it?

FRANK: Yeah, it's worth it. Goddammit, Willie, I don't want to be mad at you.

WILLIE: I'm not mad, bro. I needed to get out of the house. I wouldn't have met that lady if I stayed home.

FRANK: Look at this.

WILLIE: What is it?

FRANK: It's the radio test scores from Kelly.

WILLIE: There's at least a hundred names here. You're the first one on the list! 98 . . . ahead of Peterson, 97, Jiménez, 96. Does this mean you got a job in radio?

FRANK: The first twelve men on the list start in January. (WILLIE *shakes* FRANK*'s hand.*) You should have seen the look on Kroger's face when they posted test scores. He looked like it was going to cost him fifty bucks to shake my hand. (*Laughs.*)

WILLIE: *¡Gringo desgraciado!*

FRANK: Willie, your hand is hot. You have a fever? Are you all right? (WILLIE *shrugs.*) Where's Mama?

WILLIE: She went with Esther to get a prescription filled for me.

FRANK: Shouldn't you be in bed?

WILLIE: What for? I can be miserable here just as well as there. Anyway, I wanted to finish Junior's present. Can you wrap it for me?

FRANK: Yeah, I'll wrap it.

WILLIE: You know, the accident was the stupidest thing I've ever done. You know how the road around the lake gets all slippery in January? We took turns spinning around, except I went into the lake.

FRANK: Why?

WILLIE: It seemed like a good idea at the time.

FRANK: I've done some stupid things in my life.

WILLIE: We could slide fifty or sixty yards and just come to a nice stop. But I wanted to go further, so I gave it gas in the middle of a spin.

FRANK: That's pretty stupid.

WILLIE: (WILLIE *laughs, then coughs.*) Come on. That's funny. (FRANK *smiles.*) That's the old Frank. Frank, remember that Christmas when Papa gave you the 22, and you took me along with you to shoot at cans? God, was I excited! We walked under the trees by the San Antonio River. It was so cold I had my hands in my pockets. You shot at a couple of bottles, at some rocks. Then you handed me the 22. I think we must have seen the squirrel on that tree at the same time. He stood still. I looked at you. You nodded. I raised the 22, got him in the sights and pulled the trigger. He fell into the river, and it swept him away. We ran after him as he was carried downstream. We ran and ran till we got to the rocks and couldn't follow him anymore. We watched the river take him away. Afterwards, we walked all the way home without saying anything to each other. Remember, Frank? I tried to join up when I was seventeen. But Papa wouldn't sign for me. That was the night I got drunk with my friends and went driving around the lake. Papa probably thinks it's his fault I had the accident. They won't admit it, that I'm not getting any better.

FRANK: There's got to be a chance. You only have a cold. Come on, that's no way to talk.

WILLIE: Don't get your hopes up. You know, when they pasted me together after the accident it was like me fixing the old Ford. There were some pieces left over (*Laughs.*) I ran okay for a while, but the parts that are left have worn out. It hurts inside all the time. You can't talk about it either. You see it in people's faces. (FRANK *begins to pace.*)

WILLIE: That woman, Mrs. Watts. What did she come here for?

FRANK: She wanted to know how her son died.

WILLIE: Did he die at the Rapido River?

FRANK: Yes.

WILLIE: What happened at the Rapido River, Frank? What happened to all those men? (FRANK *turns away.*) I've seen half a dozen articles about it in the paper. And you haven't said a word. I've read all the things you did. If I were you, I'd be proud.

FRANK: You don't know what you're talking about. You have no idea what happened there.

WILLIE: Tell me, Frank.

FRANK: What difference does it make? I don't keep any secrets from you. All that's over with. It's history. I don't want to remember.

WILLIE: Are you hiding something, Frank? I don't keep any secrets from you. What did you tell that woman, Mrs. Watts, that you can't tell me? I'm your brother, Frank. (FRANK *stops pacing and faces* WILLIE.)

FRANK: I didn't want to talk to her about her son. What good would it do? He's dead just the same.

WILLIE: What happened at the Rapido River? (*Far, far in the distance the sound of mortars and machine gun fire can be heard. FRANK tries to speak, but he can't. Finally the words come, at first slowly and painfully, then in torrents.*)

FRANK: We got orders to cross the river, hold the position long enough for the engineers to put up a bridge for our tanks to cross. The brass decided to send us over at night. The river wasn't much—thirty feet wide or so. But it was deep and fast with banks that went straight down ten feet. Everything went wrong: the guys in Supply dumped our equipment five miles from the lines. They promised us replacements and they sent us three scared kids right out of bootcamp. On top of that, the fog was so thick, we couldn't keep track of the squad. The minefields weren't cleared; we lost whole squads just getting to the river. The goddamn rubber boats tore on the rocks. I don't know how the Germans could see us in the fog. We sure couldn't see them. We sent over boat after boat, and as soon as we put one in the water, the Germans would hit it . . . hundreds . . . just went under. You'd hear them scream for help, but the brass ordered us to keep going across. One of the new recruits dropped his rifle in the river and claimed he lost it. He didn't want to go. I held my 45 to his head and told him, "You're going across or you're going to die here." So he went. We lost most of my company, 130 men, and maybe 1,200 men in the division, trying to get to the other side. Those of us who got across tried to dig in, but there wasn't a bush to hide behind—nothing but rocks and mud. The Germans were so close, we could hear them talking. We could smell their cigarettes. An hour before sunrise we were out of ammo. We'd sent messengers to find out what was going on, but they never came back. Our commanding officer was dead. We were down to four men. A couple of guys put their hands on their helmets and started walking toward the German line. Before they got ten feet from me, they were shot. So me and Watts worked our way back to the river. (*Moved by* FRANK's *story*, WILLIE *is crying*.)

WILLIE: What happened?

FRANK: When we got to the river, there were no tanks, no engineers putting up a bridge . . . only more dead G.I.s. All night long we'd been defending nothing.

WILLIE: Some of the officers at the convention said the Rapido crossing was a big mistake.

FRANK: It was a slaughter. But when you're in the middle of it, you don't think like that. I could have pulled my men back, pretended we got lost in the fog. But I took my men across the river. And *none* of them ever saw morning. (WILLIE *stands*.)

WILLIE: You're the only one left. And you're the kid who couldn't kill a squirrel.

FRANK: Sometimes I have dreams. They're never exactly the same, except that I'm back there in the war. And I know it's a dream. But I keep thinking that this time I won't make it.

WILLIE: Look at me, Frank. Look at me! I'm the one who's not going to make it. But it's okay. You understand? It's okay. (WILLIE *embraces* FRANK, *then collapses in his arms.* FRANK *carries* WILLIE *to his room and lays him on the bed. Lights start to dim. A red glow begins to rise on the horizon. The mortar and machine guns are louder.* FRANK *stands by* WILLIE's *bed and looks down at his brother.*)

SCENE SEVEN

Dream sequence. The lights come up, murky and shimmering. The sound of gunfire is heard intermittently.

WATTS: Hell . . . Hell . . . Hell . . . Come on, buddy. Try to stand. Stand, goddammit!!! I got you back across. The river's behind us now. De la Cruz, are you alive? Sergeant! There's a hell on the other side. Try to stand. You're going home a hero. Yeah, Sergeant. You went across with how many companies? F, C, H Companies. B Company, E Company . . . (FRANK *speaks slowly, his voice slurred, as if he were drunk. He appears to be unaware of a wound to his chest.*)

FRANK: (*Coughs.*) Watts? Where's my wallet? My side arm? I lost my piece over there. M-my pack, it's gone. Where's my wallet? (FRANK *sits, attempts to search for his wallet.*) There's no . . . no wallet!

WATTS: You're lucky that's all you lost. Get on your feet, Sergeant.

FRANK: You aint' seen it, have you? The picture of my kid?

WATTS: Nah, I ain't seen nothing, nothing but fog, mud and the goddamn river. Can't see a living soul now. None of us could see where you was leading us. But we followed you—all the men did. They're all dead now. All of them. (JUNIOR *enters and stands near center stage, watching.*)

FRANK: Watts, I put the picture here, so it wouldn't get lost. I got to cross the river and find my kid. He's right over there, on the other side.

WATTS: That's enough, Sergeant. We got to get the hell out of here!

FRANK: I can't leave him over there.

WATTS: You're crazy! You'll get yourself killed. We got to get you some help or you'll die here like the rest of them. Our company always went first. Why? The brass didn't think any better of us meskins and redneck farmboys. We didn't mean dirt to them. We always did what we was told. And you, Sarge, you were the best of what we had. We done enough. But no more. I'm saving our butts, de la Cruz. You're my ticket out of here. Goddamn it. We're not going to die here. Let's go. (WATTS *attempts to stand, but is hit by a sniper. He staggers, falls in* FRANK's *arms. Lights start to dim.*)

FRANK: Watts . . . Watts . . . Willie . . .

PETRA: (*In darkness.*) Willie . . . Willie . . . (*Gunfire fades slowly, overlapping into the next scene.*)

SCENE EIGHT

Living room, dawn. FRANK *stands by* WILLIE's *bed.* JUNIOR, *near center stage, watches* PETRA *and* BETO *hurry up the stairs to* WILLIE's *room.*

PETRA: Willie . . .

JUNIOR: Willie? Grandma, what's the matter? Grandpa? (ESTHER *comes from behind* JUNIOR *and blocks his way.*)

ESTHER: Stay downstairs with me, Junior.

JUNIOR: What's the matter with Willie?

BETO: You just stay downstairs. Go back to bed. Esther, *por favor.* (*She takes* JUNIOR *by the shoulders.* JUNIOR *pulls away and runs past her. She follows him.*)

ESTHER: Come here, Junior! Junior? Come here. (FRANK *catches* JUNIOR *at the door to* WILLIE's *room. He takes* JUNIOR *firmly by the hand and leads him to the kitchen.*)

JUNIOR: (*Calling.*) Willie! Mama! What's the matter with Willie? Willie! (FRANK *kneels and holds his son at arm's length.* FRANK *can harldy speak.*)

FRANK: Willie is . . . dead, son. He died in his sleep.

JUNIOR: No, he didn't! You're lying! Willie! Willie! (JUNIOR *struggles to get away.*)

FRANK: Listen to me, son. I'm telling you the truth. (JUNIOR *struggles violently*.)

JUNIOR: Let me go. I want Willie.

FRANK: Willie can't be with us anymore. (FRANK *begins to sob, letting go of* JUNIOR. JUNIOR *runs to the stairs, stops and turns around toward* FRANK.)

JUNIOR: He said he'd always play with me.

FRANK: I know, son. I know you loved him. I loved him, too. (JUNIOR *runs back to his father and embraces him.* FRANK *returns the embrace. Softly.*) I loved him, too. I loved him, too. (*Lights down.*)

CURTAIN

Latina

Latina was first produced in 1980 by the New Works Division of Artists in Prison and Other Places, directed by and in collaboration with Jeremy Blahnik. After a two-week tour of California communities, Latina opened at the Pilot Theater in Los Angeles. Including the director, this production boasted an all-female production/design staff with choreography by Lynn Dally, sets and costumes by Barbara Ling, costumes by Louise Hayterby and sound by Janet Dodson. This creative team, along with a talented group of actors, moved critic Gretchen Henkel to say, "With its humor, warmth and gutsiness, Latina sings with a unity of spirit. Every element of the production has lovingly brought out the best parts of these women's stories . . . "[1] The play was an immediate success and won seven prestigious Drama-Logue awards later that year.[2]

Like many first-plays, Latina is based on the playwright's personal experience. In an interview during the run of the play, Ms. Sánchez-Scott commented, "I had known a lot of women, including myself, who were going through an obvious denial of their Latin roots, which they were trying to push into the background."[3] Speaking more directly of her experiences with the Beverly Hills domestic agency, she added, "These women made me realize that it is possible to come to terms with one's own Latinismo and to hold on to it in this society." A few years later, the playwright recalled, "These immigrant women, who had their feet on the ground, and their eyes on the stars, and their hearts full of love, strengthened me. It was like meeting at the river."[4]

Thus, Latina looks once again at the theme of cultural identity, this time, however, from a distinctly latina point of view. Sarita is the only Chicana in the play, the others are all immigrants, mostly undocumented workers. Thus, this play that centers around Sarita's personal identity crisis also encompasses the other women's problems—usually greater than hers—such as, "How will I feed my children?" rather than "Why wasn't I born an Anglo?" Fortunately, the playwright gives attention to the broader picture, both in personal and cultural terms, demonstrating some of the differences as well as similarities between women from different parts of Latin America.

To quote once again from Ms. Henkel's enthusiastic assessment of the Los Angeles production, "The dialogue, staging and design elements paint the frayed fabric of two cultures unraveling into each other. When Latina women make Los Angeles their home, Spanish jokes have English punchlines; disco intermingles with ranchero [sic] music; and tackiness and splashy color mark their styles."[5] In fact, several cultures blend into one another in one of the few Hispanic-American plays to explore beyond the differences between Chicanos and Mexicans only.[6] Sánchez-Scott gives us a taste of an arrogant Cubana who brags "I'm human, I have a green card," as well as the humility of a newly-arrived Peruana and the cynicism of a Mexicana.

When asked why there had not been more productions of *Latina*, Sánchez-Scott candidly responded, "This play poses problems for me because all of the women are maids and that is what we always play on television, in the movies. I have trouble promoting my own play if it will promote stereotypes."[7] Improperly interpreted, *Latina* could become nothing more than stereotypes, but if directed and acted with a clear understanding of who and what these women really represent, this play can enlighten an audience, even as it entertains.

Clearly, this is a play about two types of survival: economic and cultural. Unlike many other Chicano plays about loss of identity, however, *Latina* attempts to dramatize its protagonist in a sympathetic manner. Sarita is a typical "vendida," and although the playwright looks at her critically, she is, after all, the playwright herself, and the character's eventual recognition of her true culture is also the playwright's. Most other Chicano sellouts, beginning with Mingo/Mr. Sunday in Luis Valdez's *Shrunken Head of Pancho Villa*, do not change their misguided ways. They remain examples of someone who has gone astray and may never be redeemed.

As Valdez did in his first play, Sánchez-Scott mingles elements of realism and expressionism in order to draw a complete picture of her protagonists and her theme. Thus, there is no fourth wall from the inception of the play when Sarita speaks directly to the audience, inviting it to listen to her story. The opening monologue effectively creates the framework for all that is to follow, leaving no doubt that this is Sarita's play and that she has an identity crisis. As the play progresses and Sarita continues to break the fourth wall with glances at the audience or other asides, she is reminding the audience that she is only human. The flashbacks into Saritas' youth add to our understanding of the forces that have made her think the way she does.

Like the flashbacks, the asides and the moving mannequins add expressionistic elements to an otherwise realistic play. But while the flashbacks are serious, the asides and mannequin scenes give the play a sense of having fun with the audience. When Mrs. Homes brings Alma back and Sarita looks at the audience and says, "What does she think this is, the May Company?", this is a funny as well as a serious statement about how these women are treated. The maids, apparently, are nothing more than objects that can be replaced or discarded if they do not please.

When the mannequins "come alive," they exist only in Sarita's mind, like characters from Willy Loman's past that nobody else is privy to. This is an effective way of including the audience in the character's thought processes. Like the good angels in a morality play, these mannequins serve as Saritas' conscience, telling her to do what she knows is right: "If you cant's stand up for yourself, stand up for Alma." Thus we see the struggle in this Chicana's mind, giving her more dimension than most representations of a "vendida." The audience is urged not to judge her too harshly, for she does know what is right. She simply cannot act yet.

Behind all the commentaries about the Latina women are the statements about their employers, the wealthy women who hire these Latinas to clean their houses and take care of their children and their husbands. Each of the Anglo characters in the Los Angeles production were played by one actress, another comment in itself. Certainly, each of the employers, from Mrs. Homes to Mrs. Camden, have their distinctions as indivudals, but ultimately they are all alike. No matter how much the wigs, costumes, makeup and accessories change the actress playing these four women, she is still the same person underneath it all. Any actress would welcome the opportunity to play these women as an excercise in versatility.[8]

And then there's Sleazy Sánchez. By making the owner of the domestic agency another Latino, in this case a Guatemalan, the playwright is drawing attention to the fact that Latinos can be exploited by other Latinos. This even adds to the humor, for this Latino is a caricature of an actual person who is close to the playwright's understanding of his type. It seems difficult to imagine Sancho as a Jones, for there is something in the fact that he comes from the Latino community, yet is apart from it, or perhaps would like to be.

Sánchez is the ultimate entrepreneur, a mini-capitalist striving for the American Dream just as passionately as the women. But he does not consider himself a small-time player; he is diversified. And it is that diversity that causes us to laugh at him. Sánchez is nothing less than audacious, an egotistical, beer-bellied Hispanic-American who fancies himself a ladies man, surrounded, as he is, by his women. Short of being an actual pimp, Sánchez is a kind of "madame," representing his women for prospective clients, as if they were, in fact, prostitutes.

Sánchez thinks he is a realist surrounded by dreamers. "Everybody's gotta have a dream, honey. It keeps them together," he tells Sarita, who dreams of being a movie star, while he dreams of being Businessman of the Year. Unfortunately, Sánchez has a much greater chance of achieving his desires than any of the other characters. Sánchez represents the Latino small businessman, always looking for a new enterprise, continually searching for the pot of gold. When he tells Sarita "some of them thought the streets of this country were paved with gold," he is unknowingly referring to himself as well. Like so many businessmen before him, both large and small, as he exploits everyone around him, his gold will have a taint to it.

As the play progresses we learn not only about the variety of women who pass through these doors, but also why Sarita thinks as she does. The flashbacks reveal the influences of both sympathetic and non-sympathetic nuns in her youth. The nuns vary from Sister Agnes painted with a sympathetic tone, to the nameless nun who crushes Young Sarita's enthusiasm for a Mexican artist with her Eurocentric adoration of Michaelangelo. The playwright does not negate Michaelangelo's importance as much as she calls for a recognition of the contributions of Mexican artists, as well.

Approaching the conclusion of the play, the final flashback reveals a maturing Young Sarita in conflict with yet another nun, but unlike the previous sister, this nun is sympathetic to Mexican history. Unfortunately, it is too late, for Sarita's negative impressions of her people have already been firmly established. When she thinks of Mexicans or Chicanos, Sarita can only envision what are, to her, unfavorable images, such as "cholos," "grafitti," "low riders" and "Whittier Boulevard." No matter how positive this nun is about Sarita's "rich, fertile history," the teacher's enthusiasim is negated by her student's adolescent disdain for people with whom she does not want to be associated. This Young Sarita has made her choice and contiues to substitute an Anglo name for Sara Gómez, despite the nun's pleadings.

By the time Mrs. Camden enters, we have been prepared for her through her many phone calls. The playwright has carefully built up the tension in the play, leading to the protagonist's final reversal. Both we and Sarita have had enough of the grovelling to both the clients and the boss, so that when Sarita finally reacts to this arrogant, racist woman, we cheer her on. It is only a symbolic gesture when Sarita breaks down and gives Mrs. Camden a piece of her mind, but it is enough to release her anger. In telling Mrs. Camden what she really thinks of her, Sarita gains a dignity that she did not possess before. She has won the respect of the women who ridiculed her for denying her heritage, but more importantly, she discovers her own self respect.

By having the immigration agents raid the agency at the end, the playwright underscores the fact that so many of these workers are being exploited precisely because they are undocumented. The recurring theme of the exploitation of undocumented workers will not go away until some sort of solution is found. However, capitalism is based on a cheap pool of labor and as long as there is abject poverty south of the border, there will be people trying to gain a better existence in this country, no matter what the risks. As Sánchez tells Sarita, "They'll all be back," and he is correct.[9]

Not being an agit-prop play, *Latina* does not leave us with a solution to the immigration problem. But the play does indicate that people can be changed; that even a Sarita can finally recognize her true self. It is clear that the sleazy Sánchez and Mrs. Camdens of the world will continue to exploit, unless the exploited unite to do something about their condition. Even Sarita, perhaps heartened by her impending television role and her outburst, will be back on the job the next day. But history proves that we can be certain that she will not play a doctor, lawyer, teacher or judge on "Eight Is Enough." Working for the ultimate dream machine, Hollywood, Sarita will continue to portray stereotypes, but she has ceased to be one herself and that is the message.

[1]Gretchen Henkel, "Latina," *Drama-Logue*, 12–18 June, 1980, pp. 6.

[2]*Latina* was produced by California State University, Long Beach, in 1983, directed by Elena Gutiérrez as her Master's thesis project. No other companies have produced this play, perhaps because of the unusually large casting requirements. This play might be perfect for universitiy theater departments, save for the fact that I know of no program in the country with enough Latina women to successfully cast this play.

[3]Ron Pennington, "Curtain Calls," *The Hollywood Reporter*, 15 May, 1980, n.p.

[4]M. Elizabeth Osborn, *On New Ground: Contemporary Hispanic-American Plays* (New York: Theatre Communications Group, 1987), p. 245.

[5]Henkel, p. 6.

[6]Eduardo Gallardo's *Women Without Men*, set in New York's Garment District during World War II, explores the differences between Latin American women waiting for their men to come home. This serio-comic play with music was produced as a workshop by Joseph Papp's Festival Latino in 1986, but has yet to be fully-mounted. It is published in Eduardo Gallardo, *Simpson Street and Other Plays* (Houston: Arte Publico Press, 1989).

[7]From a series of telephone conversations in 1988.

[8]*Daily Variety* was very impressed with Susan Niven's several characterizations, commenting that some of her characters were "minor gems of satire." *Daily*

Variety, 12 June, 1980, n.p.

[9]The Immigration Reform Act of 1988 is supposed to deter the employment of undocumented workers, but it is too early to know how effective this new law will be. Initial indications show that although some employers are being fined, the influx of undocumented workers continues.

Milcha Sánchez-Scott

Milcha Sánchez-Scott was born in 1955 on the island of Bali, the daughter of a Colombian father and an Indonesian, Chinese and Dutch mother. Her father was raised in Colombia and in Mexico, and Ms. Sánchez-Scott grew up in a variety of international settings, because her father's work as an agronomist required him to travel a great deal. During her early school years Ms. Sánchez-Scott attended a Catholic girls school near London, where she learned to speak English.

Although Ms. Sánchez-Scott is admittedly not a Chicana by virtue of her ancestry, she was introduced to the harsh realities of being brown-skinned in the United States when her family moved to La Jolla, California. She was about fifteen and was waiting for the school bus on the first day of classes when, "A smart-alecky boy threw a pebble at me and said, 'This isn't the Mexican bus stop. You have to go to the Mexican bus stop,' " and to her chagrin, the other students joined-in with the same insulting chant. Her parents immediately enrolled her in an Episcopalian girls school. "I had never experienced racial tension, but in La Jolla we saw incredible—to us—prejudice."[1]

Having experienced her adolescence and young adulthood in Southern California, close to the Mexican border and in an area rich with Mexican customs, Ms. Sánchez-Scott could not escape the influences of her environment. One year after graduating from the University of San Diego with a degree in Literature, Philosophy and Theatre, Ms. Sánchez-Scott moved to Los Angeles where she worked in an employment agency for maids in Beverly Hills.

After the job with the maid's agency, Ms. Sánchez-Scott began to work as an actress with a variety of professional theaters in Los Angeles, including the Mark Taper Forum (*Savages*) and the Loft Studio (*A Doll's House*). Like the protagonist in the play she would soon write, Ms. Sánchez-Scott also appeared in various television programs playing "a variety of barrio women." It was while performing in a women's prison, recreating the inmates' experiences as dramatized by Doris Baizley, that Ms. Sánchez-Scott realized that some of the stories she had heard from the Latina women at the employment agency could also be dramatized. Ms. Sánchez-Scott recalls, "The idea to write *Latina* was born in a traffic jam on the Pomona Freeway. I mentioned then to Jeremy [Blahnik] that I had kept some journals and notes on Latin women. I asked her if she would put them into play form. She turned the tables on me, however, and soon I was writing *Latina* with Jeremy as my guide and mentor."[2]

Commissioned by Susan Lowenberg, Producing Director of the New Works Division of Artists in Prison and Other Places (AIPOP),[3] the actress/playwright then created *Latina*, her first play. *Latina* was first produced in 1980 to great critical acclaim.

The success of *Latina* encouraged Ms. Sánchez-Scott to continue writing and she was then commissioned by Ms. Loewenberg to write another play. This commission led to two one-acts, *The Cuban Swimmer* and *Dog Lady*.[4] Most importantly, perhaps, Ms. Sánchez-Scott was invited to join María Irene Fornés' Hispanic Playwright's-in-Residence Laboratory during the year of 1983. "That year was the best thing that ever happened to me," Ms. Sánchez-Scott recalls. "I met some extraordinary Hispanic writers. And I felt more accepted."[5] It was during that residency that Ms. Sánchez-Scott began to write *Roosters*.

Roosters is a Southwestern play about the struggles within a Chicano family in crisis: a father and son vying for dominance and a daughter looking for significance in a too brutal reality. It is a play about survival, told in a poetic style that evokes images of pure beauty and grace, contrasted with the severity of poverty and the desert. In a mixture of naturalism and the surreal, *Roosters* evokes images of magical realism both visually and linguistically. In the playwright's words, "*Roosters* is a word play."[6]

In the introduction to *Roosters*, Ms. Sánchez-Scott tells how her youth was spent in a world of fantasy, creating images in her mind, as all children do, but with a distinctly Latin American flavor.[7] This Latin American magical realism seems to come naturally to Ms. Sánchez-Scott, who recalls such imagery on a visit to the town in Colombia where she had spent Christmas holidays and summers in her youth: "Do you remember the summer all the birds flew into the bedroom?" someone asked, reminding her of "the way we say things in Colombia."[8]

Roosters is Ms. Sánchez-Scott's best-known play to date, with professional and community productions across the country. After initial development in Ms. Fornés' workshop and at the Sundance Institute in Utah, *Roosters* was co-produced by INTAR and the New York Shakespeare Festival in 1987.[9] This extraordinary play will reach millions of people on PBS's American Playhouse in 1989.

Adding to an exceptionally busy year for Ms. Sánchez-Scott, her play, *Evening Star*, was produced by New York's Theatre for a New Audience in the spring of 1988 under the direction of Paul Zimet. That same year she was Playwright-in-Residence for the Los Angeles Theater Center's Latino Lab, working closely with director José Luis Valenzuela and a core of professional Hispanic actors. This group worked collectively with

Ms. Sánchez-Scott on *Stone Wedding*, a parable in the magical realism style about a Southwestern Chicano wedding in the 1950's. The play was included in the LATC's 1988 season, following the success of *Roosters*. Most recently, Ms. Sánchez-Scott has begun work on the book and lyrics for a musical in collaboration with Gold McDermit, the composer of *Hair*. This play, as yet unnamed, will be produced by INTAR.

Ms. Sánchez-Scott has received a number of distinctive awards, including a first-level Rockefeller Foundation Playwriting Grant, a Vesta Award, given each year to a West Coast dramatist, and the Le Compte du Nouy prize. She is also a member of New York's prestigious New Dramatists. Through her plays, Ms. Sánchez-Scott is becoming an exceptional spokeswoman for Chicano and Hispanic-American issues.

[1]M. Elizabeth Osborn, *On New Ground: Contemporary Hispanic-American Plays* (New York: Theatre Communications Group, 1987): 245.

[2]Milcha Scott with Jeremy Blahnik, "An Excerpt from *Latina*," *Frontiers* (1980): 25–30.

[3]Later known as L.A. Theatre Works.

[4]*The Cuban Swimmer* and *Dog Lady* were published by TCG's Plays in Process series in 1984 and by Dramatists Play Service, New York, in 1989. *Dog Lady* was subsequently published in *Best Short Plays of 1986*. These two plays were produced by INTAR, Hispanic-American Arts Center in New York City in 1984. Other productions were seen at Rutgers University and in London in 1985. *Dog Lady* was produced by the Teatro Campesino in 1988.

[5]*On New Ground*, p. 246.

[6]From a telephone conversation with the author September 14, 1988.

[7]*Roosters* is published in *On New Ground*, pp. 243–280, and was also featured in *American Theatre Magazine* in September, 1987.

[8]*On New Ground*, p. 246.

[9]*Roosters* was produced by the Eureka Theater in San Francisco, in 1987. Since then, the following theaters have produced the play: the Guadalupe Cultural Arts Center in San Antonio, Texas; the Los Angeles Theatre Center; the New Mexico Repertory Theatre; and the Bush Theatre in London.

Latina

by Milcha Sánchez-Scott
With Jeremy Blahnik

ACT ONE

SCENE ONE

The stage is dark. Then we hear Peruvian flute music coming from a distance. We see NEW GIRL saying goodbye to a small group of PERU- VIAN MOUNTAIN VILLAGE PEOPLE. The time is dusk. NEW GIRL is carrying a satchel. She has a Peruvian shawl around her shoulders. Her hair is in braids. She has on a peasant skirt and a work shirt and sandals on her feet. The NEW GIRL's mother steps out and puts a St. Christopher medal around NEW GIRL's neck. She embraces NEW GIRL. NEW GIRL tears herself away to leave. NEW GIRL's mother falls to her knees weeping. People around her help her up to wave at NEW GIRL.

It becomes night as NEW GIRL starts her journey through the tun- nel of light. The music changes to heart beating escape tempo. At one point we see NEW GIRL paying off a policeman. Another moment a woman steals her shawl. Then a man accosts her at knife point and tries to rape her, but she escapes. Next, she is giving money to a slick city coyote, dressed in American type work clothes, who takes her to the end of the tunnel where it is night. There is only the moon and the sound and search light of an over head helicopter. We see a large barbed wire fence. The coyote roughly holds NEW GIRL by the wrist as the search-light almost hits them. They both hit the ground and crawl on hands and knees to the barbed wire fence. She crawls through. He helps her. She stands up on the other side and looks back. There is triumph in the music with a moment of Peruvian flute. The coyote waves NEW GIRL on.

The stage is dark. The music changes tempo to American city music after a moment. Car noises start coming in and lights come up on the front of FELIX SANCHEZ DOMESTIC AGENCY set.

SCENE TWO

Front of the Felix Sanchez Domestic Agency. There is a bus bench and a Wilshire Blvd. Street sign. On the actual store front the words FELIX SANCHEZ DOMESTIC AGENCY are printed in big block letters over the door and window. In the window there are two dummies, one in a white uniform holding a pink baby dummy, the white dummy looks very maternal like a Madonna, the second dummie is in a short black uniform with a white frilly apron, holding a feather duster. She looks like a naughty French maid.

It is 7:50 on a Monday morning in October, the sounds of Wilshire Blvd. traffic in the background. A few moments after the curtain rises, SARITA, a young woman of twenty-three, walks briskly up to the agency door and tries it. It is locked. She jiggles the knob and knocks repeatedly . . . no one answers.

SARITA: Christ! . . . (*Looks at watch.*) Ah no, he's late! (*To audience.*) I don't like it when he's late. I just don't like it. I have to hang around here. Which is embarrassing. I have to go sit on the bus bench, which is also embarrassing . . . everybody will think I am waiting for the bus, which means: (a) I can't drive, (b) I don't have a car, or (c) both of the above—in Los Angeles this is embarrassing. (*Turns around, looks at dummies, then back to audience.*) I could go back there and pretend to be a dummy. Yes . . . but what if I got caught? That would really be embarrassing . . . (*Pause.*) I am tired of always feeling embarrassed. Embarrassed! Embarrassed! (*She is embarrassed.*) I'm embarrassed to be standing here on the street. I'm embarrassed to be standing here on the street in front of that place. I'm embarrassed to be working in that place, and I'm really embarrassed to be here waiting for Sleezy Sanchez to open up. And, I spent the better part of an hour deciding what to wear, because I don't want to be mistaken for a maid. I'm not a maid. You thought I was a maid . . . I am not a maid or a housekeeper. Housekeeper is what polite people call their maids. (*Pause.*) I don't want to look Latina. (*Loud sound of car stopping, blare of radio with Disco sound and motor idling.*) That's embarrassing. (*Male whistle.*)

MALE VOICES: [1st.] (*off stage*) Oh, oh, oh, (*loud kissing sounds*) baby. [2nd.] Oh, Señorita, I am in love. [3rd.] Hot tamale! Hey, little beaner. [2nd.] What a cute little maid! [3rd.] Hey, señorita! Hey little maid—you sure are pretty. You want to come to my casa? (SARITA *at first looks embarrassed, then bored. She has been*

*through this before and knows how to stop it. She puts a stupid
expression on her face, picks her nose and says . . .)*

SARITA: (*Like goofy.*) Yuk, yuk. (*Loud sounds of car peeling off. From
stage right,* EUGENIA *walks on carrying a simulated leather hand-
bag and paper shopping bag with handles. She is old, but wirey and
energetic. She stands watching* SARITA.)

SARITA: (*Unaware of* EUGENIA.) See, I hate that and I hate that dirty,
stinking place! And I hate sleezy Sanchez, and I hate this stupid bus
bench . . . (*kicks bus bench*) and the illegal women who come here
everyday looking for illegal jobs . . . Well, I don't hate the
women . . . it's just that . . . I am not one of them . . . I don't want
to be identified with them. It's all very mixed up and testy with me
right now. Okay! I am not a maid, I am a counselor. Okay! . . . Oh
God, listen to me . . . I am a counselor, like it's some big deal.

EUGENIA: Buenos días, niña Sarita. ¿Cómo amaneció? (SARITA *sees*
EUGENIA, *realizes she has been watching her.*)

SARITA: Buenos días, Doña Eugenia . . . estoy bien.

EUGENIA: Ay, gracias a Dios. (*She walks up to the bus bench.*) ¿Qué te
pasa mi hija?

SARITA: Nada. (EUGENIA *takes* SARITA*'s face into her hands and
feels for a fever.*)

EUGENIA: ¿Desayunastes?

SARITA: Yes, I ate breakfast.

EUGENIA: Te ves muy pálida y emocionada . . . ¿Quieres que te haga
un yu yu?

SARITA: No. No yu yu. No me pasa nada. Estoy bien, gracias, gracias.

EUGENIA: Andale pues. (*To herself.*) Esta niña está grave. (EUGENIA
*walks away to the alley singing "Luna que se quiebre" . . . In the
alley she gets her broom and other cleaning equipment, a little tin
can, which she takes to the faucet and fills with water.*)

SARITA: (*To audience.*) She says I look pale and emotional . . . That's
Eugenia . . . the old yu yu vendor. She makes potions for everything, from everything . . . herbs, frogs . . . They call them yu yus.
She tells me she is 48 . . . more like 68. She says that so I'll send
her on a job. Actually, I don't think she cares about getting a job.
Sleezy Sanchez gives her a few dollars to clean the office. She does
a lousy job. But that's not why she comes. She loves this place . . .
the women, the gossip. (*With the clatter of trash can lids,* EUGE-
NIA *comes out of the alley with broom and tin can . . . She starts
sweeping and sprinkling water stage left. Light change. Lights
should be like morning light. Sun coming up very bright. There is a*

ritualistic quality about this. Street sounds fade and there is soft music. We see Eugenia carry out her task as if she were a village woman in Juarez, 1915.)

SARITA: (*Smelling.*) Did I hear a rooster . . . and the smell of tortillas, early morning charcoal. Oh, it's Eugenia. The way she sprinkles the water on the sidewalk . . . like it was a dirt road in front of her little shack . . . my grandmother used to do that in Mexico, my great, great, grandmother probably did it too. (*Lights bring us back to the present.*)

EUGENIA: (*Still sweeping.*) Sarita, no se te olvide que necesitamos jabón. Ese jabón Lava, eh!

SARITA: (*To audience.*) She wants me to get her Lava soap. She loves Lava soap. She uses Lava for everything . . . the windows, the sidewalk, everything. (*She pulls an imaginary microphone chord and puts on a very commercial spokeswoman's voice.*) Hi, this is Lorraine Lovely for Lava industrial soap. For years, Lava industrial soap was used by mechanics and machinists to remove grit and grime. Today, women all over America are discovering that Lava is a face soap—it not only removes pimples, it removes skin. Dead skin. Yes, that old skin that has been hanging around your face for years. Lava helps you lie about your age . . . Today, we are here in front of the Felix Sanchez Domestic Agency talking to Mrs. Eugenia Carbajal, the oldest domestic worker in America. Mrs. Carbajal, a satisfied Lava customer, is 115; she is still working. She tells the world she is 48 and Lava helps her lie. Tell our viewers Mrs. Carbajal . . . do you use Lava on other parts of your body, eh? On your tushi? Eh, en las nalguitas, eh? (*Pinches butt. EUGENIA registers mock shock and mock anger and chases SARITA towards bus bench with broom.*)

EUGENIA:¡Muchacha grosera, sangrona!

SARITA: (*On the run.*) Lava makes you cranky, too. (EUGENIA, *unable to contain her laughter, starts laughing and cannot stop. SARITA is laughing also.*)

EUGENIA: (*Barely able to get the words out.*) Lava por las nalgas . . . (EUGENIA *starts coughing. SARITA pats her back. She starts coughing and laughing. She takes hankey from pocket and wipes her eyes.*) Ay Sarita, cómo me haces reír. Mi, hija, ¿cuándo vas a salir en la televisión otra vez?

SARITA: (*This is painful.*) No sé. (SARITA *walks over to bus bench and slumps down. EUGENIA knows it is a painful subject, shakes her head and goes back to sweeping.*) (*To audience.*) She says I make her laugh. She wants to know when I am going to be on television again. I wish I knew. See, what I actually want to be . . . I mean, what I really am is an actress. Now, why should that be embarrassing? Makes me feel like I am over-reaching. I am only working here until I get . . . oh, never mind. (*Pause.*) Have you ever noticed that when you meet an actor, instead of saying, "Hello, how are you?", they give you their credits . . . I'll give you my credits. I was a barrio girl who got raped by a gang in *Police Story*, a young barrio mother who got shot by a gang in *Starsky and Hutch*, a barrio wife who got beat up by her husband who was in a gang in the *Rookies*. I was even a barrio lesbian who got knifed by an all girl gang called the Mal-flores . . . that means Bad Flowers. It's been a regular barrio blitz on television lately. If this fad continues, I can look forward to being a barrio grandmother done-in by a gang of old Hispanics called Los Viejitos Diablitos, the old devils. (*Pause.* EUGENIA *sweeps.* SARITA *looking at watch.*) Well, he's still late. I wonder what he'll be wearing—his Mickey Mouse pajamas or the ones with the sailboats. He's been wearing Mickey Mouse for the past 7 days. Oh God, for our sake, I hope it's the sailboats. (*As* EUGENIA *continues sweeping, flute music is heard as* NEW GIRL *appears. She is tired and frightened. Very cautiously, she approaches* EUGENIA.)

NEW GIRL: Psssst, seño. (EUGENIA *doesn't hear too well.*) Psssst seño. (EUGENIA *looks up.*) Señora, perdóneme, pero, ¿aquí es dónde tienen trabajos?

EUGENIA: ¿De dónde vienes mi hija?

NEW GIRL: ¿Aquí tienen trabajos en casas? ¿Aquí?

EUGENIA: Vienes de muy lejos, ¿verdad? ¿Cómo has llegado? ¿Tienes familia? Ven. (*Grabs* NEW GIRL *by the arm.*) Ay, ésta es una de las señoritas que te puede ayudar, horita te la presento. Es muy amiga mía.

NEW GIRL: No, no, mejor que no. (*Starts to run but* EUGENIA *tries to stop her.*)

EUGENIA: No tengas miedo. Aquí no llega la migra.

NEW GIRL: (*Screams.*) Ay, la migra no.

EUGENIA: (*Struggling with* NEW GIRL.) Sarita, Sarita, ayúdame.

SARITA: (*Bolts from bench.*) Now what? (SARITA *runs to* EUGENIA's *aid. There is a tussle.* EUGENIA *who has been knocked down, gets up, while* SARITA *holds on to the* NEW GIRL.)

EUGENIA: Aquí no viene la migra. Aquí le vamos a ayudar. Esta es la señorita Sarita. Yo soy Doña Eugenia Carbajal, le vamos a ayudar.

SARITA: (*Still struggling with the* NEW GIRL.) Will you stop with the introductions already. Who does she think we are, immigration? (*At the word "immigration," the* NEW GIRL *panics again and bites* SARITA.) OHHHHHHHHH! (SARITA *drops* NEW GIRL.) She bit me. (*Points at* NEW GIRL *incredulously.*) I don't believe it. Eugenia, did you see that? She bit me like some kind of animal.

EUGENIA: (*To* NEW GIRL.) Mira no más lo que hicistes. Y la señorita Sarita no más que está aquí para ayudarte. No tienes vergüenza . . . ¡Mal educada!

SARITA: She bit my finger.

EUGENIA: Ahhh, a ver mi hija. ¿Duele mucho?

NEW GIRL: Ah, dispénseme. (*Runs to her bag to get a hankie.*) Perdóneme, es que usted me dio mucho miedo. (NEW GIRL *gives hankie to* EUGENIA. EUGENIA *dips it into water can and then tries to apply it to* SARITA's *finger.*)

SARITA: Not from there. That water's dirty. It has germs. (EUGENIA *pays no attention to dirty water and applies compress to finger.*)

SARITA: Ouch!

NEW GIRL: Señorita, por favor, perdóneme. Es que no sabía.

EUGENIA: (*Looking at* SARITA's *finger and rubbing it.*) Sana, sana, colita de rana. Ay niña, no es nada.

SARITA: What do you mean, it's nothing? Human bites are very dangerous. I could catch something.

NEW GIRL: Perdóneme. Ay, todo me ha salido mal.

EUGENIA: (*Comforting* NEW GIRL.) No le hagas caso. Horita le vamos a encontrar un trabajito.

SARITA: I am not getting her a job. Look . . . (*Holds out finger.*) It's starting to swell. (*Offstage sounds of* DON FELIX *singing, "Las Mañanitas." At hearing this,* SARITA *rushes for the bus bench to her purse.* EUGENIA *frantically looks through pockets.*) Ya es tiempo. Apúrate antes de que llegue.

EUGENIA: Ay ¿dónde está mi peseta?

SARITA: (*Excitedly takes quarter out of purse. To audience*) . . . Hear that whistling? Sleezy Sánchez is coming. He only has two pairs of pajamas, the Mickey Mouse ones and the ones with the sailboats. She calls them los barquitos. (EUGENIA *brings out her quarter.* SARITA *brings out her quarter.*)

EUGENIA: (*Agonizing.*)¡Ay! virgencita! ¿Qué será, Mickey Mouse o los barquitos? (EUGENIA *crosses herself and says a prayer.* SARITA *is getting impatient.*) Andale, mujer . . . que está a punto de llegar. (*Catching herself.*) Oh Christ, we go through this every day.

EUGENIA: (*Very sure.*) Mickey Mouse.

SARITA: (*Very sure.*) Sailboats, los barquitos. (SANCHEZ *comes around the corner from stage right carrying a pot of beans, a loaf of white bread, the L.A. Times and a ring of keys. He is wearing his Mickey Mouse pajamas. He puts key into lock. They all gather their things to go in.* EUGENIA *must coax* NEW GIRL.)

EUGENIA: Buenos días, Don Alex. ¿Cómo amaneció?

MR. SANCHEZ: (*Grunts.*) Sí, buenos días. (SARITA *gives* EUGENIA *a quarter. All go in except* SARITA. *She turns to audience.*)

SARITA: I let her win.

(*She goes in.*)

SCENE THREE

Stage is dark. Store front turns to reveal Agency in three rooms: 1. front door and reception area, 2. interview room, 3. back room

DON FELIX: (*On phone.*) Carlos, Carlos, how many times I gotta tell you? 67, the line with the blue button is the Felix Sanchez Body Shop. The red button, 68, is the Felix Sanchez Domestic Wedding Chapel. Now, the new one, the one with no color is going to be the Felix Sanchez Teenager After School Discoteque. Carlos, it doesn't matter. Paint it any color you want. Now, what we got there? Over there, with you, in the downtown office? What we got there? How many girls? How many for maid jobs? Any English-speaking? One . . . you think! She said, "Excuse me?" Carlos, I don't care if she is polite. I want to know if she speaks English. Well, talk to her. Ask her something. Pues, pregúntale algo. No le hace qué, pero pregúntale algo, hombre. Ay, I gotta think of everything. Ask her, ask her in English, idiot, ask her if she has any pets. If she likes dogs. You know, start a conversation. Okay, I'll hold. (NEW GIRL *who has been standing in doorway with* EUGENIA, *has summoned up all her courage, walks up to* DON FELIX.)

DON FELIX: (*Still holding phone.*) Buenos días, Félix Sánchez a sus órdenes. ¿Cómo puedo servir a la señorita?

NEW GIRL: Elsa María Cristina López de Moreno. ¿Aquí es donde le consiguen trabajo?

DON FELIX: Sí, señorita. (*Puts his hand protectively on* NEW GIRL*'s shoulder.*) ¿Hablas inglés?

NEW GIRL: No.

DON FELIX: ¿Has trabajado como criada?

NEW GIRL: Pues, en mi país he trabajado en muchas casas y en el campo.

DON FELIX: ¿Pero aquí en los Estados Unidos?

NEW GIRL: No, señor.

DON FELIX: (*Pats her shoulder.*) No le hace. Horita le buscamos un trabajito . . . pase atrás con Doña Eugenia. (*To* SARITA.) No English, no references . . . another $60 girl, if we're lucky. Ah, don't waste your time with her. Just work with the $100 and up girls. Wait a minute, wait a minute. Why don't you teach her to count to ten in English? Yeah, just to ten. That's all she'll need.

SARITA: What?

DON FELIX: See, honey, if she can count to ten in English, we can say she speaks enough English to answer the phone.

SARITA: Oh, that's brilliant. Does Berlitz know about this innovation?

DON FELIX: We all got to start somewhere, honey. (*Smiles brilliantly at* NEW GIRL *and motions her on to back room.*) Pase, pase. . . .

SARITA: Oh, please!

DON FELIX: (*Returning to phone.*) Carlos, what did you find out? She doesn't like dogs, but she once had a cat. You asked her in English? Okay, she speaks English. So, send her up. Put her on the bus . . . the 78 bus. Now, don't forget about the phones. (*Hangs up phone.*) Sarita, I am going to . . . (*Laughs, he thinks this is funny.*) to my private office. (*Picks up paper.*) You know where I mean.

SARITA: Yeah, yeah, you're going to the bathroom.

DON FELIX: Don't forget tonight. Grand opening. Felix Sanchez Teen Disco. Wear something sexy. (DON FELIX *goes to bathroom, laughing,* SARITA *waits until he is out of ear shot, then picks up phone and dials.*)

SARITA: Oh, is, eh, Joan in? Well, this is Sara Gómez and I read . . . well . . . last Friday I read for the part of the nurse on *Eight is Enough* and, well, I wondered if Joan heard anything . . . I'll hold. (MARIA *runs in out of breath. She has a heavy accent.*)

MARIA: Ay, María Santísima. (*Flops on reception area sofa.* EUGENIA *enters and starts dusting dummies.*) I am late.

SARITA: No, who cares?

MARIA: Where is he?

SARITA: In his private office.

MARIA: Ah, he'll be there for hours.

SARITA: (*Crossing her fingers and holding them up to* MARIA.) Yes, I know, the director said I read really great. What? Too exotic? I know what that means. And you still think I have a chance for it? Well, listen, thanks for the vote of confidence, but I won't hold my breath. Goodbye. (*Starts to slam receiver down, but with controlled effort, puts it down firmly.*)

MARIA: Your agent? Do you get the part?

SARITA: They loved my reading . . .

MARIA: Of course, you are most terrific actress.

SARITA: But they think I may be too exotic for the part and they'll get back to me.

MARIA: They'll get back to you, ¿y qué quiere decir eso?

SARITA: I'll get back to you means . . . you don't know what to say. You just say it when you don't know what else to say.

MARIA: Ah, I'll get back to you . . . Ah, Sarita there is still hope, be patient.

SARITA: Too exotic, María. They say I am too exotic.

MARIA: You are?

SARITA: That means I am too dark, to unusual, they don't have people like me on their show.

MARIA: What show?

SARITA: *Eight is Enough*. I am too dark and freaky for *Eight is Enough*. They don't have stupid Mexicans playing nurses on prime time, you know. I might scare the kids.

MARIA: Oh, sí. *Eight is Enough*, that's the show with all the kids that live in the big white house, with the little white fence with all the flowers around the little fence and the kids always drinking milk in the kitchen, talking over their problems. Last week one of the girls made a dent in their papa's car. She afraid, she no want to tell him. All show she afraid. In the end, she tell him and you know what? He's not mad because insurance pay. Ay, sí, muy bonito. Ah, sure there's hope. I am positive. Sure, you'll be on that show. They're a good Catholic family, you'll see.

EUGENIA: Sí, niña, hay que tener esperanza.

SARITA: Will you two just be quiet and look who's telling me to have hope.

MARIA: Sarita! You're just upset about your agent.

EUGENIA: Tengo mis hijos, mis nietos, todos sanos, gracias a Dios. (EUGENIA *leaves*.)

MARIA: That's right, Sarita, she has her children and her grandchildren.

SARITA: Oh, yeah, where are her precious children now, huh? They don't want her around. She doesn't fit in with their lives, so she hangs around here.

MARIA: So sad, she fights to bring her children here, for a better life. She feeds them, educates them, and they turn against her. They take up new American ways and leave her and the old ways behind. Yet, she is proud of them.

SARITA: Oh, she's just a martyr and it makes me mad.

MARIA: Mad . . . Why?

SARITA: I, I . . . don't know.

MARIA: Because you really love her.

SARITA: Well . . .

MARIA: Then, why you take her home with you all the time?

SARITA: Not all the time, María. I don't know. She cleans up my apartment. Although, last time she used Lava on my walls, took all the paint off. What a mess, oh, I don't know, María. I understand her kids. I mean, all she does is tell old stories about Mexico.

MARIA: And it reminds you about when you were little girl. How many people make fun, make less of you because you are Mexican.

SARITA: No! Yes. I just don't want to end up old, Mexican, unwanted. Why couldn't she change? Learn to speak English?

MARIA: She doesn't want to, she likes to be Mexican.

SARITA: Well, I worked real hard to change, to be different from my parents.

MARIA: Ah, sure, you improve yourself, but you are *still* Latina.

SARITA: No, I'm not.

MARIA: Okay, you're not . . . you're Swedish, but Eugenia, she likes to be what she is. It's her life. (EUGENIA *returns with wet rag and lipstick and cleans dummy's faces and applies lipstick.*) What happened to your finger?

EUGENIA: Le mordió una muchacha.

MARIA: A girl bit you?

SARITA: Yeah . . . the new girl. She was so afraid. (*Looks at finger.*) Panicked like an animal.

EUGENIA: ¡Pobrecita! Vino de tan lejos. ¡Desde Perú y solita!

SARITA: Oh, I don't believe that. She's lying. All the way from Peru by herself!

EUGENIA: Sí, solita.

SARITA: (*Looking at finger.*) She was so afraid.

MARIA: She is very brave.

EUGENIA: A lo mejor la mordida le va a traer suerte.

SARITA: Eh? What?

MARIA: Maybe the bite brings you good luck.

SARITA: Hey, if I get this television part I'll . . . I'll treat you both to . . . Oh, what am I talking about? I won't get this. It's got no gangs. I only get parts with gangs in them.

EUGENIA: (*Takes quarter out of her pocket.*) A ver, mi hija, una peseta que vas a ganar esa parte.

SARITA: Okay. It's a bet. Your quarter says I get the part, my quarter says I don't. (*They place in their bets.*)

MARIA: But, Sarita, that means you're betting against yourself. (*Phones start ringing. Lights go down as* MARIA *picks up first call. We hear* MARIA *and* SARITA *answering calls. Lights go up back room.*)

MARIA: Good morning. Felix Sanchez Domestic Agency, this is Maria speaking. How may I help you, Mrs. Rick . . . ards? Oh, excuse me, Richards. Oh, yes, we having very nice maids. Oh yes, very . . . (*While in back room* NEW GIRL *sits in folding chair rather stiffly at first, eyeing the bathroom. She is afraid* DON FE-LIX *might come out. She gingerly leaves the chair and looks down the hall. She goes back to the chair when she thinks she hears noise. She sees T.V. set and examines it carefully. She pushes a button and the volume and picture come on loudly. She jumps back and turns it off quickly. She is always on the alert, checking both doors. She very carefully goes to the food area and starts to wolf down some food. As* MARIA *takes first call, she keeps eating. She is very hungry. Once again she checks both doors, then goes through closet and finds* EUGENIA*'s purse. She looks at the pictures in the wallet. She goes through agony trying to decide whether or not to take money. She takes one dollar from wallet, puts the rest of the money back into the wallet. She then reorganizes the closet and goes back to the chair.*) Honest, yes, experience, sure. First, I take the order, you tell me what you want then, I personally find the just right girl for you. Yes, I will. Then, will you pay the girl whatever salary we agree on? Yes, of course English speaking is more money. Oh, now, Mrs. Richards, we don't check if they are illegal. That is up to you, the employer. Oh yes, the agency has a fee which the employer pays. It's a three month guarantee. Well, if the first girl leaves, we find you another one, so we supply you with girls for three months. Yes, English-speaking and references: $80 to $100 a week. Your phone, yes, I'll find somebody very nice.

SARITA: Felix Sanchez Domestic Agency, Sarita speaking. Yes, sir. Yes, most of our girls come from Latin America. Yes, some speak English. Cheapest? $60 per week. How large a home do you have, sir? Oh, a trailer. No, she doesn't need her own room. How big is your trailer? Two bedrooms? Children? Two pets? One cat. (*Phone rings again.*) Please hold. Felix Sanchez Domestic Agency, Sarita speaking. Oh, yes, Mrs. Camden (*Lights dim in back room. Lights up in front room.*) I am sorry to hear that. I said I am sorry to hear that. Hey, hey, don't yell at me, lady. I don't know where she is! Look, I'll find you a replacement. Oh, maybe a day or two. Don't yell at me lady. Hello? Hello? (*To* MARIA.) Mrs. Camden. Lola didn't show up at work today. That's not like Lola.

MARIA: You think maybe la migra?

SARITA: You better call her house.

MARIA: No phone.

SARITA: Where do the kids stay?

MARIA: With the neighbor lady and she got . . .

SARITA and MARIA: No phone. (*Phone rings.* MARIA *starts to answer, then freezes.*)

MARIA: Ay, Sarita, it's the Wedding Chapel line . . . (*Practicing*) Felix Sanchez Wedding Cha . . . Oh, Sarita, please . . . (SARITA *concentrates a moment, then pushes the phone button and lifts receiver as she does,* CHATA, LA CUBANA, CLARA *and* EVITA *come in laughing and talking. They are promptly hushed by* EUGENIA *and* MARIA *as* SARITA *answers phone in low, low voice sounding like a sexy undertaker.*

SARITA: Felix Sanchez Wedding Chapel. How may I help you? . . . Oh yes, congratulations. No need for blood tests if you have been living together. Of course I can tell from your voice that you have the best intentions. The Reverend Sanchez can perform the ceremonies this afternoon at 2:00. You have the address of our wedding chapel? Congratulations. I am sure it will be a lovely ceremony. (SARITA *hungs up. Ladies all laugh and clap.*)

MARIA: Ay Sarita, you do it so beautiful.

LA CHATA: Ay, que la Sarita . . . Sarita, don't forget your friend here . . . (*Points to herself.*) needs a job with plenty of lana.

CLARA: Me too, Sarita. (*They all gather around* SARITA*'s desk. Lights dim in front area and go up in the back room.*)

MARIA: Sarita, this man with the cat, he's still on hold. See . . . (*She points to flashing button.* SARITA *sits, lifts the phone.* DON FELIX *comes out of bathroom. His hair is slicked back with pomade like patent leather. He is wearing a polyester, navy suit with white stitch-*

*ing, white shoes, a white satin tie. He closes the bathroom door
which has a broken full length mirror behind it. He preens unaware
of* NEW GIRL *watching him. He puts a white plastic carnation in
his lapel and makes dignified, reverend-like gestures in the mirror.*)

DON FELIX: Friends, we are gathered here today to join this man to this
woman . . . no, it's . . . Friends, we are gathered here today to join
this woman to this man . . . no . . . Friends, we are gathered here
to join this couple in holy matrimony today in the flower of their
love . . . (*He turns, sucks in his stomach, takes out cigar, lights it
and continues to talk to himself in the mirror.*) Yes, ma'am, I am the
Reverend Felix Silvestre Sanchez. Yes, I got a car place, I got a
domestic agency, I got a wedding chapel and, starting tonight, I will
be the owner of the Felix Sanchez Teen Discoteque . . . I don't care
what Sarita says, I am a man of success. (LA CHATA *walks into the
backroom, whistles in approval.*)

LA CHATA: She also says you're wanted in Guatemala.

DON FELIX: (*Leaving for front room.*) That's not funny. (*Lights go up in
the front room and dim in the back room.* CLARA *is on her way to
the back room.*)

CLARA: Buenos días, don Félix, ¿cómo amaneció?

DON FELIX: Buenos días, Clara, ¿la familia?

CLARA: Bien, gracias a Dios.

EVITA: Buenos días, Don Félix.

DON FELIX: Hola, Evita. I've been trying to reach you. (*He whistles in
approval.* EVITA *does pirouette, showing off her new clothes.*)
Well, things are good for you, chabelita! You are still with Mr.
Hodges, eh?

EVITA: Ay, sí . . . yesterday he took me to the May Co. and said, "Anything you want, Evita." (*The women "OOH" and "AH" and "Qué
bueno."*) I got French blue jeans, the kind when you walk away they
wish you was coming back.

DON FELIX: Oh, honey, those are my favorite.

EVITA: High, pero, real high heeled shoes. Ay, I got so many clothes, I
don't have enough days to wear them . . . and look . . . this Boluva
watch he gave me.

DON FELIX: Oh nice, very nice honey. (*He starts to leave.* EVITA
follows him a few steps out of ear shot of the other women.)

EVITA: And he says he is going to buy me an LTD . . . he says, he
says . . . Ay, it's a lie Don Félix. He used to say those things. He
used to say he would be good to me. Help me with my momma. He
used to say . . . many things, like maybe he would marry me. Ay,

Don Félix, I want another job . . . make him jealous . . . make more money.

DON FELIX: Oh, sure, honey, sure. That's why I been dying to reach you.

EVITA: He is un desgraciado! ¡Un viejo pinchi!

DON FELIX: Ah, sure, honey . . . I got just the job for you, at my new disco, the Felix Sanchez Disco. The Felix Sanchez Disco, you heard about it, no? (*Phone rings and* SARITA *answers*).

EVITA: Ay qué bruto, imbécil, ay, he makes me so mad! What disco?

DON FELIX: I been trying to tell you, honey, you could teach the kids the new steps . . .

EVITA: Ah, sí, perfect job . . . make him really jealous. All those young boys who will dance with me . . . ¡qué padre!

SARITA: (*Holding out receiver to* DON FELIX.) It's for you.

DON FELIX: Eh . . . later, honey. We'll talk later. Go practice, the opening is tonight. (DON FELIX *rushes to take the phone from* SARITA.)

SARITA: (*Holding the phone receiver without looking up from the desk.*) It's the I.R.S. (*We see* DON FELIX *pale before our eyes. He carries on phone conversation while* LA CUBANA *has been peeking through windows, careful not to be seen. She keeps this up for a few minutes. Finally, she puts on sunglasses and wraps the sweater that* EVITA *left on the sofa around her head. This catches* MARIA's *attention.* LA CUBANA *comes in again and peers through the window again.*)

MARIA: ¿Cubana, qué te pasa?

LA CUBANA: My name is Margarita, por favor.

MARIA: Margarita, ¿qué te pasa?

LA CUBANA: Sssssssh! (*Looks carefully out of window then back to* MARIA.) There's a car filled with men and they are following me.

MARIA: (*Doesn't look.*) Margarita, don't you want some coffee?

LA CUBANA: They were there yesterday and now today, waiting to get me.

MARIA: Andale, una taza de café. (DON FELIX *gets off the phone on* SARITA's *desk and is quickly walking to his own desk. His mind is preoccupied.* LA CUBANA *rushes up to him and gets in his way.*)

LA CUBANA: Ah, Don Félix, these men are outside. They're after me.

DON FELIX: Sure, sure, honey. (*She gets her big body in his way. They do a small dance trying to get out of each others way.*) Andale, Cubana, go sit in the back, honey.

LA CUBANA: Margarita. My name is Margarita! (DON FELIX *pays no attention and goes to his desk. He makes a phone call.* EVITA *and* EUGENIA *go to the back room.* LA CUBANA *waits to talk to* SARITA. MARIA *answers the phone and takes down an order.* NEW GIRL *goes out of the back room and into the front room to* SARITA's *desk, cutting in front of* LA CUBANA.)

NEW GIRL: Seño, por favor . . .

LA CUBANA: (*To* NEW GIRL) Un momento. I am first. (NEW GIRL *backs up a step. She is not dissuaded. She stands firm and looks at* SARITA.) Ay, Sarita . . . (*Points to her finger.*) ¿qué pasó con tu finger?

SARITA: Nothing . . . (NEW GIRL *takes off the medallion her mother gave her in the first scene and offers it to* SARITA.) Oh, Christ . . . Oh, put it back on. I don't want your St. Christopher medal. María, you have your diccionario?

MARIA: Sure. (*Holds up dictionary.*) *Inglés Sin Maestro.*

SARITA: Good. Take this application form and Miss Peru here. Help her fill it out. It's in English.

MARIA: Sure thing.

SARITA: And teach her to count to ten (*To herself.*) . . . why not?

MARIA: Okay dokey. (NEW GIRL *just stands there.*)

SARITA: María le va a ayudar. (MARIA *takes* NEW GIRL *by the arm. They start to go to the back room.*)

MARIA: (*To* NEW GIRL) Espérame un momento aquí. (*Hands* NEW GIRL *dictionary to hold.*) Sarita, Don Félix's appointment book . . . (*She rushes around looking for it, then finds it.*)

LA CUBANA: (*Hands on hips.*) Andale, Sarita, where is my ladies' companion job? (*Fishes green card out of her bosom and waves it at* SARITA.) I have my green card. You can't push me around like the rest. (*Phone rings and is quickly answered.*)

SARITA: Un momento, Margarita. (*Picks up phone and* LA CUBANA *stalks off to the back room.*) Yes, Mrs. Camden, I am sorry. No, I told you Lola isn't here. I am trying to get . . . hello, hello . . . (*Puts phone down.*) Ohhh, that woman, and where is Lola? (DON FELIX *gets off the phone.*)

DON FELIX: María, the appointment book.

MARIA: Ahi voy. (*Brings the appointment book to him.*) Don Félix, you have a wedding at 2:00 this afternoon.

DON FELIX: (*Looks at appointment book.*) Honey, honey, you gotta put down where. At their home, you put down their address.

MARIA: (*Getting nervous.*) At the church.

DON FELIX: What church? Where is the address? Eh?

MARIA: The wedding church. You built behind the body shop.

DON FELIX: The chapel! The chapel! The Felix Sanchez Wedding Chapel! You got it! So here . . . (*Pointing at place in the book.*) After place, you put down at the W.C., that means Wedding Chapel.

MARIA: The Chapel, sí, sí, W.C. (MARIA *takes* NEW GIRL *by the arm and they exit to back room.*)

DON FELIX: Sarita, I gotta go. (*Preening to get her approval.*)

SARITA: (*Without looking up from her desk.*) You look like a hair oil salesman.

DON FELIX: (*Visibly dejected.*) I'll be right back.

SARITA: Take your time. (*He leaves through the front door. Phone rings.* SARITA *concentrates a moment.*) Felix Sanchez Wedding Chapel. How may I help you? (*Lights start to dim.*) Oh, congratulations, I am sure. (*Front room dark. Back room lights up.*)

LA CHATA: Think of it. Don Félix doing weddings?

EVITA: Well, maybe he'll do mine.

LA CHATA: You're getting married, mi hija?

EVITA: (*Opening compact and putting on mascara.*) Maybe.

CLARA: And what are you doing here? Don't you have a job with that Mr. Hodges in the "motherless home"?

EVITA: So? ¿Y a ti, qué?

CLARA: Hmmmmph!

EVITA: Y eso. Can't a person come here on her day off? Maybe Don Félix has a better job for me.

LA CHATA: Ay, sí. (*Dirty old lady chuckle.*) She wants to get ahead. A girl should have ambition.

CLARA: A girl should live at home with her mama helping her, but instead . . .

LA CHATA: Clara, keep out of it. (EVITA *not answering, continues putting on make-up.*)

CLARA: Aren't you ashamed? I know your mamá since I come here twelve years ago in this very room. I met her twelve years ago. Of course, you wouldn't know, you was only six years old still in Mexico.

LA CHATA: Ay, Dios, I remember. I met you on that day too. My little Consuelo was only four. Ay, the three of us talking about our babies. Right here, in this very room. They was offering live-ins for $30 to $35 a week. Then it wasn't so hard for me, with my mother alive and my baby here, but for Clara and your mama, ay, times were rough, sending all their money for you kids back home.

CLARA: That's right, your mama and I was killing ourselves for $25 a week.

LA CHATA: Don't exaggerate, it was $30, sometimes $25 if the people were nice.

CLARA: Hmmmmph! We never had those nice people. Evita's mama and I, we were killing ourselves to send that money home, so you could have a crust of bread.

LA CHATA: Keep out of it, I tell you.

CLARA: Hmmmmmph! Now, look how she pays her mother back. (EVITA *gathers her things and walks out of the back room.*) I hope you choke on your Mr. Hodges!

LA CHATA: Ay, "vieja metichi," always putting your nose in people's business.

CLARA: Hmmmmmph! If her poor mother knew.

LA CHATA: I am telling you . . . keep out of it. Always meddling, causing trouble. That's why people don't like you.

CLARA: Who doesn't like me?

LA CHATA: La gente, pues . . . everybody.

CLARA: Name one person.

LA CHATA: Well, there was that woman, ay, what's the use. A person can't talk to you. Ay, I hope Sarita gets me more money.

CLARA: What woman?

LA CHATA: Never mind, never mind. Sarita says, if I got my papers . . .

CLARA: You mean that woman who used to work in the tuna factory with you? The one whose hands smell of dead fish?

LA CHATA: Forget it. Sarita says President Carter made a law that if a person is here more than seven years, a person could get their papers.

CLARA: For her own good, I tell her to use Lava soap on her hands . . . for her own good. Is that the one who don't like me?

LA CHATA: Te digo, my lips are sealed.

CLARA: I don't care, anyway. Hmmmmmmph! Aha! I know the one . . . it was the woman who was here two months ago. The one with the red hair who tried to steal my Tuesday cleaning job in Encino.

LA CHATA: She didn't try to steal your job. That stupid job. Who would want it? Only you would take two buses to Encino on your day off and two buses back to go and clean in between the tile with a toothbrush! And what for? To get a check for $20? They don't even give you cash. And how are you supposed to cash the check with no I.D.? Tell her to give you the cash every week when you come to clean, tonta!

CLARA: You talk like it's so easy. "I am not used to paying my help in cash," she says, "I should be reporting your wages," she says, "My husband wouldn't approve." She makes like she's doing me the big favor, letting me scrub her floors. "You'll just have to wait," she says, but Ernestito's school don't wait.

LA CHATA: You shouldn't be sending him to that special school. You'll make a sissy outa him. A maricón. That's what he'll be . . . the way you fuss over him.

CLARA: ¿Y tú qué sabes? You big tunapacker. You're just like my pendejo husband. I try to make him see. Xavier, I say, Ernestito is special, he got this gift from God. But that idiot, Xavier, he say, "Well, tell him to give it back." All he knows is working in the car wash, but as long as me duran los huesos, I'll work so Ernestito can have his chance.

LA CHATA: Ahhh, he's gonna end up a priest.

CLARA: And your daughters gonna end up a . . .

LA CHATA: Oyes, tú . . . keep out of my daughters. Consuelo, she's . . . she's got her own ways.

CLARA: Hmmmmph! She don't respect you.

LA CHATA: You keep this up, you'll be sorry. I'm warning you.

CLARA: Comadre, you know it's true. She don't have any use for you, you, her own mother.

LA CHATA: Cállate la trompa. I ain't gonna mix-up in my daughters life, you hear? That's the trouble with you. Always in other people's business. That's why they don't like you.

CLARA: Oh yes, well, who exactly doesn't like me, eh? Name that person.

LA CHATA: Never mind.

CLARA: Was it la vieja who . . .? (MARIA *and* NEW GIRL *sitting together in corner of backroom. They are filling in the application form. Form is in English.* MARIA *is doing the filling in and translating.*)

MARIA: A ver, "name" quiere decir nombre. (MARIA *and* NEW GIRL *both say name in unison, very slowly as* MARIA *writes it down.*)

MARIA AND NEW GIRL: Elsa María Cristina López de Moreno.

MARIA: Address? Su dirección.

NEW GIRL: (*Shaking her head.*) No tengo.

MARIA: No address? Oh, you use mine. Social security número. Oh, no worry, we use Lola's. Aquí lo tengo. (*Gets number from wallet in purse and copies it onto the form*). Do you speak English?

NEW GIRL: (*Shakes her head.*) No, no más, a ver, beefsteak, Disneylandia.

MARIA: Ay, Dios, cómo le va a faltar. Le voy a enseñar los números. (MARIA *using her fingers to teach the numbers*.) One.

NEW GIRL: Gwone.

MARIA: Two.

NEW GIRL: Tu.

MARIA: Three.

NEW GIRL: Tree. (*Sound of phone ringing in the front room. Lights start to fade in back room. Lights up in the front room.*)

MARIA: Four.

NEW GIRL: Pour. (SARITA *at desk. She calls to* MARIA.)

SARITA: María, I'm on the phone. Get the other phone.

MARIA: Mira este libro, horita regreso. (*Running to front room*.) Yes, Mrs. Camden, but . . . but, Mrs. Camden. No, Lola is not here. Ay, Mrs. Camden, you must be calm. Sarita? Oh, sure. (MARIA *hands phone to* SARITA. SARITA *shakes her head and won't speak to Mrs. Camden. This mortifies* MARIA *and leaves her helplessly tossing the phone receiver from one hand to the other as if it were hot. Silently pleading with* SARITA. MARIA *gets back on the phone.* SARITA *trying to control laughter*.)

MARIA: Ah, Mrs. Camden, you'll never guess, Sarita, she's not here. She had to go . . . Mrs. Camden? Mrs. Camden? (MARIA *replaces receiver*.) She hung up. Ay, Sarita, you made me lie!

SARITA: I made you lie? We lie here everyday. That woman is trouble. Now we have to find Lola. Maybe where her husband works.

MARIA: I'll ask St. Anthony.

SARIA: St. Anthony?

MARIA: Sure, whenever I lose something, I pray to St. Anthony and pssst, right away, I find it. Remember last week when I lose my red pen that Aunt Cecilia gave me for my birthday? I prayed to St. Anthony and right away I found it.

SARITA: But María, you never lost your red pen. It was in your hair, where you put it. Don't be silly. You would have found it without St. Anthony.

MARIA: Oh sure, silly, you call me the silly. All the time you call me the silly. You went to the big important school. You speak perfect English. You working here just for fun.

SARITA: Fun? You call this fun?

MARIA: Sure to you is fun. You always laughing at us. When I make mistake in English, you laugh, you don't help me to say it better.

SARITA: (*Starting to laugh*.) Oh, come on, María.

MARIA: No, you come on. You know what it means in my country when they say, "Es una muchacha mal educada?" (MARIA *pauses and looks at her.*) Do you? Do you know what it means?

SARITA: What is this, *Hollywood Squares*?

MARIA: Do you know what it means?

SARITA: Yes, María, I know. It means a badly educated girl.

MARIA: But not education from the books. It means you do not have manners, that you do not have respect for other people and their ways. (*This has a deep effect on* SARITA. EUGENIA *walks in with mop and pail of water. She is wearing tennis shoes. Her skirt is rolled up revealing striped socks which are held up by means of ankle garters. She has a bandana on her head. On top of that an L.A. Dodgers baseball cap on sideways. The effect is comic. She starts mopping the floor behind* DON FELIX*'s desk.*) Doña Eugenia is better educated than you.

SARITA: (*Laughing.*) Oh no, not Eugenia. Oh, St. Anthony, save me, please.

MARIA: No eres una persona seria.

SARITA: Oh, now you want me to be a serious person all the time. You don't want me to laugh?

MARIA: When I say, "No eres una persona seria," it means you are not sincere. That you do not value yourself and I don't care what you say, St. Anthony will find Lola. (*Crosses herself, folds her hands and bows her head in prayer.*)

SARITA: Better him than immigration. (EUGENIA *stops cleaning and holds mop in her hand like a staff; with the other hand she takes off the baseball cap and raises it, saying proudly*) Que Dios la bendiga y que no se encuentre con la migra. (SARITA *and* EUGENIA *both laugh.*)

MARIA: Doña Eugenia!

EUGENIA: Sí, mi hija. (*Crosses herself and folds hands in prayer. They both say a prayer out loud and in unison.*)

EUGENIA AND MARIA: En el nombre del padre, del hijo y del Espíritu Santo . . . (*Praying.*)

SARITA: Out loud? (*Lights dim and we hear church music, a chorus of little girls singing, "Oh Mary We Bring You Blossoms Today." Far right corner of the stage by the file cabinet a vision appears: An elaborate Latin altar with a large crucifix and statue of the Virgin Mary covered with flowers. A little girl in a white communion dress is led to the altar by* SISTER AGNES.)

SISTER AGNES: Say it out loud, Sarita, so God will hear.

LITTLE SARITA: Yes, Sister Agnes.

SISTER AGNES: Hail Mary . . .

LITTLE SARITA: Hail Mary, full of grace, the Lord is with thee, blessed art thou amongst women and blessed is the fruit of thy womb, Jesus. God bless grandma, Mommy and Daddy and please protect Mr. Amador, who works hard in the fields and don't let immigration catch him . . .

SISTER AGNES: No, Sarita, you can't pray for something that's against the law.

LITTLE SARITA: Oh, how about Mrs. Amador? Can I pray for all the Amador children?

SISTER AGNES: Yes, of course, you can.

LITTLE SARITA: God bless Mrs. Amador and Angie and Manuel and Trini and Louie and . . .

MARIA: Lola! (MARIA*'s voice shatters the vision. The music stops.* SARITA *turns around. Lights go up on the front room and the vision is lost.* LOLA *has just come through the front door.* EUGENIA *and* MARIA *stare at her.*)

LOLA: Buenas. What's wrong? (MARIA *and* EUGENIA *run up and embrace* LOLA.)

MARIA: We thought. We were so worried. ¿Dónde estabas?

SARITA: (*Looks up to heaven, then to audience.*) I'll never hear the end of this. (*Turns to* LOLA.) Lola, what happened?

LOLA: Nothing. Everything, I'm up to here (*indicating her neck.*) Aguantando y aguantando, ya no puedo.

SARITA: Oh, that's terrific! And what about Mrs. Camden? She wants you back.

LOLA: ¡Nunca jamás! No way José.

SARITA: Why didn't you call me? And why didn't you give her two weeks notice? At least you could have called.

LOLA: Ay Sarita, no entiendes. That job was driving me crazy I thought you would understand.

SARITA: What I don't understand is why you didn't give notice or at least call. It puts me in a bad position.

LOLA: Pero, I was the one working in the bad position. You don't think about me? (*Phone rings and* MARIA *starts to answer, until she realizes that it's the Wedding Chapel line. She struggles but she can't bring herself to answer.*)

MARIA: Sarita, please, it's the Wedding.

SARITA: I have to do everything around here. (*She concentrates a moment, lowers her voice.*) Felix Sanchez Wedding Chapel, may I help you? Congratulations, Miss Ramírez. (EUGENIA, MARIA *and*

LOLA *go to the back room while* SARITA *is on the phone*.) Yes, the Reverend Sanchez would be happy to perform the ceremony. Problems? Ay, no Miss Ramírez, we don't provide counseling service. No, ma'am, no I am not a marriage counselor. I really don't think it would help if I spoke to your boyfriend. (*Other phone rings*.) I mean that's between the two of you. Wait, wait, I can't talk to him. (*Puts hand over mouth piece and yells*.) María, María . . . (*Back to phone*.) Listen, can you hold a minute? (*Gets the other phone*.) Felix Sanchez Domestic Agency. (LA CUBANA *walks into the front room and goes to the windows and peeks out*.)

LA CUBANA: Sarita, they're still there. Come and look, in the green Chevy. The same ones, Sarita, look! (SARITA *waves her away. Lights dim in the front room and lights up in the back room.* CLARA *is knitting.* NEW GIRL *is holding yarn.* EVITA *is practicing disco steps. The radio is playing Tex-Mex Ranchera music.* LA CHATA *is singing along as* MARIA, LOLA *and* EUGENIA *enter back room.*)

EVITA: Chata, how can I practice my disco with that music?

LA CHATA: Aquí está mi Lola. Me dan ganas de hacer una party. We should have a party.

LOLA: With Alma's tamales.

LA CHATA: Y unas cervecitas Carta Blanca, ayii, ayii.

CLARA: Ay, pensamos que la migra got you. Like Hortensia, last week. (*All women say, "Ah, no."*)

LA CHATA: (*To* CLARA) ¿Y por qué no me dijiste? Important things you don't tell me.

CLARA: Porque te coges una rabia. She gets so mad.

LA CHATA: ¿Y por qué no? Makes me feel hunted, like an animal.

EUGENIA: ¿Y los niños? ¿Con quién están?

EVITA: The kids are staying with Armeda.

MARIA: Qué pena. Ay, who would take care of my baby if I got caught?

CLARA: (*Reflecting*) Ernestito, ay Chata, he would end up in the car wash with Xavier. You're his godmother.

LA CHATA: Ay, mira la chillona. Don't worry. I'll send him to interior decorating school.

CLARA: No, he wants to be a priest.

LA CHATA: What did I tell you?

EVITA: Ay, I would never see mi amorcito, el Mr. Hodges.

MARIA: Y yo. I could never go to the night school for to be a nurse.

LA CHATA: I didn't know you wanted to be a nurse.

MARIA: Sure thing. All my life, I dream to be a nurse.

CLARA: Qué bien.

NEW GIRL: (*Very upset.*) Y yo que llegué de tan lejos. (*Runs to* EUGENIA *and buries her head in her lap.*)

LA CHATA: (*To* CLARA) Look, you made her cry.

LOLA: ¿Quién es? ¿Qué le pasa?

CLARA: Es la new girl that bite Sarita.

LOLA: Good for her. That Sarita is a gringa in her heart.

EUGENIA: (*Stroking* NEW GIRL*'s head.*) Ay, ay, pobre inocente. Le abandonaron en la supermarket y le dio mucho miedo.

LA CHATA: Those damn coyotes. Leave her in la parking lot of the Ralph's. "Here is where the rich people live, you'll find a job here." No English, nobody to help her in the middle of Beverly Hills. Lucky some gardener saw her walking in circles and told her where to go.

LOLA: ¡Desgraciados! ¡Hijos del diablo! They don't care. It was the same when I came. The policeman on the road wants his mordida. What the police don't get, the bandits take. Better for them if it's a woman. Then they try to get paid in other ways or sometimes they just kill the people.

EUGENIA: Sí, a veces matan a la gente.

LA CUBANA: It should be a lesson to them to stop coming here like beggars. Get your green card, like I did, or stay in your own country. (LA CUBANA *enters the bathroom and closes the door behind her.*)

LA CHATA: (*Loudly.*) Oyeme, Cubana, I am dying to teach you a lesson.

LOLA: Ay, don't be mean. I don't like her, pero dicen que she has cancer, pobrecita.

CLARA: Es muy mentirosa. She lies. She just say about the cancer for attention. Like she say she's married, she's not.

LOLA: (*To* EUGENIA) No?

EUGENIA: (*Shakes her head no.*) No, está mala aquí. (*Puts finger to her head and makes crazy sign.*)

LA CHATA: No, she's only loca sometimes. She's from Cuba, those Cubans. Se creen mucho, like they are better than everybody.

EVITA: The ones from Colombia are the worst.

MARIA: No es cierto, I am from Colombia.

EVITA: You're the only person from Colombia I ever like.

CLARA: Los de Guatemala son los peores.

LOLA: I am de Guatemala.

CLARA: De veras, you are? I thought you was like me, from El Salvador.

LOLA: Poor people are the same everywhere. They are the ones that suffer.

LA CHATA: Ay, sí, es la vida. (*Sounds of toilet flushing as* LA CUBANA *comes out of bathroom.*)

LA CUBANA: Because you don't help yourself. You just have babies. You don't think how you will feed them. No, every year, plop, another baby and, plop, another baby. Then you come here and get on the Welfare. Help yourself, show some class, like me. (*She turns around and starts to walk out and there is a big piece of toilet paper stuck on the seat of her skirt. The women, seeing this all, point and howl with laughter.*)

LA CHATA: Ay, Señorita Margarita, help yourself to the toilet paper on your nalgas. (*The women are all laughing as* LA CUBANA *removes the toilet paper from her buns. She is shame faced.*)

LA CUBANA: ¡Cerdas! Pigs! (*Exits from back room.*)

LOLA: Qué loca. Everybody knows you need papers to get on welfare.

LA CHATA: Ay, that made me feel good. We should have a party.

EVITA: ¿Celebrando qué?

LA CHATA: What are you, a gringa? You don't need a reason for a party, see? (*She pulls a bottle of rum out of her bag.*) We got Cokes. We can make our own highballs. We got food. We got friends, the radio for music. (LA CHATA *hits the side of her head as she spots the* NEW GIRL *staring at her with wide eyes.*) Ay, I am so stupid! We got a reason for a party. We got to celebrate the arrival of the new girl. (*All the women agree and begin the party. They touch and embrace the* NEW GIRL *and stand her up on a chair.*) After what she has been through, she should have a party. (LOLA *and* MARIA *start getting Cokes from the Coke machine. Some of the women clear the chairs. Someone turns up the radio.*) Viva la new girl. (NEW GIRL *stands on her chair in the center as lights dim.* MRS. HOMES *walks into agency. As she walks into reception area* ALMA GUTIERREZ *trails behind, painfully shy.* SARITA *is on the phone.*)

MRS. HOMES: Well Alma, here we are. Why don't you sit over there, dear? (*Gestures to sofa.*)

SARITA: Yes, thank you very much, then we look forward to seeing you. (*Sees* MRS. HOMES.) Mrs. Homes, what . . .

MRS. HOMES: I am returning Alma. (*She gestures, indicating* ALMA. SARITA *looks at* ALMA. ALMA *looks up and then bows her head.*)

SARITA: Let me get your file. Would you like some coffee?

MRS. HOMES: Oh, no, thank you, no, Sara dear. (SARITA *walks to file* cabinet, *opens drawer, stage right, near edge of stage, while* MRS. HOMES *takes a hanky out of her purse and dusts the seat before sitting.*)

SARITA: (*To audience with the same gesture of the hand and voice that* MRS. HOMES *used earlier.*) I am returning Alma. What does she think this is, the May Company?

MRS. HOMES: She is as sweet as can be, but not at all suited to our lifestyle. We take great pride in our surroundings. It has become obvious that Alma has never been around beautiful things. She has no respect for my blue and white Chinese porcelain, or any of our antiques and these things are irreplaceable, you know. Where do you people get these girls? (ALMA *sits there in total disgrace.*)

SARITA: (*To audience.*) The Greyhound bus station, Ralph's Market's parking lot, the RTD bus stop.

MRS. HOMES: What was that, dear?

SARITA: (*Getting file from drawer.*) Nothing. Ah, here is your file.

MRS. HOMES: I mean, you should make sure their references are in order.

SARITA: (*Looking at file.*) According to Alma's references, she is very clean, takes a great deal of pride in her work and . . .

MRS. HOMES: Oh, she is very clean. I wouldn't allow a dirty girl in my home, but she just doesn't understand antiques and fine things. Now, I want someone who understands these things. Someone who knows how to polish silver properly, knows you wax English pine, not just Pledge it. Someone who will value and understand our fine things.

SARITA: Uh, for $65 a week it's going to be hard to find somebody like . . .

MRS. HOMES: Oh, I'll be more than happy to go higher for a proper person. I'd go to, say, $100 a week. Of course that would be live-in with Monday's off. What about a black lady. (*Excited by the idea*) Or better still, an Oriental? How much would an Oriental run me?

SARITA: H . . . How much?

MRS: HOMES: Some of our friends have Orientals. I hear and I can see they are efficient. Oh, yes, indeed, and very clean, energetic, too . . . (SARITA *walks slowly to file cabinet area down stage right.*) no grass growing under their feet, but they are moody, surely too, I hear. No, I can't have that, now, you Mexicans . . . (*At this* SARITA *turns her head with a start and looks directly at* MRS. HOMES) have the best dispositions. You people may not be the cleanest or the most energetic, but I'll say this for you . . . you know your place. (SARITA *looks at* ALMA, ALMA *looks at* SARITA *and they both bow their heads*.) One thing, though, if you get me a Mexican girl, get me one with no relatives. You see, one day they can't come because their grandmother is sick, the next week it's the husband or the kids. (*Light goes on in the file cabinet area where the dummies appear.*) You people have no sense of responsibility. (*Dummies appear at first standing very still in the same pose as they appeared in the window.* SARITA, *startled, looks to see if anyone else sees them.* ALMA *is sitting on the sofa looking dejected*.) Mr. Homes doesn't stay home when I am sick. Why, I remember when our son had meningitis, poor thing ran such a fever . . . (MRS. HOMES*'s voice fades.* SARITA *realizes that the dummies are in her mind. She turns her back on them and tries to will them away*.)

SARITA: Get back in the window. (*Turns around and they are still there. She turns her back on them again and says slowly . . .*) Get back in the window! (*At this point, the dummies move. They are still and move like people who have been in one position too long*.)

DUMMY IN BLACK: (*Stretches and reaches down in a long stretch to touch her toes.*) ¡Ay, Dios! (*Takes off her shoes and rubs her feet.*) Ay, cómo me duelen los pies.

DUMMY IN WHITE: (*Shifts the baby from one arm to the other and rocks it. With her free hand she rubs her back.*) Ay, sí, y a mí, la espalda.

DUMMY IN BLACK: Ay, it gets hot in there, this time of day! Hola, Sarita.

SARITA: Get back in the window.

DUMMY IN BLACK: Hey, Don Félix gave us the day off.

DUMMY IN WHITE: Sí, pues, he's got Orientals in the window today.

SARITA: Orientals in the window?

DUMMY IN BLACK: Sure, he's running a special. They even got a sign out there . . . CLEAN AND EFFICIENT HELP.

DUMMY IN WHITE: With no grass under their feet. Hijo, but those Orientals are mean. Did you see how the big one was looking at the baby?

DUMMY IN BLACK: Oyes, Sarita, how much money you got for those Orientals?

DUMMY IN WHITE: Ay, it isn't polite to talk about money. Don't you know your place?

DUMMY IN BLACK: (*Looks up, looks down. Looks behind herself.*) Sure, I know my place. Right here on this earth where God put me. You know your place?

DUMMY IN WHITE: Of course, I was just testing you.

DUMMY IN BLACK: Good. Does the baby know her place?

DUMMY IN WHITE: I will teach her. I will teach her not to be ashamed. I will show her the statues of Francisco de Zúñiga and she will see how it is to be a strong, proud Latina.

DUMMY IN BLACK: ¡Ayyyyy, qué vivan las Latinas!

DUMMY IN WHITE: Shhhhh, you'll wake the baby.

DUMMY IN BLACK: Ah, I was just happy that some of us know our place. Listen, Sarita, if you can't stand up for yourself, stand up for Alma.

DUMMY IN WHITE: (*Wrapping rebozo around herself.*) Come on, we'll be late. (DUMMY IN BLACK *wraps rebozo around herself.*)

SARITA: Where are you going?

DUMMY IN WHITE: Let's go to the park. The baby looks so yellow.

DUMMY IN BLACK: Ah, all babies look that way. (*Dummies disappear.*)

SARITA: Wait! (*We hear* MRS. HOMES' *voice as lights go back on center stage.*)

MRS. HOMES: And he was just yellow with the fever, but I still scrubbed and waxed the floors. The house was just spotless. You wouldn't have known any one was sick at all. Well, well, Sara . . . Sara?

SARITA: Yes.

MRS. HOMES: Now that we've raised the salary, I am sure we'll have no problem in finding someone. You know, Sara, this wouldn't have happened except that my husband is always looking for bargains. But, some people just never learn that you get what you pay for. In the end, cheap is expensive. Let that be a lesson, dear. Well, Sara, you have the idea now and I'll be hearing from you. Let's see, anything else? (*Starts to walk off and trips on* ALMA*'s paper shopping bag.*) Oh, here's your luggage, Alma. (ALMA *rises as* MRS. HOMES *hands her the shopping bag.*) Oh, goodbye, Alma dear, and good luck.

ALMA: Sí, Mrs. Homes. (MRS. HOMES *exits.* ALMA *is close to tears.*) ¿Qué es lo que hice?

SARITA: Nada, y porque . . . (ALMA *starts to cry and runs out of the front room to the back room.*) Why is she so stupid? Why couldn't she know those things? Why, why did she look that way? Like a stupid, docile Mexican, like me, just like me. Oh, God. (*Clutches her chest.*) I can't breathe. I am so angry, I can't breathe, in, out, in, out, God, it hurts. Why didn't I say something? How could I allow her to say those things to us? To both of us? (*Lights dim. Back room lights on. Women gather around* ALMA. ALMA *is crying.*)

CHATA: (*With drink in her hand. She is tipsy.*) Andale, Almita, no llores. Ay, what do you care? It's only a job. What do you care what that vieja pinchi said.

CLARA: Ssssss! You big tuna packer, cállate. Sarita's gonna be mad.

CHATA: Ay, tú. (*Mimicking.*) Shhhh, it's a hospital. Sarita's gonna be mad. Oyes tú, I'm mad. Did that vieja Mrs., Mrs. . . .

ALMA: (*Crying.*) Mrs. Homes.

CHATA: Sí, esa. Did she ever taste Alma's ento . . . ento . . .

ALMA: (*Still crying.*) Entomatadas.

CHATA: Sí, or her mole, eh? The best in all Mexico. ¡Viva Mexico!

CLARA: Be quiet you!

CHATA: Oyes tú, no me da la gana. (*Sits down and sings "Estoy en un rincon de una cantina."*)

LOLA: No llores, Almita. Cállate una rabia, pero no llores. Piensa en tu abuelita, your grandmother, the one who followed your grandfather and fought with Pancho Villa. She wouldn't cry.

CHATA: Ay, what kinda party is this? Everybody saying, "Poor Alma, poor Alma." Yo digo, ¡Viva Alma! ¡Viva México! Viva la Revolución y viva mi viejo gordo y feo, qué le hace que me dejó. (*The women all laugh.*) Andale, chabalonas. Lets go on strike, or sing songs from the Revolution, "Cama de Piedra," "Adelita."

LA CUBANA: I don't know the words to those songs. You want to sing them because I don't know the words. (*Exit* LA CUBANA.)

CHATA: (*Puts arm around* ALMA.) Andale, Almita, ponte a cantar. (*They all sing "Cama de Piedra" with* ALMA *reluctantly joining in. Then "Adelita" as* SARITA *comes back into the back room.*)

LOLA: (*To* SARITA *while women sing softly.*) Oyes, Sarita, why didn't you defend Alma? You always take the gringas' side. First me, now Alma. Why don't you ever stand up for us.

SARITA: And why aren't you more responsible? Why do you put me in these crazy positions, why can't you stay in your jobs and do your work? Why do I have to get involved?

LOLA: If I tell you, you don't hear my side. In your eyes I am wrong, because I am the maid, because I am Latin, because you are ashamed. You want that I should be ashamed.

SARITA: That's . . . that's not true.

LOLA: Then why don't you ever stand up for us? All you want to be is a gringa desteñida! (*She turns her back on* SARITA *and throws herself into singing. "Adelita" singing gets louder.*)

EVITA: (*Yelling and running to the T.V. set.*) Ay, *Viviana*, it's time for

Viviana. (Phone rings as EVITA *turns T.V. set on. Viviana theme music blares, drowning out singing.* CHATA *and* CLARA *join* EVITA *at. T.V., as* MARIA *goes to back room phone, leaving* LOLA *and* DOÑA EUGENIA *to continue singing.* NEW GIRL *tries to get* SARITA*'s attention.)*

MARIA: Ay Sarita, it's the Wedding Chapel.

SARITA: María, you have to learn to answer it.

NEW GIRL: Señorita Sarita, un trabajo, por favor.

MARIA: Ay, Sarita, please. I can't, ay Jesús, no puedo.

SARITA: No! I don't hear it, and I'm tired of doing all the work around here.

CHATA: *(Seeing T.V.)* Ay, viva *Viviana* . . . Qué sexy.

CLARA: You big tuna packer, you're drunk.

CHATA: I'm not drunk! *(Other phone rings.)*

CLARA: Sí, sí, you are, bien borracha.

LA CUBANA: *(Rushing into back room.)* Sarita, those men are still out there. You have to hide me.

EVITA: Shut up! I can't hear *Viviana.)*

CLARA: Don't tell us to be quiet. We was here, your mother and me, much before you.

MARIA: *(Frozen before phone.)* Sarita, please . . .

SARITA: Stop! *(Looks towards heaven.)* Give me a break! *(Everybody freezes and the phones stop. Then* SARITA *walks to stage apron, as all women slowly and calmly gather around T.V., taking sandwiches out of bags and passing food among themselves.* SARITA *to audience)* We need a break. *(As lights fade to dark, we hear commercials from T.V. T.V. stays on all during intermission.)*

ACT TWO

SCENE ONE

Lights go up slowly. SARITA *sits alone in front room section of stage. As we hear Atahuelpa Yupanqui singing "Le Tengo Rabia al Silencio."* SARITA *translates phrases sporadically for the audience. Very slowly lights go up on back room. As lights go up we see various debris from lunch: paper plates, napkins, empty Coke bottles and paper cups. There are also paper and plastic shopping bags, coats and sweaters, some shoes strewn about. The back room is in a general state of disarray, except the area around* CLARA*'s chair, which is very tidy. The women are sitting still listening to the song, in their various reflective moods except for* CLARA, *who is knitting. She looks at them, shakes her head in disapproval and turns down the radio as the song ends.*)

CLARA: Hmmmmmmph! Wasting time!

CHATA: (*Pouring rum into her paper cup, from the bottle by her chair.*) That is why they call him El Poeta de las Pampas. ¡Qué hombre! Cómo sabe sufrir.

ALMA: Mrs. Homes, no good?

MARIA: Sí, the poet, like San Sebastián, he suffers. (*The women, except* CLARA, *all agree with nods of their heads, a few say, "Ay sí's" and "Qué bien lo dice," "Qué bonito."*)

CLARA: (*Still knitting.*) Hmmmmmmmph!

CHATA: (*Getting to her feet, with a large gesture to* CLARA.) ¿Y tú, qué sabes? The trouble with you, Clara, is you have no soul.

CLARA: De soul, de soul don't pay my bills, only work.

ALMA: Almita, no good?

CHATA: Work, work, that's all you know. Ay, I feel it here. (*Strikes her chest and starts to sing loudly.*) Le tengo rabia al silencio por lo mucho que perdí . . . (ALMA *starts to cry, immediately comforted by* LOLA *and* MARIA. *They hug her and say things like, "Ya, ya, no llores," "Andale, Almita." At this little commotion* CHATA *sits down again abruptly.*)

ALMA: Y yo perdí mi trabajo, ay, ¿qué hice mal?

CLARA: Ya ves, ya ves, you and your singing make Almita cry.

CHATA: Me? Tú, tú, vieja! You and your long face y work, work, work.

CLARA: Hmmmph! Por lo menos I no talk of the suffering of a stupid poet. Almita don't need to hear of suffering. She need a job.

CHATA: Ay tú, Sarita will find her a job. Then she will suffer again in silence, así son los trabajos, but if it makes Almita happy . . .

LOLA: Ay, Chata, didn't you listen to the song? Didn't the poet say that those that want to be happy should be silent? (*Turning to* ALMA.) Mira, Almita, did Sarita defend you? No. So you gotta be strong and speak up to those people.

ALMA: Sí, Lola, voy a tratar de aprender.

CLARA: Hmmmmmph! Entonces te da la patada, like this one . . . (*Gesturing to* CHATA) always losing her job.

CHATA: Y a ti, ¿qué? I don't lose my jobs, I just leave them. Mira, Almita, you do like me, eh? You work for a little bit, then you take off. Ay, you have a good time. All this work, work. Life's too short.

MARIA: No te preocupes, Almita. Go to the night school for the English. Do your work and God will help you.

EVITA: (*Going up to* ALMA.) Oye, Almita, yo te puedo ayudar if you dress up, get a new hairstyle, maybe a little make up around your eyes y a little gloss on your mouth and then your eyebrows . . . (LOLA *interrupting*.) No. Just speak up.

CHATA: (*Raising her paper cup.*) Have a good time.

MARIA: Light a candle, a la Virgencita.

EVITA: Just pull your hair back.

LA CUBANA: (*Gets up from her distant chair and goes up to* ALMA.) Psssst! Pssssst! (ALMA *goes up to her.* LA CUBANA *puts her arm around her in conspiratorial fashion, looks around to make sure the others aren't listening. All of the women are straining to hear.* EVITA *gets the closest.*)

LA CUBANA: (*To* ALMA.) Get your green card and don't trust anybody, eh!

WOMEN: ¿Qué dijo? ¿Qué dijo?

EVITA: Get your green card and don't trust anybody. Big deal.

LA CUBANA: Y tú, y tú, estás jealous porque you don't have green card, green card, green card, green card? You don't have one. You want to know why?

EVITA: No, I don't want to know why.

LA CUBANA: They see you. You tell secrets and immigration knows this about you. They know, they see you telling the secrets and laughing at the people, yes, they know.

CHATA: Esa cubana está bien chiflada.

LOLA: Ay, no seas mala. Encerrada todo el tiempo in these people's homes can make you lonely and crazy.

EVITA: Ay sí, remember Josie, la negrita, se volvió loca y she was chasing la patrona all over the house trying to stab her con un fruit knife.

MARIA: ¡No! ¿Sí?

EVITA: Sí, la pobre, la llevaron al funny farm.

MARIA: (*Crossing herself.*) ¡Ay, Dios mío de mi vida!

CHATA: Y Violeta . . .

LOLA: Sí, pero Violeta wasn't crazy. It was her nerves, those people she worked for were mean, la maltrataron mucho.

ALMA: Sí, a veces así es la gente.

CLARA: Hmmmmmmph! I don't pay attention to them. I just do my job. Mira, Almita, como mi trabajo en Encino . . .

CHATA: Encino, Encino, es todo lo que sabes.

CLARA: (*Ignoring* CHATA.) The daughter complains anytime anything is missing, los sweaters, los jeans. The mother say to her, "ask the maid."

LOLA: Sí, sí, ask "the maid," tell "the maid."

EVITA: Mr. Hodges tell his friends I am the "housekeeper."

CHATA: Ay sí, housekeeper. ¿Por qué no domestic engineer? (*Laughing uproariously. All women laugh.*)

CLARA: Hmmmmph! (*Then determined to go on.*) She say, "Please tell your maid to stay out of my room." Hmmmmph! I don't pay attention, I just come and I clean. That's what they pay for. Then la mamá she say to the daughter, "From now on I want you to take care of your own things." (*Women all mumble their approval with, "Sí, así debe ser" and "tiene que aprender."*)

CLARA: Sí, entonces la hija, she say to la mamá, "Look at you. You no take care of your things. Your maids do all your work."

CHATA: Daughters are mean to their mamas.

CLARA: Y la mamá she get mad. Ay, then they fight, oh, so loud. I don't pay attention. I just keep cleaning. And el husband when he come, he no like to talk but he say to her, "Some day your maid will learn to turn off the lights in the garage." (*The women react.*)

CHATA: Pinchi pendejo, turn them off yourself!

EVITA: No, you say, "Ay, amorcito, I didn't want you to hurt your toes in the dark." (*Women all laugh.*)

CLARA: Hmmmmph! I don't pay attention. If I am sick or my boy is sick and I don't come, they try to make me feel bad. Como si fuera floja. The next day, she just gives me that look.

LOLA: Sí, una mirada que mate.

CLARA: Hmmmmmph! She don't talk to me. Then she starts, she say, "Everybody should be equal, pero the people who like to be equal, they have to be responsible and work hard at their job."

CHATA: (*Gives the raspberries.*) Oyes, a tu patrona le gusta hablar.

CLARA: Sí, she like to talk. Eso de everybody equal. She go to meet with the other women, they talk everybody equal y de los husbands y como los hombres le tratan mal. They talk how the woman must be equal to men. Then she come to me and say, "Clara, you and me, equal." Hmmmmmph! I don't pay attention. (*Silence.*) She don't know nothing. I been taking three buses every day to clean houses for fifteen years and she . . .

CHATA: Comadre, you ain't equal to her. Any pendejo can see that.

CLARA: Sí, pues, but she likes to pretend. But I don't pay attention. I just do my job. (*There is a moment of silence when* CLARA *sits down.* MARIA *crosses herself, more silence.*)

CHATA: (*To* CLARA.) Mira lo que hace. You put everybody in a bad mood. Andale, muchachas. What happened to our party? Evita, go put the radio on the Cuban station.

LOLA: Ay, it's so slow today. Aren't the jobs coming in? (*All the women agree.*)

NEW GIRL: ¿Cuándo nos van a conseguir trabajo?

MARIA: Hay que tener paciencia. Sometimes it's slow, pero yo les voy a hacer un special prayer and you will see. All the ladies will be coming to get you.

EUGENIA: Sí, sí, hay que tener paciencia, mucha paciencia. (*She picks up her bag, rummages through it.*)

ALMA: Ojalá que sí.

MARIA: ¡Claro que sí!

EVITA: (*Seeing* DOÑA EUGENIA *with her bag.*) Ay, Almita, María's prayers son muy fuertes, pero maybe Doña Eugenia can make a special yu yu so you get a job right away. Maybe a special one for me?

CHATA: Y para la new girl, a yu yu for her too.

NEW GIRL: Ah sí, un yu yu. (*All the women get very excited. They surround* EUGENIA *and sit on the floor except for* LA CUBANA *who stands up from her seat and starts walking out the door.*)

LA CUBANA: I already have a job. (*The women sit on the floor in a semi-circle, holding hands, and intensely watch* EUGENIA *as she rummages through her shopping bag.*)

EUGENIA: (*Takes out an herb from her bag.*) Yerba santa para la garganta . . . no.

LA CUBANA: (*Pausing just before she gets to the door.*) Don Félix told me that Sarita already has a job for me as a lady's companion in Bel Air and I start . . . (EUGENIA *gives* LA CUBANA *a powerful look and a soft gesture of her hand to sit down.* LA CUBANA *sits down quietly on a chair nearest the door.*)

EUGENIA: (*It is a different* EUGENIA *speaking in a rich, serious voice.*) Alma, piénsalo bien ¿de veras, quieres trabajar?

EVITA: (*Very excited.*) Sí, sí, Doña Eugenia. She wants a job with a nice lady and kids. She's good with kids and I want . . .

EUGENIA: (*Sternly to* EVITA.) No le hablo a usted. Alma Gutiérrez, ¿quieres trabajar?

ALMA: (*Pauses, then with strength and belief.*) Sí. (*Lights go down in the back room and come up in the front room.*)

SARITA: Something is going on here, I can feel it. (*She stands very still and sniffs the air until the end of the song.* DON FELIX *bursts through the front door with confetti sticking to his sticky hair and all over his clothes a few colorful paper streamers here and there.*)

DON FELIX: (*Walking to his desk.*) What a wedding. Ay, honey, you should have been there. The bride, this big she was . . . (*Stretches his arms out to indicate width of bride.*) Una gorda sabrosa y chichones hasta aquí . . . (*Stretches his hands out to indicate huge breasts.*) Ay, her skin so smooth. She was delicate. When she got excited, she trembled all over y el novio, un hueso, a real skinny runt, he was. (*Laughing.*) I hope he's going to be all right. (DON FELIX *sits at desk absorbed in the yellow pages of phone book.* SARITA *starts to pace back and forth in front of his desk.* DON FELIX *finally looks up.*) Something bothering you, honey?

SARITA: (*Still pacing.*) No! (DON FELIX *continues to look for phone number.*)

DON FELIX: You sure nothing's bothering you, honey?

SARITA: (*Still pacing.*) Absolutely nothing's bothering me, honey! (*To audience.*) First, the new girl bites me. Then, I lose a job on *Eight is Enough* because I am too exotic. Without any warning whatsoever, Lola quits her job with Mrs. Camden. Mrs. Camden calls and yells at me. Mrs. Homes returns Alma, insults us and now wants me to find her a cheery Chinese person or a docile Mexican with no relatives. La Cubana is now well into an advanced state of paranoia and is seeing things. Chata is getting drunk. María is mad at me because I don't believe in St. Anthony. Lola's mad at me because, because, well, skip that one. (*Turns back to* DON FELIX.) The jobs aren't coming in. Mrs. Camden is screaming for a replacement today and where are you? Behind the body shop marrying Laurel and Hardy.

DON FELIX: Ay, honey, is that all? First of all, Mrs. Camden you don't have to worry about because we already have the money. She'll just have to wait for a replacement and the rest you just make up some M.B.'s.

SARITA: M.B.'s! M.B.'s! I . . . I (SARITA *turns and talks to audience with her back to* DON FELIX.) I don't believe this. His solution to every problem is an M.B. A make believe.

DON FELIX: (*Talking to the back of* SARITA *as if she were facing him.* Give them an illusion. Make up some hope, honey, make up a job.

SARITA: (*To audience.*) He does that just before they leave for the day. He makes up a perfect job for each of them so they'll come back the next day. When they do come back, of course, the make believe job is no longer available. It's all bullshit! But they keep coming back and coming back. What I can't figure out is, do they really believe it or do they want him to think they believe it so they keep him coming back?

DON FELIX: (*To* SARITA*'s back.*) I know you think it's bullshit. Everybody's gotta have a dream, honey. It keeps them together, like all those huddled masses that came to Ellis Island. They had their dreams, some of them even thought that the streets in this country were paved with gold. (*Lights up slowly in the back room. Women, except for* LA CUBANA, *sitting on floor around* EUGENIA, *holding hands. Every now and then* EUGENIA *says the name of an ingredient, making up yu yu.*)

SARITA: (*To audience.*) M.B.'s should be for big dreams, not for some piddley maid's job to keep your family on this side of starvation.

DON FELIX: Now, take me for example. I got a dream that I'll be businessman of the year. I'll be the speaker at the Rotary Club luncheon. (*He has made microphones out of paper cups placed on his desk pen set. The effect is of a speaker on a podium. He taps a glass of water on his desk, tapes the microphones.*) Testing, one, two, three, testing, one, two, three. As a young boy in Guatemala, we didn't have a lot. (*He takes a pause. The phone rings and shatters his dreams. He answers it.*) Felix Sanchez Domestic Agency, Don Félix speaking. Oh, Carlos, sí hombre. (LA CUBANA *enters front room and goes up to* SARITA.)

LA CUBANA: Oyes, Sarita, a mí me prometieron ese trabajo de ladies companion. It's my job.

SARITA: What job?

LA CUBANA: My job as a ladies companion.

SARITA: Ladies companion? (*Looks at heaven.*) Give me a break, will you? (*She walks to her desk as the other phone rings.*)

LA CUBANA: (*Running after her.*) Sí, sí, my lady's companion job.

SARITA: (*Hand on phone about to pick it up.*) Believe me, Margarita, I haven't had a call for a lady's companion since the Bronte sisters left town.

LA CUBANA: (*Reaches over, picks up the receiver of the ringing phone and slams it down. Ring stops.*) No! Yo sé, you're on their side. They all hate me because I have a green card y la Doña Eugenia make yu yu por Almita to find job. Por eso, you're giving Almita my job, my lady's companion job.

SARITA: Calm down. Where did you get the idea I had a lady's comp . . . (*Looks at* DON FELIX *who has quickly gotten off the phone. He looks at them both sheepishly.*)

LA CUBANA: Tell her, Don Félix, how you promised me the job with the rich, lonely old lady in Bel Air.

DON FELIX: (*Suddenly in an awful hurry.*) Sí, sí, con su pe miso, voy al baño.)

SARITA: (*Angrily to* DON FELIX, *enunciating every word.*) Which "rich," "lonely," "old lady," in Bel Air?

DON FELIX: (*To* SARITA.) M.B. honey, M.B. (*In stage whisper.*) Use your imagination. (DON FELIX *exits to bathroom.*)

SARITA: (*Gritted teeth.*) An M.B.

LA CUBANA: M.B.?

SARITA: A, sí, sí, M.B., which means, "Muy bien," which means, as you know, "very good." I remember now thinking it was a terrific job for you, Margarita, but unfortunately the old lady . . . she . . . she died. This morning. So, she won't be needing you for the job.

LA CUBANA: She didn't die! My old lady didn't die! You're just giving the job to Almita!

SARITA: I swear to you the old lady is dead. And that's the truth.

LA CUBANA: ¡Cerda! ¡Mentirosa! ¡Puñetera! ¡Bullshit!

SARITA: Ay, Margarita, such language from a ladies companion. Remember who you are.

LA CUBANA: I know who I am. I am Cuban y I have a green card, ¿y tú? You are pocha. Mexican trying to be gringa. That's why the television people no want you, they know, they see, television people they see everything, they watching you. Even when the television is off, they watching you. They see how you lie, how you don't stand up for Almita, how you are afraid to speak up to the gringas. The television people no want you to be on the shows because you are dark face, pocha prieta, who don't tell the truth.

SARITA: Okay, okay, you want the truth; there is no lady's companion job. There is no job. Don Félix just made it up and even if there was a lady's companion job, you, you would be the last person to get it. You're fat, lazy, overbearing, obnoxious, a hypochondriac, paranoid and crazy.

LA CUBANA: No! No! You lying.

SARITA: Oh yes, and you smell bad.

LA CUBANA: No, no.

SARITA: Yes, yes, let's have the "truth." You want to know what you smell like?

LA CUBANA: No es cierto, mentirosa.

SARITA: You smell of sweat, urine, buggers and cheap perfume.

LA CUBANA: No, no, mentiras, no más mentiras.

SARITA: Yes, yes, you do, you stink! I've sent you on countless interviews. People think you're a joke, a big smelly joke. God only knows, I've tried, I've tried, I have really tried. Nobody wants you either. (*They are both stunned.* SARITA, *with hand over her mouth as she watches* LA CUBANA *sink slowly into the chair by her desk, tears streaming down her face. Her lower lip trembling, gently but firmly and rhythmically, she pounds her clenched fist against the desk, muttering . . .*)

LA CUBANA: No, no es cierto, mentiras, nomás se burlan de mí, todo el mundo se burla de mí; me quitan todo.

SARITA: Oh, please . . . I didn't mean it, you got me so angry. It just came out. (SARITA *crouches down and gently takes* LA CUBANA*'s fist to stop the pounding.* LA CUBANA *turns and looks at* SARITA. *For a moment the two women look at each other. Lights softly up back room as we see more yu yu ceremony.*) Don't pay any attention to me. You know, for an idiot, no one can out do me.

LA CUBANA: Only me. Everybody always make fun of me. Since I was a little, little girl, todo el mundo se burla de mí.

SARITA: Margarita, not the whole world, don't exaggerate, and not when you were a little, little girl.

LA CUBANA: Sí, that's true.

SARITA: There was always somebody holding you, kissing you, calling you la consentida.

LA CUBANA: Mi papi use to call me Amorcita, o Corazón o Mi Reina. We used to go to the beach every Sunday and make a barbacoa, a goat, a pig.

SARITA: Ah, geez, look at you. You got snot coming down your nose, mascara running, here. (*Hands* LA CUBANA *Kleenex from desk.* LA CUBANA *wipes her eyes and blows her nose loudly.*)

LA CUBANA: Sarita, I will never be a lady's companion?

SARITA: I . . . I don't know.

LA CUBANA: But they say in this country anything is possible.

SARITA: Yeah, look at Charo, "Cuchi, cuchi," uhhh sick!

LA CUBANA: And I am Cuban, I am somebody.

SARITA: Absolutely!

LA CUBANA: Sí, absolutely.

SARITA: Margarita, what exactly do lady's companion do?

LA CUBANA: Oh, many things. They talk, they are friends, they take care of each other. I show you. I will be the companion and you can be the lady.

SARITA: (*With a cockney accent, scratching herself.*) "Me mother was a lady."

LA CUBANA: (*Bringing* SARITA *a paper cup from the desk.*) Here, Sarita, you are the lady and I bring you your morning coffee.

LA CUBANA: Andale, Sarita, you start.

SARITA: Okay, okay. (SARITA *concentrates for a moment.*) "Ah, good morning, Magarita." (*Takes a pretend sip of coffee.*) "Oh, delicious coffee."

LA CUBANA: It's Colombian. Would you like me to take you to the park? It's a beautiful day.

SARITA: "Not just yet, maybe later. How are you feeling Margarita?"

LA CUBANA: Ay, lady, it's the cancer. Last night alone in my bed, I felt it like, ay . . . like feathers on my arms . . . (*She strokes her upper arms sensuously*) On my neck, on my thighs, and even, even there (*Quickly points to her genital area.*)

SARITA: "Oh, that nasty cancer!" Wait a minute, hold it. You can't talk to the lady about cancer. Nobody's going to hire you if you keep talking about cancer. People don't like to hire people with cancer. So, don't talk cancer, okay?

LA CUBANA: Sí, okay.

SARITA: Anyway, it really isn't cancer, Margarita. It's, it's, well, I feel that way a lot. Especially after I see a Robert Redford movie and I have to go home alone.

LA CUBANA: Ah, sí . . . (*Pause.*) So the lady, do the lady again, Sarita.

SARITA: Okay, okay, I'll do the lady.

LA CUBANA: Ah lady, I like Ricardo Montalbán, ay "the rich Corinthean," he looks just exactly like my husband.

SARITA: "The astronaut?"

LA CUBANA: Sí, he is on a secret mission. (MARIA *comes to doorway of front room.*)

SARITA: "Another one!"

LA CUBANA: Sí, he can't even come to see me. Maybe he don't want me anymore.

SARITA: "Margarita, he just doesn't want to . . . to . . . blow his cover; it must be very difficult for him, without you." What am I saying? Hold it, time out. Listen, Margarita, two things you have to remember, number one, don't talk cancer, number two, don't talk about your astronaut husband. No secret missions, none of that stuff, okay?

LA CUBANA: Sí, lady, okay?

SARITA: All right, now, go on, go on. (SARITA *takes another sip of her coffee, holding her cup in a lady-like fashion with an exaggerated pinkie sticking out. She turns and sees* MARIA, *dismisses her with a "Hmmmmmph!")*

LA CUBANA: A ver, ah sí, is it time for the park now, lady?

MARIA: José y María, ¿qué está pasando aquí?

LA CUBANA: Sarita is pretending she is the lady and I am the companion.

MARIA: (*In disbelief, pointing to* SARITA.) She is the lady?

SARITA: Sí, pobre, pero de tan buena familia. (*We hear car horn honking, just as* MRS. LEVINE *walks through the front door, harried and smoking one of her shermans.*)

MRS. LEVINE: Oh, María, thank God you're here. I need a replacement right away. (*Car horn beeps.*) Those guys in the car are going to drive me crazy! (*She turns and goes out the door.*)

LA CUBANA: (*To* MRS. LEVINE, *as she is leaving.*) Ah, you saw them, too? María, María, ya ves, she saw those men in the car, too. The ones I saw this morning, the ones that are after me.

SARITA: Margarita, Margarita, rule number three, we don't talk about strange men in cars who are after us, you don't see them, okay?

LA CUBANA: Sí, lady, but . . .

MARIA: (*Interrupting.*) Sí, sí, Margarita, and go to the back and tell, ah, tell . . . ay, Sarita, who would be good for this job? She don't need English.

SARITA: Almita, she needs it.

MARIA: Sí, pues, Margarita, go tell Almita to get ready, y que si Dios quiere le tengo un trabajo. (*Lights go up in the back room.* LA CUBANA *runs to the back and runs into* DON FELIX *on his way to the front.*) Mrs. Levine, she always needs a replacement, the girls just leave her.

SARITA: Well, Alma stays through anything. I am going to make sure she gets this job. (SARITA *goes to back room and runs into* DON FELIX *who is going into the front room. We hear a car horn again and off stage voice of* MRS. LEVINE.)

MRS. LEVINE: Robert! Bernard! Knock it off. (MRS. LEVINE *comes through the front door, takes a few steps into the front room, the horn blows again. Phone rings,* MARIA *answers.* MRS. LEVINE *sticks her head out the door and yells at the kids as* DON FELIX *walks up to her.*)

MRS. LEVINE: I told you two to knock it off.

DON FELIX: Ah, lovely Mrs. Levine. Such a pleasure to see you again.

MRS. LEVINE: Oh, I'll bet it is. If you could find somebody that would even stay a week. Nobody has stayed a week. (*During* MRS. LEVINE*'s last speech*, NEW GIRL *has sneacked out of the back room. Phone rings*, DON FELIX *answers it*. MARIA *gets off the phone*.)

MARIA: The same money, Mrs. Levine?

MRS. LEVINE: Yes. No, ten dollars more if she stays the week.

MARIA: Ah, I have the just right girl for you. Excuse un momento. (MARIA *goes to the back room. The car horn beeps again.* MRS. LEVINE *sticks her head out the door and yells at the boys as* NEW GIRL *cautiously approaches* MRS. LEVINE.)

MRS. LEVINE: Knock it off, boys. Do you hear me, Robert? Don't stick your leg out the window . . . the traffic. Do you hear me? Get your leg back in the car. (MRS. LEVINE *closes the front door, turns around and finds herself face to face with* NEW GIRL.)

NEW GIRL: Perdóneme, Señora, me fijé que usted busca a alguien que le ayude en la casa y pues yo soy trabajadora buena. Yo sé hacer todo en la casa. Por favor, señora. (*Car horn beeps*.)

MRS. LEVINE: Oh, I am sorry. I don't speak Spanish too well. I just took one year in high school. (*In a very slow, broken Spanish with a heavy American accent*.) Yo me llamo Stephanie. (*Car horn beeps*.) Niños. Muy mal. Excuse me. (MRS. LEVINE *sticks her head out the front door and yells*.) If you boys don't stop that, I am taking all of your privileges away, do you hear me? (MRS. LEVINE *closes the front door, turns around and faces the* NEW GIRL.)

NEW GIRL: (*Talking rapidly*.) Yo me llamo Elsa María Cristina López de Moreno. A mí me encantan los niños. En mi país yo tengo tres hermanitos, viven con mi mamá. Mi papá se murió y me he propuesto a mantenerlos. (*Car horn beeps again*.)

MRS. LEVINE: I got your name, I think, but I missed all the rest. I just took one year. All I can remember is the lesson on Isabel.

NEW GIRL: Isabel?

MRS. LEVINE: (*Slowly*.) ¡Hola, Isabel! ¿Cómo está usted? Yo estoy bien. Yo voy a la biblioteca. Of course, I can say other Spanish phrases: niños watchando T.V.? . . . lavando los windows? . . . Vacuuming aquí . . . (*Car horn beeps*.) Excuse me, yo spanko los niños. (MRS. LEVINE *goes out the front door*. NEW GIRL *waits for her by the front door*. DON FELIX *is still on the phone as lights get brighter and voices get louder in the back room*. EVITA *is putting the finishing touches on* ALMA*'s face and hair*. SARITA *brushes off* ALMA*'s skirt*.)

SARITA: ¡Apúrate! ¡Apúrate!

CHATA: Sarita, what's all the fuss for? La Mrs. Levine, she's lucky to get anybody. I am telling you, Sarita, those kids son diablitos, it ain't such a good job.

SARITA: I want Alma to look responsible, neat, professional. Then Mrs. Levine and her kids will respect her.

CHATA: I am telling you, those kids don't respect nothing.

CLARA: Hmmmmph! Carmela left Mrs. Levine porque los kids, they tie firecrackers around the toilets.

CHATA: Sí, Alma, cuidado when you sit down, eh? Ay Evita, you put too much pencil on her eyebrows. She looks like she got one line straight across.

SARITA: Sí, Chata's right, here Evita, wipe it off. (EVITA *wipes off the eyebrow pencil.* ALMA *stands very still as the women appraise her. She has on her own skirt and blouse but all of* SARITA*'s accessories, except for her own shawl.* SARITA *gives* ALMA *a long critical look. All the women look at* SARITA *for the final judgement. All except* LOLA, *who just sits there with arms crossed across her chest.*) Hmmmm, something is wrong, I know. Here, Alma, take my sweater. Give me your shawl. (*They exchange.*) Much better. Now don't forget what I told you. Don't look sad. Pretend you're Hazel. Don't mention your relatives and don't get nervous. María, don't forget to say what a good cook she is.

CHATA: All this fuss, for La Levine.

CLARA: Hmmmmph! A lo menos, it's a job.

MARIA: Mira, Alma, los weekends off y te dan $85, si duras la semana.

ALMA: Qué bien, sí, sí, yo lo duro. (*All women wish* ALMA *good luck in Spanish.* SARITA, MARIA, ALMA *start to leave the back room, suddenly* ALMA *stops.*) ¡Mi yu yu! ¿Dónde está mi yu yu? (EUGENIA *gets the yu yu and hands it to* ALMA. *They get to the front room just as* MRS. LEVINE *returns to the front room.*)

MARIA: Mrs. Levine, this is Alma Gutiérrez. I have good references on her.

MRS. LEVINE: Hola, yo me llamo Stephanie. (ALMA *and* MRS. LEVINE *shake hands. A very dejected* NEW GIRL *leaves the front room.*)

ALMA: Mucho gusto, señora. (*Car horn beeps.*)

MRS. LEVINE: Niños, muy malos. (ALMA *looks out the front door, turns back to* MRS. LEVINE.)

ALMA: Ay qué chulos, muy bonitos. (*Car horn beeps.* ALMA *opens the door, sticks her head out and yells out the door.*) Oigan chavalitos, les voy a dar una buena patada si no se me portan bien. (*All honking stops.* ALMA *puts her head in the door as* EUGENIA *comes into the front room with* ALMA*'s paper bag.*)

MRS. LEVINE: Oh, María, could she come home with us now?

MARIA: Oh, I am sure. (EUGENIA *brings paper bag to* ALMA, *hugs her as* MRS. LEVINE *signs another contract and makes out and gives check to* MARIA. SARITA *goes to the back room. Visually, we see* SARITA *tell the women that* ALMA *got the job. The women all cheer.* CHATA *pours herself another drink. In the front room,* MARIA, EUGENIA *wave goodbye to* ALMA *and* MRS. LEVINE *as they exit.* NEW GIRL *returns to front room with broom and vigorously attacks cleaning the front room.* EUGENIA *and* MARIA *look at check.* DON FELIX *gets off the phone and grabs the check from* MARIA *as* SARITA *comes into front room.*)

SARITA: Hey, María, we did it. Did you see Alma's face? She looked so proud and confident. I gave away half my clothes, but we did it.

MARIA: It was God and Doña Eugenia's yu yu.

SARITA: Sure it was.

MARIA: Sí, sure it was. Doña Eugenia say Almita would find job with nice lady and kids. She makes special yu yu.

SARITA: Oh, yu yu, shmu yu.

MARIA: Sarita, Lola is right. You really are a . . . you don't respect the old ways.

SARITA: Listen, I believe in hard work. I can't do it all the time, but I know that's what gets you what you want. Not yu yus.

DON FELIX: Sometimes it does, sometimes it doesn't. Me, I believe in this . . . (*Kisses* MRS. LEVINE*'s check.*) But I don't like to take any chances. That's why I am going to ask Doña Eugenia to make me a special yu yu for the disco opening tonight.

SARITA: God save us from the yu yu disco . . . (*Sees the* NEW GIRL *passionately scrubbing the walls.*) What is going on here? What's with Miss Peru?

NEW GIRL: No se nota, pero yo soy muy fuerte. Yo soy trabajadora buena. Por favor, señorita Sarita, necesito un trabajo. Mire, mire, yo sé . . . (*Very slowly in broken English.*) I don pay atencion, watchando T.V., lavando los windows, one . . . two . . . three . . . (EUGENIA, MARIA, DON FELIX *watch in amazement as* NEW GIRL *continues counting. Slowly lights change as* SISTER *appears, and a younger* SARITA *appears, and a younger* SARITA *jumps up and down, waving her arm at* SISTER.)

YOUNG SARITA: Sister! Sister, I know, I know the answer . . . Francisco Zúñiga, the statues of the Latina women, on page 324, were done by

Francisco Zúñiga and he is Mexican. The statues are made of bronze, not pink marble and Mr. Zúñiga made them to sit outside on the earth. They're tough, they sit outside, through the rain, the wind, the snow, even tornadoes. They look soft, like my Grandma's lap, like you could hug them, but they are hard and strong and heavy . . . 2, 4, 6 even 100 strong men couldn't move them, not even Mr. Amador's truck.

SISTER: That's enough, Sarita.

SARITA: They would need a bulldozer.

SISTER: I said that's enough, Sarita. Now, class, turn to page 375 and look at those extraordinary statues of Michael Angelo. (SISTER *disappears. Lights dim, music from back room radio gets louder.* LA CUBANA *and* EVITA *are dancing to Cuban music, with* LOLA, CLARA *and* CHATA *looking on.* LA CHATA *is drinking,* CLARA *is knitting,* LOLA *is sitting there with arms crossed, lost in thought.*)

CHATA: Chiiii, mira esa Cubana chiflada, sí, sabe bailar.

CLARA: How fine Almita looks. That was smart of Sarita to make Almita look good.

LOLA: Smart? ¿Eso también quieres? ¿Que Sarita le viste al gusto de los gringos? She don't stand up for Almita when they insult her and then your preciosa Sarita dressed her up, so she won't look too Latina for the gringos.

CLARA: Sarita was helping.

LOLA: (*Interrupting.*) No entiendes. She is so ashamed that she don't think Almita looked good enough to clean the gringa's toilet.

CHATA: Ay, Lola, ¿qué te pasa? (LOLA *angrily gets up and goes to the bathroom slamming the door shut.*)

CLARA: Hmmmmmmph! She needs a job.

CHATA: ¡Ay tú! Work, work, maybe she's having trouble with Roberto. (*Sipping from her cup, she becomes reflective.*) Comadre, men are nothing but trouble. That pinchi gordo of mine, even took my T.V. when he left me.

CLARA: Hmmmmmmph! Maybe you're lucky. My Xavier stays, but he runs around, viejo vago, but I don't pay attention. I work, I have my boy. (*Music has stopped,* EVITA *flops down on the chair next to* CHATA *as* LA CUBANA *fixes herself some beans with white bread from the table with bean pot.*)

CHATA: (*To* EVITA.) Oyes, Evita, this gringo, Mr. Hodges, he don't give you trouble?

EVITA: Claro que sí, todos los hombres give trouble.

CLARA: Todos son iguales.

EVITA: Pero los gringos son cobardes. Men here, they are afraid, afraid of their hearts, their feeling, of the women. Doña Eugenia give me this . . . (*Fishes down into the front of her blouse and pulls out a little yu yu bag.*) I put this under Mr. Hodge's pillow for ten day then we will be married.

CLARA: Hmmmmmph! Evita, forget it.

EVITA: Sí, you will see, in the church in a white satin dress with little, little pearls here. (*Touches her neckline area.*) With . . . with sleeves to there. (*Points to spot on upper arms.*) Long white gloves con botones de pearls, toda de blanco, toditita de blanco voy a estar.

CLARA: Hmmmmmph!

EVITA: And on my head, a crown, a crown of pearls, the bridesmaids in long pink velvet dresses with powder blue sashes, carrying yellow tea roses and baby's breath and the grooms all twelve of them in white pants with a blue stripe down the leg and powder blue jackets.

CHATA: Ay, no, Evita, white jackets, more simple.

EVITA: White jackets then. I will keep it simple. But my mamá, my mamá will wear a yellow lace dress with an orchid corsage. (*Turns to* CLARA.) And you, Doña Clara, if you would come, I would get for you an orchid corsage and you could sit next to mamá, please?

CLARA: Maybe I could get the day off.

CHATA: (*Getting very melancholy.*) The day I met my first husband, Emilio, was two days after my sixteenth birthday. I shaved my eyebrows to look like Lola Beltrán. I cut off my trenzas and did my hair like María Félix in "El Rapto." I was living with my sister and mother on Soto Street. I walked down the block to the little mercado and there he was . . . ¡hijo! ¡Guapísimo estaba! Y me dice, "Mamacita, ¿a dónde vas?" Ay, he was a real lady killer. Divino estaba. Me puso loca and pretty soon he did me the favor and I got the big belly. My uncle Rufino told him he was gonna cut off his balls if he didn't marry me. So, we got married, but not by the priest. So, mamá said we weren't really married. She cried, poor thing (*Crosses herself*) and that no good Emilio didn't even have the pantalones to stick around after Consuelo was born. (*Turns to* CLARA.) Clara, I really had feelings for Emilio. All the rest, the guy from Pep boys, the Samoan bartender, what was his name?

CLARA: Nickie, big Nickie.

CHATA: Ah is, big Nickie, even that gordo, when they left I feel lonely, bad. But I don't feel them in my heart like Emilio. Ay, comadre, people always leave me. Pero, it's the ones that leave me and stay in my heart, like Emilio and Consuelo, that hurts. (CLARA *drops knitting and embraces* CHATA.)

CLARA: And me? I am not in your heart? I am here. I don't leave.

LA CUBANA: I met my husband when I was living in Miami at the space center. (MARIA, EUGENIA *and* NEW GIRL *come into the back room.* EUGENIA *takes* NEW GIRL *to far corner of the back room.*)

EUGENIA: No te preocupes, mi hija. Sarita te va a ayudar y yo voy a hacer un yu yu muy fuerte para que te encuentres un trabajito. (EUGENIA *and* NEW GIRL *secretly sit in far corner of the room as* EUGENIA *makes yu yu for* NEW GIRL.)

MARIA: (*To* CLARA.) ¿Qué le pasa a Chata?

CLARA: Hmmmmmmph! Los hombres son diablos.

MARIA: No todos, some husbands is very good. Pobrecito, my husband works so hard y también es muy dulce con la niña.

EVITA: Ay sí, María, qué suerte tienes, your husband is so good. Always happy.

CLARA: Sí, María, es verdad. ¿Cómo le haces?

CHATA: Ay you, how do you think she does it?

MARIA: (*Interrupting.*) I pray to Santa Bárbara, for me you pray to Santa Bárbara.

CHATA AND EVITA: ¡Santa Bárbara!

MARIA: Yes, you pray to Santa Bárbara and she will send you a good man.

CHATA: With big fingers?

MARIA: Big fingers?

CHATA: Sí, if they have big fingers that means they have a big . . . cosa . . .

EVITA: No, Chata, it's the feet, if they have big feet.

MARIA: ¡No! ¿Sí? Ay, Chata, you can't ask Santa Bárbara to bring you a man con . . .

CLARA: Hmmmmmph! It's the nose! (*Lights start to dim and go up in the front.*)

CHATA: ¿Ah, tú qué sabes? It's the fingers.

LA CUBANA: On the moon it gets bigger porque no tiene gravity to hold it back.

EVITA: My cousin Chuyita is married to this man with big feet and she say . . . (*We hear another, "¡No! ¿Sí?" from* MARIA *as lights go down in the back room and up in the front room.* SARITA *is on the telephone.*)

SARITA: Yes, *Eight is Enough.* Well, I wondered if they had made any decision. Yes, I'll hold. (*Second phone rings.* DON FELIX *answers it.*)

DON FELIX: Felix Sanchez Domestic Agency. Mr. Felix Sanchez speaking, ah, lovely Mrs. Camden, so good to . . . (SARITA *gets* DON FELIX*'s attention, shakes her head and points to herself indicating that she isn't in.*) Yes, yes, but of course, the contract? Oh, no refund; yes, of course. One of our many counselors will be happy to help you through this difficult situation. Goodbye, Mrs. Camden. We look forward to seeing you.

SARITA: (*Still on hold.*) Oh, please, tell me she isn't coming.

DON FELIX: I am afraid so, honey.

SARITA: Why don't you just give her a refund?

DON FELIX: Me? Refund? Just get her a replacement, honey. (DON FELIX *leaves for back room.*)

SARITA: (*Mimicking* DON FELIX.) Just get her a replacement, honey . . . one of your many counselors will help. (*Into telephone.*) Hello, not yet? Yes, I'll call back. (*Slams receiver down and takes a deep breath.*) I wish I were Betty in *Father Knows Best*, or I wish, I were in *Mayberry* with Sheriff Taylor, Barney, Goober, Aunt Bea, Opie. We'd all be in the kitchen, eating one of Aunt Bea's famous pies, "What's that, you say you took first prize with this pie over at Mt. Pilot?" (MARIA *enters front room.*)

MARIA: Sarita, Don Félix wants . . .

SARITA: Oh, María, you're just in time. (*Clearing path for Aunt Bea.*) "Careful, don't drop it now, Aunt Bea." Look, María, a peach pie, (*Pad of paper on* SARITA*'s desk had become the pie. They both look at it intently.*) all warm from the oven with a tender, flakey, golden crust. Oh wait, "Yes, Aunt Bea, María would love a scoop of vanilla ice cream right there on top." Wouldn't you, María? (SARITA *looks up and sees* MS. HARRIS *as* MARIA, *is still concentrating on pad.*)

MS. HARRIS: Uh, make mine chocolate. I'd have to have chocolate.

SARITA: With peach pie?

MS. HARRIS: With anything, I am really into chocolate.

MARIA: I am María, this is Sarita, she is always playing the games, making us laugh, ha, ha. Can we help you Mrs. . .

MS. HARRIS: Oh hey, it's Cindy, Cindy Harris. We're neighbors. I'm into Public Relations. We're just down the street. I just got this great promotion. My girlfriend Silvia, she's the one who told me about you, she went into the hot tub business with her boyfriend, who is a total jerk. Anyway, I got her job. But my boss, he's a real sweetie, says I am going to have to put in a lot more time, so I need somebody to look after my two kids, since my ex, the ultimate Virgo, will only take them on weekends. I really can't afford anybody, but Silvia said most of your women were . . . well, you know, illegal.

SARITA: We're not responsible for . . .

MS. HARRIS: Oh, hey, listen, it doesn't bother me. I mean I wouldn't dream of asking, it's not my business. Everybody's gotta do what they gotta do. I mean, as far as I am concerned, she doesn't even have to speak English. It would be nice, but I hear that's more expensive. I just want somebody young, clean, bright. I mean, I don't want one of those fat ones with the gold teeth. I always see those kind at the bus stop. God, I don't see how anybody can let themselves go like that and I guess they think the gold teeth are pretty. Anyway, I've never had a maid before, I mean, what do we do? Do you just send somebody? Could I get her today? Could I get somebody for $50 a week?

MARIA: (*Taking a form and starting to fill it in.*) I explain everything, but first, I must put the little cross in this little box for child care. Cooking?

MS. HARRIS: Not much, they're into Mrs. Paul's Frozen Fishsticks. Do you think you have somebody?

SARITA: Hmmmm, no English, not fat, clean, young, bright for $50 a week. I don't know.

MS. HARRIS: Today? For $55?

MARIA: Sarita, the new girl. She is young, clean and she don't got gold teeth. She would go for $55, since this would be the first time she work . . .

SARITA: (*Interrupting.*) The first time she's worked for a single parent. She's always worked in large families. She's great with kids, but she wouldn't go for less than $65 a week, too bad. She's very clean, energetic, bright, got her own teeth too.

MS. HARRIS: I could go to $60.

SARITA: And you wouldn't be sorry, she's perfect and a Taurus. They're great with kids, right María?

MARIA: Ah sí, sí, the new girl is the best one for you and she is from Peru! (*Lights come up slowly in back room.* EVITA *and* LA CUBANA *are showing* DON FELIX, LOLA *and* NEW GIRL *some new disco steps. On the radio "Disco Inferno." As* EUGENIA, CHATA *and* CLARA *sit on the side line* CLARA *is mending* DON FELIX*'s disco pants on her lap.*)

MS. HARRIS: New girl? From Peru? She didn't just get here, did she?

Because Sylvia said they're not any good when they first come here.

EVITA: (*Dancing with* LA CUBANA.) See, this one's the Latin Hustle.

SARITA: Oh, no, I can assure you she's been here a while. No problem, I'll get her, you'll see for yourself.

CHATA: Ay, I don't like this music. I like the Cuban music better or . . .

MARIA: Ah sí, sí, no problem, I explain contract. (*Lights dim but not out, front room. Exit* SARITA.)

CHATA: (*Picking up one of* DON FELIX*'s disco chains from chair next to her.*) Don Félix, how come you have this little gold razor blade on a chair?

CLARA: (*Shaking out* DON FELIX*'s pants.*) Aquí están sus pantalones, no debe romperlos otra vez.

SARITA: (*Entering back room.*) Quick, I think we got Miss Peru a job.

DON FELIX: Make sure María gets a check. I better go. (*Fast exit into front room.*)

SARITA: (*To* NEW GIRL.) A ver, ¿cómo se llama otra vez?

NEW GIRL: Elsa María Cristina López de Moreno.

SARITA: No, no más dile a la señora, Elsa Moreno.

NEW GIRL: Sí, Elsa Moreno.

SARITA: Okay, now we have to make her look like she's been here a couple of years.

LOLA: ¿Y por qué? Why we have to do that, because you say it?

SARITA: Why? Because the client doesn't want someone who just fell off the turnip truck, that's why!

LOLA: Ah sí, you always please the gringo lady, pero yo no!

CHATA: (*To* CLARA.) Ay comadre, fíjate, they're using turnip trucks to bring them in now. (*Radio volume gets louder with* "Latin Hustle.")

SARITA: Evita, you fix her hair. Margarita, get some lipstick. A ver, Elsa, quítale la falda y ponle la mía . . . (*The women all gather around* NEW GIRL *and* SARITA. LOLA *sits disapprovingly to the side.* CHATA *is too tipsy to stand, but yells instructions from the side.*)

CHATA: It's better with the belt.

EVITA: Ay, ¿dónde está mi hair spray? (*Finds spray and sprays.*)

CHATA: Here, put one of Don Félix's disco chains on her for luck.

LA CUBANA: Ay, Evita, why you spray my face?

CHATA: This one with gold razor blade. It ain't going to help Don Felix if he gets into a fight.

EVITA: Pues, if you will remove your big Cuban nalgas.

EUGENIA: (*To* NEW GIRL.) Mi hija, no te pongas nerviosa, todas las cosas van a salir bien.

CHATA: My Gordo love to fight, that's why my daughter didn't like him.

LA CUBANA: Mira, no me faltes respeto, eh.

CLARA: Es más ladylike without the belt.

EVITA: Qué cute.

CHATA: Ay qué mi Consuelo. She was such a cute baby. Look just like her father.

SARITA: Elsa, si te pregunta la señora, le dices que estás aquí más que dos años, okay?

ELSA: Sí, sí. Más que two años.

CHATA: Smart too, she wants to be somebody.

CLARA: Qué barbaridad, too much lipstick.

CHATA: She's going to the Brymann School for to be a dental assistant.

EVITA: Mira, Sarita, la Cubana se freakió con el lipstick and el blusher.

CLARA: ¡Mira no más, cómo le pintó la cara a esta pobre criatura!

SARITA: Ay Margarita, you went crazy with the blusher. Here wipe it off.

LA CUBANA: Así, me gusta, se ve muy apasionada.

SARITA: She's not supposed to look passionate, she's supposed to look bright and responsible.

CHATA: Every day she say I ain't gonna be like you, cleaning houses, getting drunk. I ain't nothing like you, she say.

LOLA: ¿Qué dices, Chata?

CHATA: Mi hija, ay mi Consuelo, y la perdí. "I ain't gonna be like you," así me dice.

LOLA: Ay, Chata, es mejor que tomes un café. Horita te lo traigo. (*As* LOLA *goes to get* CHATA*'s coffee, women stand back from tight circle. We see an Americanized version of* NEW GIRL, *with a new slick hair style, make-up and* SARITA*'s clothes. Off to the side we see a different* SARITA, *with* NEW GIRL*'s clothes.* SARITA *looks stunned at* NEW GIRL *as others stand back and exclaim, "Qué guapa," "Qué bien se ve," as* NEW GIRL *struts around the room.*)

EVITA: Ahi va la new girl.

CHATA: (*Looking at* NEW GIRL.) Consuelo.

SARITA: No, it's not right. I made a mistake.

LOLA: You make terrible mistake. Didn't you have eyes to see she was beautiful the way she was? (DON FELIX *enters back room.*)

DON FELIX: Hurry up, honey, I got her to sign the contract and give me the check and she hasn't even seen the merchandise. (*Sees* NEW GIRL *and whistles.*) Ay, honey, we shoulda asked for more money. (DOÑA EUGENIA *gives* NEW GIRL *a hug.* NEW GIRL *shows her the yu yu around her neck, then drops it into her blouse.* DOÑA

EUGENIA *says goodbye, "Buena suerte," "Qué te vaya bien, hija," "Mucho cuidado, mi hija."*)

NEW GIRL: Muchas gracias a todas.

DON FELIX: Andele, señorita. (*Presenting his arm to her.*)

NEW GIRL: *With arm on* DON FELIX*'s hand, looks back at* SARITA, *with one hand reaching out to wave.*) Seño Sarita, muchas gracias, lo agradezco mucho.

SARITA: Oh no, please. Let's change her back. (*As* NEW GIRL *leaves on* DON FELIX*'s arm,* CHATA *reaches out.*)

CHATA: No te vayas, Consuelo.(EUGENIA *puts her arm around* SARITA. *All women except* CHATA *stand around the door as though they could still see her.*

SARITA: (*to* EUGENIA) She was beautiful the way she was.

EVITA: Ay, Sarita, she looks much better now. (*We see* NEW GIRL *going into front room with* DON FELIX, *timidly shaking hands with* MS. HARRIS, MARIA *interpreting and giving final instructions.*)

CLARA: No, I like her the way she was. She had more . . .

LOLA: Dignidad.

CLARA: Sí, eso es.

LA CUBANA: Now she looks good. She looks Cuban.

EVITA: Ay tú, Cuban, she don't look Cuban. I know what Cubans look like porque I been looking at one all day and I am telling you she don't look that bad.

LOLA: (*To* SARITA.) Are you happy now? You and all your changes. I am tired of all this changing.

CHATA: Ya perdí mi Consuelo.

EUGENIA: Andale, Chata, tómate el cafecito.

CLARA: Hmmmmph! Mira, Lolita, esto no es nada. You want to hear about changing, I will tell you. That no good daughter de la Chata, Consuelo, she changed her name on the papers for the school.

LOLA: Consuelo changed her name?

CHATA: Sí, pues, María Consuelo Sandoval de García. Ahora se llama, Connie Gar.

SARITA: Your daughter is now Connie Gar?

CLARA: Connie Garr (*Trilling the r's.*) Two R's . . . Garrrrr.

CHATA: You shut up. (*We hear front room phone ring and* DON FELIX *answers. We see* NEW GIRL *saying goodbye to* MARIA *and then starts to leave out the front door with* MS. HARRIS. *Second phone line rings and* MARIA *answers.*)

MS. HARRIS: (*Going out the door.*) Elsa Moreno. I'll just call you Elsie.

NEW GIRL: Sí, Elsie. (*Exit* NEW GIRL *with* MS. HARRIS.)

CHATA: Ay, I'm gonna be sick.

CLARA: ¿Ya ves? ¿Ya ves? ¿Qué te dije? Evita, get a wet towel. (*EVITA goes to bathroom as* LOLA *and* CLARA *make* CHATA *drink coffee.* DOÑA EUGENIA *massages her head,* LA CUBANA *fans her and* MARIA *enters the back room.*)

MARIA: Sarita, you got a phone call, it's your agent. (SARITA *starts to take it on the back room phone and changes her mind, goes to the front room.*)

DOÑA EUGENIA: Buena suerte, mi hija. (SARITA *goes into the front room.* DON FELIX *is on the the other phone.*)

DON FELIX: (*Into the phone.*) Sí, sí, pues mira, las pagué la semana pasada.

SARITA: (*Into the phone.*) Hello . . . I did? (DON FELIX *looks over at* SARITA, *knods his head in affirmation.*) I'll be there, that's great, thank you, okay, goodbye.

DON FELIX: Okay, Carlos. I'll be right over. (*Hangs up phone.*) You got the part?

SARITA: Yes, I got the part.

DON FELIX: Honey, I gotta change for the disco. I can see it now, your name in lights over the Million Dollar Theatre: Sara Gómez. No. Sarita Gómez. No, no, something special like Estrellita Gómez. No, ay, I'm late. (*He turns to exit, takes a few steps, then turns.*) Estrellita Espan . . . Eh! Eh, think about it. (DON FELIX *exits to back room, lights change as* SISTER *appears.*)

SISTER: Sara, Sara Gómez.

SARITA: (*Drops her shawl and becomes a twelve year old Sarita.*) Yes, Sister.

SISTER: Is this your paper? (*Shows* SARITA *paper.*)

SARITA: Yes, Sister.

SISTER: It's a very good paper. Why did you sign it Donna Reed? And last week it was Gidget. Sara Gómez is a beautiful name.

SARITA: It's a dumb name. It's Mexican.

SISTER: Oh, Sarita.

SARITA: Ah, Sister, you don't understand. I seen it on television.

SISTER: You *saw* it on television.

SARITA: Yes, I saw it on television on *Father Knows Best.* There's Kathy, Betty and Bud, and then there's Mr. Ed, the talking horse, David and Ricky Nelson. Even on *Leave It to Beaver* the people have names like June and Ward Cleaver, Eddie Haskel . . . I never saw anybody named Jesusita, Rubén or Sara Gómez.

SISTER: A rose by any other name would smell as sweet. Can't you see that Sara Gómez is a special name?

SARITA: No. When you think about it, Sister, "the Beaver" is a real weird name for a kid. I'll bet he's going to have trouble with it when he grows up.

SISTER: Sara, read your history books, then you will see what a rich, fertile heritage you have. Why, just look at California, filled with Hispanic names: San Francisco, Santa Barbara, Los Angeles, San Fernando . . .

SARITA: San Fernando . . . Whittier Boulevard.

SISTER: Father Junipero Serra . . . Ramona.

SARITA: Cholo wagons . . . Graffitti . . . Gangs

SISTER: El Camino Real, San Luis Obispo.

SARITA: Homeboys, Low riders, Chebbies.

SISTER: Sara, Sara, listen to me. The first governor, the very first governor of California was a man named Pío Pico.

SARITA: Sara Pico. (*Trying it out.*) No, I'm staying with Donna Reed. (SISTER *disappears.*) No, Sara Gomez, SARITA GOMEZ!!!! (*Phone rings.* SARITA *answers.* MARIA *and* LOLA *coming into front room.*)

MARIA: Lola, Lola, ¿ya te vas?

LOLA: Sí, I go before la Mrs. Camden comes y tu amiguita Sarita dresses up somebody for her.

MARIA: Ay Lola, no digas eso. Sarita's trying to help.

LOLA: Sí, I see how she helps by taking away what we are.

SARITA: (*On phone.*) Shsssh! Yes, Mrs. Walker, a good basic cook. Nothing fancy.

LOLA: Sí nothing fancy. (*Going to* SARITA *and phone.*) We got fancy, too, Mrs. Sarita can make us anything you want.

SARITA: Be quiet. I am sorry, Mrs. Walker.

LOLA: She'll dye our hair, change our names, anything you want, Mrs.

SARITA: (*With hand over mouthpiece.*) Will you shut up?

LOLA: No, I will not shut up, gringa! ¡Gavacha!

SARITA: And don't call me names.

LOLA: Gringa, gavacha, imbécil.

MARIA: (*Taking* LOLA *aside.*) Ay, Lola, ¿qué te pasa?

SARITA: Hello, hello, Mrs. Walker? She hung up.

MARIA: Ay, tanta rabia, it's very bad for your heart.

SARITA: (*Slamming down phone.*) Well, I hope you're satisfied. That might have been a good job for Clara you just lost us.

LOLA: ¡Qué bien! ¡Me alegro! One less chance for you to take away our dignidad, our pride.

SARITA: Don't point your finger at me. You haven't done anything all day but bitch and moan and walk out on your job. Did you come here for work? Well, pride doesn't get you work. Haven't you learned that?

LOLA: No. Ay, Dios must have saved me from that lesson. But not you, you have no pride. (SARITA *hangs up phone*.) New Girl, the way she was, ay, I think of my country, going to the fields to bring Roberto his food every day. On my bare feet, the sun on my back, the earth smell y entonces I would see him there in the fields. Esa vista me mataba: his beautiful brown body, strong, disfrutando el trabajo. My heart would stop, this feeling would enter my body, ay, I don't know how to say, me invadía. He look up y me dice, "¿Qué trais, mujer?" and I stand there, shy, my head a little away so he don't see my face. But I feel at the moment, every day, en these moments, that I belong here on this earth. (*Points to floor*.) I belong to him, my family, God. That is pride. (LA CUBANA, EVITA, *holding up* CHATA. EUGENIA *carrying the shopping bags, comes into the front room*.)

MARIA: Estabas young and in love, touched by the noble fever.

CHATA: Ay, comadre, you would have been better for a touch of typhoid.

EVITA: Vamos a llevar a Chata a su casa.

CHATA: Ay que mi chavalona de Guatemala, yo soy pura Mexicana.

EVITA: Tell Don Felix, I'll meet him at the disco.

CHATA: Disco no . . . (*Starts to sing*.) "Mexico lindo y querido, si me muero lejos de ti. Que digan que estoy dormido y que me traigan aquí." (*Sees* SARITA.) Un party to celebrate Sarita's T.V. job. Sarita, you ask for cash, no checks.

MARIA: Ay, sí, Sarita, Don Felix told us. I am so stupid.

EUGENIA: Ya ves, yo te hice un yu yu.

LA CUBANA: She going to be big movie star and I will be her companion.

EVITA: Y yo le voy a hacer su make-up.

LOLA: Ay sí, congratulations, Sara Smith. Aren't you going to change your name, dye your hair, change your eyes, insult yourself, your family . . . (*All women mumble,* "*Ay Lola,*" "*No seas así.*" MRS. CAMDEN *enters*. CHATA *falls down on the couch*. EVITA *and* LA CUBANA, DOÑA EUGENIA *gather by the couch and stand very still*.)

MARIA: Mrs. Camden!

MRS. CAMDEN: Well, I see my maid is here, Sara.

LOLA: I am not your maid.

MARIA: (*Taking* LOLA *away to other end of front room.*) Cálmate, Lola, pórtate con dignidad.

MRS. CAMDEN: Oh, you people. What you are doing is criminal and unethical and I'm not about to put up with it.

SARITA: Mrs. Camden, I will get you a replacement.

MRS. CAMDEN: You people don't seem to understand that when a busy person pays for competent, reliable help, they expect a competent, reliable person, comprende? (CHATA *sits up from couch.*)

CHATA: Mira tú, vieja pinchi . . . (EVITA *puts her hand over* CHATA's *mouth and pushes her back down on the couch as* LA CUBANA *sits nearly on top of her.* EUGENIA *next. They giggle.*)

MRS. CAMDEN: Ah, let me tell you something . . . (*Looking at everyone.*) You people think you are so downtrodden. Well, you bring it all on yourselves. Most of you know nothing about running a modern house. The repair bills I've had to pay for all the appliances you people have broken would support your families in Mexico. Most of you can't even take a simple phone message . . . no sense of responsibility.

SARITA: Mrs. Camden, I think . . .

LOLA: *Tearing herself away from* MARIA's *grip and interrupting* SARITA.) And you, and you come here to insult us. Don't worry, Sarita will find you a replacement, she is very good for that.

MARIA: (*Taking* LOLA *firmly aside.*) Tranquila, tranquilamente.

MRS. CAMDEN: That maid (*Pointing to* LOLA.) with no previous warning, quit. It is customary to give two weeks notice. She didn't even call.

LOLA: You look at me like I'm a machine. So I act like machine. Machine don't give notice.

MRS. CAMDEN: Oh, we treated you very well, you took advantage of it. (*Addressing all women, even* SARITA *on the phone.*) Understand, please, that she had her own room and bath with her own T.V. It is a very lovely room. I am sure she has never seen anything like it before in Mexico. She had nothing, so out of the goodness of my heart I bought her some nice uniforms. She eats the same food we eat. I gave her the advantages and protection of my home and this is the way she thanks us? (LA CUBANA *gets up from* CHATA *and stands by window, every now and then looking out.*)

LOLA: Why, no one in your house call me by my name. I hear you, your husband, the children, all of you speak about me as your Mexican maid. Always you say, "Ask the maid, tell the maid." Each day you make me more nobody, more dead. You put me in nice white uniform so I won't offend your good taste. You take away my name, my country. You don't want a person, you want a machine. My name is Lola. I am from Guatemala.

MRS. CAMDEN: She is an illegal. She is an alien. And if I wanted to, I could call immigration on her so fast it would . . .

SARITA: It would what, Mrs. Camden?

LA CUBANA: (*Looking out window.*) Be quiet, they'll hear you.

SARITA: Mrs. Camden?

LOLA: This legal-illegal is the business of governments, but God put me, a human being, in this world. I am here because my children must eat. (CLARA *and* DON FELIX *in his disco outfit enter front room.*)

CLARA: Sara, don't forget I am looking for work.

DON FELIX: Ah, you must be the lovely Mrs. Camden we've heard so much about.

MRS. CAMDEN: (*Looking at* CLARA.) Sara, is this my replacement?

SARITA: No. No, Mrs. Camden.

CLARA: Sarita!

SARITA: We will give you a refund, Mrs. Camden.

DON FELIX: No refund. No, Sarita, ¿estás completamente loca? No refund, Mrs. Camden.

MRS. CAMDEN: And who are you?

SARITA: ¡Juan Revolta! (*Phone rings.* MARIA *answers.*)

LA CUBANA: Ay, Don Félix, please look. They are after us. Ay, apúrate. Ven a ver. (*She rushes up to* DON FELIX *and pulls his arm.*)

MARIA: Don Félix, it's for you. An emergency, Carlos say.

DON FELIX: (*Going to phone.*) No refund. No refund.

MRS. CAMDEN: You'll hear from my lawyers. You, whatever you are, and your illegal aliens. (SARITA *clutches her chest and has trouble breathing.*)

SARITA: Oh, oh, you! (*Pointing to* MRS. CAMDEN.) You, you. All my life, you, you hypocrite! You talk "legal," you hired her because you didn't want to pay the salary a legal person gets.

MRS. CAMDEN: Why should I? My taxes support your people's welfare.

SARITA: You! Your support? No! You depend! You're cheap, you're greedy. You want their labor, their cheap abundant labor. You don't care about the "legalities," sí, your "legalities, "chinga tus legali-ties." If you did care, you wouldn't be here whining for me to get you a maid.

MRS. CAMDEN: Whining? This person is crazy. I don't deal with your kind. Mr. Sánchez? Mr. Sánchez!

DON FELIX: (*On the telephone.*) Sí, sí, ah, just a moment, Mrs. Camden.

MRS. CAMDEN: Mr. Sánchez.

DON FELIX: (*On telephone.*) Un momento, Carlos. Yes, Mrs. Camden.

MRS. CAMDEN: Mr. Sánchez, what can we do to solve this matter?

DON FELIX: Do not worry, Mrs. Camden, I will take care of this matter myself. I will personally deliver to your home a fresh maid.

MRS. CAMDEN: In the morning promptly at 10.

DON FELIX: Yes, exactly at 10. It's been a pleasure serving you. (*Continues on telephone.*) Carlos, when did you give them the money?

MRS. CAMDEN: I am glad to see someone takes pride in their work. (*Turns and starts to walk to front door.*)

SARITA: Pride! Pride? (SARITA *goes after* MRS. CAMDEN *ready to tear her apart. As* SARITA *takes a swing at* MRS. CAMDEN*'s back,* LOLA *grabs* SARITA*'s arm, throwing her off balance, which causes* MRS. CAMDEN *to turn around.*) Let me go, let me go, I say. You pink, colorless pig!

MRS. CAMDEN: This person is crazy!

MARIA: Hurry, lady, hurry. You must leave. (*Fast exit*, MRS. CAMDEN.)

LOLA: Sarita, I only wanted you to stand up for us, not to kill the woman. Andale, un abrazo. (SARITA *collapses into* LOLA*'s arms.*) Ahora, sí, eres una latina completamente latina.

MARIA: (*Crossing herself.*) Ay Dios mío de mi vida, you were going to kill her, Sarita. That's a sin. Un pecado muy grave. (DONA EUGENIA, *who has been holding on to* CLARA *during fight, goes to* SARITA *and comforts her with* LOLA. CLARA *goes to* CHATA *and wakes her.*)

CLARA: ¡Chata! Wake up.

CHATA: ¿Qué? ¿Qué pasó?

EVITA: ¡La Sarita se freakió!

DON FELIX: Está seguro, Carlos. I gave them the money myself.

LA CUBANA: Look, they are getting out of their cars. (EVITA *goes to the window.*)

EVITA: ¿Quiénes son? ¡Don Félix! ¡La migra!

DON FELIX: (*Looking up from phone.*) No. No puede ser. I fixed it. I fixed it. (*To telephone.*) Carlos, hombre, call my lawyers. (DON FELIX *drops the phone and runs to the window and looks.*) ¡Sarita! ¡Viene la migra! Immigration! (*General commotion as lights start to dim.* LOLA *is torn out of* SARITA*'s embrace by* CHATA. *All women run towards back room exit. Except* LA CUBANA *who stands still holding green card.* DON FELIX *is at file cabinet putting papers into briefcase.* SARITA *walks slowly to stage apron.*

As lights get dimmer we hear voices of immigration officers herding the women. Women's screams and protests are heard. Some women call Sarita with requests to call relatives. CHATA *singing "Mexico Lindo."* DON FELIX, *carrying briefcase, and* LA CUBANA *run after* SARITA *onto stage apron as curtain falls behind them.* SARITA *has back to them as she faces audience.*

DON FELIX: Don't worry, honey. They can't touch you. You're free to go and my lawyer says they can't hold me. I didn't break the law. I didn't bring them up here.

LA CUBANA: And me, what about me, Sarita?

DON FELIX: Honey, you got a green card. You got no problems. I'll see you tomorrow, Sarita. Sarita! They'll all be back. They just put them on the bus and drop them on the other side. When they get the money, they'll be back. You'll see. (*Putting his arm around* MAR-GARITA, *they walk off the stage.*) Listen, Margarita, tomorrow there's this job with an old lady . . . (SARITA *walks over and sits on the bus bench. Flute music, helicopter lights and sounds, barbed wire fence as we see creeping towards the fence another new girl and her coyote.*)

The Shrunken Head of Pancho Villa

Although *The Shrunken Head of Pancho Villa* was first written when Valdez was still an undergraduate, he revised the script when he directed the play for the Teatro Campesino in 1968 and again in 1970.[1] Therefore, this is not a student exercise, reproduced here as an historical document alone. This is a historically important work, but more significantly, *The Shrunken Head of Pancho Villa* is just as artistically valid today as when it was first conceived.[2] When the Teatro performed this play at the Radical Theater Festival held at San Francisco State College in 1968, one critic observed, "Row by row the audience came to its feet. . . . I too, rose, though I'm sure I wasn't the only one casting about for some more direct, less traditional way to react to what I knew had been . . . the premiere performance of a major new American play."[3]

The *San Francisco Chronicle* reviewers were also exuberant in their praises saying that the play, " . . . has more punch and grit than the last dozen burnt offerings by ACT [American Conservatory Theatre] or the art houses. . . . The whole thing is so good, in fact, that after one act you want to go out to a quiet bar and rest your head. Or maybe saddle up Old Paint and join the Villistas."[4]

In theatrical terms the play can work quite well, even with university actors. Of the University of Washington production directed by Rubén Sierra in 1977, a Seattle critic observed, " . . . although the play provides no resolution to the complex of Chicano problems, it provides a generally entertaining—and sometimes enlightening—evening in the theater."[5] Entertaining, yes, and thought-provoking. Obviously, this play is not as accessible as, say, Valdez's *Actos*.

In 1984, Prof. Manuel Pickett directed the play at California State University at Sacramento. The mostly Chicano audience thoroughly enjoyed the play the night this observer witnessed the production.[6] However, Prof. Pickett was cautious of the symbolism and added director's notes in order to clarify the imagery, particularly of the cockroaches. He told this writer, "The audiences loved the humor—which they could relate to—but I did not want Chicanos to be offended by the image of the cockroaches."[7]

When asked why he chose to produce this play, Prof. Pickett answered, "I directed it because I saw it as a classic work and it was a challenge. The play explores political realities of the time that are examples of what Chicanos were doing in the 60's." Further, Dr. Pickett was interested in demonstrating to his students and to his audiences that "There are different approaches to theater that can be used in teatro; not just the acto or realism, but a genre that is not usually associated with Chicano theater." For Prof. Pickett the play was "a very good example of extremes."

The Shrunken Head of Pancho Villa is not a realistic play, as the playwright indicates in his notes preceeding the script. It is a surreal vision, a mixture of the real with the unreal, the natural with the unnatural. This play is, in fact, written in the Latin American tradition of magical realism, conceived long before the North American fascination with this literary genre. In magical realism, anything can happen and nobody has to explain it to anyone else. Therefore, when events in this play begin to veer from conventional reality, the characters are nonplussed about it, though the audience may not be so complacent.

In an interview in 1987, Valdez called this play absurdist and compared himself to the central figure of Belarmino:

> In a metaphorical sense that was me back in the early 60's. That's the way I felt—that I had no legs, no arms. By 1970, when I got to Bernabé, I was the idiot, but I'd gotten in contact with the sun and the moon and the earth. Fortunately, out of these grotesque self-portraits, my characters have attained a greater and greater degree of humanity.[8]

The characters in this play are human, but they represent exaggerations of humanity in Valdez's attempt to paint as broad a picture of his people as possible. Cruz and Pedro can be seen as archetypical Mexican parents and their three children are surely cast from similar molds in many Mexicano/Chicano households. These characters are all extensions of reality created to more clearly reflect that reality on stage. Although the characters are central to an understanding of the Chicano condition, whether in 1964 or 1989, these people must be seen within the broader context of the society that surrounds them.

No matter what form his plays and actos have taken, Valdez has always written about the Chicano family in crisis, because for him, the family represents the Chicano's link with his roots, his culture and his language. However humble, the Valdezian home is the safe place, a haven from exterior threats to the family. Yet those exterior threats are centered within his characters who fight or succumb to assimilation through linguistic and cultural disintegration. The characters' internal struggle is externalized, as when Mingo comes on with a face that is half brown and half white or Joaquin returns without a head.

The audience does not realize that this play is going to go beyond reality when the curtain first rises. The bodyless character of Belarmino is the play's first unnatural element, yet we do not know of his "condition" until the end of the first act when Domingo runs out of the bedroom screaming "He's only a head!" The other family members have known this and have not reminded Domingo, precisely because he has returned to the fold a changed man. Domingo has been altered in the Marines and they know that he is no longer a part of their family, especially when he cannot even remember his sister's name nor remember his oldest brother.

Domingo is Valdez's first characterization of a "vendido," a type that the playwright will return to in later works. To any Mexican/Chicano in the audience, this sellout is immediately recognizable: the Mexican or Chicano who denies his heritage in an effort to "pass" in an Anglo society. Since the Mexican became a foreigner in his own land, the "vendido" type has been a popular comic figure, ridiculed in corridos and vaudeville sketches from Texas to California.[9] Thus Valdez's first sellout has his historical roots, just like his brother, Joaquín.

Diametrically opposed to the Anglo-cized Domingo stands the tough street youth, Joaquín. Joaquín is the street bandit, the Robin Hood of the barrios, and is thus Valdez's protagonist in this early play about cultural identity. But although Joaquín is more connected with his Mexican heritage, he cannot speak Spanish, indicating that he exemplifies the Chicano who has been educated in the United States. Joaquín represents many young Chicanos, first generation U.S. citizens who cannot speak their parents' native tongue. His English is not that good either, making him a victim of society's greatest influence on a child's formative years: the schools.

As Prof. Pickett observes, Valdez enjoys extremes in this play, contrasting the two brothers as well as the distinctions between the generations represented. On a scale of assimilation from immigrant to "acceptable," Valdez shows us the spectrum, from the Mexican parents through degrees of assimilated children. While Joaquín relates more as a Chicano and has some consciousness of urban struggle, Lupe does not want to be Mexican, yet she is not as assimilated as Mingo.

Each of the children goes through a cultural and political transformation. Mingo's transformation into Mr. Sunday is extreme, but so is Joaquín's transformation into a social bandit. Even Chato and Lupe metamorphose into carbon copies of Pedro and Cruz. When Lupe gives birth to another bodyless head, the playwright suggests that there will be no improvement in their condition—one generation will succeed another—unless they wake up and see the possibilities. Belarmino says it all when he asks his mother to connect him to the headless Joaquín.

As a young Chicano student responding to the Eurocentric world of

Anglo American theater, Luis Valdez wrote a play that not only questioned the status quo, but argued for a re-definition of his people. The playwright's image of the Chicano is that of a people whose daily struggles for survival are represented by an insatiable bodyless head, a people whose surreal lives seem extraordinarily ordinary. The dialogue is right out of any barrio home, although the image of cockroach-infested walls and a head covered with lice is not a positive one, if seen as a realistic picture of a typical Chicano family.

Betty Diamond reminded the reader that the cockroaches, "while pervasive and very real tenants of old buildings, are at the same time symbols of yet another psychological aspect of barrio life—the will to endure and the desire to rebel."[10] Chicanos have certainly demonstrated a will to endure and the constant influx of their brothers and sisters from all of Latin America will not cease despite new immigration laws. 'We are as ubiquitous as cockroaches,' Valdez is telling us, 'and we will endure.' "

[1]The Teatro revived the play again in 1970–71, with a core of young actors who would eventually dedicate their lives to Teatro Chicano, including Félix Alvarez as Chato, Phil Esparza as Mingo, Manuel Pickett on sound and trumpet, Luis Valdez as Pedro, and the future Mrs. Lupe Valdez as Lupe. The production toured northern and central California.

[2]Two other student productions of this play have been produced since the initial version at San Jose State University in 1964: the School of Drama of the University of Washington in Seattle in 1977 and the Theatre Arts Department of California State University at Sacramento in 1984.

[3]Donna Mickelson, " 'The Shrunken Head' Triumph," *San Francisco Express Times*, 9 October 1968, p. 38.

[4]Michael Grieg and Charles Howe, " 'The Head'—Powerful," *San Francisco Chronicle*, 30 September 1968, p. 47.

[5]Wayne Johnson, " 'Head of Villa' is Lively Fare," *Seattle Times*, 24 January 1978, p. A–11. Prof. Sierra directed the production for the School of Drama with members of his student/community troupe, Teatro Quetzalcoatl.

[6]Prof. Manuel Pickett directed the play for the Theatre Arts Department of California State University at Sacramento in collaboration with his student/community troupe, Teatro Espejo, in 1984.

[7]From a telephone conversation with Mr. Pickett, 18 December 1988.

[8]David Savran, "Border Tactics: Luis Valdez Distills the Chicano Experience on Stage and Film," *American Theatre*, January, 1988, p. 17.

[9]For more on the early *carpas* see Nicolás Kanellos (ed.) *Mexican American Theatre: Then and Now* (Houston: Arte Publico Press, 1983): 7–15 and 41–51.

[10]Betty Ann Diamond, *Brown Eyed Children of the Sun: The Cultural Politics of the Teatro Campesino* (Ann Arbor: University Microfilms, 1977): 130.

Luis Valdez

 # 23.89'
29 yrs.

In the twenty-three years since he founded the Teatro Campesino, Luis Valdez and his troupe have gone through a number of changes. Initially, the Teatro Campesino was just that, a farmworker's theater, dedicated to the education and entertainment of striking farmworkers struggling against the powerful machine of California agricultural interests. Today, that theater group is no longer a collective made up of actual farmworkers, but rather a producing organization capable of employing artists in any number of theaters. From the fields to the stages of prestigious theater companies, Valdez has made an odyssey few theater artists in the United States can claim.

No other individual has made as important an impact on Chicano theater as Luis Valdez. Indeed, as evidenced in the introduction to this book, it is impossible to discuss Chicano theater without talking about Valdez, for he initiated this vital movement. With Valdez's serious move into filmmaking in 1987, confirmed by the success of *La Bamba*, more has been written about this man than any other Chicano in the arts. But even before his name became a household word, Mr. Valdez's work as a playwright and director had placed him firmly in the history books of theater in the United States.

Born in 1940 to a migrant farmworker family in Delano, California, Valdez might have succumbed to the fate of so many migrant workers' children of the period and become another school drop-out. Instead, Valdez not only graduated from high school, but he was awarded a scholarship to San Jose State College in northern California. Early in his youth, Valdez had discovered the fascination of the theater and writing. By the end of his freshman year in college, he "made the plunge" and changed majors from math and physics to English, with an emphasis on playwriting. Valdez's first full-length play, *The Shrunken Head of Pancho Villa*, was produced by the Theater Department in 1964, launching him fully into the theater.

After college, Valdez worked with the San Francisco Mime Troupe, discovering the effectiveness of commedia dell'arte as an educational and entertainment tool. When he went to work with the Farm Workers Union in 1965, Valdez had no idea of what would ensue, but he knew that he could be an integral part of an important labor movement. He was returning to his roots, both politically and spiritually, conscious of the hard life of the farm worker and armed with a potential tool to combat that existence: theater. The result of his first meeting with those striking workers is, as they say, "history." His involvement with the Farm Workers Union became the first phase of the Teatro Campesino's career and the beginning of the Chicano theatre movement.

Valdez worked with the Farm Workers Union from 1965 to 1967 and made the difficult decision to leave that organization when he realized that he needed to work on his craft as a theater worker. Once separated from the union, the director/playwright and his troupe could focus on their development as theater workers rather than union organizers. The Teatro had made a national impact while still a part of the union and Valdez now had to find independence for himself and his troupe.

The choice to leave the union movement initiated the second phase of the Teatro Campesino's development under Valdez. It was no coincidence that when the Teatro Campesino separated from the union, their first acto, *Los vendidos*, dealt with the identity of the Chicano.[1] Now that his theater was no longer intimately connected to the farmworker struggle, Valdez could dedicate his efforts to exposing the problems beyond the fields; *Los vendidos*, a satirical look at the typical Mexican-American sellout, seemed ideally suited to that purpose. This issue has always interested Valdez, beginning with the character of Domingo/Mr. Sunday in *The Shrunken Head of Pancho Villa*.

During this second stage, politics came before economics, as the Teatro members joined with Valdez in a kind of monastic poverty, living collectively and earning very little beyond subsistence level. Valdez had surrounded himself with a dedicated core of individuals with varying degrees of theater training and experience, sometimes frustrating his optimum growth as a playwright and director. Nonetheless, in time the director/playwright would develop a very proficient company capable of performing a unique style of theater that combined elements of the acto, street theater, myth, indigenous music and dance.

Although he and his troupe were working collectively from the beginning, the individual playwright in Valdez was anxious to emerge. Discussing the process of writing plays outside of the group, Valdez recalled, "I used to work on them with a sense of longing, wanting more time to be able to sit down and write."[2] In 1967, the playwright did sit down and write an anti-war mito, *Dark Root of a Scream*.[3] This contemporary myth takes place during a wake for a Chicano who died in Vietnam, an ex-community leader who should have stayed home and fought the battle in the barrio. The dead soldier becomes a symbol of all Chicanos who fought in a war that the playwright himself objected to. "I refused to go to Vietnam," Valdez told an interviewer twenty years later, "but I encountered all the violence I needed on the home front: people were killed by the Farm Workers' strike."[4]

In 1970 Valdez wrote his second mito, *Bernabé*. This one act play is the tale of a town fool, Bernabé, who is in love with *La Tierra* and wants to marry her. Bernabé is a wonderfully written play that brings together myth and history, contemporary figures and historical icons. The play tells its audience that Chicanos not only have a history of struggle, but are that struggle. Bernabe "marries" *La Tierra* and becomes a whole person, symbolically representing all men who love and respect the earth.[5]

In 1970, even as Valdez, the playwright, was scripting his individual statement about the Chicano and his relationship to the earth, Valdez, the director, was guiding the collective creation of an acto dealing with the war in Vietnam: *Soldado Razo*.[6] Reflecting the influences of Bertolt Brecht's theories, *Soldado Razo* carefully explored some of the reasons young Chicanos were willing to go fight in Vietnam. This acto complemented and expanded the earlier mito, *Dark Root of a Scream*, by looking at the same issue but from a different viewpoint and in a distinct style. In Valdez's words, the acto "is the Chicano through the eyes of man," whereas the mito, "is the Chicano through the eyes of God."[7] While *Soldado Razo* methodically demonstrated the eventual death of its central figure, *Dark Root of a Scream* picked up the action after the soldier's death and explored its cause from a mythical distance.

Valdez had begun to explore his indigenous Mexican roots years before and his developing philosophy was naturally emerging in these plays, as well as in the Teatro's collective work. In 1973 Valdez wrote a poem, "Pensamiento Serpentino," in which he tried to define his neo-Maya philosophy, a way of thinking that was determining the content of his latest collective creation: *La carpa de los Rasquachis*. The poem began:

> Teatro
> eres el mundo
> y las paredes de los
> buildings más grandes
> son nothing but scenery.[8]

In other words, to Valdez, Chicano theater was and is a reflection of the world, a universal statement about what it is to be a Chicano in United States society.

Among the many artistic achievements of the Teatro Campesino during the 1970's, one major work stands out: *La carpa de los Rasquachis*. Developed over a period of years, *La carpa de los Rasquachis* stunned the audience at the Fourth Annual Chicano Theater Festival in San Jose, California, in 1973.[9] This production became the centerpiece of the Teatro for several years, touring the United States and Europe many times to great critical acclaim. But even as *La carpa de los Rasquachis* was touring, Valdez had begun to make the transition into his next phase: the mainstreaming of Chicano theater, or, if you will, "the infiltration of the regional theaters."

This phase marked an important turning point in Valdez's relationship with the Teatro Campesino as he began to write for actors outside of the group. Valdez's development as a playwright and director led to the historic play with music, *Zoot Suit*, first produced in Los Angeles in 1978. This experience introduced Valdez to the Hollywood Hispanic and non-Hispanic talent pool and suddenly brought him into contact with a different breed of artist. With a large population of professionals at his disposal, Valdez's vision had to expand. No longer surrounded by sincere, but sometimes limited talent, Valdez could explore any avenue of theater he desired.

The director/playwright had not abandoned his theater company. The Teatro Campesino was still touring and *Zoot Suit* was produced by both the Teatro Campesino and the Center Theatre Group of Los Angeles. But this was a first step towards an individual identity that Valdez had previously deprecated by working in a collective. His collaboration with a non-Hispanic theater company and subsequent move into Hollywood filmmaking was inevitable; it was the natural course for a man determined to reach as many people as possible with his message and with his art. Theater was his life's work, it was in his blood, but so was the fascinating world of film and video.

Zoot Suit was not Valdez's first exposure to filmmaking, either in front of or behind the camera. In high school, Valdez had been a regular on a local television station as a ventriloquist, writing his own material and performing it.[10] In 1969 the Teatro Campesino produced a film of Rodolfo Gonzalez's epic poem, "I Am Joaquin,"[11] and in 1973 Valdez adapted *Los vendidos* for an NBC broadcast.[12] After several successful tours of *La carpa de los Rasquachis*, Valdez revised this play for Public Television and re-titled the one-hour program *El Corrido* in 1976.

Thus it was only natural for Valdez to write and direct the motion picture version of *Zoot Suit* in 1981, although it was not easy to secure the financing after the play's critical and economic failure in New York in 1979.[13] The motion picture did not fare well at the box office, but did receive a Golden Globe Award and it became a kind of "art film" for some observers. Never one to work on a single project at a time, Valdez had also been writing and directing another play, *El fin del mundo*, from 1975 to 1980.[14] This play explored man's relationship to the earth, this time in an extended *corrido* style that Valdez and his troupe had explored for years, combining traditional Mexican music and lyrics to dramatic action.

The *corrido* style reached its apex when in 1983 Valdez wrote and directed a collage of *corridos*, appropriately titled *Corridos*. The Teatro Campesino produced a fully professional version of this production at the Marine's Memorial Theater in San Francisco in a very successful six-month run. *Corridos* won all of the Bay Area Critic's Association awards for that year and was then produced in conjunction with the Old Globe Theater of San Diego, California, for four weeks, followed by a limited run in Los Angeles. In 1987, Valdez directed a video version of *Corridos* for a PBS national broadcast later that year.

Prior to his taping of *Corridos*, Valdez had directed the sleeper hit of the summer of 1987, *La Bamba*, which finally opened the doors that had been so difficult to penetrate for so many years. "When I drove up to the studio gate," Valdez related, following the success of his film, "the guard at the gate told me that the pastries were taken to a certain door. The only other Mexican he ever saw delivered the pastries."[15] Security guards will surely know his name now.

All of this interaction in Hollywood, and his own sense of history, inspired Valdez to write his most recent play to date, *I Don't Have to Show You No Stinking Badges!*, first produced by the Teatro Campesino and the Los Angeles Theatre Center in 1986.[16] This play was written for a fully-equipped theater and four actors, one of whom is a Japanese-American dancer/actress. The production requires a realistic set, designed to look like a television studio setting, including video monitors hanging above the stage to help the audience make the transfer from theater to "live studio audience."

Badges! focuses on a middle-aged Chicano couple who have made their living as "King and Queen of the Hollywood Extras," playing non-speaking roles as maids, gardeners and the like. The couple has been very successful, having put their daughter through medical school and their son into Harvard Law School. They have, in effect, accomplished the American Dream, with a suburban home complete with swimming pool, family room and microwave.

The conflict arises when their son comes home from Harvard unexpectedly and announces that he has dropped-out, alienated from the Ivy League reality in which he was the single Chicano student. To make matters worse, he decides that he will become a Hollywood actor. Both parents, his girlfriend and the audience know by now that his fate will be the same as his parents', playing "on the hyphen": bit parts as thieves, drug addicts and rapists.

The production of *Badges!* represented the beginning of the fourth phase for Valdez and his company. The Teatro Campesino was no longer a full-time core of artists, living and creating collectively under Valdez's direction. Instead, the company began to contract talent only for the rehearsal and performance period. The Teatro Campesino has thus become a producing company, with Valdez at the helm as Artistic Director and writer. The Florida and San Diego versions of *Badges!* were directed by Valdez's Associate Artistic Director, Tony Curiel, partly for practical reasons (Valdez was working on *La Bamba*) as well as the fact that Valdez began to focus his efforts more on writing and directing films.[17]

The Teatro Campesino still exists, but in a different form than when it first began, although it seems to have come full circle. In the summer of 1987 the group produced *Fin del mundo* as the culmination of a teen workshop, thus staying in touch with and encouraging the next generation of artists. For several years the December production of *La Virgen del Tepeyac* has included professional guest artists as well as a company of community members ranging in age from pre-school to grandparents. This new Teatro Campesino in San Juan includes people from all walks of life—school children and professional actors—in a play that dates back to the sixteenth century. It is that same Teatro Campesino that co-produced fully professional productions of *I Don't Have to Show You No Stinking Badges!* in three cities outside of San Juan.

Valdez's odyssey from the fields to the mainstream could not have been predicted, yet the course was inevitable. Ever conscious of his responsibility, both to himself and to his community, there is no reason to believe that Luis Valdez, writer-director-filmmaker will ever forget his roots.

[1]See *Los vendidos*, in *Actos by Luis Valdez and el Teatro Campesino* (Houston: Arte Publico Press, 1989).

[2]David Savran, "Border Tactics; Luis Valdez Distills the Chicano Experience on Stage and Film," *American Theatre* (January, 1988): 18.

[3]*Dark Root of a Scream* is published in Lilian Faderman and Omar Salinas, eds., *From the Barrio* (San Francisco: Canfield Press, 1973): 79–98; and *West Coast Plays* 19/20 (Los Angeles: California Theatre Council, 1987): 1–20.

[4]Savran, p. 21.

[5]*Bernabé* is published in Roberto Garza, *Contemporary Chicano Theatre* (Notre Dame: University of Notre Dame Press, 1976): 30–58; and *West Coast Plays* 19/20 (op. cit.): 21–51. For a discussion of this play see: Betty Diamond,

Brown-Eyed Children of the Sun; *The Cultural Politics of El Teatro Campesino*, (Ann Arbor: University Microfilms, 1977): 146–159, and Jorge Huerta, *Chicano Theater: Themes and Forms* (Tempe: Bilingual Review Press, 1982): 195–199.

[6]*Soldado Razo* is published in *Actos*, pp. 131–145; and *West Coast Plays* 19/20, pp. 53–66.

[7]Luis Valdez, *Actos* (Houston: Arte Publico Press, 1989).

[8]Luis Valdez, *Pensamiento Serpentino* (Houston: Arte Publico Press, 1989).

[9]For more on Luis Valdez's Neo-Mayan period and *La carpa de los Rasquachis*, see Jorge A. Huerta, *Chicano Theater*, pp. 192–207; and Francoise Kourilski's excellent account of that piece, "Approaching Quetzalcoatl: The Evolution of El Teatro Campesino," *Performance* (Fall 1973): 37–46. See also: Carlos Morton, "The Teatro Campesino," *The Drama Review*, 18 (December 1974): 71–76 and Theodore Shank, "A Return to Aztec and Maya Roots," *The Drama Review*, 18 (December 1974): 56–70.

[10]Savran, p. 17.

[11]See Rodolfo Gonzales, *I Am Joaquin* (New York: Bantam Books, 1972).

[12]This television version of *Los vendidos* was only telecast in Chicago and Los Angeles because the network did not believe that there would be any interest outside of these major centers of Mexican-American population.

[13]The Los Angeles production of *Zoot Suit* ran almost one year, setting a record for its time; the New York production could not survive the generally disastrous reviews of the New York critics. For a sampling of the reviews, see: Clive Barnes, " 'Zoot Suit' Proves Moot," *New York Post*, 26 March 1979, pp.71,77; Richard Eder, "Theatre: 'Zoot Suit,' Chicano Music-Drama," *New York Times*, 26 March 1979, sec. C, p. 13; Walter Kerr, " 'Zoot Suit' Loses Its Way in Bloodless Rhetoric," *New York Times*, 1 April 1979, sec. 2, pp. 3,20.

[14]Luis Valdez did not always direct his plays; the 1978 version of *El fin del mundo* was directed by his sister, Socorro. For more on this play, see Diamond, pp. 207–234; and Huerta, *Chicano Theater*, pp. 207–213.

[15]On January 30, 1988, Valdez was the featured speaker at the Albuquerque Hispanic Chamber of Commerce Annual Banquet. Earlier that day, the director held a press conference to discuss his work. The present author attended both functions.

[16]The Los Angeles production of *I Don't Have to Show You No Stinking Badges!* was followed by productions at the Burt Reynolds Dinner Theater in Jupiter, Florida, that same year and the San Diego Repertory Theatre in 1987. See Luis Valdez, *Zoot Suit and Other Plays* (Houston: Arte Publico Press, 1990).

[17]Valdez will continue to write a play "every two years" for the Teatro Campesino, according to the troupe's managing director, Phil Esparza, in a presentation for the Association for Theatre in Higher Education convention in San Diego, California, August 5, 1988.

The Shrunken Head
of Pancho Villa

by Luis Valdez

A mi padre, Francisco "Pancho" Valdez

CHARACTERS

PEDRO, the jefito, an old Villista con huevos.
CRUZ, the madre, long-suffering but loving.
JOAQUIN, the young son, a vato loco and a chicano.
LUPE, the daughter.
MINGO, the son, a Mexican-American.
BELARMINO, the oldest son.
LA JURA, a police officer.

SCENE

The interior of an old house: a large, imposing two-story building sagging
into total dilapidation. The front room with tall cracked windows; doors to

a stairwell and the kitchen; and an adjoining room with a curtained doorway, once a study now also a bedroom. This front room, which is the center of the play's action, has been repainted with a true Mexican folk taste. Bright reds, yellows and blues try to obscure the shabby, broken-down "chingado" quality of it all.

NOTE ON STYLE

The play is not intended as a "realistic" interpretation of Chicano life. The symbolism emerging from the character of Belarmino influences the style of acting, scene design, make-up, etc. The play therefore contains realistic and surrealistic elements working together to achieve a transcendental expression of the social condition of La Raza in los Estados Unidos. The set, particularly, must be "real" for what it represents; but it must also contain a cartoon quality such as that found in the satirical sketches of José Clemente Orozco or the lithographs of José Guadalupe Posada. In short, it must reflect the psychological reality of the barrio.

PROLOGUE

FRANCISCO VILLA, born 1878—died 1923.

Campesino, bandit, guerrilla, martyr, general, head of Northern Division of the Revolutionary Army, and finally an undying legend.

He is born and christened Doroteo Arango in the town of Río Grande, state of Durango. In 1895, when he is 17, he is outlawed for killing an *hacendado*, a landowner—a member of the ruling class who had raped his sister. He is caught, but escapes and he takes the name of Francisco Villa. Thus, during the years between 1896 and 1909, the legend of Pancho Villa is born. The legend of the providential bandit: rob the rich to give to the poor. And the poor give him their faith.

The year 1910 brings the beginning of the Mexican Revolution. Pancho Villa enlists his band of men as a guerrilla force. Minor victories grow into major victories: San Andrés, Camargo, Juárez, Torreón, Zacatecas, Irapuato, Querétaro. The bandit force becomes a Revolutionary

Army with horses, trains, cavalry, artillery and a mass of 50,000 men. The peasant outlaw evolves into one of the most brilliant military strategists of our century.

November 27, 1914: Pancho Villa and Emiliano Zapata meet in Mexico City. It is a triumph for the poor, the campesinos, the disinherited. Pancho Villa tries out the presidential chair, yet neither he nor Zapata are compromising types. They are not politicians.

1915: Against the recommendations of his advisors, Woodrow Wilson, President of the United States, recognizes the rival Carrancista government and permits Carranza to transport troops over American soil and thus outflank Villa's División del Norte at Agua Prieta. Villa is defeated. It is the beginning of the end.

1916: Villa retaliates with a raid on Columbus, New Mexico. He is declared an outlaw by the Carranza government, and Wilson sends General John J. Pershing into Mexican territory on a "punitive expedition" looking for Pancho Villa. Pershing fails, and Villa resumes his guerrilla warfare. His military strength, however, is flagging.

1919: Emiliano Zapata is murdered on April 10 in Chinameca.

1920: July 28. Francisco Villa surrenders the remains of his army to the government. He settles in Canutillo to live peacefully.

July 23, 1923: Pancho Villa is ambushed and he dies in the streets of Parral, Chihuahua. His body is dumped into an unmarked grave. Three years later it is disinterred and the corpse is decapitated. The head is never found. This is the story of a people who followed him beyond borders, beyond death.

ACT ONE

A sharp-stringed guitar plays "La Cucaracha." It is afternoon. PEDRO, the aged father of the family, is asleep on a broken-down couch. He is on his back—his paunch sagging—and snoring loudly. He has a long, drooping white moustache and toussled white hair. The guitar concludes "La Cucaracha" with a sharp, final note. PEDRO, as if on cue, shouts violently!!

PEDRO: (*In his sleep.*) ¡¡VIVA VILLA!!
BELARMINO: (*Screams from the curtained bedroom. It is the cry of a full-grown man. He starts singing with vengeance.*) Aarrrrrgh!

155

      (*Sings*.)¡La cucaracha! ¡La cucaracha
      Ya no quiere caminar
      Porque le falta, porque no tiene
      Marihuana que fumar!

CRUZ: (*Running from the kitchen.*) Dios mío, you see what you do, hombre? You have wake up your own son! (BELARMINO *repeats "La Cucaracha," getting louder and more viciously impatient.* CRUZ, *distraught, runs into the curtained bedroom. From off.*) Belarmino, Belarmino, my son, go to sleep. Go to sleep. A la rurru, niño, duérmete ya. (BELARMINO *dozes off singing and is finally silent.* CRUZ *emerges, sighing with relief.*) ¡Gracias a Dios! He's asleep! (*To* PEDRO, *a harsh whisper.*) Be quiet, you old loco! You know he always wakes up hungry. I got enough trouble catching your son's lices so they don't eat us alive! You are crawling with them already.

PEDRO: (*In his sleep.*) Señores, I am Francisco Villa! (*Scratches.*)

CRUZ: Sweet name of God.

PEDRO: ¡Pancho Villa!

CRUZ: Pedro!

PEDRO: I am Pancho Villa!

CRUZ: Yes, with lices!

PEDRO: ¡Viva Villa!

CRUZ: Qué hombre. (*She goes to him.*)

PEDRO: VIVA PANCHO VEE-

CRUZ: (*Pulls his leg.*) ¡PEDRO!

PEDRO: Yah! (*He wakes up.*) Uh!

CRUZ: Stop shouting, hombre.

PEDRO: Uh. (*He goes back to sleep, scratching his belly.*)

CRUZ: Viejo loco. Pancho Villa. I don' know what goes through that head he gots. (JOAQUIN *rushes in and stops, panting against the door. His shirt is torn.*) ¡Joaquín! What happen to you?

JOAQUIN: Nothing.

CRUZ: What did you do?

JOAQUIN: Nothing.

CRUZ: What happen to your shirt?

JOAQUIN: Nothing!

CRUZ: Don' you know nothing but nothing?

JOAQUIN: (*Pause.*) I beat up some vato.

CRUZ: Another fight, my son?

JOAQUIN: I never start it. Dumb gavacho. He come up to me and says "Heh, Pancho!"

PEDRO: (*In his sleep.*) Uh?

CRUZ: You hit him for that?

JOAQUIN: Well, how would you like it, man? I wasn' looking for no trouble. I even take Pancho Villa at first, which was bad enough, but then he call me a lousy Pancho, and I hit the stupid vato in the mouth.

CRUZ: ¡Dios mío! (*Pause.*) What is wrong with you hombre? Don' you think? You on patrol!

JOAQUIN: Parole.

CRUZ: Sí. (*Sighs.*) And mañana it will be the jail again, no? How come you this way, hijo? Your brother Mingo, he never fight so much.

JOAQUIN: He was pus-pus.

CRUZ: (*Miserable.*) Don' you know nothing else? Your brother he's coming from the war today with muchos medals, Joaquín. That is not so pus-pus. If he fight, he do it in the right place. Only you turn out so lousy.

JOAQUIN: (*Fiercely.*) I ain' lousy, ma!

CRUZ: (*Pause.*) You goin' to hit me in the mouth too, my son? (JOAQUIN, *starts to go.*) What you doin'?

JOAQUIN: Splittin'!

CRUZ: Joaquín!

JOAQUIN: (*He stops.*) Stop bugging me, jefita!

CRUZ: (*With deep concern.*) What trouble you so much, hijo?

JOAQUIN: The gavachos.

LUPE: (*Comes in from the kitchen.*) Mamá, the beans are ready! You wan' me to bring 'em?

CRUZ: No, Lupe, Belarmino is asleep.

LUPE: What happened to our favorite jailbird?

JOAQUIN: Shut up!

LUPE: Been out duking again, huh? Rotten pachuco.

CRUZ: Guadalupe, don' say that.

LUPE: It's true. He barely got outta jail yesterday, and now look at him. He don' even care that Mingo's coming home from the war. I bet he's just jealous.

JOAQUIN: Of what?

LUPE: His medals.

JOAQUIN: Screw his medals!

CRUZ: Joaquín! Don' you even feel glad your brother's come home alive

157

and safe?

JOAQUIN: Simón, it makes me feel real patriotic.

LUPE: Liar! Just wait till Mingo gets here. He'll cool your bird. Lousy hoodlum.

JOAQUIN: Lousy, huh? Well, how about this? (*He grabs* LUPE *and pretends to set a louse loose in her hair.*) Ha! Who's lousy now, man?

LUPE: Ayy, Mamá! Mamá!

CRUZ: Haven' you do enough already, muchacho?

JOAQUIN: I was only joking.

CRUZ: But Belarmino . . .

JOAQUIN: I was only joking, man! I don' got no piojos.

LUPE: That's what you think.

JOAQUIN: Shut up!

LUPE: You lousy Mexican!

CRUZ: Stop it, señorita. Din't I tell you to go water the beans?

LUPE: No!

CRUZ: Go water the beans. (*Pause.*) Andale. Go, Guadalupe. (LUPE *exits.*)

JOAQUIN: And stay out!

CRUZ: You stop too, Joaquín. Wha's wrong with you, anyway? Are you as loco as your padre?

JOAQUIN: Loco?

CRUZ: Making noise! This morning your poor brother he eat 50 plates of beans and 100 tortillas. This afternoon I find 30 lice on him—do you hear, hombre? 30! My poor Belarmino, some of this days if he don' eat us out of the house, his lices they will do it. (*She turns and notices* JOAQUIN *scratching his head.*) Joaquín, what you doing?

JOAQUIN: (*Stops.*) What? (*Lowers his hand.*)

CRUZ: You was scratching your head! Blessed be the Señor! Come here, sit down.

JOAQUIN: (*Guiltily.*) What?

CRUZ: (*Inspecting his head.*) Dios mío, this all we need.

JOAQUIN: (*Angry.*) What?

CRUZ: For you to catch the lices, muchacho.

JOAQUIN: (*Tries to rise.*) Lices!

CRUZ: Don' move. (JOAQUIN *remains still.*) Joaquín! I think I find one! No . . . sí . . . sí! It is one. It gots little legs!

JOAQUIN: (*Jumps up.*) Let's see.

CRUZ: Put him up to the light, my son. (*Pause.*) It is . . . one lice, no?

JOAQUIN: A louse.

CRUZ: What is that?

JOAQUIN: One lice.

CRUZ: May the Señor help us all! (BELARMINO *grunts*.) Ay. Now he's waking up again. I better fix his frijolitos. (*Exits to kitchen.*)

JOAQUIN: Me too, huh, señora? My pipes are rumbling.

PEDRO: Sí, mi general. I hear the rumbling. The gringos got cannons y aeroplanos, pero no se apure . . . mi general! ¿Qué pasó con su cabeza? ¡Muchachos, abusados! ¡Alguien se robó la cabeza de Pancho Villa! Ayyy.

JOAQUIN: (*Shaking him.*) Pa! ¡'Apá!

PEDRO: (*Awaking.*) Uh? What?

JOAQUIN: You have a nightmare.

PEDRO: How you know?

JOAQUIN: You shout. Something about Pancho Villa and his head. I don' know. It was in Spanish.

PEDRO: Huh. (*Sits up.*) Where's your madre?

JOAQUIN: In the kitchen.

PEDRO: Frying beans no doubt, eh? Only I never get to try 'em. The loco in the room over there always eat 'em first. Curse the day all my sons was born starving in the land of the gringos! (*He finds an empty wine bottle under the couch.*) Ah, here it is. No, hombre, my little bottle is dead. Oye, my son, you got enough maybe for one . . . bueno, you know, eh?

JOAQUIN: Nel, I'm sorry, jefito.

PEDRO: No, don't start wis your "I'm sorrys." Don' you find work yet?

JOAQUIN: Work?

PEDRO: Field work.

JOAQUIN: You mean like farm labor?

PEDRO: Man's work!

JOAQUIN: Cool it, ese, I just get here. They work me enough in the can. I pull off more than a year wisout pay.

PEDRO: Bueno, it's your own fault. For your itchy fingers . . . stealing tires.

JOAQUIN: What tires?

PEDRO: Pos what ones? They din' catch you red-handed?

JOAQUIN: Simón, but it wasn' tires. They arrest me for a suspect together with nine other vatos. Then there at the station the placa gives us all matches, and the one wis the short one was guilty. They catch me red-handed! But I din't swipe no tires.

PEDRO: No, eh? Well, I hope maybe you learn something.

JOAQUIN: No sweat, jefito. I learn to play the guitar.

PEDRO: Tha's all?

JOAQUIN: Nel, I sing too. Honest. Loan me your guitar, I show you.

PEDRO: No, Joaquín, I don' like to loan that guitar. I have too many year with it, since the Revolución! Qué caray, what happen if you break it. Ees too old.

JOAQUIN: What about when I fix it that time?

PEDRO: When?

JOAQUIN: When you smash it on Mingo's head.

PEDRO: Oh, sí. But the baboso he talk back to me, tha's how come. Bueno, qué caray, go bring it, pues—I want to see if you really know how to play it.

JOAQUIN: Orale. (*He goes into the side room and comes out with an old guitar.*)

PEDRO: What you play? ¿Corridos, rancheras?

JOAQUIN: Rhythm and Blues.

PEDRO: (*Pause.*) What about "Siete Leguas"?

JOAQUIN: What about it?

PEDRO: You see, you don' know nothing.

JOAQUIN: What's "Siete Leguas"?

PEDRO: "Seven Leguas"! How you say leguas in . . .

JOAQUIN: Uh, leagews.

PEDRO: What?

JOAQUIN: Lea-gews.

PEDRO: That's right. "Siete Leguas." The song of the horse of Pancho Villa. The horse he mos' estimated. (*Solemnly.*) He ride that horse until the day he die.

JOAQUIN: The general?

PEDRO: No, the horse. After that Pancho Villa buy a Chivi. Maybe it was a Ford? No, it was a Chivi. 1923! That was the year they kill him, you know. A revolutionary giant like he was.

JOAQUIN: Aah, he wasn' a giant.

PEDRO: Oh, caray, you don' know, my son! Francisco Villa was a man to respect. A man to fear! A man con muchos . . . ummmhh (*Whispering.*) huevos. He rob from the rich to give to the poor—like us. That's why the poor follow him. Any time he could rise 50,000 men by snapping his fingers. You should have see what he do to the gringos.

JOAQUIN: The gavachos?

PEDRO: No, the gringos. In them times they was only call gringos. Not gavachos. Pancho Villa have 'em running all over México.

JOAQUIN: What was they doing in México?

PEDRO: Chasing him! But they never catch him. He was too smart, eh? Too much cabeza. He ride on Siete Leguas and stay in the mountains. Then he ride his men around the back, and they kill gringos until they get tired! Sometimes they even get more tire' than picking potatoes, but they go back to the mountains to rest.

JOAQUIN: (*Impressed.*) Hey, man, tha's too much.

PEDRO: I myself ride with him, you know. See this scar? (*Points to his neck.*) From a bullet. And listen to this: ¡VIVA VILLAAA!

CRUZ: (*In the kitchen.*) ¡Pedro, hombre! You wake your son!

PEDRO: (*Shouts back.*) Oh, you and that crazy loco! (*To* JOAQUIN.) Huh, that stinking madre of yours! All she live for is to feed that bean belly! He has curse my life.

JOAQUIN: What about Pancho Villa? When he got the Chivi? I bet he run down a lotta gavachos, huh? Squashed 'em!

PEDRO: (*With exaggeration.*) ¡Oh sí! He . . . (*Pause.*) The Chivi? No, hombre, when he get the Chivi, then they get him. Right in Chihuahua too, in Parral. He was just driving down the street one day, not bothering nobody, when they shoot him down and kill him. (*Mournful pause.*) So . . . they bury him, and then in the night three years later, somebody come and—ZAS! They cut off his head.

JOAQUIN: His *head*?

PEDRO: Chattapí (*Whispering.*) You want Belarmino to hear?

JOAQUIN: How come they cut off his head? Who done it?

PEDRO: Pos, who you think?

JOAQUIN: ¡Los gavachos!

PEDRO: (*Nods.*) Maybe they still even got it, too. To this day nobody has find it.

JOAQUIN: Híjola, how gacho, man. (*Pause.*) How did that song goes?

PEDRO: "Siete Leguas"?

JOAQUIN: Simón.

PEDRO: (*Sings.*) "Siete Leguas, el caballo que Villa más estimabaaa."

JOAQUIN: (*In his room.*) ¡Ay, yai, yai, yai!

PEDRO: Oh-oh, now we do it.

CRUZ: (*Entering.*) What have you do, hombre?

PEDRO: Nothing. (BELARMINO *yells and howls, sings "La Cucaracha."*)

CRUZ: No, eh? (*Shouting back.*) Lupe, bring the tortillas!

PEDRO: We eat now?

CRUZ: You wait!

PEDRO: I don' want to wait! (BELARMINO *yells*.)

CRUZ: Lupe, bring the beans too! (*She goes into the bedroom*.)

PEDRO: I don' got to wait! I wan' to eat—EAT! ¡Quiero tragar! (LUPE *comes out of the kitchen with beans and tortillas. JOAQUIN grabs a tortilla with a laugh*.)

LUPE: You pig!

PEDRO: (*Turns around*.) Pig?

LUPE: I meant Joaquín. (*She goes into the bedroom quickly*.)

PEDRO: ¡Sinvergüenzas! Who's the boss here, pues? Who buys the eats!

CRUZ: (*Inside the room*.) ¡El Welfare!

PEDRO: And before that?

CRUZ: Your son, Mingo.

PEDRO: Mingo? (*Throws his arms out in a helpless gesture*.) So this is what I get, eh? In 1927 I come here all the way from Zacatecas. For what? CHICKENSQUAT? Everybody talks back, that . . . that loco in there eats before his padre does, and Mingo. .. Mingo . . . where's Mingo?

JOAQUIN: (*Eating the rolled up tortilla*.) Not home from the war yet. (MINGO *walks into the room through the front door. He is in a soldier's uniform and carries a sack with his stuff in it*.)

MINGO: Somebody say war?

LUPE: (*Peeking out of* BELARMINO's *room*.) Mamá, Mingo's home!

CRUZ: (*Coming out with the bowl of beans*.) My son! (*She embraces him and cries*.)

PEDRO: Bueno, bueno, lemme see him. He's my son, too!

MINGO: Hello, Pa. (*Offers his hand*.)

PEDRO: ¿Halo qué? Give me one abrazo, I'm your padre! (*He hugs him*.) Tha's it—strong like a man. Look, vieja, see how much medals he gots?

LUPE: Hi, Mingo, remember me?

MINGO: Sure. ¡María!

LUPE: ¡María!

MINGO: (*Pause*.) ¿Rosita?

LUPE: ¡Lupe!

MINGO: Oh, yeah, Lupe.

PEDRO: And over here you got your brother Joaquín.

MINGO: Hi, punk. Shake.

JOAQUIN: Orale. (*They shake hands*.)

CRUZ: Well, my son, sit down. Rest. You must be tired.

MINGO: Not at all, Mom.

CRUZ: ¿Tienes hambre?

MINGO: What's for dinner?

CRUZ: Papas con huevos.

MINGO: What else?

LUPE: Huevos con papas.

MINGO: Is that all?

JOAQUIN: Papas a huevo.

MINGO: No, thanks. I had a steak in town.

CRUZ: Oh. Well, thank God, you have come home safe and sound. (*She takes him to the couch.*) Look, sit down over here. Tell us about . . . (*She sees the wine bottle.*) Pedro hombre, this dirty bottle!

MINGO: Still at it, huh, pa?

PEDRO: No, only from time to time, hijo. For the cough. (*He coughs.*)

LUPE: Tell us of the war, Mingo.

CRUZ: What's wrong with you, woman? Your brother he want to forget such things. It already pass, gracias a Dios.

PEDRO: Huh, it pass? You mean we don' suppose to know where the muchacho was? War is war! If the sons fight today, we fight yesterday. Mira, when I was with Pancho Villa, we kill more Americanos than . . .

MINGO: ¿Americanos? Americans!

BELARMINO: (*In his room.*) ARRRRRGGHH!

MINGO: (*Alarmed.*) What the hell's that?

CRUZ: ¡Belarmino! Lupe, please give him the beans that was left. I had forgot he didn' finish eating.

MINGO: Mom, who's Belarmino?

CRUZ: (*Surprised.*) Pos . . . you know, hijo. You don' remember?

PEDRO: Of course, he remember! Caray, how he's going to forgot that animal? Don' let him bother you, my son. Come here, tell me your plans. What you going to do now?

MINGO: Well, 'apá, I been thinking. (*Long pause.*)

PEDRO: He's been thinking, qué bueno. What you been thinking, hijo?

MINGO: I been thinking I wanna help the family!

CRUZ: ¡Ay, mijito! (*She embraces him. PEDRO shakes his hand.*)

MINGO: As a matter of fact, I got a surprise for you. I bet you didn't expect me till tonight, right? Well, you know how come I'm home early? I bought a new car!

JOAQUIN: A new car!

CRUZ: A new car!

LUPE: (*Reentering.*) A new car! (BELARMINO *grunts three times, mim-*

icking the sound of the words, "A new car.")

CRUZ: ¡Dios mío!

LUPE: We didn't even hear you drive up!

MINGO: Natch. She's as quiet as a fly in the beans. Mom, sis, hold on to your frijole bowl. There she is! (*Points out the window*.) A new Chevrolet!

LUPE: A Chevi! ¡Mamá, un Chevi!

CRUZ: Blessed be the name of the Señor. That one is ours, Mingo?

MINGO: All ours, only forty more payments to go. (*Everyone looks out the window except* PEDRO.) What's wrong, pa? Ain't you going to look?

PEDRO: For what? They going to come for it in two months.

MINGO: Not this baby. I'm gonna keep up all my payments.

PEDRO: Tha's what I used to say. I never make it.

MINGO: I know, but I ain' you. (*Pause*.) I mean, it wasn' necessary, Dad. Give me one good reason why you didn't keep good credit. Just one!

PEDRO: (BELARMINO *grunts hungrily in his room*.) There it is.

CRUZ: Guadalupe, go. (LUPE *exits to room*.)

MINGO: (*Pause. Everybody dejected*.) You know what's wrong with you people? You're all defeated! Just look at this place! Well, it ain't gonna get me down. I learned some skills in the Marines, and I'm gonna use 'em in the best place I know to get ahead!

PEDRO: Where?

MINGO: The fields.

JOAQUIN: At farm labor? (*Laughs*.) You going to be a farm laborer?

MINGO: Listen, you cholo.

CRUZ: Cállate el hocico, baboso.

MINGO: What's he ever done but land in jail, Mom? What you ever done? (JOAQUIN *blows a raspberry in his face*.)

CRUZ: Joaquín, es-stop it.

MINGO: You drop-out. You high school drop-out!

CRUZ: Mingo, please.

MINGO: You know what you're gonna end up like? Like the old man—a stinking *wino*!

PEDRO: WHAT!

MINGO: (*Embarrassed pause*.) Aw, come on, Dad. I din' mean nothing bad. Look, let's face it, okay? You're just a wino, right? Like I'm a Marine. What's wrong with that? There's a million of 'em. Today I was even going to buy you a bottle of

Old Crow.

PEDRO: Whiskey?

MINGO: Damn right. $6.50 a quart. It's better than that 35 cent stuff you been drinking. From now on it's nothing but the best for us. Only, we gotta be realistic. Plan everything. Okay, Tomahawk, you'll be working with me. You got a job now?

JOAQUIN: Chale.

MINGO: You mean Dad's the only one working?

PEDRO: (*Pause.*) Eh . . . no, I don' work neither, Mingo.

MINGO: Then how do you support yourselves?

JOAQUIN: How come you don' tell him, Pa? The jefitos are on welfare, ese.

MINGO: Welfare? WELFARE! (*He turns away, sick.*)

CRUZ: We always been poor, my son.

MINGO: (*Determined.*) That's true, Mom. But now things are gonna be different. I'm here now, and we're going to be rich—middle class! I didn't come out the war without learning nothing.

JOAQUIN: Then how come you going back to the fields? Nobody get rich in that jale.

MINGO: No, huh? (*He embraces* CRUZ *and* PEDRO.) Well, thanks to this old man and old lady, who were smart enough to cross the border, we live in the land of opportunity. The land I risk my life for. The land where you can start at the bottom, even in the fields, and become a rich man before you can say . . .

BELARMINO: ARRRGGGHHH! (LUPE *comes running with her blouse torn on one side.*)

LUPE: AY! Mamá! He ate all the beans then he try to bite me!

CRUZ: Por Dios. The poor man.

LUPE: The poor man? He's a pig. Look at the hole he made.

CRUZ: All right pues, I see it.

LUPE: And he give me his piojos.

CRUZ: No matter. Go bring more tortillas!

MINGO: Wait a minute, *wait a minute*! Mom, for the last time, who's in there?

CRUZ: Your older brother, hijo. Belarmino.

MINGO: Brother? I don't remember no other brother. What's wrong with him? How come he shouts?

PEDRO: Ay, pos 'tá loco el baboso.

CRUZ: (*Surprised.*) He's sick . . . but you should know. You used to play with him when you was little.

MINGO: Ma, don' lie to me. Are we so poor we gotta take in braceros?

Or maybe it's a wetback you're hiding?

JOAQUIN: (*A whisper to* PEDRO.) Or maybe he's suffering from shell-shock?

MINGO: I ain't suffering from nothing, man!

JOAQUIN: Take it easy, carnal, cool it.

MINGO: Well, Ma, is that guy a wetback?

CRUZ: No, he's your brother.

MINGO: Brother, huh? We'll soon find out! (*He charges into the bedroom.*)

BELARMINO: (*After a pause.*) ARRRRRRRGGGGHH.

MINGO: (*Running out.*) ARRRRGGGGHH! He ain't got a body. He's just a . . . HEAD!

Curtain.

ACT TWO

Three months later. The walls of the house are moderately speckled with red cockroaches of various sizes. LUPE *is standing behind* PEDRO, *who is asleep on a chair, delousing him. On an old sofa in the corner, a white lace veil covers* BELARMINO—*like a child. The radio is blaring out frantic mariachi music,* "La Negra." LUPE *finds something in* PEDRO*'s hair.*

LUPE: (*Gasps.*) Lousy cucaracha!

CRUZ: (*Shouting from the kitchen.*) Negra, shut off the noises, diablo! (*Pause.*)¡Negra! Belarmino is sleeping!

LUPE: Mama, stop calling me negra.

CRUZ: Shut off the noises, sonavavichi!

LUPE: (*Shuts off radio.*) Okay, pues, I did, man! (BELARMINO *grunts from under the veil.*) What you want? (BELARMINO *grunts louder.*) No, no more radio. Didn't you hear mi 'amá? Go to sleep! (BELARMINO *grunts again.*) Ay, that stupid cabeza! (*She removes the veil and* BELARMINO *is seen for the first time: he is the head of a man about 30-35 years old. That is all. He has no body. He has long hair and a large mustache. His black eyes are deep and expressive. The head is otherwise only distinguished by its tremendous size. A full eighteen inches in diameter.*)

166

BELARMINO: (*Singing.*) "¡La Cucaracha!"

LUPE: Shut up! (BELARMINO *laughs idiotically.*) Idiot, because of you I'm like a slave in this house. Joaquín and Mingo and e'rybody goes to town but they never let me go. I gotta be here—ready to stuff you with frijoles. Like a maid, like a negra.

CHATO: (*At the front door.*) Hi, negra.

LUPE: (*Covering* BELARMINO.) What did you call me?

CHATO: N—othing.

BELARMINO: ¡Cállate el hocico!

CHATO: Why!

LUPE: Mi papá, he's asleep.

CHATO: Oh! Heh, tha's Belarmino behind there, huh?

LUPE: Where at?

CHATO: Under that velo. (*Points to veil.*)

LUPE: No! My brother's a man, how can he fit in there?

CHATO: You know. (*He laughs.*)

LUPE: Look, Chato, if you come to make fun of us, you better cut it out, man. Belo's sick, he don'—(BELARMINO *grunts.*) Okay, okay, hombre. In a minute. Here, have a cockroach. (*She takes a cockroach off the wall and gives it to him.*)

CHATO: (*Open mouthed.*) How come he eats cockroaches?

LUPE: Because he's hungry, dumbbell.

CHATO: I'm not a dumbbell!

LUPE: Oh, no, *you're* real smart. Only you don't even know how to read or write. You think we din't go to the second grade together? Menso.

CRUZ: (*In the kitchen.*) ¿Guadalupe?

LUPE: Sí, mamá? (*She makes a sign to* CHATO *not to say anything.*)

CRUZ: Who vou talking to?

LUPE: Belarmino, Mamá. I'm cleaning his cucarachas.

CRUZ: Okay pues, don' let him eat 'em.

CHATO: (*Looking under the veil.*) En la madre, what a big head.

LUPE: (*Turning, whispering furiously.*) What you doing? Let him alone! Nobody tell you to come in. Get out!

CHATO: How come?

LUPE: Because.

CHATO: Huy, huy qué touchy. Come on, esa. Don' play hard-to-get.

LUPE: (*Menacing the fly-spray pump.*) Look stupid, I'll hit you.

CHATO: Okay, don't get mad. I come over to see Mingo. He don't pay me yet.

LUPE: Liar. He said he paid you two days ago.

CHATO: What days ago? I been searching for a week for him. He haven't pay me nothing. I go to the rancho, he ain't there. I come over here—same story. This whole thing is beginning to smell. (BELARMINO *farts loudly.*) ¡Sacos! De potatoes. Heh, wha's wrong with this ruco?

LUPE: None of your business. Pig!

CHATO: Din' he just learn to talk too?

LUPE: No!

CHATO: Joaquín says he sings "La Cucaracha."

LUPE: He's crazy, man.

BELARMINO: (*Singing.*) ¡LA CUCARACHA, LA CUCARACHA!

CHATO: ¿No, qué no? That cat do okay.

LUPE: Oh, how you know? I'm sick and tired of this freak. Feeding him beans, taking out his louses. Listening to that stupid little song. That's all he knows. He don' talk. If he wants to eat, he still shouts or grunts like he's doing it all my life. I almost can't stand it no more!

CHATO: (*Putting his arm around her.*) Okay pues, mi honey. Don't cry. Some of these days I'm going to take you away from all this.

LUPE: What all this?

CHATO: This poverty, this cucarachas, this . . . this . . .

LUPE: This what?

CHATO: You know . . . Belarmino. I don' say nothing, but . . . well, there's the Raza, no? El chisme. People talk.

LUPE: (*Sobering.*) What they say?

CHATO: Well, you know . . . dicen que tu carnal es una cabeza.

LUPE: Una what?

CHATO: Cabeza.

LUPE: Sorry, guy. I don' speak Spanish.

CHATO: Una HEAD! (PEDRO *wakes, goes back to sleep with a grunt.*) Tha's what they say. No arms, no legs, no nothing. Just a head. (*Laughs.*)

LUPE: You black negro! You dirty Mexican! (*She attacks* CHATO.)

CHATO: Orale, hold it there! (*He grabs her.*)

LUPE: Let me go, Chato.

CHATO: Who's a dirty Mexican!

LUPE: You, and ugly too. And more blacker than an Indian.

CHATO: Huy, huy, huy, and you like cream, uh. I'm dark because I work in the fields all day in the sun. I get burn! But look here. (*Shows her his armpit.*) See? Almost tan.

LUPE: You're loco.

CHATO: Chure, loco about you, mi vida. Don' make me suffer. I don' care if Belarmino's a cabeza.

LUPE: Chato, mi papá'll wake up.

CHATO: So what? Te digo que te quiero, que te amo, que te adoro.

LUPE: My mother's in the kitchen.

CHATO: Tú eres mi sol, mi luna, mi cielo . . .

LUPE: Chatito, por favor.

CHATO: Mis tamales, mis tortillas, mis frijoles

CRUZ: (*Entering from the kitchen.*) GUADALUPE!

LUPE: (*Matter-of-factly.*) Mi mamá.

CHATO: (*Turns.*) Buenas tardes. (*He runs out.*)

CRUZ: Sí, buenas tardes, you shameless goddammit! (*Turns.*) ¡Pedro!

PEDRO: (*In his sleep.*) ¿Sí, mi general?

CRUZ: Pedro, hombre, wake up.

PEDRO: ¡Viva Villa!

CRUZ: You old loco.

PEDRO: Viva Pancho Vi—(CRUZ *pulls his leg.*) Yah! Uh? ¿Qué pasó?

CRUZ: ¡Chato!

PEDRO: (*Jumps up.*) Chato? (*Pause.*) ¿Chato who?

CRUZ: He was after Lupe, hombre.

PEDRO: (*Heads for kitchen.*) Where's he at?

CRUZ: (*Pulling him back.*) He went that way! Go, hombre! Serve for something!

PEDRO: Where's my rifle! WHERE'S MY GUN?

LUPE: (*Throws herself upon him.*) ¡No, Papá!

PEDRO: You chattap! WHERE'S MY GUN, WOMEN!

CRUZ: (*Pause.*) You don' got a gun, Pedro. (*Silence.*)

LUPE: I din' do—

PEDRO: CHATTAP! Dios mío, how lousy. (*He grabs his wine bottle beside the chair.*) You see? This is what I get for coming to the land of the gringos. No respect! I should have stay in Zacatecas. (*He heads for the door.*)

CRUZ: Pedro, where you going?

PEDRO: Where I feel like it, sabes? To look for work.

CRUZ: At sundown?

PEDRO: La night shift, mujer! Maybe I go back to Zacatecas.

CRUZ: Oh sí, hitchi-hiking.

PEDRO: ¡Cállate si no quieres que te plante un guamaso! ¡Vieja desgraciada! (MINGO *enters dressed in new khaki work clothes, complete with new hat and boots. He carries a clipboard with papers and a money box.*)

MINGO: Home sweet home! E'erybody yelling as usual? What was

Super-Mex running for?

CRUZ: Who?

MINGO: Chato. He come flying outta here like the immigration was after him.

CRUZ: He was after Lupe.

MINGO: (*To* PEDRO.) Where were you, man?

CRUZ: Your padre was asleep.

MINGO: (*Deliberately*.) Oh.

PEDRO: (*Sensing disrespect*.) Oh, what?

MINGO: Oh, nothing . . . Dad.

PEDRO: Some of this days, cabrón, you going to say "oh, something else." Then we see who's boss around here. (*To* LUPE). I take care of you later, señorita. (*He exits*.)

CRUZ: Dios mío, that old loco. Now he won' be home until it is so late. Then he gots to cross the tracks in the dark. (*To* LUPE.) You *see*? You see what you do?

LUPE: I din' do nothing! Chato grabbed me!

MINGO: What you mean he grabbed you? Just took a little grab, huh?

LUPE: No, he was telling me about Belo. The whole neighborhood's talking about him! They say he don' got no arms or legs or nothing. That he's a . . .

CRUZ: What?

LUPE: You know what. (*Uncomfortable pause*.)

CRUZ: No, I don' know. My son is sick! How can they say such things?

MINGO: Forget 'em, Ma. They do it from envy.

LUPE: Envy, of Belo?

MINGO: Of me! Since they always pass the time drunk or begging on welfare, they can't stand a man who betters himself. But they ain't seen nothing yet. Mom, sit down over here. I got something to tell you. You too, negra.

LUPE: Don' call me negra, Mingo.

MINGO: Can't you take a joke?

LUPE: No!

MINGO: Sit down. (*She sits*.) Okay, now. Ma, remember that place where we picked prunes for so many years? On Merde Road? (CRUZ *nods*.) Well, it's called Merde Boulevard now. They cut down the orchard and built new houses on the land. They got a big sign up: Prune Blossom Acres. And right under it: No Down Payment To Vets. You know what it means, Ma? I'm a vet and we're gonna get a new house!

LUPE: A new house! Mamá, a new house!

MINGO: (*Laughs.*) I thought that'd grab you. Well, Mom, what do you say? Shall we move outta this dump? (CRUZ *is silent, she stands.*) Heh, what's wrong?

CRUZ: This ain't a dump, Mingo. It is the house of your padre.

MINGO: Padre, madre, so what? I'm talking about Prune Blossom Acres. America's at out doorsteps. All we have to do is take one step.

CRUZ: What about Belarmino?

MINGO: Somebody can carry him, what else? Put him in a shoebox.

LUPE: He don't fit in a shoebox.

MINGO: Not a real shoebox, stupid. A cardboard box. We can put holes in it so he can breathe. That ain't no problem.

CRUZ: I know, Mingo, but . . . it is not the same. In this barrio they don' care.

MINGO: I care!

CRUZ: And the gringos?

MINGO: Whatta you mean, gringos?

CRUZ: Who else lives in new houses?

MINGO: Americans, Ma. American citizens like me and y . . . (*Pause.*) Aw, whatta you trying to do? Get me defeated too? You wanna spend the rest of your life in this stinking barrio? What about all the gossiping beanbellies? You know they're laughing at this head.

CRUZ: This what?

MINGO: (*Pause.*) Shorty.

LUPE: That's not what I heard.

MINGO: You shut up, sister.

CRUZ: His name ain't Chorti, Mingo.

MINGO: For pete's sake, Ma, I'm trying to help out here! He's my brother, so I call him Shorty. What's wrong with that? He's short. The important thing's the lies people are telling about us, about Shorty, about me. I don't owe them peons nothing.

JOAQUIN: (*Standing in the doorway.*) Simón, just pay Chato what you owe him. Come on in, ese, don' be chicken.

MINGO: And what do I owe him?

JOAQUIN: His pay.

CHATO: Buenas tardes. (*He hides behind* JOAQUIN.)

CRUZ: You say that before, sinvergüenza! (CHATO *runs out again.*) You dare to come in after he try to steal our respect!

CHATO: (*Reentering.*) Aw, I din't come to steal nothing. I come because you robbing me!

CRUZ: What?

CHATO: Well, maybe not you, but Mingo. Tell you right off the bat,

Doña Cruz, this vato's nothing but a crooked contractor!

MINGO: Crooked?

LUPE: ¿Mingo?

CRUZ: My son?

BELARMINO: AAARRRRGH!

CRUZ: (*To* BELARMINO.) Ay no, my son, not you. You ain't crooked.

MINGO: What the hell you trying to say, Chato?

JOAQUIN: What you think, you din't hear him? He says the big war hero's a thief just like e'rybody else! So you was going to get rich working in the fields, uh? Free country and all that chet! Simón, I believe it now. Anybody can get rich if he's a crooked farm labor contractor. Only this time it's no dice, ese. Chato's my friend. Pay him.

MINGO: I already paid him! If you don't believe me, look here in my paybook. Here's everybody that received their wages. See . . . what's signed here? (*He shows* CHATO.)

CHATO: I don' know, ees in Spanish.

MINGO: Spanish? It's your name, stupid. Chato Reyes. You sign it yourself.

JOAQUIN: Nel, carnal, we got you there. Chato don' know how to read or write.

MINGO: (*Pause.*) Of course he don't know—that's how come his "X" is here instead of his name. See? (*He shows the "X".*) Okay, Chato, if you want to prove that this ain' your "X" or that I haven't paid you, you got to take me to court, right? But just to show you I ain't crooked, I'm gonna pay you again. Sit down. (CHATO *and* MINGO *sit down.*) All right, how many days do you work?

CHATO: Four.

MINGO: Four days, at ten hours each, is 40 hours. 40 hours at 85 cents an hour is . . . $34, right?

CHATO: Sí, muchas gracias.

MINGO: One moment, social security.

CHATO: But I don't got a card.

MINGO: You an American citizen?

CHATO: Simón.

MINGO: Good. You can still pay. That's $15, plus a dollar fine for not having a card. That leaves $18, right?

CHATO: Simón, gracias.

MINGO: Hold it, income tax. 50% of 18 is 9. That leaves you $9, correct?

CHATO: Orale, gra . . .

MINGO: The lunches. Five tacos at 40 cents each, one chili pepper at 15 cents and a large-size cola at 35 cents . . . that's $2.50 a day. $2.50 for four days are . . .

CHATO: Heh, cut it out!

MINGO: What's wrong, a mistake?

CHATO: Simón, that ain't right! I don't pay for mordidas.

MINGO: (*Standing up.*) ¡Mordidas! What you referring to?

CHATO: Pos what? The tacos. They have bites.

CRUZ: Bites?

CHATO: Mordidotas.

LUPE: Oh-Oh, I know who done 'em.

CRUZ: You shut up, woman. (*To* MINGO *smiling.*) I don't know who could have do it, my son. I put 'em in new every day.

MINGO: Well, (*He sits.*) one cent discount for each taco for the bites are . . . 39 cents five times. $1.95, plus the chili pepper, the Coke, etc . . . $2.45 a day. For four days that's $9.80. You had 9 dollars; you owe me 80 cents.

CHATO: OWE?

MINGO: There's the proof. Pay me. (CHATO *looks at the paper.*)

JOAQUIN: Lemme see that, ese. (*He takes the paper.*)

MINGO: (*Taking the paper from* JOAQUIN.) How about it, Chato? You pay me or what you gonna do?

BELARMINO: AARRRRRRRRRGGGGGGHHHHHHH!

CRUZ: ¡Ay, mijo! (*She goes to quiet* BELARMINO.)

CHATO: I see you! (*He runs toward the door.*) And ees true what I say! You stupid, chet contractor! T'ief!

MINGO: Thief! You come here and say that, you little . . .

CHATO: ¡Ay! (*He runs out.*)

BELARMINIO: AARRRRRGGGGGHHH!

CRUZ: Mingo, please, don' make so much fuss.

MINGO: Fuss? What you talking, señora? Din' you hear what . . .

CHATO: (*Peeking in again.*) I forget to say somet'ing. Stay wis you stinking head! (*He ducks out quickly.*)

CRUZ: Stinking head? ¡Pos mira que jijo de . . .! (*At the door shouting.*) ¡Arrastrado! ¡Analfabeto! ¡MUERTO DE HAMBRE!

MINGO: Mom!

CRUZ: YOU GODAMMIT!

MINGO: Okay, Ma, that's enough! (*He pulls her back.*)

CRUZ: He call your brother a stinking head. (BELARMINO *farts sonorously.* JOAQUIN *leaves.*)

LUPE: ¡Ay! It's true! (*Everybody moves away from* BELARMINO *except*

CRUZ.) It's true. He's disgusting.

CRUZ: And what you think you are, estúpida? Don' think I forget what you do with Chato, eh? Go make tortillas.

LUPE: For what? Belarmino eat 'em all?

CRUZ: No matter, go do it.

LUPE: He eats all the lunches.

MINGO: Lunches?

CRUZ: Don' talk back, I tell you. Go make tortillas!

LUPE: Oh no! I'm not a tortilla factory.

CRUZ: Pos, mira que . . . (CRUZ *starts to hit* LUPE.)

MINGO: Wait a minute, WAIT A MINUTE, MA! What's this about the lunches?

LUPE: It's Belarmino, Mingo. We make 200 tacos for the lunches tomorrow and he already eat 150! He never gets full. That's why Chato's tacos have bites, because mi 'Amá give 'em to Belo.

MINGO: You give 'em to him, Ma? The tacos we sell to the men?

CRUZ: He was a little hungry, my son.

MINGO: A little hungry! What about all the beans he's already eating? You seen the bills at the store lately? He's eating more and more every week.

LUPE: And that's not all. He's also crawling wis more and more lices! And he eats cucarachas, and he stinks! I can't stand him no more. He's just a stupid . . . HEAD!

CRUZ: (*Pause. She slaps* LUPE.) Your brother is not a head.

MINGO: I oughta knock your stupid lips off.

LUPE: (*Anger, disgust.*) Go to hell. I'll never use 'em! Give 'em to Belo so he can eat *more*! I rather get married so I can suffer in my own house, even if it's with the ugliest, most stupidest man in the world. It can't be worser than this. One of this days Belarmino's gonna grunt or yell for his frijoles, and I won't be here to stuff his throat. You going to see! (*She goes out crying.*)

JOAQUIN: (*Reenters.*) Ma? This a piojo?

MINGO: ¿Piojo? A louse!

JOAQUIN: One lice.

CRUZ: This ain't a piojo, my son. Ees one little . . . cucaracha, que no?

BELARMINO: ARRRRGGGHHH!

CRUZ: Ay! (*She removes* BELARMINO's *veil.*) ¡Dios mío!

MINGO: What the hell's on his face?

JOAQUIN: Cucarachas! (BELARMINO's *face is covered with cockroaches of various sizes.*)

BELARMINO: (*Smiling, singing.*)
  ¡LA CUCARACHA, LA CUCARACHA!
  YA NO PUEDE CAMINAR
  PORQUE LE FALTA, PORQUE NO TIENE
  ¡MARIHUANA QUE FUMAR!

ACT THREE

SCENE ONE

Later that same night. BELARMINO *is on top of an old table, asleep.*
JOAQUIN *staggers in drunk, singing, smoking a hand-rolled cigarette.*

JOAQUIN: (*Singing.*)
        I'm gonna sing this corrido
        And I'm feeling very sad
        Cause the great Francisco Villa
        Some vato cut off his head.

        La Cucaracha, la Cucaracha
        She don' wanna go no more
        You give her pesos and marijuana
        Cuca open up her door! (*Sees* BELARMINO, *moves toward him.*)

        When they murder Pancho Villa
        His body they lay to rest
        But his head somebody take it
        All the way to the U.S.

        La Cockaroacha, La Cockaroacha
        She don' wanna caminar
        Porque le falta, porque no tiene
        She's a dirty little whore!
(*Pause.*) Heh, Belo? You awake, ese? Come on, man. Get your butt up! Oh yeah . . . you don't got one, huh? (*Laughs.*) So what? Get up! (*Pulls his hair.*)

BELARMINO: (*Roars.*) ¡LA CUCARACHAAA!

JOAQUIN: Tha's all you know, huh stupid! (*Mocks him.*) "¡Cucaracha!"
(*Pause.*) Oh, a real one, eh? They even coming outa your nose, ese.
Look at her . . . she's a dirty little whore. A putita. (*Holds out the
small cockroach with his fingers in front of* BELARMINO's *eyes.*)
¡Puuuteee-ta! (*Laughs, throws it down, squashes it.*) Well, what you
looking so stupid about? It was only a stinking cockaroach. Dumb
Mexican . . . not you, ese, this stupid cucaracha I squash. They
love to be step on. (*Laughs.*) You know what happen tonight, man? I
been all over the barrio running away from vatos. Simón, all my
friends and camaradas. Like a big chingón I get 'em at work with
Mingo, and he chisel 'em. Now I'm the patsy and they wanna knife
me. Even Chato. He's telling e'ybody you're a head, ese. (*Laughs.*)
With no guts.

BELARMINO: (*As if disembowled.*) ARRRGGGGHHHH!

JOAQUIN: (*Whispering.*) Heh, MAN, CUT IT OUT! Shhh, the jefita's
gonna hear. Okay, you ask for it! (*He covers* BELARMINO *with his
coat.*) Shhh. (BELARMINO *yells, muffled.* JOAQUIN *laughs.*)
Come on, ese, be a sport. You wan' me to throw you out the window? (BELARMINO *stops shouting.* JOAQUIN *gives him a tug.*)
Heh? (*No response.* JOAQUIN *peeks under the coat.*) You awright?

BELARMINO: Simón

JOAQUIN: (*Covers him quickly.*) Dumb head. (*Pause.*) Heh, he say
something. He's learning to talk! (*Uncovers him again.*)

BELARMINO: ¡Cabrón!

JOAQUIN: Spanish.

BELARMINO: (*Grunts.*) Uh, ¡toque! ¡Toque, cigarro!

JOAQUIN: What, you want' a toke? (*He holds out the cigarette.* BELAR-
MINO *puffs on it eagerly.*) No, man don't just puff on it. You gotta
inhale it. See, like this. (JOAQUIN *inhales.*) Take in a little air wis
it.

BELARMINO: (*Grunts*). Uh-uh, ¡toque! (JOAQUIN *holds out the cigarette again.* BELARMINO *puffs noisely, then sniffs vociferously.*)

JOAQUIN: How do you like it, bueno?

BELARMINO: (*Holding his breath.*) Bueno.

JOAQUIN: (*Laughs.*) Chet, man, you just as bad as me. A lousy Mexican!

BELARMINO: ARRRGGGGHHH! (JOAQUIN *covers him with his
coat.*)

CRUZ: (*Runs in the front door.*) ¡Joaquín!

JOAQUIN: Hi, Jefita.

CRUZ: What you doing? Where's Chorty?

JOAQUIN: (BELARMINO *grunts under the coat.*) He went out to take a piss.

CRUZ: Wha's that?

JOAQUIN: What? Oh, that—my coat. (BELARMINO *grunts.*)

CRUZ: Válgame Dios, do you got Belarmino in there, Joaquín?

JOAQUIN: Nel, there's nobody under here. (*Lifts coat.*) See? No body! (*He laughs.*)

CRUZ: ¡Belarmino! (*She goes to him.* BELARMINO *grunts, moans, breaths hard.*) He shrink . . .

JOAQUIN: (*Moving away from* BELARMINO.) Don' let him fool you, jefita. Maybe you think the vato grunts and tha's it, but he talks. (CRUZ *looks at him.*) No chet, I mean no lie. He do it. And it's not only "La Cucaracha." He swing in pure words, huh, ese? Simón, he just barely talk to me. Go on, ask him something.

CRUZ: (*Emotionally.*) Mijito . . . my Chorti, ees true? You can talk at last? Ees me, your madre. Speak to me! (BELARMINO *grunts.*) Ay, Dios, he can talk inglés.

JOAQUIN: That was a grunt. Come on, Belo. Talk right. (BELARMINO *laughs idiotically.*) Nel, ese, don' act stupid. This is the jefita. She want to hear you talk. (BELARMINO *grunts and makes idiotic noises.*) Come on, man!

BELARMINO: ARRRGGGGH!

CRUZ: Tha's enough, Joaquín. You scare him. I don' know how you can make fun of your poor brother.

JOAQUIN: But he can talk, señora. He's faking.

CRUZ: Tha's enough! Din' I tell you not to bother him? I have enough to worry with your sister. She run out like crazy this afternoon, and haven' come back. Maybe she want to elope with Chato?

JOAQUIN: Pos, so what? Chato's a good vato.

CRUZ: A good vato. An ignorant who let the contractors rob him!

JOAQUIN: Simón, and who's the contractor? Mingo!

CRUZ: Shut up, liar! Thief!

JOAQUIN: T'ief?

CRUZ: Since you was born you have give me nothing but trouble. Going out in the streets at night, coming late, landing in jail. I don' got no more hope in you. Or in Lupe. The only one who haven' come out bad is my poor Chorti who's only hungry all the time. Why don' you rob something for your brother to eat, eh? Serve for something. (*Weeps.*) Válgame Dios, nobody care about my poor sick Belarmino. Only his madre. (*She starts to go out.*)

BELARMINO: Mamá.

CRUZ: (*Without turning.*) No, don' call me, Joaquín.

JOAQUIN: But I din' . . .

CRUZ: No, I tell you, comprende, sanavavichi! I got to be out in the street. Maybe with the help of the Virgen, your sister come back. (*Exits.*)

BELARMINO: Pobre viejita.

JOAQUIN: Pobre nothing! If you care so much, how come you keep your mouth shut when it count?

BELARMINO: (*Brusquely, furiously.*) ¡No seas torpe! Si todo el mundo se da cuenta que puedo hablar, van a saber quien soy. O mejor dicho, quien fui. Me vienen a mochar la lengua o ¡toda la maceta de una vez! ¿Que no sabes que estamos en territorio enemigo?

JOAQUIN: Orale pues, cool it, ese! You don't gotta make a speech. (*Pause.*) Man, what a trip! You know what? I think I been smoking too much. You din' really say all that, right? Simón, it's all in my head.

BELARMINO: Pos, quién sabe lo que dices, vale.

JOAQUIN: What?

BELARMINO: Que no hable inglés. El totache. Háblame in espanish.

JOAQUIN: Sorry, man, I don' speak it. No hablo español.

BELARMINO: Mendigos pochos. (*Pause.*) Mira, chavo . . . ah, you . . . mexicano, ¿no?

JOAQUIN: Who me? Nel, man, I'm Chicano.

BELARMINO: No seas pendejo.

JOAQUIN: Who you calling a pendejo?!

BELARMINO: You, tú, tú Mexican! ¡Pendejo! Mira, espérate . . . ahhh, you Mexican, me Mexican . . . ahhh, this one familia Mexican, eh? ¡Mingo, no! Mingo es gringo. ¿Comprendes?

JOAQUIN: Heh, yeah, now you talking my language!

BELARMINO: Mingo ees gavacho, ¿eh?

JOAQUIN: Simón, and a t'ief.

BELARMINO: Okay maguey. Now . . . you don' puedes atinar quién soy?

JOAQUIN: Wait a minute man . . . Slower, I can't do what?

BELARMINO: Atinar.

JOAQUIN: Atinar . . . that's *guess*. I can't guess what?

BELARMINO: Quién soy.

JOAQUIN: Who you are. (*Pause.*) Who?

BELARMINO: Pos guess. You have hear . . . el Pueblo de Parral?

JOAQUIN: Parral?

BELARMINO: ¡Chihuahua!

JOAQUIN: Oh, simón. Tha's the town where they kill Pancho Villa and they cut off his . . . (*Pause.*) HEAD.

BELARMINO: Exactamente.

JOAQUIN: Did you ever have a horse?

BELARMINO: Siete Leguas.

JOAQUIN: And a Chivi?

BELARMINO: One Dodge.

JOAQUIN: 1923?

BELARMINO: Simón—yes.

JOAQUIN: (*Pause.*) I don' believe it. You? The head of Pancho . . .

BELARMINO: Belarmino, please! (*Secretively.*) Muchos carefuls. I only trust you. Ees one secret político ¿comprendes?

JOAQUIN: (*Shocked.*) Simón, I don't tell nobody. (*Pause.*) Only the jefita. MAAA! (*He runs out the front door.*)

BELARMINO: OYE! (*Alone.*) ¡Chi . . . huahua! ¡Qué feo no tener cuerpo, verdad de Dios! (PEDRO *is heard in the kitchen, yelling and singing drunkenly.* BELARMINO *feigns sleep.* PEDRO *enters with a wine bottle, and cartridge belts criss-crossed on his chest.*)

PEDRO: (*Sings.*)
"¡Adiós torres de Chihuahua,
Adiós torres de Canteraaa!
Ya vino Francisco Villaaa,
Pa' quitarles la frontera.
Ya llegó Francisco Villa
A devolver la fronteraaa!"

(*Shouts,*) Ay, yai, yai, YAI! I'm home, cabrones. Your padre is home, come out! Come out from your holes! I am home!! (*Pause.*) Where's e'rybody at? (*He goes to* BELARMINO.) Oye, Wake up, loco! (*He pulls* BELARMINO's *hair.*)

BELARMINO: (*Opening his eyes.*) ARRRRGGH! ¡LA CUCARACHAA!

PEDRO: (*Furiously, in case of insult.*) What?

BELARMINO: Cucaracha.

PEDRO: (*Pause.*) You know "Siete Leguas"? (*Sings.*) "Siete Leguas el caballo que Villa más . . ."

BELARMINO: AY, YAI, YAI!

PEDRO: Heh, you do that pretty good, cabrón. (CRUZ *runs in the front door.* JOAQUIN *follows her.*)

CRUZ: Pedro, what are you doing?

PEDRO: I am talking to my son.

CRUZ: Talking? (*She glances at* JOAQUIN.)

JOAQUIN: Din' I tell you? He can talk, huh Pa? (BELARMINO *grunts and spits at* JOAQUIN.) Orale, carnal, take it easy. You can trust the jefitos . . . (BELARMINO *spits, hits* JOAQUIN*'s shirt.*) ¡Un pollo! (*He exits upstairs.*)

CRUZ: It ees true, Pedro, my son talks?

PEDRO: Who? This animal? No, wha's wrong wis you, not even with a gallon of vino. (BELARMINO *laughs idiotically.*) You see? How can this idiota talk? He don' know nothing.

CRUZ: He is still your son, Pedro.

PEDRO: Pos, who knows, ¿verdad? A man almost forty years old which he don' even know his own padre? That is no son. You got this one for you, woman.

CRUZ: Tha's not true, Pedro. He look like you.

PEDRO: Oh yes, the face!

CRUZ: And the hair, the eyes, the mustaches.

PEDRO: CHICKENSQUAT! Those are things a madre notice. A padre he wants a son with a strong back. And arms and legs to help him work! You cheat me, woman. Caray, I will never forget the day Belarmino was born. 1928 and my first son! They run to the field to get me, and when I arrive . . . there you was with the niño in your arms . . . his big eyes looking out, his mouth open . . . with ears, a nose, and mucho hair, everything his madre want. Then I open the blanket: NOTHING. *Nothing for his padre! Dios mío, what a lousy son*!

CRUZ: (*Hurt.*) Yes, lousy, but it hurt me to have him.

PEDRO: Pos, I give him to you then. For your pains. I give 'em all to you. Joaquín, Mingo, Lupe, and the head, for good measure. (JOAQUIN *enters with guitar.*) Anyway, I'm going across the border. My carrilleras and my 30–30 is all I take. Wis that I come, wis that I go.

JOAQUIN: And your guitar, jefito?

PEDRO: You keep it, hijo. Of all my sons, I like you the most, because you're the only one who understand the Revolución. Maybe this guitarrita serve to remind you of your padre . . . when he's dead.

CRUZ: You're crazy, viejo.

PEDRO: Well, you will see. I going back to Zacatecas, to my tierra, to die.

CRUZ: (*Relieved.*) Okay, pues, go die! I don' care. Right now I'm worry about my Lupe. (*She wraps her shawl around her neck.*)

PEDRO: Where you going, to the street again like a crazy loca?

CRUZ: I'm going over to Señora Reyes house. Maybe Chato come back. I don' even know what to think, Dios mío. (*Exits*.)

PEDRO: Stinking vieja.

JOAQUIN: Heh, Pa, can I go to Mexico with you?

PEDRO: For what? You din' come from over theres, you was born heres.

JOAQUIN: So what, maybe I gotta get outta town? I mean the U.S.

PEDRO: Can you ride a horse?

JOAQUIN: No, pero . . .

PEDRO: Or eat chili peppers?

JOAQUIN: No, but . . .

PEDRO: Ah! And tortillas, my son. How to know a good woman by her tortillas. You got to know. One don' buy burro just because she gots long eyelashes.

JOAQUIN: Okay pues, but you know what? I find the head of Pancho Villa.

PEDRO: (*Pause*.) When?

JOAQUIN: Today . . . tonight!

PEDRO: You crazy. How you going to find the head of the general? Pos mira . . . go say it up in the sierra, ¡qué! Where they believe you.

JOAQUIN: You wanna see it?

PEDRO: (*Pause*.) ¿El general?

JOAQUIN: Pancho Villa himself.

PEDRO: You sure ees him? How you know? He don' be in bad shape?

JOAQUIN: He's like new.

PEDRO: (*Lowers his head emotionally*.) I don' believe it . . . after so many years? Just imagine, to rescue the general's head from the hands of the gringos, then to take it back to Mexico con honor! In a big train like the old days! Qué caray, maybe even the Revolución break out again! Maybe they give us a rancho—in Zacatecas. ¡Ay, yai, yai! Think we better be careful, my son. (*Pause*.) Oye, you hide it good? If we lose that head again . . .!

JOAQUIN: Nel, he's here in the house.

PEDRO: Who know about it?

JOAQUIN: Nobody, just me and you, and the general.

PEDRO: General? He's dead.

JOAQUIN: He ain' dead.

PEDRO: What you mean, hombre? They kill him.

JOAQUIN: Not all of him.

PEDRO: Yes, all of him!

JOAQUIN: Nel, he lives. Pancho Villa lives!

PEDRO: (*Pause*.) You chure?

JOAQUIN: Simón, and there he is! (*Points to* BELARMINO.)

PEDRO: (*Scandalized.*) ¡Belarmino! ¡Pos, qué jijos . . .! What you think-ing, baboso? Laughing at your padre?

JOAQUIN: No, jefito! He prove it to you himself. Just give him a chance! (*Goes to* BELARMINO.) Heh, general. ¿General Villa?

PEDRO: (*Pulls his hair.*) Wake up, bruto.

BELARMINO: AARRRAAGGHH!

JOAQUIN: Uh, general, here's one of your Villistas . . . my jefito. You know him already, tell him something, okay? Just a word or two.

BELARMINO: (*Smiles.*) UHHH.

JOAQUIN: He's warming up.

PEDRO: For what, more frijoles? No, Joaquín, this go beyond a joke. I never going to forgive you this.

JOAQUIN: But he's Pancho Villa, 'Apá. He tell me.

PEDRO: What I care what this animal tell you? How he's going to be the great Centauro del Norte? Pancho Villa was a giant, a legend, a big hombre!

JOAQUIN: Simón, and this is a big hombre's head.

PEDRO: CHICKENSQUAT! Not in one thousand years can you compare this chompetita to the head of my general! Men like Pancho Villa ain't born no more, just lousies like this one. And cowards! T'iefs! Useless cabrones! Tha's all I got for sons.

MINGO: (*Standing in the front.*) And we're only chips off the old block, no Pa? (PEDRO *turns toward* MINGO *who is dressed in casual bowling clothes. He also carries a bowling bag.*)

PEDRO: Pos, you tell me. What block you talking about?

MINGO: Skip it. What was the yelling about?

PEDRO: This pachuco . . . lying to his padre.

JOAQUIN: I din' lie, jefito.

PEDRO: Chatap! Pos, this one . . . still at it, hombre? (*To* MINGO.) What you think he was saying, my son? That Belarmino is my Gen-eral Villa! Mira . . . lousy goddamit. (*To* JOAQUIN.) Why don' you be smart like your brother here. He don' go around wis stupid babosadas. He is a serious hombre con respeto y dinero.

JOAQUIN: Orale, cool it pues.

PEDRO: Culo . . . ¿¡a quién le dices culo!? I still haven' die, cabrón. I still the boss in this house.

JOAQUIN: Okay, okay. Keep your house. (*Gets the guitar and heads for the door.*)

PEDRO: Oye, oye, and my guitarra?

JOAQUIN: You give me it. Want it back?

PEDRO: No, for what I want that junk?

JOAQUIN: Here. (*Gives him the guitar*.) I get a new one. Orale, carnal, hand over 75 bolas.

MINGO: Bolas?

JOAQUIN: Bones, maracas, bills, ese.

MINGO: Seventy-five dollars? What the hell for?

JOAQUIN: My cut, ese! I get the workers, you screw 'em, we split the take.

MINGO: You're crazy.

JOAQUIN: Simón, real loco. But I ain't stupid. All the vatos in the barrio go to work for you because I ask 'em.

MINGO: So what? I paid you 50 cents a head for that truckload you round up and that was it.

JOAQUIN: Nel, ese, you din' tell me you was going to burn 'em. Like Chato! Social security, income tax . . . that's a lotta chet, mano. You got itchy fingers too, qué! You pocket them coins yourself.

MINGO: (*Calm.*) Can you prove it?

JOAQUIN: I see you do it!

MINGO: Then call the cops. Go on! Who you think the law's gonna believe, me or you?

JOAQUIN: (*Pause.*) Eh, jefe, you loan me your guitar?

PEDRO: Now you wan' it back, eh? Bueno, take it. (JOAQUIN *grabs the guitar and lifts it to smash it on* MINGO*'s head.*) FOR YOU TO PLAY IT!! (JOAQUIN *stops.*)

JOAQUIN: Don' you see he's cheating us?

PEDRO: I don' see nothing!

JOAQUIN: The general see it!

PEDRO: ¡No qué general ni nada! (JOAQUIN *leaves with the guitar.*) Useless! Huh, as if all people don' be crooked. No hombre, we all looking to see what we scratch up. (*Drinks from his bottle. It is empty.*) Chihuahua, it is finish. Bueno, no matter? Tha's how come we got money—for necessaries. Of all my sons I like you the most— porque tienes inteligencia, hijo, lo juro por los cielos. Andale, my son, let loose one pesito to go for more. But this time we get a big one, eh?

MINGO: No, señor.

PEDRO: Bueno, a small one, pues.

MINGO: No! Don' you understand? There's no money for booze.

PEDRO: Mira, mira, don't play the crooked contractor wis me, eh? I ain' Joaquín. All I ask is for 35 centavitos.

MINGO: I don't give a damn. That money ain't gonna support your habit. I want this family to be decent and that's how it's gonna be.

PEDRO: Oh sí ¿eh? Well, who are you to decide everything? I'm your padre.

MINGO: You're nothing. If it wasn' for me, we'd still be in the gutter, like usual. Confess it. You could never handle Shorty's hunger. You had to drag us all to the fields together with mi'amá. And for what? We still ended up owing the store just to feed the head! That head's a pushover for me. From now on, I'm in charge here and you can do what you damn well please.

PEDRO: (*Pause.*) Pos, I think I damn well please to give you some chingazos well-planted, ¿sabes?

MINGO: If you can. Don' forget I was a Marine.

PEDRO: And I was a Villista!

MINGO: You want me to give you a judo chop?

PEDRO: (*He runs to the door.*) ¡Joaquín! ¡Joaquín! Bring me my guitarra!

MINGO: The guitar? You going to play or fight?

PEDRO: I going to smash it on your head, pendejo!

MINGO: What's the matter, old man? Not so good with your fists anymore? Been picking fruit too long? Come on, gimme a try! This hand only broke a Chink's red neck once. WHACK! Come on, wetback, get a taste of an American fighting man overseas! Come, farm laborer! Greaser! Spic! Nigger! (*Pause.*) ¡GRINGO!

PEDRO: (*The dam breaks.*) ¡VIVA VILLAAAAA! (PEDRO *leaps on* MINGO *and they wrestle.* MINGO *quickly subdues him, giving him a couple of efficient judo chops. He pins him down and sits on him.*)

MINGO: All right, green-carder, you give up?

PEDRO: Cabrón.

MINGO: What?

PEDRO: ¡Cabrón!

MINGO: That's what I thought you said.

PEDRO: ¡Joaquín!

MINGO: Hee ain't coming back, man. You think he wants that guitar smashed? Besides, you ran him out. You better give up. What you say? No hard feelings? Look, I'll even get up. (*He rises.*) Come on, Pete, be a sport. Don't be a bad loser. (*Nudges him with his foot.*) Come on, I don't like to see you sprawled out like that.

PEDRO: Get away, cabrón! Get away!

MINGO: Okay, stay down. I don't give a damn. (*Exists.*)

PEDRO: Now I don't got any sons . . . except Belarmino. He was the first. I like him the most. Besides, he always remind me of Pancho Villa. (*He gets up and removes his cartridge belts.*) Eh, my son? You see this carrilleras? They're from the Revolución. They don' got any bullets, but I give 'em to you, eh? (*He places the belts around* BELARMINO.) Now you look like the general. You remember Pancho Villa? There was a man, a giant . . . he rob the rich to give to the poor. You should have see him when we take Zacatecas. (*He begins to walk around the room imagining the scene he describes.*) All the trains, the smoke, the people climbing all over like lices. (*Laughs.*) Caray, there was nothing like the trains. (*Train whistle in the distance.*) They would gather at the crossings. (*Under his voice: "Marcha de Zacatecas."*) Here comes Pancho Villa, they would say. ¡Ahí viene Pancho Villa! And mi general he would come to the back of the car. ¡VIVA VILLA! ¡VIVA VILLA! Here come Pancho Villa! (*One final war cry.*) ¡A ZACATECAAASS! *The music is like the sound of a train pulling in.* PEDRO *runs out in the direction of the train whistle. The sounds end abruptly and all that remains is the ringing of a small bell at the distant railroad crossing. This fades into the sound of a church bell. Light and sound fade.* BELARMINO *is left illuminated by a single ray of light. He screams, a sorrowful cry of death. Darkness. Curtain.*

SCENE TWO

The front room. Morning. Church bells. A guitar plays "Siete Leguas." A procession in black enters. CRUZ *in mourning,* MINGO *holding her. Then* LUPE *and* CHATO, *carrying* BELARMINO *wrapped in a sarape.*

LUPE: I'll put Belarmino away, Mamá. (*Goes into bedroom.*)
CRUZ: (*Sitting on the couch.*) The señor knows what we shall do now, my sons.
MINGO: Pa was a good guy.
JOAQUIN: You liar!
MINGO: You insulting his memory already? (*Pause.*) I'll let that one go this time.
LUPE: (*Reentering.*) He's asleep.
CRUZ: He was tired, poor man.
MINGO: I don' think we shoulda take him.
CRUZ: It was his padre, my son.
MINGO: He sang "La Cucaracha," din't he? Pa was my Pa too, Ma. I wanted him to have a good quiet funeral. What was the name of that

185

other "bit" you did?

JOAQUIN: "Siete Leguas."

MINGO: What?

JOAQUIN: Seven . . . leaguews. (*He chokes up with grief.*)

CHATO: That's okay, ese, e'rybody like what you did.

LUPE: It was so sad to see them let mi 'Apá down into his grave and all the time Belarmino singing "La Cucaracha." E'rybody think you like it like that, Mamá.

CRUZ: We should have had a wake.

MINGO: You still on that, Ma? The funeral parlor did the job.

CRUZ: They din' let me see him.

MINGO: There was nothing left to see. I mean, what you expect them to do? That train hit him. I'm not even sure it was him when I identified him. Maybe it wasn't. Maybe he went back to Mexico like he always wanted? That's possible.

JOAQUIN: Why don't you shut up!

CRUZ: We should have had a wake! (*She breaks down crying.*)

LUPE: Chato, help me. (LUPE *and* CHATO *take* CRUZ *upstairs, crying.*)

MINGO: Everything's gonna be okay, Ma. You'll see. I ordered him a stone with his name in Spanish, and a saying: "Here lies our Dad, By Angels Guarded . . . " (CRUZ *has gone upstairs.*)

JOAQUIN: Tried to feel sad but only farted. (*Laughs until he cries.*)

MINGO: (*Going over to him, whispering.*) What the hecks the matter with you, Tomahawk? Pa's dead. Don't you appreciate that? (*Pause.*) Heh, are you crying?

JOAQUIN: Lemme alone, ese.

MINGO: Listen, Joaquín, things ain't been the best between us, but maybe we ought to sit down and talk, huh? Man to man? I'm your legal guardian now.

JOAQUIN: What you mean?

MINGO: I'm responsible for you. For the whole family. I wanna help you, Tomahawk.

JOAQUIN: Help me what?

MINGO: Help you. You wanna join the Marines? I'll sign for you. Sure, the service'll make a man outta you. Look what it did for me. How about it?

JOAQUIN: Nel, I awready tried. They don' like my record.

MINGO: That bad, huh? Well, how about night school? (JOAQUIN *makes a face*.) Okay then, come and work with me.

JOAQUIN: I awready worked with you.

MINGO: You still think I cheated your friends?

JOAQUIN: I know it!

MINGO: Boy, that's rich. You know what's wrong with you? You can't imagine anybody making an honest buck. This is a free country, man. There's no law against making money.

JOAQUIN: How about being a Chicano?

MINGO: Is *that* what's eating you?

JOAQUIN: How come we're poor? How come mi jefito die like that?

MINGO: Not because he was a Mexican!

JOAQUIN: You ever have the placa work you over in jail, ese? Rubber hoses on the ribs? Calling you greaser! Mexican bastard!

MINGO: I've never been in jail remember?

JOAQUIN: You're still a greaser.

MINGO: Why, you little punk, don't aim your inferiority complex at me. You're so twisted with hate you can't see straight.

JOAQUIN: Simón, I'm cross-eyed. But you wanna be a gavacho so bad, you can't see nothing. You hated mi 'Apá. You hate all of us! You and your new clothes and bowling ball and shit. Well, take a good look, ese. We're greasy and lousy, but we're your family!

MINGO: Damn rights, my family! But you don't have to be greasy and lousy!

JOAQUIN: You don't have to be a gavacho!

MINGO: Listen, man, there's only one thing I ever wanted in this life. That's not to be poor. I never got that until I become a Marine. Now I want it for the family. Is that so bad? You wanna go on this way, with that stupid head eating and stinking and farting?

JOAQUIN: He's the general!

MINGO: Come off it, buddy. Shorty ain't Pancho Villa. He's nothing but a mouth. I know, I have to feed it.

JOAQUIN: If you ever feed him nothing again, I'll kill you.

MINGO: Okay. But how are you going to feed it? On welfare, like the old man used to do it?

JOAQUIN: You don' even respect mi 'Apá now! When he's dead!

MINGO: That's a damn lie! I loved that old wino.

JOAQUIN: Pinchi buey.

MINGO: What did you call me!!!

JOAQUIN: ¡Pinchi puto desgraciado!

MINGO: You talk to me in English!

JOAQUIN: (*Swings guitar at him.*) FUCK YOU! (*Runs out.*)

MINGO: (*Running to the door.*) You goddamned delinquent! I'd turn you in if Pa wasn' dead today.

Curtain.

ACT FOUR

Six months later. It is winter. The walls of the house are covered with red cockroaches of various sizes. LUPE is studying the walls. Carrying a fly-swatter. She is pregnant, but is nevertheless knocking down cockroaches energetically and capturing them in her apron. BELARMINO is on top of an old, broken-down TV set. His eyes are wide open, following every move that LUPE makes. The door to the side bedroom is new and has "Private" painted on it in big black letters.

LUPE: Cucarachas . . . big fat cucarachas. There's one! (*She knocks it down.*) Gee man, this is a big one!

BELARMINO: NARRH!

LUPE: No, you pig! This is mine and I'm gonna eat it by myself.

BELARMINO: NAAARRRRGGGH!

LUPE: ¡Pediche! You ain't hungry. You just don' want me to have it, huh? Well, now you going to have to eat it! And I hope you choke! (*She crams it into* BELARMINO's *mouth.*)

CRUZ: (*In the kitchen.*) Guadalupe?

LUPE: ¿Sí, Mamá? (*She backs away from* BELARMINO.)

CRUZ: (*Enters.*) Did Belarmino shout? (BELARMINO *spits out the cockroach.*) ¡Una cucaracha!

LUPE: It's not my fault, man. I can't watch him all the time.

CRUZ: Ay, little woman. Go bring the tortillas.

LUPE: There's no more.

CRUZ: And the dozen there was?

LUPE: I ate 'em. (*Pause.*) Well, what you want? I was hungry! Besides, there's plenty of food there—bread, steaks, milk, eggs, orange juice.

CRUZ: It all belong to Mingo.

LUPE: Sure, pure American food. Well, what about us? Are we suppose to eat cucarachas? (*Angry.*)

CRUZ: No! Now stop this foolishness and go make tortillas, ándale.

LUPE: Tortillas . . . I should work in a taco bar. (*Exits, angry.*)

CRUZ: (*Loud voice.*) And don' touch Mingo's food! (BELARMINO *growls.*) Sí, my son, I know. She coming with your frijolitos. You mus' be very hungry, no? You have eat nothing for days. (*Pause.*) Here. Eat one little cucaracha, eh? But don' spit out the shell. I don't want your sister to know. Here.

MINGO: (*In the kitchen.*) Aha, I caught you!

CRUZ: ¡Mingo! (*She turns, searching for him. Noises come from the* kitchen. *A chair falls, a glass breaks. We hear the voices of* MINGO *and* LUPE, *arguing.*)

MINGO: Drinking my orange juice, eh? What you eating?

LUPE: None of your business!

MINGO: What's that?

LUPE: Give 'em back!

MINGO: You crazy?

LUPE: Gimme 'em back!

MINGO: Oh no, sister, we're going to see Ma.

LUPE: No, Mingo, please—ay!

MINGO: Shut up! (MINGO *comes in from the kitchen, pushing* LUPE *in front with her arm twisted behind her back.* MINGO *is dressed in fashionable casual clothing.*) Heh, Ma, you know what this pig was eating?

CRUZ: (*Resigned.*) Cucarachas.

MINGO: How do you know?

CRUZ: What's wrong with you, woman? You want to kill that child you carry? You going to be a madre.

LUPE: I'm not either. I don' got no baby. Only a belly full of cockaroaches! And I'm still hungry. We never have any meat in this house! (*Exits.*)

MINGO: (*Shouting after her.*) Meat? Well, tell your Chatito to get a goddamn job! How d'yuh like that? What's her husband for? Just to keep her pregnant? Tell the bum to go to work.

CRUZ: It is winter, Mingo. There's no work in the fields.

MINGO: Then to the breadlines, lady. The welfare department. Anyway, that's all they know.

BELARMINO: (*With rage.*) ARRRRRGGGGGGH!

MINGO: Heh!

CRUZ: Belarmino, behave.

MINGO: (BELARMINO *stares at him with hate.*) Look at him, señora, look! He's enraged! Well, now I seen everything. This freak getting insulted. (BELARMINO *growls with rage..*)

CRUZ: My son, calm down!

MINGO: Let him blow his top. He can't do nothing, anyway. Maybe he's been eating my food, too, no Ma? You sure you ain't slip him one of my T.V. dinners?

CRUZ: No, Mingo, your poor brother he haven' eat nothing in four days.

MINGO: So what?

CRUZ: Look how skinny he is. He's shrinking on me, and he still don' wanna eat nothing.

MINGO: Maybe he knows something I know.

CRUZ: (*Suspiciously.*) What?

MINGO: (*Calmly, deliberately.*) That he ain't got no guts.

CRUZ: (*Alarmed.*) Don' say that!

MINGO: It's a fact.

CRUZ: No!

MINGO: Look at him!

CRUZ: He's sick.

MINGO: (*With meaning.*) He ain't got a body, señora. (CRUZ *stares at him unbelievingly.*) Let's face it, okay? He's a head. (CRUZ *turns away shaking her head.*) You gotta accept it, Ma. Shorty's a head and that's it.

CRUZ: No!

MINGO: (*Angered.*) Then, where's all the food going that he's eating? I become a contractor to make more money, but each week that I make more, he eat more. Last week it was $127. By himself! Beans and tortillas!! He blew my whole check. (BELARMINO *laughs.*) Shut up!

BELARMINO: ARRGGH!

MINGO: All these years we been poor and stinkin', working the fields, for what? To stuff his fat belly which he don't even got! What kinda stupid, useless life is that? I don't wanna end up like Dad. I wanna get outta this slum!

CRUZ: Por favor, Mingo, no more.

MINGO: Look, Ma, I wanna help you. I'll even let Lupe and Chato freeload on us for the winter, if you do one thing.

CRUZ: What?

MINGO: Stop wasting money on beans and tortillas. Admit Shorty's a head.

CRUZ: No!

MINGO: Ma, it's nothing but dumb pride. Be realistic. Be practical.

CRUZ: (*Determined.*) My son is not a head!

MINGO: (*Pause.*) Okay, suit yourself. Just don't expect me to pay the bills at the store no more. (*Adds quickly.*) But don't worry, I'm still gonna help the family—with my example. See that little red sports car in front of the house? It's mine.

CRUZ: Yours?

MINGO: I trade it in for my Chivi. I also took 200 bucks outta the bank and bought new clothes. See? Everything new. You should see how great it feels! Instead of the head, I'm spending money where it counts: on self-improvement. And with my credit, I can get anything else I want. Thirty dollar shoes, color T.V., a Hi-Fi stereo, a new bowling ball, steak dinners, cocktails! I can even go to college. Sure, State College! The G.I. Bill will foot the bill. Heh, you get that? G.I. Bill foot the bill? I know it's below your mental intelligence to comprehend the simplicity . . . (*During his speech* MINGO*'s voice changes from a Chicano accent to the nasal tones of an Anglo; he also begins to talk down his nose at his mother.*)

CRUZ: ¡M'ijo!

MINGO: (*Coming to his senses.*) ¿Qué?

CRUZ: What about us?

MINGO: Well . . . hustle! Din't Joaquín go to work?

CRUZ: He say he have little jobs to do.

MINGO: What little jobs?

CRUZ: I don' know.

MINGO: What about mi 'Apá? He can still work. Where is he, boozing again?

CRUZ: (*With fearful surprise.*) ¡Tu padre está muerto!

MINGO: ¿Muerto? Dead? (*Laughs.*) You're kidding.

CRUZ: For six months. That train kill him. (*She crosses herself.*) But . . . how did you forget? Wha's happen to you, Mingo?

MINGO: Six months?

JOAQUIN: (*Outside the house.*) ¡Viva mi jefito! (*Shouts of Viva.*) ¡Viva Pancho Villa! (*More Vivas.*)

BELARMINO: ¡AY, YAI, YAI, YAI, YAI! (*Outside the house we hear the music of a band. Drums and trumpets sound with revolutionary enthusiasm.*)

MINGO: What the hell's that? (*Goes to the front door.*)

CRUZ: Mariachis.

MINGO: The hell, it's a pachuco band.

CRUZ: No, ees a Charro. It's . . . Joaquín!! And Chato!

A police siren sounds in the distance. There is immediate confusion outside. "En la madre, the fuss!" "Le's go!" "No, don' run!" etc. Various voices, besides the voice of JOAQUIN *and* CHATO, *indicate there is a small group of young men outside, which now breaks out running in all directions.* CHATO *runs in, frightened, dressed in huarache sandals and white Mexican peasant clothing. He wears a straw hat, and carries a drum and a trumpet. He enters tripping over his feet, making noise, trying to hide.*

CRUZ: Chato, hombre, wha's happen?

CHATO: The placa!

MINGO: The police? What did you do?

CHATO: I din' do nothing!

JOAQUIN: (*Outside.*) Open the door, sergeant!

CRUZ: Joaquín!

JOAQUIN: (*Still outside.*) Sergeant, the door!

MINGO: How come you're dressed like that? You look like a peon.

JOAQUIN: (*Still outside.*) ¡CHATO!

CHATO: Yes, my general! (*He opens the door.*)

JOAQUIN: It's about time, *corporal!* (JOAQUIN *enters dressed in the traditional costume of the Mexican charro, complete with a pair of cartridge belts crisscrossed on his chest. Hanging from one shoulder on a strap, he carries a 30–30 carbine. On his shoulders he carries two big sacks, one on each side.*) Here you are, jefita. (*He lowers the sacks.*) One hundred pounds of flour . . . and a hundred pounds of beans, like I promised you.

MINGO: Where did you get this?

JOAQUIN: I'm sorry, I don' speak gavacho.

MINGO: Don't act stupid, where did you get these sacks? You swipe 'em, huh?

JOAQUIN: (*Ignores him.*) And this is for you, jefita. (*From his jacket he pulls out a beautiful white rebozo—a shawl.*)

CRUZ: Where did you got this, hijo?

MINGO: He swipe 'em, don' I tell you, señora? (*He grabs* JOAQUIN *by one arm.*) You going to have to return them!

JOAQUIN: 'Tas lucas, gringo.

MINGO: ¿Gringo?

JOAQUIN: Mingo el gringo.

BELARMINO: (*Joyfully.*) ¡AY, YAI, YAI, YAI!

JOAQUIN: VIVA VILLA! (*To* BELARMINO.) And this is for you, mi general. A box of cigars. (*He offers him one.*) You wan' one! (BELARMINO *smiles, grunts affirmatively.*) Orale, pues.

CRUZ: No, Joaquín, your brother don' smoke.

BELARMINO: (*Growling.*) ARRGH!

CRUZ: (*Backs up.*) Ay, Dios.

JOAQUIN: At your orders, mi general. (*Gives him a cigar.*) Qué le haga buen provecho y qué . . . (*Pause.*) Corporal, a match! (*Chato comes forward with a match.*) ¡Qué viva la Revolución! (BELARMINO *smokes contentedly, making a lot of smoke.*)

MINGO: I don't believe it. (*Laughs.*) So this is the general, eh? Who the hell do you think you are? The Cisco Kid and Pancho?

CHATO: No, He's Pancho. (*Points to* BELARMINO.)

MINGO: You lousy clown! I oughta call the cops right now.

CRUZ: No, Mingo.

MINGO: Don't worry, señora. The cops are already after 'em. I bet they even end up in jail tonight. For thiefs!

JOAQUIN: And you? You're the one that oughta be in jail for cheating the jefitos, the family, La Raza! You pinchi sell-out traitor!

CRUZ: Joaquín!

MINGO: No, no señora. Let him spill the beans.

JOAQUIN: We rob the rich to give to the poor, like Pancho Villa! But you . . .

MINGO: I worked to fill all of your stinking bellies! Especially your beloved general there. I got tired of stuffing his guts with . . .

JOAQUIN: What guts?

MINGO: (*Pause.*) I won't argue that.

JOAQUIN: Simón, because he don' got any. He's a head and tha's all.

CRUZ: No, head, no

JOAQUIN: The head of Francisco Villa! ¿No, mi general?

BELARMINO: (*Triumphantly.*) ¡AY, YAI, YAI!

LUPE: (*Entering.*) ¡Ay! (*She doubles up with pain.*) ¡Ay, Mamá!

CHATO: Mi honey! (*He goes to her side.*)

CRUZ: Lupe, wha's wrong?

MINGO: It's the cockaroaches she ate.

LUPE: ¡Ay! Ay, Mamá, help me.

CRUZ: Sí, m'ijita. Diosito santo, maybe she's going to have the baby?

CHATO: Baby?

CRUZ: Sí, hombre, your son. Help me with her.

CHATO: Heh, ese, I going to have a son.

CRUZ: Joaquín, no you . . . Mingo! Go call the doctor!

JOAQUIN: Nel, jefita. I'll go!

MINGO: Not dressed like that! I'll go!

JOAQUIN: Dressed like what?!

MINGO: Like a stinking Mexican!

JOAQUIN: You dirty cabrón, I'm proud to be a stinking Mexican! You're dress like a gavacho! Through and through!

MINGO: You're the one that's through, Mex! You can't even bring a sack of beans home without stealing it!

JOAQUIN: Simón, but I swipe from the supermarket, not the poor! It's no crime to be a thief if you steal from thiefs!

MINGO: Who told you that?

CRUZ: (*Entering.*) ¡Mingo, pronto! Go bring the doctor! Your sister . . .

JOAQUIN: Who you think? The one and only who knows. And that ain't all! He also tell me that he wasn' hungry for food all this time. He was hungry for justice!

MINGO: (*Laughs*.) Justice?

JOAQUIN: Social justice!

CRUZ: ¡M'ijos!

MINGO: What social, stupid? You don' even know what the word means!

JOAQUIN: That's what you think, but we've had it wis your bones, ese! We're going to get rid of all the gavacho blood-suckers like you. The contractors, the judges, the cops, the stores!

MINGO: Bandit!

JOAQUIN: Simón, like Pancho Villa!

MINGO: You want me to give you a judo chop?

JOAQUIN: ¡Pos ponte, ese!

CRUZ: Hijos, por favor . . .

MINGO: Greasy, low, ignorant, lousy . . .

JOAQUIN: ¡Viva la Raza! (*They start to fight*.)

CRUZ: ¡HIJOS DE SU CHINGADA MADRE! (CRUZ *is holding the 30–30 carbine*.)

MINGO: Ma!

CRUZ: Shut up! Now you going to calm down and sit down like hombrecitos or I pump holes in you! (*Ferociously*.) Okay, MARCH! (*She pushes them toward the sofa, with the carbine*.) Caramba, if you want to fight like dogs, tha's how they going to treat you.

MINGO: But I din't.

JOAQUIN: Yo no hice . . .

CRUZ: ¡Silencio! (JOAQUIN *and* MINGO *sit on the sofa*.) Now you, Mingo, you goin' for the doctor, and bring him here, understand? Don' make me beg you again. And you, Joaquín. You goin' to take off that crazy clothes and you going to return everything you steal.

JOAQUIN: For what? So the fuzz can get me? Nel, jefita, I'm sorry. I rather go to the mountains and take the general with me. My jefito rode with Pancho Villa, now it's my turn!

CRUZ: NO!

JOAQUIN: Simón, ¡Viva la Revolución!

CRUZ: No, I tell you! Ees time you know . . . . your padre never was in the Revolución.

JOAQUIN: Chale.

CRUZ: He was in Arizona all those years, working in the mines. For the gringos.

JOAQUIN: Aaah, tha's a lotta chet. And the scar he have here in the neck, from the bullet?

CRUZ: Belarmino bite him there before you was born.

JOAQUIN: (*Desperate.*) And this cartridge belts? And this 30–30? You going to tell me they're not from the Revolución?

CRUZ: No, because they are.

JOAQUIN: Okay, then, mi 'apá use them. Who else could have use them?

CRUZ: (*Pause.*) I use them, Joaquín! (JOAQUIN *and* MINGO *are shocked.*) Sí, mis hijos, your madre rode with Pancho Villa! And tha's how I'm certain Belarmino ees not the general. (*Someone knocks at the door rudely. Silence, another knock.*)

POLICE: (*Outside.*) Okay, I know you're in there! Open up!

JOAQUIN: (*Runs to the window.*) ¡La jura!

MINGO: The cops! Din't I tell you, señora? They're looking for him!

CRUZ: ¡Ay Dios! My son, pronto, hide. (*She puts the sombrero over* BELARMINO.)

MINGO: No, Ma! How can you tell him to hide? It's the law! (*He peeks out the window.*) For Pete's sake, this is embarrassing. All the neighbors are watching.

POLICE: (*Knocking furiously.*) OPEN UP IN THE NAME OF THE LAW, GODDAMMIT!

CRUZ: Mingo, do something.

JOAQUIN: Don' ask nothing from that sonavavichi, jefita. (*More knocks.*) Open the door!

CRUZ: No, Joaquín, they get you. (*More strong knocks, then the sound of glass and wood breaking.*) ¡Ay Dios!

POLICE: (*Entering with his club.*) What the hell's going on here? (*The* POLICEMAN *is dressed in a uniform that half resembles a highway patrolman's and half, a soldier's. He wears a helmet with the letters "MP" printed in black. As soon as he barges in,* JOAQUIN *takes the carbine from* CRUZ.)

JOAQUIN: (*Lifting the rifle.*) Put your stinking gavacho hands up!

CRUZ: ¡Joaquín!

JOAQUIN: (*The* POLICEMAN *goes for his gun.*) Ah! Don't try it, man! I fill you full of holes!

POLICE: You're gonna regret this, boy.

JOAQUIN: Tha's what you think, man. (*He takes the officer's gun.*) Heh, wait a minute. Wha's that on your hat . . . MP? Ain't you a city cop?

POLICE: What's the difference? You pachuco no le gusta mucho los cops, right? Maybe it's Military Police—maybe its Mexican Patrol. We're looking for a couple of suspects. Supermarket thieves. "El Ladrón de los Supermercados."

CRUZ: ¿Ladrón? Ay no, forgive him, señor! He's a good boy. Him and Chato din' do nothing.

POLICE: Who's Chato?

CHATO: (*Entering the room.*) Heh, Doña Cruz, my wife is very . . . (*Sees the officer.*) . . . lonely! (*He exits.*)

POLICE: Heh!

JOAQUIN: Ah, ah! Cool it, gringo!

POLICE: You cholos are in mucho hot water, you savvy that? When did you swipe the car outside?

JOAQUIN: What car?

POLICE: The red sports car!

MINGO: (*Entering from his room.*) Sports car? Oh, no officer, that's my car!

POLICE: Who the hell are you?

MINGO: (*Pause.*) NOBODY! I don't have nothing to do with these people. I just room here. I'm a college student.

CRUZ: Tell him, Mingo, explain . . . you got the words.

MINGO: What my landlady here means, officer, is that the punk you want is right there. He's the Supermarket Thief.

JOAQUIN: Simón, ees me! But so what, you can't do nothing! Maybe the Revolución break out right now. What you say, General? We go to the mountains?

BELARMINO: ¡AY, YAI, YAI, YAI!

POLICE: Now what?

JOAQUIN: ¡Pancho Villa!

POLICE: What the hell's going on in this place?

JOAQUIN: I'm going to blow you to pieces, that's what. One side, jefita!

CRUZ: Oh, Joaquín, that carabina don' shoot. It don' got bullets.

MINGO: It's not loaded.

POLICE: Not loaded?! (*He tries to jump JOAQUIN.*)

CRUZ: NO! (*She steps in front of the officer.*) Por favor, señor, don' take him.

POLICE: Get outta my way, lady!

MINGO: Get away, landlady!

JOAQUIN: Hold 'em there, jefita! (JOAQUIN *pulls gun. He runs to* BELARMINO.)

CRUZ: Joaquín, what you doin'?

JOAQUIN: I'm going to the mountains with my general!

CRUZ: No, hijo, you drop him! (MINGO *knocks down* JOAQUIN*'s gun.*)

JOAQUIN: ¡VIVA LA REVOLUCION!

POLICE: Why you little son of a . . .

CRUZ: JOAQUIN!

MINGO: I'll help you get him, officer!

POLICE: (*Chasing* JOAQUIN.) I warn you, punk! It'll go worse for you resisting arrest! (*Everyone chases* JOAQUIN *around the room, trying to catch him and* BELARMINO. CHATO *peeks in.*)

CHATO: Heh, ese, throw it over here! Over here! (JOAQUIN *throws* BELARMINO *like a ball.*)

MINGO: Stay out of this, Chato!

CHATO: (*To* JOAQUIN.) Run, ese, run!

JOAQUIN: Not wisout the general!

CRUZ: Gimme him, Chato!

JOAQUIN: Throw it back, ese! (CHATO *throws* BELARMINO *back to* JOAQUIN, *but* CRUZ *catches him. The police officer nabs* JOAQUIN. CRUZ *takes* BELARMINO *back to the TV set and examines him. In a corner of the room, the officer beats* JOAQUIN.)

CHATO: ¡Orale, watcha eso! (*The officer pulls out handcuffs.*)

CRUZ: No! Not those, señor! (*She goes to* JOAQUIN, *leaving* BELARMINO *on top of the T.V. set.*) Por favor, he's my son, señor! ¡M'ijo!

POLICE: Sorry, lady, I'm only doing my job. (JOAQUIN *resists and the officer beats the sadistic hell out of him.*) It's only my job.

CRUZ: (*Embracing* JOAQUIN.) ¡Hijo, m'ijo!

POLICE: Lady, I . . . (*Tries to pull her away.*)

JOAQUIN: Leave her alone!

POLICE: Shut your mouth, boy! (*He pulls* CRUZ *away.*) All right, señora.

CRUZ: ¡Joaquín!

JOAQUIN: (*Blood on his nose.*) Don' worry, jefita. I ain' scared of 'em. You'll see. I going to return with 50,000 vatos on horses and Chivis! Lemme go, huh? (CRUZ *silently makes the sign of the cross on* JOAQUIN'*s forehead with her thumb.*)

POLICE: Okay, boy, let's go!

MINGO: Here's your gun, officer.

POLICE: That's okay, boy. Just put it in my holster.

JOAQUIN: I'm coming back, jefita! I'm coming back! ¡VIVA VIL-LAAAAAA!

CRUZ: ¡Joaquín! Joaquín, my son!! (*She weeps at the front door. Silence.* MINGO *approaches* CRUZ.)

MINGO: (*Pointing to* BELARMINO.) Look, señora, there's your son.

CHATO: ¿Hijo? ¡Hijo de su! Lupe's gonna have my son! We need a doctor! Orale, brother-in-law, loan me your sports car to go fast. Ees for your carnala.

MINGO: What are you talking about?

CHATO: Tu sister, Lupe.

MINGO: I don't have a sister.

CHATO: ¡La negra!

MINGO: ¿Negra? Not my sister, boy. You trying to be funny? I just room here.

BELARMINO: ¡DESGRACIADO!

MINGO: Who said that?

CHATO: Not me.

BELARMINO: ¡TRAIDOR A TU RAZA!

CRUZ: Ees Belarmino. He's talking!

MINGO: What did he say?

BELARMINO: ¡LAMBISCON!

MINGO: Obscenity, obscenity.

BELARMINO: ¡CABRON!

CRUZ: ¡Ay Dios! (*Crosses herself.*) Belarmino, don' say that!

BELARMINO: ¡PENDEJO!

CRUZ: ¡Ay Dios! (*Crosses herself.*)

MINGO: I'll shut him up! (*He approaches* BELARMINO.)

BELARMINO: ¡BABOSO!

CRUZ: ¡Ay Dios, mi Chorti! (*She approaches* BELARMINO.)

BELARMINO: ¡SINVERGUENZA!

CRUZ: Ees the devil!

CHATO: Nel, ees the general!

MINGO: I'll fix this general!

BELARMINO: AARRRGGHH! (*He bites* MINGO.)

CRUZ: Dios. (*Crosses herself.*)

BELARMINO: (*Getting up steam.*) AMERICANIZADO, DE-SECHADO, DESARRAIGADO, DESVERGONZADO, INTERE-SADO, TAPADO . . .

CHATO: Go, go, General!

BELARMINO: ¡AGARRADO, EMPAPADO, FIJADO, MALHA-BLADO, TROPEZADO, AHOGADO, CHIFLADO!

MINGO: Shut up! Shut up! Speak English! (CHATO *whistles.*)

CRUZ: Chato, don' do that, por Dios! Go bring the doctor! And a priest!

CHATO: Priest?

CRUZ: Tell him to bring Holy Water! Andale, run! (CHATO *exits.*)

BELARMINO: ¡NI SABES QUIEN SOY! ¡NI SABES QUIEN SOY!

MINGO: Speak English! Speak English!

BELARMINO: ¡PANCHO VILLA!

MINGO: SPEAK ENGLISH! (*Goes on repeating.*) SPEAK ENGLISH!

SPEAK ENGLISH! SPEAK ENGLISH! SPEAK ENGLISH!
BELARMINO: (*Simultaneously with* MINGO.) ¡PANCHO VILLA, PANCHO VILLA, PANCHO VILLA, PANCHO VILLA!
CRUZ: (*Simultaneously, kneeling, crossing herself hysterically.*) ¡¡DIOS, DIOS, DIOS, DIOS, DIOS, DIOS, DIOS, DIOS!!

Curtain

ACT FIVE

Two years later. A Winter night. The walls of the house are still covered with cockroaches. Some of them have grown to a tremendous size. CRUZ *is sitting on the sofa with* BELARMINO *to her side. A kerosene heater is nearby flickering with a weak, useless flame and heating absolutely nothing. Everything looks more run down than ever.*

CRUZ: (*Singing sadly.*)
    Adiós torres de Chihuahua
    Adiós torres de Cantera
    Ya vino Francisco Villa
    Pa' quitarles la frontera
    Ya llegó Francisco Villa
    A devolver la frontera.
(BELARMINO *is snoring.*) Ay, my little Chorti. What a good hombre you are. I would not be sorprise if some of these days the Señor he give you a big body for being so good, no? Not a little body but a great big body with arms and legs strong like a macho. Tha's how Pedro always want you to be. May God keep him in peace. (*Crosses herself. We hear a terrible cry more animal than human coming from the kitchen.* CRUZ *rises and calls.*) Guadalupe, what you doing to the niña? (*More cries.*) ¡Lupe! (*The cries stop.*) Don' you know how to feed her yet? (*Lupe enters with a small bundle. She looks like* CRUZ *in hair style and dress, having taken on the role of a mother.*)
LUPE: How can I feed him? He bit the nipple on the bottle and ate it. Look, he's all cover with bean soup.
CRUZ: What is she shewing?
LUPE: A cucaracha. (*Pause.*) Oh, don' look at me like that, man. He like 'em. At least I peel off the shell first.
CRUZ: Qué muchacha. What kind of little mother you be, eh? You want

to kill her?

LUPE: He's not a her, Mamá!

CRUZ: How you know? He don' get mustaches. His uncle Chorti was born wis mustaches.

LUPE: I don' care. I know. I'm his madre.

BELARMINO: (*In his sleep.*) La tuya.

LUPE: There he goes again, man.

CRUZ: He's sleeping.

BELARMINO: (*Dreaming.*) Señores, I am Francisco Villa.

LUPE: See? He's dreaming just like mi 'Apá used to do it.

BELARMINO: ¡Pancho Villa!

CRUZ: My son?

LUPE: Why don' you pull his leg. (*Laughs.*)

CRUZ: You chattap. You think your son gots so much?

BELARMINO: I am Pancho Villa.

CRUZ: No, my son, you're Belarmino.

BELARMINO: ¡VIVA VILLA!

LUPE: Shut him up, man! He's scaring my baby. Pull his ear!

BELARMINO: VIVA PANCHO VI . . . (CRUZ *pulls his ear.*) ¡YAH-aay jijos! Who pull my ear?

CRUZ: I do it, my son. You was having a bad dream.

LUPE: And it gets worser every day. Look like that's all you learn to talk for. I'm Pancho Villa! ¡Pancho Villa!

BELARMINO: I also talk something else, babosa jija de la . . .

LUPE: Ah ah. Speak English. Without English there's no welfare.

BELARMINO: How I'd like to keek your butt.

LUPE: Well, try it . . . Shorty! (*Laughs.*)

CRUZ: Stop it, negra. You shoulda have more respect for your older brother. Since Mingo leave and Joaquín's in jail, he's the man of the house.

LUPE: The head of the house.

BELARMINO: Shattap! Your madre's right. I'm in charge.

LUPE: Of what? Starvation?

CRUZ: (*Sighs.*) If Mingo was here, we wouldn't have to worry about nothing. He always work so hard.

BELARMINO: Chure, on us! Forget Mingo, señora. Mingo go away forever. I'm here and I take care of you now. Just wait till the Revolución.

LUPE: What Revolución? What we need is welfare so we can eat.

CRUZ: I only pray to Dios Nuestro Señor that Joaquín come back from jail serious . . . Ready to marry and settle down and support a family.

BELARMINO: Sí, like *our* family, for one ejemplo, no? ¡Huevonas! I know what you up to. You itching for Joaquin to come so he can support you! Well, what happen to all that pedo about welfare? We got a right to it. I'm disable.

CRUZ: They want to come to investigate first.

BELARMINO: To investigate? Wha's that?

LUPE: They wanna see how come you don' get a job.

BELARMINO: Huy, pos let 'em come. I don' hide nothing.

LUPE: You got nothing to hide.

BELARMINO: (*An angry burst.*) Tú ya me estás cayendo gordo, ¿sabes? ¡Vale más que te calles el hocico! ¡Yo mando en esta casa y me tienes que guardar respeto! ¡Malcriada, Pendeja, Malhablada!!! (*Pause.*) Chihuahua, what a relief. There's nothing like saying what you got to say in Spanish. Like chili in the beans. But I say the same thing in English if you push me, eh? You goddamit!

LUPE: Ay, okay pues. Don' bite me.

BELARMINO: Well, don' come too close. Ma? What time is Joaquín coming from the jail?

CRUZ: I don' know, my son. I'm worry already. Chato go to get him this morning and ees already night. (*There is a knock at the door.*) ¡Ay! Maybe tha's him?

LUPE: No, I bet it's the welfare man.

CRUZ: No, ees my son. I feel it's Joaquín.

LUPE: No, señora, why should Joaquín knock? He lives here.

CRUZ: But maybe he's . . .

BELARMINO: Bueno pues, don' just argue. Open the door!

CRUZ: (*Hesitant.*) Ay Dios. You open it, Lupe . . . I can't do it.

LUPE: (*Opens the door.*) There's nobody.

CRUZ: Nobody? (*She goes to the door.*)

BELARMINO: Look outside, maybe he's outside! Stinking viejas! If I had your legs I would have already run around the house. You don' see nobody?

CRUZ: Nothing. I wonder who it is? (LUPE *crosses the door.*)

CHATO: (*Outside.*) Orale, don' close it! I'm coming!

LUPE: It's Chato! (CHATO *enters, dressed in* PEDRO*'s old clothes. He has a mustache now, and in appearance and behavior he has begun to resemble* PEDRO.) What a joke you trying to pull, hombre? Knocking at the door.

CHATO: What door? ¡Vieja sonsa! I din' knock.

BELARMINO: Where's Joaquín?

CRUZ: Yes, Chato. Where's my son? (CHATO *says nothing.*)

BELARMINO: Well talk, hombre!

CHATO: I din' find him.

CRUZ: What?

CHATO: I went to the prison door and wait, but he din' come out.

CRUZ: Ay no, my poor son! They din' let him come out!

LUPE: Din' I tell you? He haven' change. He do something and they take away his parole.

CHATO: They din' neither! I ask 'em. They let him out today.

BELARMINO: Then where's he at? Baboso, maybe you miss him.

CHATO: Nel, I notice good all the vatos that come out. Joaquín wasn't nobody of 'em. I mean . . . nobody look like Joaquín.

BELARMINO: ¡Me lleva . . . ! What you think Joaquín look like? Like Joaquín! A muchacho wis arms and legs! Did you look good by the road? Maybe he come walking?

CHATO: Nel, I look up and down. I even run outta gas and have to leave my carrucha by the road. I din' have even enough to buy a gallon of gas. (*Pause.*) Don' worry, Doña Cruz. Maybe Joaquín come in the bus or something. He'll come today. (*Pause.*) What about here? Did the welfare vato come? (*There is another knock at the door.*)

CRUZ: Ees my son! (*She goes to the door and opens it.*)

BELARMINO: Ees him? (*Pause.*) How do he look? ¡No la jodan pues! Tell me who is it?

CRUZ: Ees nobody. (*She closes the door. There is another knock at the door. Stronger this time.*)

BELARMINO: ¡Epale! They knocking over here, señora! (CHATO *opens the door to the side room,* "MINGO's room". MINGO *is standing in the doorway. He is dressed in a professional gray suit and is carrying a briefcase. He wears a smart hat and glasses, shoes shined, etc. His face is unusually pale: in fact, it almost looks bleached.*

MINGO: Good evening. Is this the home of Mr. Belarmine?

LUPE: Who?

MINGO: Belarmine, I believe it is?

LUPE: Oh, you mean Belarmino!

BELARMINO: Abusada, raza, es el vato de la welfare.

LUPE: Yes, this is the home of Mr. Belarmino. Come in please.

MINGO: (*With an Anglo accent.*) Muchas gracias. (*Enters, takes off his hat.*)

CRUZ: (*Approaching* MINGO, *awed.*) Mingo? My son, my Domingo! (*She leaps at him and hugs him.*) You come home!

MINGO: I beg your pardon!

LUPE: (*Trying to pull* CRUZ *away.*)Mamá! Please! This gentleman isn't Mingo! Mingo's gone! (CRUZ *backs up.*) This is my mother, please excuse her. She thinks you're my brother who went away.

CRUZ: (*Touching* MINGO's *face.*) ¿Cómo te llamas?

MINGO: (*Pause.*) Mi nombre is Sunday, señora.

LUPE: You speak Spanish?

MINGO: Un poquito. It's part of my job.

LUPE: You see, Ma? He's call Sunday, not Domingo. Let him talk with Belarmino.

MINGO: Gracias, let me see . . . Usted es Mr. Belarmine?

CHATO: No, him.

MINGO: Him?

BELARMINO: Quihubole, chavo.

MINGO: Mucho gusto. I have here your application to receive county welfare aid, and oh, do you speak English?

BELARMINO: Oh yes, more better than a gringo.

LUPE: ¡Belo!

MINGO: Ha, ha. It's okay, I don't mind. It may surprise you to know that I'm Mexican-American and fully aware of the sympathies of the culturally deprived. Now Mr. Belarmine, all we want and need before your case goes through is a few personal facts about yourself for our records. ¿Me entiende?

BELARMINO: (*Nods.*) Pícale a la burra.

MINGO: Well, for example. You've applied for our disability coverage, so we need to know who you sleep with.

BELARMINO: ¿Qué?

MINGO: Do you sleep alone?

BELARMINO: None of you bis'ness! Pos mira . . . sonavavichi!

LUPE: Belo!

MINGO: I'm sorry, but we need to know.

CRUZ: He sleep with me.

MINGO: Oh yeah? And where's your husband, señora?

BELARMINO: Está muerto.

MINGO: Let her answer please!

CRUZ: He is dead.

MINGO: Well, I don't mean to question your traditional moral values, but don't you think it's wrong just to shack up with this fellow? You're both old enough to know better. Why don't you get married?

CRUZ: Because he's my son!

MINGO: Oh. Oh!

BELARMINO: Cochino.

MINGO: Well, what kind of disability do you have?

BELARMINO: Pos take a good look.

MINGO: (*Pause.*) Hmm. You did have a rather serious accident, didn't you? Have you tried to find any work at all?

BELARMINO: Doing what, being a fútbol?

MINGO: Do you have any stocks or bonds or private property?

BELARMINO: Huuuy.

MINGO: Well?

BELARMINO: Nothing, nada, ni madre!

MINGO: Good. I guess that does it. We have your application with all other facts and with this, we'll be able to push your case through. But there's just one more thing.

BELARMINO: Pues sí, there's always just one more thing.

MINGO: I would suggest you get a haircut.

BELARMINO: Haircut?

MINGO: A crewcut.

CRUZ: No! No, señor, please. Not his hair! When he was born like he is, I promise the Virgin never to cut his hair if she let him live.

MINGO: Oh, I see. An old supersti—religion, huh? Well, I was only thinking of your health. I know it's hard in these barrios to keep the city clean, but we gotta give it that old 100% try, know what I mean? I'm going to let you in on a little secret, maybe you'll feel better. Once a long time ago . . . I was poor too. That's right. I also used to live in a lousy dump with cockroaches, a lot like this one. Everything was almost exactly like this . . . but that was a lotta years back . . . in another barrio . . . another town . . . another time. (*Snapping out of it.*) Now I'm middle class! I got out of the poverty I lived in because I cared about myself. Because I did something to help myself. I went to college. So now I'm a social worker helping out the poor! Which means that I want to help you to take full advantage of what our society has to offer. There's nothing to lose and everything to gain, believe me!

BELARMINO: I believe you. When do the checks come?

MINGO: Oh, I figure in about thirty days.

BELARMINO: Thirty days!

LUPE: But we don' got nothing to eat.

MINGO: I'm sorry but that's the best we can do.

LUPE: What about Aid to Needy Children?

MINGO: What needy children?

LUPE: My baby. (*She shows him the baby.*)

MINGO: Cute. But what does he need?

LUPE: Look. (*She opens the blanket.*)

MINGO: (*Double take at* BELARMINO *then at the baby again.*) Another one! What happened?

LUPE: He's sick. Like his uncle.

MINGO: Runs in the family, huh? Well, I'll tell you. There's a good chance you might be able to get some kind of help, but nothing before 30 days at least.

BELARMINO: Okay, that do it! Señora, fry me some cucarachas! I hungry.

CHATO: Don' worry, Doña Cruz. I bet Joaquín gets some coins.

MINGO: Joaquín who? Another man in the family?

BELARMINO: Simón limón, more man than you think! Es más hombre que la ching . . .

CRUZ: ¡Mingo! Oh, Joaquín, no-Lupe, ah, tú—Chorti!

MINGO: Joaquín . . . ? Oh yeah! I forgot! Where is this Joaquín? (*No one says anything.*) Okay, let me put it different. Where was this Joaquín? In prison?

CHATO: How you know?

MINGO: And he was just released today?

CRUZ: Yes, on patrol.

BELARMINO: Parole.

MINGO: What's he like? Tall, short, light, dark?

CRUZ: Yes, tha's him! Why?

MINGO: Because tonight when I was coming across town I passed by this good looking Mexican walking along the road. It was pretty cold, so I gave him a lift. He'd just gotten out on parole this morning.

CRUZ: Joaquín, ees my Joaquín!

CHATO: Where's he at?

MINGO: Outside in my car. I forgot he came with me. I'll go get him.

CRUZ: ¡Ay Dios! My son is outside!

MINGO: Oh, another thing. It looks like the prison term helped him a lot. He seems very reformed, rehabilitated. Lots of spunk. A clean cut American boy! Be right back. (*He exits.*)

BELARMINO: ¡AY, YAI, YAI! Now you going to see the Revolución burst out! Joaquín is back!

CRUZ: (*Overexcited.*) ¡Viva la Revolución! (*Pause.*) I mean Gracias a Dios, my son is back.

LUPE: I bet you pass up Joaquín when he was walking, huh? ¡Menso!

CHATO: ¿Cómo que menso? ¿Quieres que te meta un guamazo en el hocico? Huh, pos mira. Who's the boss around here pues? (*He goes to door.*)

CRUZ: You hear what the social worker says, Lupe? My Joaquín is change, he's serious and reform.

BELARMINO: He don' say that. He say he got lots of spunk. He's revolutionary!!

CHATO: (*At the window.*) Here they come! (*Pause.*) ¡Qué caray! Tha's not Joaquín!

CRUZ: What?

LUPE: (*At the window.*) ¡O no, Joaquín!

BELARMINO: ¿Qué? What you see?

MINGO: (*Opening the door.*) Okay, folks, here he is! (MINGO *comes in.*) Well, Jack, come in. This is where you live.

CRUZ: (*Standing in the doorway.*) Dios mío, my son. (*She weeps. JOAQUIN comes into the house. He is well dressed, BUT HE HAS NO HEAD.*)

BELARMINO: Chingado, they got him.

MINGO: You see? Rehabilitated. He even grew a little. Congratulations, Jack, I know you'll make it. Well, I guess I better be on my way. Don't forget the crewcut and general cleanliness, okay? Buenas noches. (*Exits.*)

LUPE: I don' think he looks so bad, Mama. He look cleaner.

CHATO: Quihubole, ese. (*Shakes* JOAQUIN's *hand.*) No wonder I din' reco'nize him on the road.

LUPE: You shut up. I think Joaqu—Jack's gonna be okay, Ma. He can still find a job in the fields. Now we can all plan together for the future. Like my son, he's not going to have a poor life like us. I'm going to make sure he study so he can go to college someday like Mr. Sunday. With the help of God, my son will grow to be a decent man. Maybe someday he even find a body he can . . . (*Pause.*)

BELARMINO: (*Quickly.*) Heh, señora, bring Joaquín over here! I want to see him. Pos what you know? Look at the big arms he gots . . . and the big body! Oye, Ma, I got an idea.

LUPE: No you don't! I see him first!

BELARMINO: What firs'? I got years waiting for him! Anyway, he don' even fit that little head you got.

CRUZ: What you two arguing?

BELARMINO: Pos what? There's the body and here's the head. Le's get together! Pick me up!

CRUZ: But how, hombre? Joaquín's your brother.

BELARMINO: Pos there you are. We keep it in the family. Pick me up somebody!

CRUZ: No, Belarmino.

BELARMINO: Orale, Chato, gimme a lift!

CRUZ: No, I say!

LUPE: See? He's mine, huh, Mamá?

CRUZ: Neither his or yours or nobody but me. Joaquín is mine. Buenas noches. Come on, my son. (*Exits with* JOAQUIN.)

BELARMINO: Heh! Wait, señora! Wait one minute!

CRUZ: ¡Cállate tú, cabezón!

LUPE: You see, stupid? We both lose! Come on, Chato. (*Exits*.)

BELARMINO: (*Shouting after* LUPE.) Both lose, eh? Bueno, we see who have more pull wis the old lady! Stinking woman! They don' understand Revolución for nothing. We men must carry on the fight. We machos! No, Chato?

CHATO: Simón, we machos!

LUPE: (*Shouting*.) Chato, come to bed!

CHATO: Oh, that vieja apestosa! Buenas noches, ese.

BELARMINO: Buenas noches. (CHATO *exits*.) Well, here I sit . . . broken hearted. But tha's okay cause I still got time to wait. Sooner or later, the jefita gots to come across wis Joaquín's body. All I need is to talk sweet when she give me my beans, eh? In other words, organize her. Those people don' even believe who I am. Tha's how I wan' it. To catch 'em by surprise. So don' worry, my people, because one of this days Pancho Villa will pass among you again. Look to your mountains, your pueblos, your barrios. He will be there. Buenas noches.

Curtain

Brief History of the
Teatro de la Esperanza:
The First Four Years

El Teatro de la Esperanza began as a student group, initially named Teatro MECHA, at the University of California at Santa Barbara in 1969. The present author became the director of Teatro MECHA in the fall of 1970.[1] Because there were no available plays by or about the Chicano experience until the following year, the troupe collectively created its own *actos*, developing sketches in the style of the Teatro Campesino.[2] Under the guidance of the director, the students improvised scenes based on their experiences as university students, far from the realities of their individual barrios.

The actos that resulted from the group's initial workshop dealt with a variety of themes important to the students, such as separation from family and racial conflicts with non-Chicano students, professors and high school teachers.[3] These initial actos were mostly exercises, although the group performed a few of the more salient examples for MECHA meetings and conferences. Initially intended as the cultural arm of the organization, Teatro MECHA included a dance component dedicated to performing Mexican folklorico dancing. In the beginning of the troupe's evolutin as a teatro, the dances were the best part of the performances, as the director struggled to build cohesion among a disparate group of teatro aficionados with little or no theater experience.

In the spring of 1971 the troupe attended the second annual Chicano Theater Festival, organized by the Teatro Campesino in Santa Cruz, California. Following this historic event the troupe became involved in the formation of a national network of teatros called TENAZ, acronym for El Teatro Nacional de Aztlán.[4] This new relationship with other teatros and particularly with Luis Valdez and the Teatro Campesino opened new doors for the group, exposing the members to first-hand encounters with the leader of the developing teatro movement.

Guided by a board of directors representing a variety of teatros from several states, TENAZ began to organize quarterly meetings and yearly festivals and workshops. Teatro de la Esperanza became a major force in this important organization, hosting meetings and participating on the board of directors.[5] Through these regional gatherings, the theater groups were exposed to one another and to groups and individuals from the burgeoning political theater movement in Latin America. Although the Latin Americans boasted a far more developed dramaturgy, their plays were not yet appropriate for most Chicano groups, because teatros were anxious to perform themes close to the Chicano experience in this country.

When Luis Valdez's collection of actos was published in the spring of 1971, the students produced three of the Teatro Campesino's early pieces with great success: "Los vendidos," "The Militants" and "La quinta temporada."[6] These now classic actos served as a springboard for the developing troupe, demonstrating the effectiveness and economy of the acto form. People who had seen the Teatro Campesino were thrilled to witness another group's efforts at the popular form; those who had never seen a teatro were equally enthusiastic in their responses to what was for them a new form of theater.

The Teatro produced these actos for the final meeting of the MECHA membership in the last week of the 1971 spring quarter. The Teatro had produced "The Militants," Valdez's biting satire of the excesses of the Chicano movement, in an effort to expose the stupidity of in-fighting. But it was unfortunately too late to teach these campus radicals anything, as half of the MECHA membership walked out at the end of this historic meeting, only to form a separate organization, La Raza Libre.

Six of the twelve Teatro MECHA members wanted to remain in the teatro, although their political allegiance went with the new group. When the leadership of MECHA told the director that the six dissidents had to go, he and those six students joined the splinter group and founded El Teatro de la Esperanza. The newly-formed opposition group became a part of a new community center, La Casa de la Raza, and invited the Teatro de la Esperanza to join it in this exciting effort. The Teatro now had a new home in the community while also maintaining its university base.

During the first summer in La Casa, the troupe remodeled a small room at the back of this former warehouse into a little theater with seventy seats and a small stage. The teatro members taught workshops in Chicano theater techniques to a group of teenagers, who also helped in the remodeling efforts. This new relationship with the Casa proved beneficial to all parties and the group was then invited to be the resident teatro.

By the following year the group remodeled a larger auditorium, capable of accomodating almost two hundred people. The teatro had a permanent home, shared with other active community projects, such as a clinic, employment office, library and central clearing house for information relevant to the community. The troupe worked all summer at the Casa and returned to the university the following fall with a renewed vision and a very important sense of community involvement.

After its first successful summer at the Casa, the troupe was able to continue performing its repertoire of Teatro Campesino actos on campus.

With living examples of well written actos to emulate, students in the director's "Introduction to Chicano Theater" courses began to script their own versions of actos, the most successful of which the teatro subsequently produced. Following in the footsteps of the Teatro Campesino, which had given all teatros permission to produce its actos, the Teatro de la Esperanza published its anthology in 1973, also granting production rights to any groups that wanted them.[7]

After three years of producing actos, the troupe decided to explore the docu-drama format in order to grow beyond the acto form. None of the teatro's brief pieces were suited for a major production, nor were they docu-dramas. Though the Valdezian acto is very effective and entertaining, its brevity, coupled with the sometimes allegorical and fantastical premises of the genre, limit its scope. Thus the group felt the need for theater pieces that presented rounder characters than the acto offered, in situations that expressed the people's historical condition within a documentary framework.

The director had been greatly influenced by Bertolt Brecht's theory and technique, as well as by the documentary nature of Latin American plays created by groups such as El Teatro Experimental de Cali and that theater's director/playwright Enrique Buenaventura. Having also been influenced by the Teatro Campesino's creative processes and communal lifestyle, the group worked to form a nucleus of members with the experience, commitment and understanding of the collective process to enable them to create a major piece of theater. Over the years, many students worked with the Teatro, revolving around a core of individuals for whom teatro was not an "elective course."

By 1974 the core membership of the Teatro had been together for almost four years and had developed the infrasturcture necessry to embark on a major collective creation. The nucleus of actors were Drama majors, serious students of theater who had elected to produce Chicano theater as a way of life, rather than as an avocation.[8] However, unlike the Teatro Campesino, El Teatro de la Esperanza did not have a resident playwright, and there were very few plays by or about Chicanos that the troupe felt suitable for production.

When the group began to plan a production for its 1974 spring season, the only anthologies of Chicano plays in print were the aforementioned *Actos* and Esperanza's own anthology. Neither of these collections offered full-length plays in any genre, much less documentary pieces recording historical or current events. The few plays that had recently been published by individual playwrights were also limited in scope and development. Thus, the Esperanza troupe recognized the need for a play that

210

went beyond stereotyped characters and fictitious situations, addressing current problems in a manner that would educate and entertain.

Having analyzed Brechtian techniques and the Latin American collective tradition, the members of the teatro were ready to create a Brechtian documentary and began to research current events in order to find a theme to dramatize. When the teatro was invited to a candlelight vigil for three residents of nearby Guadalupe who were being incarcerated, the teatro members realized that they now had a topic of national significance to dramatize. The three individuals involved had been convicted of "disturbing the peace" in the town of Guadalupe, when, in fact, they had been singled-out in an attempt to suppress political activty and union organizing among the mostly Mexican and Chicano population of that community.

Armed with newspaper articles, personal interviews and a report published by the U.S. Commission on Civil Rights, the teatro members began to dramatize events crucial to an understanding of what had transpired in this central California farm community.[9] The town of Guadalupe, though rural, was a microcosm of Chicano culture, politics and the problems faced by the poor Mexican and Chicano in the U.S. including inadequate schooling, drug and alcohol addiction, low income and a recurring cycle of repression and defeat. The result of that investigation was *Guadalupe*.

The research and documentation phase of the collective process was based on assessing a variety of incidents revealed through the published materials, as well as conducting interviews with residents of *Guadalupe*. Conflicts would be improvised in the rehearsal room and then scripted by one of the actors based on the variety of dialogues that had transpired around a central conflict. The scene between the drug addict and his wife, for example, was the result of an interview with one of the mothers who told the group that her son had, in fact, prostituted his wife for drugs. Such a conflict is ripe for dramatization and the actors worked on a variety of dialogs until the right mixture of pathos and tension was achieved.

Personal observation became crucial to the creation of *Guadalupe*, for the group did not want an audience to doubt the truth in any of the episodes being dramatized. When the troupe visited the local parrish, the Spanish priest noted their presence and, almost as if to taunt them (for he knew why the group was in Guadalupe—everybody did), piously admonished his congregation, "¡Ustedes que siguen a César Chávez, irán directamente al infierno!" Naturally, the group was thus moved to demonstrate through a scene the collusion between this representative of the Church and the few families who controlled the wealth in *Guadalupe*.

The teatro worked from January to May developing *Guadalupe*, premiering the play on Cinco de Mayo of 1974. This docu-drama placed Teatro de la Esperanza at the forefront of Chicano theaters, demonstrating a form that had not yet been explored by any other teatro. *Guadalupe* ushered-in a period of developing professionalism for the teatro, a turning-point for the troupe and for Chicano theater in general. The further development of this teatro continues in the introduction to *La víctima*.

[1]For a study of the early development of El Teatro de la Esperanza from 1970 to 1973, see Jorge A. Huerta, "The Evolution of Chicano Theater," unpublished doctoral dissertation, University of California at Santa Barbara, 1974, chapters 4–6 and Appendices.

[2]For examples of the acto form, see Luis Valdez, *Actos del Teatro Campesino and Luis Valdez* (Houston: Arte Publico Press, 1989).

[3]One of the most prevalent themes among Chicanos in all parts of the country was the problem of little or no encouragement from high school counselors. Anywhere this author went to lecture and demonstrate the origins of Chicano theater it was always possible to get students in the audience to improvise the classic conflict between the Chicano who wants to go to college and the counselor who feels that the student should take technical courses, because "you people work so well with your hands." See "La vida de Juan Masa," a representative acto, in Jorge Huerta, "The Evolution of Chicano Theater," pp. 413–417 .

[4]For more on the formation of TENAZ, see Jorge Huerta, "The Evolution of Chicano Theater," Chapter III. The term "Aztlán" is a Nahuatl word which means "the land to the north—the land from whence the Aztecs came." Because of the Chicano student movement's early nationalism, some leaders (including Valdez) looked to the south for their cultural and historic references.

[5]Teatro de la Esperanza continues to be TENAZ's leading example of a community-based yet professional full-time producing teatro.

[6]These three *actos* are included in Luis Valdez's *Actos*.

[7]These early works are in Jorge A. Huerta, *El Teatro de la Esperanza: An Anthology of Chicano Drama* (Santa Barbara: El Teatro de la Esperanza, 1973). Each of the *actos* is preceeded by a brief introduction which offers information about its author and the evolution of the script itself.

[8]The original creators of *Guadalupe* were, Estela Campos, Mike Cordero, Rodrigo Duarte-Clark, Joey A. García, Marta Hernández, Ginger and Jorge Huerta, Arturo Madrid, Romelia V. Morales, Santiago E. Rangel, José G. Saucedo and Hilda Peinado. Adjunct members of the troupe were Ron and Gregg Huerta, aged 4 and 6, respectively.

[9]One of the major documents that inspired *Guadalupe* was *The Schools of Guadalupe. . . A Legacy of Educational Oppression* (Sacramento: California State Advisory Committee to the U.S. Commission on Civil Rights, 1973). For a more thorough discussion of the creation of Guadalupe, see Jorge A. Huerta, "El Teatro de la Esperanza: Keeping in Touch with the People," *The Drama Review*, 21 (March 1977): 37–46, and Huerta, *Chicano Theater: Themes and Forms*, (Arizona: Bilingual Press, 1982): 140–153.

Guadalupe

Critical reaction to *Guadalupe* was immediate and generally positive when the play premiered in 1974. For critics of Luis Valdez's neo-Maya philosophy, as expressed in the Teatro Campesino's *Carpa de los Rasquachis*, *Guadalupe* was a welcome relief.[1] After prefacing his review with an indirect reference to the Teatro Campesino's "retreating to the search for idealistic individualistic 'solutions,' " Jorge González observed, "Guadalupe . . . is unrefutable evidence that [Teatro de la Esperanza] has chosen to be a mirror of the conditions and aspirations of the Chicano people."[2] Though González felt that "the play suffered somewhat from lack of cohesion," he praised *Guadalupe* for not confusing its audience and was especially impressed "with the group asking the audience at the end of the play to criticize their performance."

Of the performance during TENAZ's Quinto Festival de los Teatros Chicanos: Primer Encuentro Latinoamericano held in Mexico City that summer, Juan Miguel de Mora was enthusiatic in his praise and somewhat prophetic in his vision: "Por su estructura escénica y por sus actuaciones, es evidente que este grupo muestra un adelanto notable en el camino hacia el teatro bien hecho y que si sigue trabajando tesonoramente y con disciplina artística, podrá ser pronto el mejor de los teatros chicanos."[3]

After the successful tour of Mexico, the director and his wife, who was the musical director, left the group, confident that the members were ready to be independent of a single director. The group continued to evolve and continued working on its script. In the spring of 1975 the teatro performed its newly-revised version of *Guadalupe*, prompting Ellen McCracken to observe, "The Chicano movement's search for aesthetic expression has understandably turned to the epic theatre of Bertolt Brecht, in which entertainment and education are necessary functions of one another. The success of this combination is unquestionably evident in *Guadalupe*."[4] Obviously aware of Brecht's insistence that the audience not be lulled into complacency, McCracken was impressed with *Guadalupe*'s use of Brechtian narration, observing: "The audience is encouraged to keep its eyes on the unfolding narration because *Guadalupe* begins with its own ending. . . . "

Writing about the Sexto Festival de los Teatros Chicanos, held in San Antonio in 1975, Nicolás Kanellos stated, "*Guadalupe* . . . has brought the various elements of Chicano theatre to their perfection," concluding that this piece was "a masterpiece of the genre."[5] Alongside the Teatro Campesino's still-evolving *Fin del mundo*, also performed at the festival, *Guadalupe* did, indeed, seem the epitome of clarity. While Valdez's latest creation searched for meaning in indigenous myths, Esperanza' s documentary held no surprises.

In Brechtian fashion, *Guadalupe* demonstrates the problems faced by the townsfolk through carefully crafted scenes designed to keep the audience's attention and objectivity. Humor is intertwined with pathos as the actors recreate the common humanity of the people involved while also ridiculing the power structure. The villains wear masks while the protagonists do not. Each episode builds upon the previous to create a fabric of intertwined vignettes leading to the inevitable incarceration of the Mexican and Chicano activists.

Another Brechtian technique aimed at keeping the audience's objectivity is the use of "breaks" in the action wherein an actor will interject a quote from a document or newspaper or an actual person in order to highlight the theme of the scene being presented. For example, the emotionally packed scene in which the teacher derides the student for speaking Spanish is interrupted when the actress playing the teacher steps out of character and quotes a statement that reveals the school system's attitude towards the Mexican people. Thus, the audience is continually reminded that this is a play based on actual facts. As Brecht insisted, the audience is never allowed to sink back into subjectivity without being continually reminded of the socio-political basis of all human conflict.

The musical leitmotif was inspired by both Brecht and the Teatro Campesino's use of musical narration. Music has always been a part of Chicano theater since the Teatro Campesino created its first strike song which depicted the farmworkers' struggles and triumphs in typical corrido fashion.[6] Just as the Mexican corridos narrated historical and topical events, so, too, did the Teatro Campesino's adaptations of these traditional songs. However, in adapting the corridos to fit their thematic needs, the Teatro Campesino singers recalled Brecht's *verfremdungseffekt*, whereby the viewer is presented with something familiar in an unfamilar fashion.[7]

Guadalupe thus employs familiar corrido melodies altered to tell another story. The audience members are thereby forced to pay closer attention to the lyrics, since these deviate from what they are accustomed to hearing. The play and each of its episodes are framed by musical narrative designed to move the action forward as well as to comment upon that action. The well-known corrido "Valentín de la Sierra" opens the play, but instead of the traditional lyrics, the song depicts the characters and events the audience is about to see.

Guadalupe was well-received by audiences in both the U.S. and Mexico. The company always conducted a discussion with the public after the play to hear its reactions to the events portrayed and to hopefully generate meaningful debate about the issues depicted. It was clear to the teatro members that the problems in the town of Guadalupe were not unique to that community, but they wondered if their audiences would recognize similar situations in their own backyards.

At one East Los Angeles performance, a mother in the audience said, "I knew that these things happened when I was a little girl, but I had no idea they were still doing this to kids." Another lady in the theater immediately interjected, "Señora, what you saw on that stage is happening right around the corner at Hillside School!" Whether those parents did anything to combat the problems in their own schools is unknown. They were, however, made to think about it, at least, for the moment.

When the teatro toured Mexico in the summer of 1974, the audience response was similar, but couched in the framework of Mexican images of what the United States is like. When the actors would ask them if they still wanted to go to the United States, the members of the audience generally said "Sí." The Mexicans were not ignorant of the injustices heaped upon their people in the U. S., but they were willing to risk that fate for the opportunity to earn a better living than was possible in their homeland. They were most fascinated by the differences between the Mexican and the Chicano as portrayed in the play and asked about those differences and the reasons behind them.

Because the teatro members chose to dramatize a recent and still evolving issue, they could not deviate too far from the truth. They wanted their audiences to appreciate the fact that what they were seeing was no fabrication, but rather, the result of the American Dream gone sour. If people questioned the veracity of the situations, the teatro members could literally "throw the book at them" by giving them the government report that documented the events as they occured.

Following the initial success of *Guadalupe*, both at home and in Mexico, the docu-drama continued to evolve into the script included here. While the troupe was on tour in Mexico, the play was televised nationally on the government's Canal 13 and was condensed and adapted by the teatro and José Luis Ruiz for National Educational Television in 1975.[8]

Guadalupe served the teatro well for two years and has not been revived by the troupe since its initial productions. Ten years after Esperanza's final production of *Guadalupe*, José G. Saucedo directed the piece for the Guadalupe Cultural Arts Center in San Antonio, Texas, in 1986. On leave from the group at the time, Saucedo was one of only two of the original creators of the play still with the teatro in 1986.[9] With his intimate knowledge of the script and his continued growth in the teatro, Saucedo accomplished what few directors can with non-professional actors: a successful production.

Perhaps because it was not produced with salaried actors, and thus not excessively expensive, Saucedo used twenty-two people in his remounting of *Guadalupe*. Jorge Piña, who produced the production, had seen the original and commented, "I was overwhelmed by it at the time. That show was very simply staged, though, and I think we're really opening this production up."[10] Without the exigencies of having to tour, the producers could mount a stationary production, but they could also have ruined the beauty of the original conception of sparseness. According to one critic, they did not ruin the play, giving proof to the old axiom that a good play can survive any number of "concepts."

Any fears this author had about Saucedo's mass approach to *Guadalupe* were placated by Bruce-Novoa, a respected critic of Chicano theater. Bruce-Novoa had not only seen the original version of this play, he had seen it several times, and he did not look forward to a poorly-produced revival of what he had termed "a classic of Chicano drama."[11] What he found, however, delighted our critic, giving full credit to the guest director's vision and to the "classic" status of *Guadalupe*.

Finally, Bruce-Novoa's praises confirm this author's belief that *Guadalupe* is not a dated play. The critic's thoughts are best summed-up in the following excerpt: "Saucedo has managed to mold actors into a group capable of performing, almost without flaw, a complex script, full of quick changes of rhythm and tone . . . while most things from the '70s seem embarrassingly passé, 'Guadalupe's' message remains fresh and, yes, relevant."

Although conditions have improved in *Guadalupe* since the first performance of this play, there is still much work to be done there and in all the barrios in this country. Perhaps *Guadalupe* can make a difference.

[1]See the biography of Luis Valdez in this book and footnote 4 in that section for more information on Valdez's neo-Maya philosophy and his *La carpa de los Rasquachis*.

[2]Jorge González, "Chicano Theatre Explores Drama of Guadalupe Life," *Santa Barbara News and Review*, 24 May 1974, p. 20.

[3]Juan Miguel de Mora, "Guadalupe," *El Heraldo de México*, 7 de julio de 1974, p 8D.

[4]Ellen McCracken, "Guadalupe," *Educational Theatre Journal* (December 1975), p. 554.

[5]Nicolás Kanellos, "Sexto Festival de los Teatros Chicanos," *Latin Ameri-*

can Theatre Review (Fall 1975), p. 81.

[6]Early in its development the Teatro Campesino adapted the popular song "De colores" to suit its huelga needs. The original lyrics begin "De colores, de colores se visten los campos en la primavera." The Teatro changed these to: " . . . de colores se visten los ricos en la primavera." Rather than singing about the beauties of springtime, the revised lyrics tell of the riches being gained by the growers and farm labor contractors at the expense of the miserable farmworkers.

[7]For an example of a corrido adapted to an *acto*, see "Huelgistas" in Valdez, *Actos*.

[8]The Mexican version of the videotape is in the teatro's archives. The PBS version can be rented through the teatro.

[9]Mr. Saucedo left the Teatro permanently in 1988 after establishing himself as an important director of Chicano/Hispano theater in the Southwest. He is now based in San Francisco and has formed a new group, *El Taller*, in collaboration with Lalo Cervantes and Anita Matos.

[10]David Scott, "Controversial 'Guadalupe' bows," *San Antonio Light* 14 Septemebr 1986, n.p.

[11]Bruce-Novoa, "S.A. Revival Does Justice to 'Guadalupe,' " *San Antonio Light* 20 September 1986, n.p. For Bruce-Novoa's earlier observations about *Guadalupe*, see: Juan Bruce-Novoa and David Valentin, "Revolutionizing the Popular Image: Essay on Chicano Theatre," *Latin American Literary Review* (Spring-Summer 1977): 42–50.

Guadalupe

by El Teatro de la Esperanza

SCENE ONE

CORTEZ: (*Walks to center stage, shouting angrily.*) Hey, bring in a couple of those guards and close those doors. I want a couple of men down here in the front row, and someone to watch these exits. (*Addresses the audience.*) My name is Marcos Cortez and I've come here to talk about the truth behind the Chicano Movement. Before I begin, let me bring to your attention some rumors that I've heard . . . rumors concerning some parents of Guadalupe who have formed a little group against the teachers of this school. This type of action appalls me, makes me ashamed to call myself Spanish. No other country offers children a free education. I say that, instead of speaking against the teachers, the parents should work with them. Or perhaps, if these parents don't like the way things are here in this country, they should go back to Mexico where they came from. (*To a woman in the audience.*) Wouldn't you agree, Mrs. González?

VIRGIE: No, I don't.

CORTEZ: Too often it is assumed that if a child is having trouble at the school, that it's the fault of the teacher. If the parents would spend more time with their kids instead of letting them run wild on the streets like animals, there would be no trouble.

SRA. BECERRA: What do you know about Guadalupe? You live in Santa María.

CORTEZ: Con permiso, señora, con permiso. I have been to the schools here, and I've seen the teachers at work. They offer the same fine education and standards to all of the children, just as it should be. I have always felt that a child should not be shown special favor just because he is a so-called minority. In fact, he should be encouraged to work twice as hard as the others in order to prove that he is just as good as the next child. I worked hard and, because of the education

I received, I am proud to stand before you as one of this county's leading citizens. (*Someone in the audience*: You're a vendido!!!) Because I worked hard, I'm a vendido? When are you people going to stop making excuses for laziness? (*Audience reacts noisily.* COR-TEZ *tries to quiet them down.*) Obviously you women in the Chicano movement don't know your place. Why aren't you in your home taking care of your children where you belong?

VIRGIE: We are taking care of our children. What do you think we're doing here?

SRA. MORENO: ¡Mandamos a nuestros hijos para que los eduquen, no a que los maltraten!

CORTEZ: The teachers have much to put up with. The children can hardly speak a word of English, they act disrespectful, and some of these children come to the classes looking and dressed like pigs. (*Someone in the audience*: The only pig in this town is you. *Quieting the audience.*) Now the question is: who is to blame for the formation of this little group against the teachers? It is groups such as MECHA, the Brown Berets and the United Farmworkers who are deliberately and willfully deceiving and mis-informing the community. (*Unfolds three flags: Nazi, Communist and UFW.*)

VIRGIE: The board told us this was not going to be a political meeting. You are making this meeting political.

CORTEZ: I am not a politician, señora. I am here as a concerned citizen to inform the "good" people of this community. We, as self-righteous Americans, cannot allow ourselves to be deceived by such self-interest groups. (*General uproar.*) Just as the people in Italy followed Musolini, just as the people in Germany followed Hitler, you will be making the same mistake if you allow yourselves to follow César Chávez and the United Farmworker's Union! (*Different character in the audience*: That's not true! ¡Sáquenlo, no sabe lo que dice! ¡Qué viva la huelga! ¡Qué viva! ¡Qué viva César Chávez! *Everyone joins in shouting "¡Qué viva César Chávez! The shouting is abruptly cut off by the beat of a drum.*)

VIRGIE: (*In the audience.*) Esta junta de padres y maestros se llevó a cabo el 16 de marzo de 1972 en Guadalupe, California. Los siguientes sucesos antecedieron esta junta.

CORTEZ: (*On stage.*) This parent-teacher meeting took place on March 16, 1972 in Guadalupe, California. The following events led up to this meeting. (*Drums roll while actors walk on stage. They move into position for first song.*)

SEÑORAS Y SEÑORES: Señoras y señores, venimos a cantar

Aquello que el gobierno no puede ocultar.
En todos los pueblitos también en la ciudad
Hay gente que el sistema no quiere respetar
La historia de los pobres, a quien les quita el pan
La historia de la Raza, Chicanos en Aztlán.

Escuchen nuestra historia, basada en la verdad
Presenta muchas cosas que son realidad
Problemas se resuelven no sólo con hablar
Su ayuda es necesaria para poder pelear
Unidos venceremos, hay que tomar acción
Escuchen este hecho y pongan atención.

SCENE TWO

DEMONSTRATOR: Un habitante de Guadalupe por cuarenta años, dice "Vivimos en un campo de concentración." (*Singer/musician narrates in song as the other members of the company pantomime picking the crops. The lyrics are sung to the music of "Valentín de la Sierra."*)

FIRST VERSE: Voy a cantar un corrido
De un pueblo muy escondido
Llamábase Guadalupe que de repente
Fue bien conocido.

SECOND VERSE: Toda la gente del pueblo
trabaja entre los "files"
Día tras día sudando
y siempre no tienen pa pagar los biles. (*Farmworkers begin to talk while working. Musical accompaniment continues under dialogue.*)

SR. MORENO: Oiga, Vicente, no se le olvide lo de la junta que va a haber en la empacadora.

CHICANO: What did he say?

VIRGIE: Don't forget about the meeting in the packing house.

CHISMOSA 1: Oye, que va a haber junta.

CHISMOSA 2: ¡Ah!

THIRD VERSE: Oiga, usted, mi comadrita
Un chisme le voy a contar
Pásese usted a mi casa
y del vecino podemos hablar.

POMPIS: Comadre, are we going to the meeting?

FRUTI: ¡Qué meeting ni qué meeting! Tú, Pomposa Merones, no le busques tres pies al gato porque le hallas cuatro.

POMPIS: Ay, Fruti, just for a few minutes.

FRUTI: No, ni un minutito.

POMPIS: Pero . . .

FRUTI: No hay pero que valga.

POMPIS: Don't you want to know about what's happening? La Virgie has been inviting everybody.

FRUTI: Usted lo que quiere es andar de chismosa.

POMPIS: Agua fiestas.

FOURTH VERSE: Andan los dos de la greña
                          El pocho y el mexicano.

MEXICANO: Oye, Chente, ¿Oíste del pleito que hubo en la high school ayer?

CHICANO: Yeah, I heard something happened. What was it?

MEXICANO: Fíjate que unos buscapleitos agarraron a un mexicano y lo dejaron allí por muerto. Eran esos chicanos; tú sabes, ¡los pochos!

CHICANO: Well, I'm a Chicano. Are you calling me a Pocho?

SECOND PART OF FOURTH VERSE: Somos iguales, comprendan,
                          Mejor sería que nos demos la mano.

FIFTH VERSE: La educación de los niños
                          No vale ni un centavo
                          Sólo ayudan al gringo
                          y al mexicano lo echan para un lado.

VIRGIE: ¿Por qué no fuiste a la escuela hoy?

FRANKIE: I didn't feel like going. I don't like that place. They treat me bad over there and they make me feel stupid.

VIRGIE: ¿Por qué?

FRANKIE: They say I work out here like an animal.

VIRGIE: ¿Y por qué te avergüenzas de trabajar en el campo?Este trabajo es más importante que el del ranchero. Si no fuera por nosotros, nadie comería.

SIXTH VERSE: Lo que pasa en Guadalupe
                          Existe en todos los barrios
                          Nos tienen esclavizados
                          Pues nuestra vida depende de salarios.

SR. MORENO: Bueno, Kiko, entonces te quieres meter en la unión ¿sí o no? Sabes bien que tenemos muchos problemas.

KIKO: Bueno, aunque las condiciones no sean muy buenas, yo necesito mi trabajo.

SEVENTH VERSE: Unos curas de la iglesia
        Sólo quieren comprender
        Que el dinero es lo primero
        Y Dios y los pobres se quedan después.

FRUTI: Pompis, ¿qué día vas a ir a la jamaica?

POMPIS: Ay, Fruti allí le sacan a uno hasta lo que no tiene.

FRUTI: Pero, fíjate que el Padre Cruz dice que la iglesia necesita nuevos santos, un altar nuevo, flores, candelabros . . .

POMPIS: Fruti, no le hagas caso a ese viejo gachupín. Sí, ese padrecito debería ser como el curita de Santa María que anda por allá piqueteando con los trabajadores.

FRUTI: El lugar de los padres está en la iglesia.

POMPIS: No lo creas, comadrita. Los padres no son cosa sagrada.

EIGHTH VERSE: Son armas de este gobierno
        La migra y la policía
        Dicen que sirve al pueblo
        Pero a lo visto es otra mentira.

CHICANO: Mira, ¡ahi viene la migra!!! Ha, ha, don't believe me, I was just kidding.

FARMWORKER: ¡No estés chistoseando!

CHICANO: I thought you'd gotten your papers fixed. You know, they picked up fifty workers in Santa María. Last week . . .

MEXICANO: Pues sí, como ya no los necesitaban. A mí ya van dos veces que me llevan.

CHICANO: Well, why don't you stay where you belong? Can't you take a hint?

NINTH VERSE: Se dice que hay muchas drogas
        Por calles y por cantinas
        Mientras cerveza unos toman
        Otros se pican con la heroina.

VIRGIE: Doña Pomposa me dijo que te vio juntándote con esa bola de pachucos.

FRANKIE: Doña Pomposa, what does she know? Those guys are my friends.

VIRGIE: ¿Y qué clase de amigos son esos que toman píldoras y cochinadas?

FRANKIE: We were just going for a cruise, that's all.

VIRGIE: ¿Qué? ¿Quieres acabar como tu hermano el Jessie?

FRANKIE: Don't compare me to him, gah . . .

TENTH VERSE: Oiganme bien, compañeros
                   Tenemos que organizarnos
                   Ya basta de sufrimientos,
                   Unidos con fuerza, ya no hay que dejarnos.

KIKO: Oye, Juan, dime un poco más de esta unión, pues.

J. MORENO: Esta noche hay trabajo en la empacadora. Allí nos vamos a reunir.

KIKO: ¿Y qué van a hacer?

MORENO: Vamos a discutir las quejas de todos los trabajadores.

KIKO: No van a hacer nada. Es pura habla. De lo dicho al hecho hay mucho trecho.

MORENO: ¿Cómo que no? Acuérdate que el que no habla, Dios no lo oye.

KIKO: Pero a mí no me gusta ese borlote. Cuando termine la co-rrida, yo me voy pa México. (*Whistle to end the workday blows. Farmworkers begin to walk out of the fields while the sound of a machine begins to be heard. People freeze.*)

DEMONSTRATOR: Un campesino de Guadalupe dice: "Estamos ante una red de poder."

SCENE THREE

Farmworkers begin to move into the packing house. There is talking and laughing. Women stand behind the conveyor belt waiting to sort the tomatoes. Men begin to pass the boxes of tomatoes to be dumped onto the belt.

MORENO: ¡Andenle mujeres, a trabajar!

OCHOA: ¡Ahi les va una caja!

VIRGIE: Apurarse, ¿y pa qué? Para acabarse uno más pronto.

SRA. MORENO: Por lo menos aquí hay techo y no estamos allá en el solazo.

SRA. BECERRA: Oye, Virgie, what happened to this meeting you and Moreno were talking about?

VIRGIE: Nothing has happened yet, but we're going to have it.

SRA. BECERRA: Well, when is it going to start?

MORENO: Pues, ahorita, señora.

FUENTES: What about Bob? He might hear us.

VIRGIE: Ah, don't worry about Bob. We'll keep an eye out for him.

BECERRA: So what's the big secret? Are you planning to get us into trouble or something?

VIRGIE: Cálmate, Toña. No seas tan escandalosa.

OCHOA: Oye, Moreno, ¿pos de qué van a hablar?

MORENO: De nuestros problemas.

OCHOA: ¿Cómo que nuestros problemas? A mí no me metan en sus líos.

MORENO: Mira, Salvador, todos estamos en la misma joda. Trabajamos todo el día en los files y luego "overtime" aquí en la empacadora; y apenas nos alcanza pa la comida. Hay que hacer algo.

OCHOA: ¿Como qué?

FUENTES: En Santa María the campesinos organized with the Union.

OCHOA: Uh . . . pos de Guatemala a guatepeor. Si se ponen en huelga, les va peor.

MORENO: Pero fíjate, que ahora les pagan mejor y las condiciones las han mejorado. Hay que juntarnos para cambiar las cosas aquí en Guadalupe.

VIRGIE: That's right. This town has gotta change; they treat us like animals here.

SRA. BECERRA: Oh, come on, Virgie, it's not that bad.

VIRGIE: The hell it ain't. We work for nothing and our kids, they don't have a chance either. Those schools don't teach them anything.

SRA. BECERRA: But that's because the kids just don't want to learn.

VIRGIE: But how can they learn if they're always getting hit.

SRA. BECERRA: Oh, they don't hit them that much.

VIRGIE: Listen to this woman. ¿Ya se te olvidó el moretón que le hicieron a tu hijo?

SRA. BECERRA: Well, it was pretty bad. But knowing my Freddie, he probably deserved it.

SRA. MORENO: A mi Lupita la golpearon también.

FUENTES: ¿Por qué?

SRA. MORENO: Porque no sabía la respuesta a una pregunta que le hicieron.

FUENTES: ¿No más por eso?

SRA. BECERRA: She must have done something. They don't hit them for nothing.

SRA. MORENO: No, si mi Lupita se porta muy bien. ¿Verdad, Juan?

SR. MORENO: Sí, si nuestra niña es estudiante muy buena.

SRA. BECERRA: If she's such a good student then why did they flunk her last year?

SRA. MORENO: Pues, francamente no sé, porque mi Lupita traía muy buenas calificaciones—puras A's y B's.

SR. FUENTES: She got A's and B's y no la pasaron?

SR. MORENO: Y eso le pasa a otras familias también.

SR. FUENTES: Well, that doesn't make sense.

SRA. BECERRA: That's kind of strange.

VIRGIE: And that's not all. I haven't told you about my Frankie.

SRA. BECERRA: Well, what did he do this time?

VIRGIE: I know my Frankie's no angel, but two days ago he came home with stitches!

SR. MORENO: Están oyendo lo que dice la Virgie. Ya no hay que dejarnos. Esa gente no quiere educar a nuestros hijos.

OCHOA: ¿Y pa qué necesitan tanta educación? Mejor pónganlos a trabajar.

SR. MORENO: Eso es lo que quieren, Salvador. Como no tenemos educación, nuestro trabajo le sale barato al patrón.

OCHOA: Pues, aunque no tenga educación, yo tengo mi trabajo.

SR. MORENO: Pero, comprende que les conviene que seamos analfabetas y por eso no quieren educar a nustros hijos.

OCHOA: A mis hijos sí los están educando.

SR. MORENO: ¿Ah, sí? Entonces dime, Salvador, ¿por qué tienen a tus hijos en las clases de los retrazados mentales?

OCHOA: A mí me dijeron que eran clases especiales.

SRA. MORENO: Sí, Salvador, son clases especiales. Pero especiales para los niños retrazados mentales.

OCHOA: Es que mi hijo no habla inglés.

SR. MORENO: Pero entiende, Salvador, que esa no es razón para que metan a tus hijos en esas clases. Deberían de tener profesores bilingües para que les enseñaran el inglés. (*The conveyor belt stops abruptly and workers react to it.*)

FUENTES: ¡Ahi viene el Bob!

BOB: What the hell happened here?

SRA. BECERRA: The machine's no good.

BOB: You're lucky it works, or else you'd be out of a job. What do you think is wrong with it, Ochoa?

OCHOA: Amen.

BOB: (*Examines machine.*) Um, it's that goddamn gearbox again. I'll have to go and check up on it. Take your break now. I'll be back in a while. (*Exits.*)

SR. MORENO: Ya se fue. Miren, tenemos que hacer algo. Hay que juntarnos y hablar con los otros.

VIRGIE: But how do we get the parents together? They're afraid to come to these meetings?

FUENTES: Of course they're afraid, but if you people take the first step and start voicing your complaints, then they won't be afraid, because they'll see that they're not the only ones.

SRA. BECERRA: Some people might.

VIRGIE: But how do we voice our complaints?

FUENTES: You can get a list of complaints from the parents and take them before the Board of Education or to the Superintendent of schools.

SRA. BECERRA: They won't listen to us.

FUENTES: They'll have to listen to you, if you do it officially. You should form a Comité de Padres and choose a spokeman to voice your complaints.

SRA. BECERRA: Who's going to do that?

FUENTES: Well, it has to be one of you. Perhaps you, Sra. González?

VIRGIE: No, no, no. I get too excited and besides I've been to see that superintendent too many times.

FUENTES: What about you, Sr. Moreno?

SRA. MORENO: Anda, Juan. Tú.

SR. MORENO: Bueno, si todos estamos de acuerdo que le entremos a esta cosa juntos. (*All nod in agreement except* SALVADOR.)

VIRGIE: Claro que sí, Juan.

FUENTES: If we organize, we'll be strong and we can back you up.

OCHOA: ¿Y qué pasa si te quitan el trabajo?

FUENTES: Por eso, hombre, we have to do this together. They can't fire all of us.

VIRGIE: Tenemos que apoyarnos unos a los otros.

SRA. MORENO: Acuérdate que es para el bien de nuestros hijos, Salvador.

SR. MORENO: ¿Qué dices, Salvador? ¿Estás con nosotros?

OCHOA: No, no sé. Tengo que pensarlo.

FUENTES: ¡El Bob! (*Enter* BOB.)

BOB: The machine is broken for the day. Just finish up these last boxes. And I'll see you tomorrow at the same time. (*Exits.*)

SR. MORENO: Bueno, tenemos que juntar las quejas y llamar a los padres.

FUENTES: Right away!

SRA. MORENO: Nosotros avisamos a las señoras de la otra empacadora. (*They go offstage talking as "Chismosas's Song" Begins.*)

En este pueblecito

Pues periódico pa' leer no hay
Pero sí tenemos dos chismosas
Con quien todo el chisme cae

Si el chisme es muy poco
Pues ahorita le ponemos más
Que al cabo la verdad no importa
Lo que vale es la sabrosidad

Acerque usted la oreja
Prometa no decir
Que el chisme es un secreto
Que jure no repetir.

SCENE FIVE

In the supermarket. FRUTI *walks in stage right and begins grocery shopping.* POMPIS *walks in stage left and is surprised to see* FRUTI.

POMPIS: ¡Ay Frutis! ¿Qué haces aquí?

FRUTI: Pues, tú sabes, buscando los sales.

POMPIS: Sí pues, ahora sí hay muchos sales. Como la gente no tiene trabajo.

FRUTI: Y dime, comadre, How are you today?

POMPIS: Ay, pues, pretty good, comadre. Si amanecí en la gloria.

FRUTI: Ay, ese esposo tuyo. Que fuera tan amoroso el mío. Qué dichosa eres, mujer.

POMPIS: ¡Frutis! The things you say.

FRUTI: Pos, a lo menos quítate esa sonrisa de la cara before I send you to the priest.

POMPIS: To the priest? Como si fuera tan religiosa. The only time I go to church is when somebody dies or gets married. Al cabo ni vale andar de santa, comadre. Fíjate lo que le pasó a Doña Lupita que anda más en la iglesia que ni en su propia casa.

FRUTI: ¿Qué le pasó?

POMPIS: You don't know?

FRUTI: ¡No, dime!

POMPIS: ¿De veras no sabías?

FRUTI: I told you que no, mujer! ¡Andale, dime, que no me aguanto!

POMPIS: Bueno pues, te diré todo. You know Doña Lupita's two older boys?

FRUTI: ¿Los más greñudos?

POMPIS: Esos meros, el Bobby y el Eddie. The other night they came home and Doña Lupita wasn't there, andaba allá en la iglesia mitoteando con las estatuas. When they got inside, the policemen came and surrounded the house. Los agarraron por surprise. Así como en la T.V.

FRUTI: ¡No!

POMPIS: ¡Sí! Fue una bola de chotas. Unos cherifes, otros del highway patrol hasta dicen que unos eran de la F.B.I.

FRUTI: Pero, ¿por qué los agarraron?

POMPIS: Pos, déjame contarte. You know what they found in the house?

TOGETHER: ¡Drogas!

POMPIS: Hallaron píldoras coloradas, píldoras amarillas, mariguana, píldoras blancas, píldoras de todos los colores del rainbow! ¿Pero no sabes lo peor?

FRUTI: ¡Ay comadre! ¿Pero qué puede ser peor?

POMPIS: ¡Hallaron unos paquetes de heroína!

FRUTI: ¿Paquetes de harina?

POMPIS: ¡Heroína, mujer!

FRUTI: Ah, pues, como la fregada harina es tan cara. Yo dije pues . . .

POMPIS: Pos, anyway, they took them to the jail in Santa Barbara.

FRUTI: ¿Hasta allá?

POMPIS: Sí. You know they were selling the drugs right here in Guadalupe? Se hacían un buen negocito. Bueno, así dice la gente. What I don't understand is where do they get all these drugs?

FRUTI: Comadrita, eso yo lo sé, ven pa'ca. Esto, Pompita de mi vida yo lo vi, nadie me lo contó. Yo trabajo con ese mentado Eddie, allá en la packing house. Un día el Eddie vino y me enseñó $4,000 dólares.

POMPIS: Four thousand dollars, comadre?

FRUTI: Ay Pompita, se me antojaron y quise arrancar con ellos. Pero, como soy mujer decente, me detuve.

POMPIS: ¡Andale, comadre, dime!

FRUTI: Bueno pues, después del trabajo iba yo caminando para mi casa sin molestar a nadie. De repente que veo al Eddie parado en la esquina, esperando a no sé qué o a quién. Dije yo, aquí hay algo y de mensa me voy de pasada.

POMPIS: ¡Andale! ¡Apúrate!

FRUTI: Yo luego pensé en ti y dije: "¿Qué pensará mi comadre Pomposa si me voy sin saber el chisme?"

POMPIS: Pues, con una fregada, Fruti, ¡me dices el chisme o te doy con este chorizo!

FRUTI: De repente que pasa un carrazo por delante de mí. Un Cadillac con dos catrines adelante.

POMPIS: ¿Un Cadillac, comadre?

FRUTI: ¿Que no me estás oyendo?

POMPIS: Sí, bueno pues, ¡sigue, sigue!

FRUTI: Bueno, se estacionó el Cadillac en la esquina y se baja uno de esos que se creen muy "fufurifufus".

POMPIS: Sí, ya los conozco.

FRUTI: El Eddie le da los $4,000 al catrín y el catrín le da una caja.

POMPIS: Four thousand dollars for a box, comadre?

FRUTI: Sí, comadre, la caja era así chiquititita. Así como el tamaño del jabón Zest.

POMPIS: Ay comadre, ya pareces T.V. commercial.

FRUTI: Esto yo lo vi. ¡Nadie me lo contó! Pero dicen que este Cadillac pasa por Guadalupe una vez por mes. Lo que yo no puedo acabar de comprender es por qué los policías siempre agarran a estos tontos de los pueblos chicos y no a los meros que vienen de las ciudades grandes a vender esta cochinada.

POMPIS: Comadre, me extraña que siendo araña no me la sepas tejer.

FRUTI: ¡Oyeme! ¡No te mandes, eh!

POMPIS: Mira, espérame . . . . (POMPIS *walks down stage to see if anyone is around*.) Por ahi se dice que el jefe de policía agarra sus buenas mordiditas de los narcotraficantes. (*Both freeze*.)

DEMONSTRATOR: Corruption in Guadalupe is wide-spread. On May 16, 1974, the Guadalupe Police Chief is sentenced from one to four years in a state prison for accepting bribes from narcotics pushers. (*They unfreeze*.)

FRUTI: ¡Oh! Pues con razón, comadre. Y ahora la Doña Lupita que se cree tan santa.

POMPIS: ¡Qué funny! I remember when Doña Lupita tenía al Bobby y al Eddie como altar boys. ¿Y ahora qué les dirá el padrecito?

FRUTI: ¡Pos, lo mismo! Que le recen a Dios y, si no, pues que se vayan mucho a la fregada. Ahora oigo que la Virgie se cree "Miss Community," como si no tuviera hijos drogadictos iguales a los de Doña Lupita.

POMPIS: You know, comadre, there are a lot of people involved in that comité. Remember the meeting que tuvieron en la packing house?

Tú no me dejaste ir y yo que quería estar tan involucrada.

FRUTI: ¡Ay sí, tú! ¿De dónde me saliste tan intelectual? Tú lo que quieres es meterte en lo que no te importa, así como la vieja chismosa de Doña Becerra que siempre anda . . . ¡Ay Señora Becerra! ¿Cómo está?

SRA. BECERRA: Muy bien, gracias. Doña Fructosa, Sra. Morones, ¿ya sabían que hay otra junta hoy en mi casa?

FRUTI: ¡Mire señora Becerra! Déjeme darle un consejo. Usted como mujer debe saber su lugar. Su responsabilidad es quedarse en su casa, atendiendo a su marido y a sus hijos . . . lavar, planchar . . .

POMPIS: ¡Cállate, Fruti!

FRUTI: Hacer de comer, coser . . .

POMPIS: ¡Ay, Fruti, mira qué barato está el Campbell soup!

FRUTI: ¡Hummm!

SRA. BECERRA: Doña Fructosa, le agradezco mucho su consejo. Pero como le iba diciendo, están las dos invitadas a la junta esta noche. ¡Ah! Don't buy lettuce.

FRUTI: Pompis, vamos a comprar lechuga, que al cabo está en barata.

POMPIS: No, mejor vamos a comprar unos cherries.

FRUTI: ¿Cheris? Ay, comadre, ya mero se me olvidaba decirte.

POMPIS: ¿Qué?

FRUTI: ¡No sabes quién anda, pero sí, bien llena de agua!

POMPIS: ¡Dime todo; dónde, cómo, quién y con quién!

FRUTI: Pos déjame decirte que . . . (*Both exit stage left. Last verse of chismosas's theme song.*)

> Acerque usted la oreja
> Prometa no decir
> El chisme es un secreto
> Que jure no repetir
> El chisme es un secreto
> Que jure no repetir.

SCENE SIX

Two Low Riders stand stage left, a young Chicano and his girl.

DEMONSTRATOR: The Guadalupe police chief says: "There are only three to five heroin addicts and they are constantly under surveillance. There is no drug problem in Guadalupe." (*Music to "Mr. 21" begins. Low Riders turn on radio and cruise downstage, then turn stage right. They cross entire stage while "Mr. 21" is being sung.*)

CHICANO: Eh, watcha la Mary. (*She slaps him on shoulder. He puts arm around her. They exit stage right. JESSE enters stage right. While song "Mr. 21" is still playing, he squats down at street corner and has a cigarrette. Enter FRANKIE stage right.*)

FRANKIE: Hey, Jesse what's happening?

JESSE: Not much, ese.

FRANKIE: So what happened to you last night? Mom waited up and everything.

JESSE: I got hung up at a friend's house.

FRANKIE: Yeah? Boy or girl? (*He laughs, but JESSE doesn't.*) Well, you should have called or something, you know.

JESSE: So how's Mom. She all right?

FRANKIE: She's fine. Just a little worried about you, though. How's Terry?

JESSE: She's okay. (*Pause.*) Don't you have something to do?

FRANKIE: Don't you?

JESSE: Don't get smart, Frankie. I'm waiting for someone, all right? Why don't you go to the show or something?

FRANKIE: The show! I've already been to the show, man. Two times even.

JESSE: So, go see something else.

FRANKIE: What something else? The next closest show is in Santa María. Your car running?

JESSE: No, it's been messed up lately. Besides, I sold it to Mocho.

FRANKIE: Sold it to Mocho? You mean you sold the "Angel Baby"?

JESSE: It's none of your business.

FRANKIE: Hey, vato, you all right?

JESSE: Yeah, it's just a stomach ache or something.

FRANKIE: Sure. Tell me about it.

JESSE: I don't have to tell you nothing. What are you doing around here anyway, Frankie? Aren't you supposed to be in school?

FRANKIE: I got sent home again.

JESSE: How come?

FRANKIE: They said I threatened the teacher, but I just yelled back that's all.

JESSE: What were you yelling back for?

FRANKIE: 'Cause he called me a liar.

JESSE: So?

FRANKIE: So, I don't like no one calling me a liar and I don't like no one poking me in the chest, like this. (*Pokes* JESSE.)

JESSE: All right!

FRANKIE: Me and Chuy have been thinking of quitting.

JESSE: What do you mean quitting?

FRANKIE: Yeah, quitting! He's got an uncle down in Texas who'll give us a job in a warehouse.

JESSE: Don't be stupid, Frankie. You better stay in school.

FRANKIE: For what?

JESSE: So you won't have to hang around the streets all day long.

FRANKIE: You seem to be doing all right.

JESSE: Well, I'm not. Hanging around is all I can do. (*Enter* VIRGINIA.)

VIRGIE: Mira no más. (*Looking at* FRANKIE.) Ahorita me las arreglo contigo. (*Turns back to* JESSE.) What happened to you? ¿Por qué no veniste? I came home early from Moreno's meeting, pero nunca llegaste. Te había hecho un caldito para que cenaras, pero nunca llegaste.

JESSE: I was busy, Mom.

VIRGIE: Busy? ¿Y no pudiste llamarme? Estaba preocupada. Pensé que algo te había pasado.

JESSE: I'll call you next time, all right?

VIRGIE: Bueno pues. Y tu esposa, ¿Cómo está? La última vez que la vi estaba muy preocupada.

JESSE: She's all right. You know Terry, she's always worried about something.

VIRGIE: Y el trabajo ¿cómo va?

JESSE: Pues, I'm not working anymore. But I'm looking for a job. In fact, this afternoon I got an appointment.

VIRGIE: Bueno, pero cuídate m'ijo. Estás tan pálido y te me haces más delgado. Everytime I see you, you seem to get skinnier. (*To* FRANKIE.) ¿Y tú? The school called me and said they'd sent you home.

FRANKIE: Yeah. I had a bad cough. (*Coughs.*)

VIRGIE: They said they sent you home because you were yelling at the teacher.

FRANKIE: Yeah, that too.

VIRGIE: Y ¿qué pasó?

FRANKIE: A teacher caught me downtown during lunch break and said I was cutting. I wasn't cutting, though. I was up on Main Street looking for a job. So he said I was insubordinative and a liar. I told him, "Hey, man, you got no right to call me a liar." So then they sent me home. (*Pause.*) God, no one believes me!

VIRGIE: I believe you, m'ijo. Pero a ver qué nos dice la escuela. The last time I went to see them they didn't want to listen to me, but they're going to have to listen because I'm not the only one. And Frankie, if you have a cough, you should be inside.

FRANKIE: I'm just going to talk to Jesse for a minute. I'll be right home.

VIRGIE: Bueno pues. Pero, hijos, stay out of trouble. Cuídense. (VIRGINIA *exits.*)

JESSE: Is that what really happened?

FRANKIE: Yeah.

JESSE: That place hasn't changed much, has it?

FRANKIE: Nothing changes around here. Hey man, you feel like getting loaded?

JESSE: Get out of here, Frankie.

FRANKIE: No, really man, I know where we can get some stuff.

JESSE: What do you know about "stuff"?

FRANKIE: I know plenty about it. Some of the guys use it in the car club.

JESSE: Do you always gotta do what your punky-ass friends do?

FRANKIE: Cut the act, Jesse, you're not my father.

JESSE: Look at me, Frankie.

FRANKIE: Ah, give me a break.

JESSE: I said look at me. You want to end up looking like me? Huh? Answer me, Frankie!

FRANKIE: I'm not gonna end up looking like you, man, 'cause I can handle it.

JESSE: You can handle it! You can't handle shit!

FRANKIE: You're wrong, Jesse. You can't handle shit. (*Exposes* JESSE*'s arm. They freeze.*)

DEMONSTRATOR: The director of the Community Action Commission states: "Forty heroin addicts voluntarily present themselves before the Mental Health Board to demand a methadone program." (JESSE *and* FRANKIE *unfreeze.*)

JESSE: Let go! You think it's so easy bumming around the streets? Well it's dead, Frankie, you hear me, man? This is all I can do carnal, but you still got a chance. Don't blow it on something like this. Make something out of yourself. (*Enter* MOCHO.) Hey, Mocho, I thought you'd never show up.

MOCHO: Ese, el Mocho de Guade always shows up, carnal. Y ese Morrillo, who is he?

JESSE: That's my carnalito, Frankie. He was just leaving. You got the stuff, Mocho?

MOCHO: Simón. I got the chiva. You got the money this time?

JESSE: Well, not exactly.

MOCHO: Este vato, what do you mean "not exactly"?

JESSE: I scored a couple of typewriters that we can sell, ese.

MOCHO: Watcha, vatito. What do you think I am, the flea market? I deal in cash "dando, dando". So either you got it or you don't.

JESSE: Como on, Mocho. I'll have it for you in a while.

MOCHO: How about your carnalillo over there?

JESSE: Ah, he's never got any money.

MOCHO: Este tecato tapado. ¿Que si se filerea? You know, does he turn on?

JESSE: He's only fifteen, Mocho.

MOCHO: I know a lot a guys who started at fifteen. Don't we, Jesse?

JESSE: He's just a kid.

MOCHO: Mira, vato, por si yo no quiero. I don't have to take your damn typewriters. You need a fix? Orale, pues. I need customers. (*To* FRANKIE.) Hey, Frankie, your big carnal over here says you're a pretty cool dude. Want to go for a little cruise?

JESSE: Get out of here, Frankie.

MOCHO: Shut up! I'm talking to him, not to you. So how about it, big man. Wanna go for a little cruise?

FRANKIE: (*Hesitates.*) Um . . . no.

MOCHO: ¡Pinche cherry, ese! (FRANKIE *crosses angrily to* MOCHO *but* JESSE *comes between them.*)

JESSE: Forget it, Frankie. It's only talk.

FRANKIE: I'm not afraid of that guy.

MOCHO: Ese, Jesse. Ahi te calmo en tu carrucha, while you baby-sit your carnal.

JESSE: Yeah, Mocho. I'll be there in a minute. (*Exit* MOCHO.)

FRANKIE: See you later, Jesse.

JESSE: Yeah, later Frankie. (*Scene opens with noisy entrance of action creating a bar atmosphere. Last actor is a drunk Mexican who enters stage right singing, "Estoy en el rincón de una cantina, oyendo la canción que yo pedí." Actors freeze.*)

DEMONSTRATOR: In Guadalupe there is one park, one cinema and nine bars. (*Background music starts.*)

BOB: Well, Rita, looks like we're gonna have another busy night.

RITA: Yeah, Bob. I sure hope I get some good tips.

BOB: Just let the men get a little drunker and they'll loosen up with the money.

RITA: Say, Bob, what's this talk going around town about your workers and this parents committee they are forming? It seems to me that things are really beginning to happen here in Guadalupe.

BOB: So you've heard about it, too? Well Rita, it's just a couple of troublemakers, I guess. But, I'd sure like to know who's behind all this. I thought maybe you'd know something.

RITA: Sorry, I just heard some of the men growling about it. But, I can't say I know any more than you.

CHICANO: Hey, Rita! How about a cerveza over here. We just got paid today and I feel like celebrating.

MEXICANO: ¡Andale, Rita, trainos una cerveza!

RITA: ¿Ya le quieren comenzar?

SALVADOR: Rita, ese Bob es bien codo, no nos paga bien por el trabajo.

RITA: Oye, Salvador, por ahi dicen que estás metido con ese borlote de los padres.

SALVADOR: ¿Qué?

RITA: Tú sabes, sí, hombre, eso de las escuelas y como maltratan a los niños.

SALVADOR: ¿Quién te dijo?

RITA: Pues por ahi lo oí. Tú sabes, Salvador, que Guadalupe es un pueblo muy íntimo.

MEXICANO: Y por ahí me dijeron Mamacita, que tú eras una mujer muy íntima.

CHICANO: Hey, Rita! ¿No te enojas cuando esos guys hacen sus cracks?

RITA: Look, Rudy, it's all part of my job. Que digan lo que digan. Al cabo they're drunk and they're having a good time.

CHICANO: How can you be so nice to those guys? They don't have any class.

RITA: Ay, Rudy, no les hagas caso. Es que están borrachos.

CHICANO: I don't like wetbacks. They sneak across the border and take away our jobs. And on top of it, el Bob cree que son good workers.

RITA: Well, Rudy, I guess they gotta make a living too.

CHICANO: I got friends who need jobs too, but Bob prefers those wetbacks. Besides, they're lousy workers. All they ever do is complain. I wonder what Bob would say if he knew that Salvador is in the middle of that parents' committee? Bob doesn't know that these people are a bunch of huevones.

SALVADOR: Oiga, Rita venga pa'cá. ¿No me puede decir cómo le puedo arreglar los papeles aquí a mi compa?

RITA: ¿Pa' qué?

SALVADOR: ¡Pos, por si lo agarra la migra!

RITA: No te hagas el tonto, que tú sabes que en Guadalupe la migra no molesta a nadie.

MEXICANO: ¡Ja! ¿Cómo que no? ¿El otro día no se llevaron a cincuenta de Santa María?

RITA: Pues, es que han de haber sido trabajadores malos.

MEXICANO: ¡Ah no! ¡Si a nosotros nos hacen trabajar como burros!

RITA: Pos yo no sé. Por ahi me dijeron que los mexicanos son muy flojos y malos pa'l trabajo.

MEXICANO: ¿Y quién jijos del chirriondo te dijo eso, mujer?

RITA: Cálmate. Yo no más te digo pa' que se pongan abusados.

MEXICANO: Mira, Salvador. Yo te apuesto que ese pocho desgraciado que está ahi aplastado, fue el que le dijo a Rita que éramos unos huevones.

SALVADOR: Porque está borracho, hombre, y no sabe lo que dice.

MEXICANO: ¡No, Salvador! Esa gente no es de confianza. Yo no sé como tú te revuelves con ellos en el famoso comité ese en que andas ahi.

SALVADOR: Es que, sí, hay razón. ¿Que no ves que, sí, hay muchos problemas?

MEXICANO: ¡No, no! Mira, el otro día, golpearon a m'ijo en la high school. Ahora tú, explícame por qué.

SALVADOR: Pues, quizá confundieron a tu hijo.

MEXICANO: ¡Confundieron, madre!

BOB: Hey, Rudy, is the conveyor belt working any better? I had some of my men fix it, but I'm not sure if it is still acting up.

CHICANO: Oh yes, Mr. Frazier! It was working much better today. It didn't stop once.

BOB: Call me, Bob, my workers are my friends.

CHICANO: Okay, Bob!

BOB: That's better. Say, you wouldn't happen to know who's behind this committee business, would you?

CHICANO: No, sir. All I heard is that some of the parents are upset because the teachers don't speak Spanish.

BOB: Well, if you hear anything, be sure to let me know.

CHICANO: Sure, Bob!

BOB: Hey, Rita! Let's keep our customers happy. How about another beer over here?

MEXICANO: ¡Mira! Ahí está ese cabrón, mitoteándole al patrón lo que le dijo a Rita.

SALVADOR: Cálmate hombre. Está borracho.

MEXICANO: A mí me importa puro sorbete. ¡Yo le voy a reventar la boca! (POLICEMAN *enters stage left.*)

POLICEMAN: Hey, Bob, how is it going?

BOB: Chuck! How are you?

POLICEMAN: Business looks good tonight.

BOB: Chuck, what has me worried is this bunch. Rita get the man a drink.

POLICEMAN: Not while I'm in uniform.

BOB: Listen, Chuck, come over here.

SALVADOR: Rita, trainos otra cerveza.

CHICANO: Andale, Rita, how about another one here?

MEXICANO: Oye, jijo de madre, esa cerveza la pedí yo. (*The* MEXICANO *gets up and scuffles with the* CHICANO *and the* POLICEMAN *interferes.* POLICEMAN *grabs the* MEXICANO.)

POLICEMAN: It looks like I'm gonna have to take this one in.

BOB: Take it easy, Chuck. Let the man go. It's only a friendly brawl.

POLICEMAN: I don't know. It looked like it was pretty serious to me. Do you speak English?

MEXICANO: Me no speaky notin.

POLICEMAN: I said do you speak English?

MEXICANO: Me no sabe.

POLICEMAN: I'm afraid I'm gonna have to see his papers.

BOB: Come here, Chuck. Rita, liven up the place. We'll have a round on the house. Chuck, I meant I'd be needing your help later. And besides, you're not the immigration. But, anyway, here's something for your troubles. (*Everybody freezes.*)

DEMONSTRATOR: A farmlabor contractor says: "The rancher makes an arrangement with the border patrol to pick up the illegal aliens one day before payday." (*Theme song gets louder as policeman exits stage left.*)

MEXICANO: ¡Ajúa! Oiga no más, Salvador. Esa música me trae recuerdos de mi terreno. Esta sí que la bailo con la Rita. ¡Rita! ¡Véngase a echar una chancleada! (CHICANO *gets up to take* RITA *from the* MEXICANO.)

CHICANO: Hey, wetback, leave this woman alone. (*Pushes* MEXICANO.)

MEXICANO: ¡Pocho jijo de tu China Mariz! Ahora, sí, te voy a reventar el hocico. (*Fight starts and freezes in meaningful tableaux. Theme song continues and actors exit.*)

SCENE SEVEN

DEMONSTRATOR: The Guadalupe priest says: "Those who follow César Chávez will go to hell." (*Parishioners enter stage left and take their positions stage left. They sing.*)

    Señor, ten piedad de nosotros
    Señor, ten piedad de nosotros
    Señor, ten piedad, Señor

Ten piedad de nosotros. (PRIEST *enters stage left and stands before the parishioners.* MR. BRADLEY, *a teacher, enters stage right and stands downstage right.*)

PRIEST: En el nombre del Padre, del Hijo y del Espíritu Santo. (*Freeze.*)

MR. BRADLEY: Ready, begin, "I pledge allegiance to the flag . . . " (*Freeze.*)

PRIEST: Pónganse de pie para el Santo Evangelio. (*Freeze.*)

MR. BRADLEY: ". . . with liberty and justice for all." (*Freeze.*)

PRIEST: Y le dijo Tomás al Señor, "Mi Señor y mi Dios." Y Jesús le dijo a Tomás, "Tú crees en mí porque me has visto, pero bien aventurados son aquéllos que creen en mí sin haberme visto." Esta es la palabra de Dios.

PARISHIONERS: Bendita sea la palabra de Dios.

PRIEST: Hínquense, mis hijos. (*Freezes.*)

MR. BRADLEY: Children this morning we will . . . (JUANITA *walks in.*) Juanita, you're late. Come here. Sit right here. (*Pulls her down onto chair.*) Why were you late? (JUANITA *doesn't answer.*) Well, I see you aren't going to talk with us. But you will answer me! Where is your homework?

JUANITA: (*Nervous.*) I didn't do it today, Mr. Bradley.

MR. BRADLEY: You didn't do it today? Why not?

JUANITA: I had to take care of my brothers and sisters.

MR. BRADLEY: Don't you have a mother?

JUANITA: You know she works late.

MR. BRADLEY: (*Slaps her on the head.*) Don't you ever speak to me that way. Now get up in front of the class. (*She shakes her head, afraid.*) I said . . . (*Freezes as he grabs her by the hair.*)

DEMONSTRATOR: The report to the Civil Rights Commission states: "In Guadalupe the Mexican-American is considered an inferior being, a beast of burden, and as such he is expected to act stupidly occasionally and to need a good switching to set him straight."

PRIEST: El Santo Evangelio de hoy nos enseña la gran importancia de la fe. En Guadalupe tenemos muchos problemas causados por esta falta. Señora, cállese por favor. ¿Que no ve que estamos en la casa de Dios? Aquí la gente ha perdido su fe en su país y en sus líderes. Ya han visto esto del comité. Este grupito de padres de familia quiere echarle la culpa a la mesa educativa por los problemas de la escuela. Quieren culpar especialmente a los patrones, a los rancheros que son tan buenos. Han hecho tanto por Guadalupe, sin mencionar lo mucho que han hecho por esta parroquia. Hasta los hijos siguen el mal ejemplo de los padres. ¿Han oído del "walkout"? No quieren respetar ni obedecer a sus profesores que son tan buenos . . .

MR. BRADLEY: I said get up! (*Pulling her up by the hair.*) Now you listen well, Juanita, and the rest of you. You have come to school to get an education. The most important part of education is discipline. When you go to work, whether you finish school or not, you will have to be on time—even in the fields. Isn't that right, Juanita?

JUANITA: Yes, teacher.

MR. BRADLEY: It's Mr. Bradley.

JUANITA: Yes, Mr. Bradley.

MR. BRADLEY: Now I'll take you to the office and you will receive a month's detention. If you are late again, you will be suspended. (*Addresses class.*) You've seen what happens to those who get out of line, so behave while I'm gone. (*Pushes* JUANITA.) You, let's go! (*Exit* JUANITA *and* MR. BRADLEY.)

PRIEST: Vayan en paz. La misa ha terminado.

PARISHIONERS: Demos gracias a Dios.

PRIEST: En el nombre del Padre, del Hijo y del Espíritu Santo. (*Parishioners, who are on their knees, begin picking tomatoes as "Vida de Muerte Lenta" is sung.* PRIEST *Exits.*)

> Aquí siguen trabajando
> Condiciones no van cambiando
> Si quieren cambiar su vida
> Campesinos fórmense en liga.
>
> El pobre sigue sufriendo
> Y el rico lo está oprimiendo
> Ya basta de esta malicia
> Gente, luchen por justicia.
>
> Lo que ven en esta obra
> Por el mundo está pasando

Con la lucha de los pobres
Va la fuerza aumentando.

El trabajo no comienza
En el corazón de otro
Si el sistema romperemos
Saldrá el cambio de nosotros.

Poco a poco va creciendo
La conciencia del obrero
Va exigiendo el campesino
La justicia al ranchero

No dejemos que nos exploten
Nuestro esfuerzo que no lo corten
Aunque digan que es muy difícil
Nuestra lucha no será inútil.

Todos tienen que tomar parte
Por sus hijos no hay que dejarse
Con la ayuda de todo el pueblo
Formaremos un mundo nuevo.

SCENE EIGHT

DEMONSTRATOR: In January of 1972, two hundred elementary school
students walked out in protest and said: "We want Mexican teachers
and to be treated like human beings." (*Chismosas's theme song begins as both chismosas come out from opposite ends into their gar-
dens.*)
En este pueblecito
Pues periódico pa' leer no hay
Pero sí tenemos dos chismosas
Con quien todo el chisme cae.

Acerque usted la oreja
Prometa no decir

Que el chisme es un secreto
Que jure no repetir.
POMPIS: Ay, comadre, ahi va la Rosie.
FRUTI: Ay, Rosie. (*Waves toward the street.*)
POMPIS: Vieja atascada. ¿Has visto como tiene la casa?
FRUTI: Como chiquero de puercos, comadre.
POMPIS: ¡Ay, ay, un topo, un topo is eating my radishes!
FRUTI: ¿Un topo?
POMPIS: Sí, it's your topo.
FRUTI: Lo siento, comadre, pero en mi jardín no hay topos.
POMPIS: I'm sorry, comadre, but this topo came from there. (*Pointing toward* FRUTI*'s garden.*)
FRUTI: Bueno, olvídalo, Pompita. El topo nos pertenece a las dos. Ay, pero te tengo un chismesito.
POMPIS: Ah, no. You have to wait your turn. Ahora me toca a mí.
FRUTI: Pos, échamelo, Pompita.
POMPIS: Abre bien los oídos, pues. Last Saturday at the cantina there was this big fight. Ah, pero qué pleito. Unos chicanos se pelearon con unos mexicanos . . .
FRUTI: Ya lo oí, comadre.
POMPIS: Después vino la chota . . .
FRUTI: No te digo que, ya lo oí.
POMPIS: ¿Y después qué?
FRUTI: (*Hits* POMPIS.) Comadre, ya lo oí.
POMPIS: Pero ¿Cómo? Si apenas me lo contó la Concha.
FRUTI: Uh, ese chisme está reviejo.
POMPIS: Pues, you should have let me told it anyway. Nada más para contarlo.
FRUTI: Pues, cuéntamelo. A ver si hay algo nuevo.
POMPIS: No, ya para qué. Ya no tiene chiste.
FRUTI: En ese caso yo te cuento el mío.
POMPIS: Andale, pues.
FRUTI: ¿Sabías que anoche tuvieron una meeting en la casa del Sr. Moreno?
POMPIS: Ah, esa meeting de los padres? Fíjate. I almost went. Nada más para ver lo que estaban haciendo, tú sabes.
FRUTI: Pues sabes que van a hacer trouble.
POMPIS: What are they going to do?
FRUTI: No sé, pero dicen que la Virgie y el Sr. Moreno van a quejarse al superintendente.
POMPIS: ¿De qué?

FRUTI: Pues que no tratan bien a los niños, que les pegan.

POMPIS: That's what I thought. Es true, you know. Pero, ¿qué van a ganar con quejarse? (*Goes back to her garden.*)

FRUTI: Lo que le encanta a esta gente es el escándalo y el barullo.

POMPIS: Ay, otra vez el topo asqueroso. Mira, comadre, tiene la mismita cara de Nixon.

FRUTI: Mujer, no seas escandalosa. A ver, ¿qué me decías?

POMPIS: Ya se metió el condenado. Mira, a mí me parece raro lo del Sr. Moreno. A mí me cae bien. I mean, I respect the man, don't you?

FRUTI: Oh, sí. Yo lo respeto mucho. Pero si ese viejo metiche se quiere meter en es mitote, pues que lo haga y que vaya con Dios. Ah, y hablando del diablo, ahi viene. (*Waves to* SR. MORENO.) Buenas tardes, Sr. Moreno. Ponte trucha, comadre. Ahora vamos a saber the real truth.

POMPIS: Just like in the movies?

FRUTI: Just like in the movies! (*They run out through their gate.*)

POMPIS: Sr. Moreno, espere un momentito.

SR. MORENO: Buenas tardes, Sra. Morones, Doña Fructuosa. Perdone que vaya de tanta prisa, pero voy a ver al superintendente. ¿No oyeron de la junta anoche en mi casa?

POMPIS: Sí, como no. Vimos a la Sra. Becerra en el supermercado, pero ahora queremos saber todos los details.

SR. MORENO: Hemos juntado una lista de quejas de muchos padres. Ah, suplicamos que firmen la lista para que nos apoyen. Hay que traer un cambio.

POMPIS: Sí, desde luego. Deme la pluma.

FRUTI: No firmes, te vas a meter en un lío.

POMPIS: Sí, sí firmo.

SR. MORENO: Gracias, Doña Morones. Y usted, señora, piénselo. Es para el bien de sus hijos también.

FRUTI: Sí, gracias lo pensaré. Buenas tardes. (SR. MORENO *exits.*) ¡Qué bonito, Pompita! Nada más eso me faltaba que me pusieras en ridículo con ese viejo.

POMPIS: Ay Fruti, forget it. Además, hay que ponernos a pensar. All the trouble in the schools, the kids walking out and everything. ¿Qué está pasando, comadre?

FRUTI: Yo te digo lo que está pasando. Los niños de hoy no tienen respeto a nada ni a nadie.

POMPIS: Pero, Fruti. Two hundred walked out. Doscientos chavalitos.

FRUTI: Han de haber sido veinte y la gente le puso otro cero.

POMPIS: Eran doscientos, comadre.

FRUTI: Te apuesto que los padres planearon todo.

POMPIS: No, no es cierto. The kids, ellos solos. They did it themselves. I know because my kids were in it. All they wanted were bilingual teachers and not to get hit so much.

FRUTI: Pues vale más que los míos no anden en ese barullo porque me los traigo a la casa de las orejas. (*Pulls* POMPIS's *ear.*)

POMPIS: Comadre, a veces los niños tienen razón. Remember when we used to go to school and they used to hit us? (*Hits* FRUTI *from the back.*) We didn't like it, did we? And maybe the parents could do something.

FRUTI: Yo lo dudo. Pero a ver qué pasa cuando vayan el Sr. Moreno y Virgie a ver al superintendente. Yo dudo que pase algo.

POMPIS: Comadre, creo que su phone está ringing.

FRUTI: Ha de ser mi comadre Bartola. ¡Vieja chismosa! Me cae como patada en la panza pero a ver que trae esta vez. Ahí me va a tener toda la santa tarde en el teléfono.

POMPIS: Me cuentas ¿eh? (*Both exit opposite ends. Chismosas's song concludes.*)

> Acerque usted la oreja
> Prometa no decir
> El chisme es un secreto
> Que jure no repetir.

SCENE NINE

MR. MORENO *and* VIRGIE *have been waiting to see the* SUPER-INTENDENT.

LILY: Mr. MacCarthy . . . ah . . . Mr. MacCarth . . . there are some people here to see you. It's Moreno and that loud lady, Mrs. González.

SUP: Not today Lily, not today.

LILY: Mr. MacCarthy, they've been waiting for a while. These parents have gotten so agressive ever since that walkout.

SUP: I guess I'll have to deal with them. Show them in, but come back to translate.

SR. MORENO: Siéntate aquí, Virgie.

SUP: Good afternoon. Lily, ask them what I can do for them this time.

LILY: El superintendente dice que ¿qué puede hacer por ustedes esta vez?

SR. MORENO: Señorita, dígale al Señor MacCarthy que venimos representando al comité de padres para discutir el mal trato de nuestros hijos en las escuelas.

LILY: Mr. MacCarthy, he says they are here representing some sort of committee, to discuss the problems of the school . . . about the mistreated children.

SUP: Well, as I recall, the last time you were here we discussed this matter quite thoroughly. I don't understand what more can be said.

LILY: Sr. Moreno, el superintendente dice que esta cosa la discutieron anteriormente.

VIRGIE: Señorita, hablamos bien el inglés. (*To* SUPERINTENDENT.) That's all you did Mr. MacCarthy, talk.

SUP: Miss Treviño is your elected representative. Why doesn't your committee voice your complaints to her?

SR. MORENO: She is not representing us. She represents you.

VIRGIE: We have gone to her many times. She does nothing; that's why we formed the comité.

SUP: ¿Comité? Who are these people? And if they have complaints, why haven't they come to me? But just so that we can maintain accurate records why don't we all speak into this recorder? And Lily, take notes.

SR. MORENO: Mr. MacCarthy we do not wish to be recorded.

SUP: Now, now, Mr. Moreno, this is a mere formality for accuracy of filing records. Now, who are these people and what are their names?

MR. MORENO: I don't have to tell you that Guadalupe's educational standing is the lowest in the state of California.

SUP: If we didn't have so many low ability students the ratings would be higher.

VIRGIE: The ratings would be higher if the students had bilingual teachers to help them instead of putting them in the EMR classes, because they do not understand English.

SUP: I don't see the advantage of Mexican-American teachers. And besides there is a low turn-over of teachers and there are no slots available.

VIRGIE: You think that two hundred children walked out because the schools are so good?

SUP: Surely, some of these kids were put up to it. They are not at a level to carry out strikes.

VIRGIE: We wish we would have thought of it ourselves.

SR. MORENO: All we are asking is that you look into the schools. Children are being mistreated, they are not learning anything, they are treated worse than animals.

SUP: Mr. Moreno, if you are referring to the disciplinary procedures employed by our teaching staff, all I can say is that discipline is an essential part of the educational process.

MR. MORENO: We agree discipline is necessary. But we don't believe a child ought to get hit simply because he does not understand English.

SUP: Oh now! Children do exaggerate, don't they, Miss Treviño?

TREVIÑO: Oh yes, they do!

VIRGIE: Do you call taping of the mouth and knocking their teeth out discipline?

SUP: These are serious accusations of which, I assure you, none have been brought to my attention.

MR. MORENO: Tell me, Mr. MacCarthy, why is it that the children are not allowed to use their forks in the cafeteria?

SUP: Lily, would you please tell him that the last time he was here, he was very interested in preserving the culture.

LILY: Sr. Moreno, el superintendente dice que la última vez que estuvo usted aquí estaba muy interesado en eso de la cultura.

SUP: Tell him that we were simply trying to comply with his demands by taking away their spoons and forks and letting them eat with their hands, as they are accustomed to at home.

LILY: Les quitaron los tenedores porque, como usted bien sabe, nuestra gente come con las manos. (*Freeze.*)

DEMONSTRATOR: A Guadalupe teacher says: "If we gave forks to the students, they'd just use them to stab one another."

SR. MORENO: If you were really concerned about our culture, you would hire bilingual teachers for our children.

VIRGIE: Here is a list of complaints, signed by two-hundred parents.

SUP: File it, Lily. I believe your time is up. I've got much to do and I'm sure you do too.

SR. MORENO: I must tell you that the parents are angry and that we will not stand for this any longer. We will keep pushing for our demands.

SUP: Lily, show them to the door.

VIRGIE: Don't bother, we know the way.

SR. MORENO: ¡Vámonos!

LILY: How rude!

SUP: Lily, call a meeting of the board immediately. Tell them it's an emergency! (SUP *exits stage left and* LILY *stage right while flute and guitar are playing.*)

SCENE TEN

DEMONSTRATOR: A Guadalupe school teacher says: "My Anglo students learn quicker. I don't know if it is environment or heredity." (*Unfreeze.*)

TEACHER: Class, as you recall me telling you earlier, today is a special day. Today is Guadalupe's birthday and to celebrate this special day she has prepared a special report on her name, which is the same as our town's name, right Guadalupe? (*Spoken with an Anglo accent.*)

STUDENT: Mr. Morgan, it's Guadalupe.

TEACHER: That's what I said, dear "Guadalupe." Now class, I want you all to pay attention as she gives her report. Come up here, dear, so everyone can see you better. That's right. Now stand straight and remember, enunciate.

STUDENT: Yo les voy a contar la historia de la Santa Virgen de Guadalupe porque así . . .

TEACHER: Guadalupe! Your report was supposed to be in English not Spanish! Not everyone understands Spanish.

STUDENT: But everyone here understands Spanish.

TEACHER: I don't understand or speak Spanish, so why don't we have the report in English?

STUDENT: But Carlitos and Rosario don't speak English and neither does María.

TEACHER: Your report will be done in English or it will not be done at all. Do I make myself perfectly clear?

STUDENT: Yes, Mr. Morgan.

TEACHER: You may continue.

STUDENT: Well, many many years ago there was an Indian named Juan Diego. He was walking on the hill of Tepeyac. He was going to mass. When all of a sudden a miracle happened. Above the sky there appeared la Santa Virgen de . . . I mean the Virgin de Guadalupe. She was a beautiful lady, she had long black hair and big brown eyes and she was real "morenita." She told Juan Diego that she would take care of all the sick and the poor . . .

TEACHER: Guadalupe, your report was supposed to be on Guadalupe the town, not the saint.

STUDENT: But, I wanted to write a story on the Virgen 'cause that's who I was named after, not this town.

TEACHER: But this is a public school and we can't bring in our religious legends, just because we're named after them.

STUDENT: It's not a legend, Mr. Morgan. Our people believe in the Virgen.

TEACHER: Oh, I'm sure they do. But she has little to do with the history of this town . . .

STUDENT: Well, I tried to write a story on this town, Mr. Morgan, but I couldn't. There was nothing nice to say.

TEACHER: Look at me, Guadalupe. I said, look at me. You're a deceitful little girl and I'm very ashamed of you. I demand that you apologize to me and to this classroom immediately.

STUDENT: But Mr. Morgan.

TEACHER: You will apologize now!

STUDENT: I'm sorry class. (*Both freeze. Flute and guitar with "Vida de Muerte Lenta" theme.*)

SCENE ELEVEN

After a moment, actors return to their places at sidelines and "Mr. Twenty-One" begins as theme music to the next scene. JESSE *enters stage right.* MOCHO *enters opposite.*

JESSE: Hey Mocho, what took you so long?

MOCHO: Ese, Jesse, why in this alley, carnal?

JESSE: This is the back of the restaurant where my wife works.

MOCHO: Tu jainita, and what the hell do we want with your jainita?

JESSE: Hey Mocho, she's got the money.

MOCHO: ¿Sabes qué, vatito? You pull this on me every goddamn time!

JESSE: You got the stuff, don't you?

MOCHO: ¡Simón! It's you that always screws up.

JESSE: Take it easy, Mocho. She'll have the money.

MOCHO: ¿Sabes qué? She better have the money, ese. I told you I don't like to carry the stuff around, ese. Y si me tuercen por tu culpa . . . ¡vas a marchar! (*Enter* TERRY.)

JESSE: Hi, babe! How was your day? You remember Mocho, don't you? Mocho, this is my old lady.

TERRY: What's he doing here?

JESSE: What do you mean what's he doing here? He just walked me over here. That's all. Come on, act nice. So where's your check?

TERRY: We didn't get them today.

JESSE: Look, this ain't no time for games, goddamn it! Now, where is your check at?

TERRY: I told you, I didn't get paid today. Our checks don't come until tomorrow.

JESSE: Until tomorrow? Hey babe, listen.

MOCHO: Como on, ese. ¡De volada, carnal!

JESSE: Hey be cool, Mocho, you'll get your money.

MOCHO: I always do.

TERRY: What the hell are you doing with Mocho, Jesse? Is he selling you some more of his stuff?

JESSE: Don't act like that, and don't talk so loud, huh? Where's your tips at, Terry?

TERRY: I don't have any.

JESSE: This ain't the time to hold out on me, babe. I need the money bad!

TERRY: I left them inside.

JESSE: Well, go get them.

TERRY: We haven't got any food in the house, the rent is due, and all you think about is your goddamn fix!

JESSE: Don't lecture me, Terry. Just get in there and get me those tips!

TERRY: I told you, they're inside and the place is closed until tomorrow!

JESSE: I can't wait until tomorrow!

MOCHO: Neither can I! (*Starts to exit.*)

JESSE: Wait up, Mocho!

TERRY: Let him go, Jesse. You don't need him. When are you going to quit, huh? When are you going to quit? (*To* MOCHO.) We don't have any more money. Why don't you leave him alone? Just leave us alone.

JESSE: Shut up, Terry. Shut up! (*To* MOCHO.) Wait a minute, Mocho. I'll get you the money.

MOCHO: Guacha, ese, I don't have to put up with all this jive!

JESSE: Look, she always has some stash hidden away at home. Just don't go, please, Mocho.

MOCHO: ¿Y qué esperas, ese? ¡Tiéndete de volada!

JESSE: You got some money at home, Terry? I know you always have some stashed away, don't you?

TERRY: I don't have anything. Jesse, look, why don't you come home with me? I can help you.

JESSE: Listen, Terry, I'll quit. I swear to God I'll quit. Just help me this one last time, babe. Please, Terry, you've got to help me!

TERRY: I told you, I don't have anything!

JESSE: Listen, Mocho, my old lady gets paid first thing in the morning. Why don't you set me straight until tomorrow? What d'you say, Mocho? I swear I'll give it to you in the morning.

MOCHO: I don't work that way.

JESSE: I'm hurting bad, Mocho.

MOCHO: I'm not a loan company, ese!

JESSE: Please! Just a little something until tomorrow.

MOCHO: ¿Sabes qué, carnal? I'll get you a filerazo for a small price.

JESSE: Sure, Mocho! Anything you say!

MOCHO: Ese, Jesse, tu ruca está de aquéllas, carnal. She's a fine looking chicky-doo!

JESSE: Hey, Mocho, she's my wife.

MOCHO: I don't mind.

JESSE: You don't understand.

MOCHO: ¡Nel, ese! You don't understand. I always get what I want and when I want it. So, te dejas caer con la feria o ¡córtate!

JESSE: (*Crosses to* TERRY.) Hey listen, babe.

TERRY: Let's go home, Jesse.

JESSE: I need a favor.

TERRY: What kind of a favor?

JESSE: Mocho thinks you look nice. You always look nice, babe.

TERRY: What are you saying?

JESSE: Mocho wants you to go have a drink with him, that's all.

TERRY: Jesse! I'm your wife, not your whore!!

JESSE: Keep it down! Are you going to help me or not?

TERRY: When are you going to quit?

JESSE: This is the last time, Terry, I swear it. You gonna help me?

TERRY: Jesse . . .

JESSE: Huh? Are you gonna help me?

TERRY: I just want you to quit.

JESSE: I said, are you going to help me? Answer me, Terry, or I'll break your goddamn neck! (*Pushes her.*)

TERRY: All right!!

JESSE: She'll do it, Mocho. (*Grabs the heroin from* MOCHO *and exits.*)

MOCHO: (*Tries to help her up and she pulls away.*) ¡Orale, esa! We're going for a little walk. (TERRY *pulls away with anger.*) Come on, you little bitch! Aquí vas a caminar morra. And you better be nice. You'll be real nice. (TERRY *and* MOCHO *exit.*)

249

SCENE TWELVE

The School Board is frozen stage left. The members of the comité are frozen stage right. DEMONSTRATOR *walks across stage singing:*

> Por ahi se oye de una junta importante
> El comité de padres ya se va a juntar
> Pues los políticos ya andan con sus movidas
> Vamos a ver cómo se van a organizar.

SUP: (*School Board secret meeting unfreezes.*) I apologize for calling you on such short notice, but I felt it necessary to act immediately. We, as the School Board, must consider this serious matter.

TREVIÑO: For God's sake, Kent, what is it?

POLICE CHIEF: Have they cut our funds or something?

SUP: No, but today I was confronted by Mrs. González and Mr. Moreno. They gave me a list of signed complaints. Their people are organized. They've got the momentum and they want to do something.

TREVIÑO: They can't do anything.

BOB: They already have. A couple of my workers have already joined that comité. Next thing they'll be bringing in the Chávez Union.

SUP: He's right. We have to think of the good of our community.

POLICE CHIEF: Next time they meet at that Moreno house, we'll patrol the area more heavily.

BOB: That hasn't worked.

POLICE CHIEF: Then let's take legal action. This conspiracy must stop.

SUP: What kind of legal action did you have in mind, Chuck?

CHIEF: Whatever is necessary.

BOB: Legally, they haven't done anything wrong.

CHIEF: One time is all it takes.

TREVIÑO: Look, those people always start something, but they never finish it. Why, it's just a passing fad for them. Believe me, I know.

BOB: Then why don't you talk to them?

TREVIÑO: Oh, ah, well, what will I say? They won't listen to me, even though I have tried representing them on the school board.

BOB: They may not listen to you, but they might listen to someone like . . . ! (*School Board Freezes. Comité unfreezes.*)

VIRGIE: ¡Marcos Cortez! Why are they bringing that fool to speak?

SR. MORENO: Quieren desacreditar el comité.

SRA. MORENO: Dios mío, ¿será tanto lo que pedimos?

OCHOA: No entiendo. ¿Qué tiene que ver el Sr. Cortez con el PTA?

FUENTES: I'm not sure. The first time I heard about him he was in Salinas making some strong speeches against the Union.

OCHOA: Y ¿qué pasó?

FUENTES: Well, the farmworkers were pretty upset, but what could they do? They knew it was supposed to make the Union look bad.

SRA. BECERRA: The ranchers probably paid him to talk.

SRA. MORENO: ¿Pensará que somos la Unión?

OCHOA: ¿El comité?

FUENTES: Aha, I think so.

SRA. BECERRA: Well, we support the Union but the comité isn't the Union.

VIRGIE: We know that, but they don't.

OCHOA: Y ¿qué pitos toca este Sr. Cortez?

VIRGIE: Es del John Birch Society. Son muy conservadores y racistas.

SRA. MORENO: Y dicen los letreros que va a hablarnos sobre la verdad del movimiento chicano.

VIRGIE: What does he know about Chicanos? I don't understand why the PTA is all of a sudden so concerned with Chicanos. ¿Cuántas veces nos dejaron para lo último en sus agendas?

SR. MORENO: No sé. Pero tienen al pueblo descontento.

SRA. MORENO: ¡Qué cosas están pasando! Hasta en la escuela andaban los policías buscando bombas. Así me dijeron los niños.

VIRGIE: Who wants to bomb the school?

SRA. BECERRA: Well, you know the PTA never calls special meetings.

SR. MORENO: Por eso tenemos que resolver esto. (*Comité freezes, School Board unfreezes.*)

CHIEF: They won't listen to that Marcos Cortez. Why, he doesn't speak for them.

BOB: Exactly!

CHIEF: Huh . . . oh, I see.

TREVIÑO: Should Marcos Cortez be invited to our next city council meeting?

CHIEF: Yes. Get the whole crowd of them while me and my boys are ready to crack some heads.

BOB: I don't think they'll come to a city council meeting.

SUP: Well, since they're so interested in the schools, why don't we invite Mr. Cortez to a PTA meeting? Eh, Treviño? I want you to set it up. Advertize it big. I want all of those people there. (*School Board freezes. Comité unfreezes.*)

SRA. BECERRA: Can't we do anything? The people are pretty mad.

SR. MORENO: Bueno, es obvio que es un ataque directo al comité.

Quieren silenciarnos.

SRA. BECERRA: That's right. They want to crush anything that will destroy their "clica."

OCHOA: Lo sé, pero como trabajamos para ellos, tenemos que jugar sus juegos o adiós al trabajo. Ya vieron lo que me pasó a mí. Creo que ya no se puede cancelar la junta.

SR. MORENO: Entonces no nos queda más que decidir si iremos a la junta.

ALL: Claro que sí.

VIRGIE: And I'll tell that Marcos Cortez exactly what I think of him.

SR. MORENO: No, Virginia es mejor dejar que diga lo que quiera.

VIRGIE: But he doesn't know what he is saying.

FUENTES: It's the best thing. Let him talk all he wants.

SRA. BECERRA: But people aren't going to stay calm.

SR. MORENO: It's up to us to keep them calm. Bueno, al fin estamos todos de acuerdo de no excitarnos en la junta. Ya sabemos como repartirnos entre la comunidad. Animo, compañeros, y vámonos. (*Comité begins to move offstage towards the audience. Then freezes enroute.* DEMONSTRATOR *once again sings.*)

DEMONSTRATOR: Fíjense bien en todo lo que está pasando abran los ojos, que nos tuercen la verdad. (*Comité unfreezes and walks into the audience.* ALICIA TREVIÑO *comes downstage.*)

TREVIÑO: Good evening. It's so nice to see so many of you here tonight at this PTA meeting. My name is Alicia Treviño. Alicia Treviño, your representative on the School Board. Anyway, I'll be your hostess for tonight's special meeting. Tonight we have a very special guest who has come to speak to you on the truth behind the Chicano Movement. But before we begin please stand for the flag salute. Please stand! "I pledge allegiance to the flag of the United States of America and to the republic for which it stands, one nation under God with justice and liberty for all." Thank you. Father Cruz will now lead us in a prayer. Father Cruz. (FATHER CRUZ *comes downstage.*)

FATHER CRUZ: Qué gusto me da ver a tanta gente en esta junta. ¡Pero qué tanto más me diera ver algunos de ustedes en la misa este domingo! Bueno, recemos. Señor, esta noche es una gran ocasión para nosotros. Tenemos al Sr. Marcos Cortez que va a hablar de algo muy importante. Por eso, Señor, bendice a Marcos Cortez. Señor, a veces esta gente no escucha lo que debe escuchar. Por eso, Señor, bendice a Marcos Cortez.

AUDIENCE: A César Chávez.

FATHER CRUZ: En el nombre del Padre, del Hijo y del Espíritu Santo. (*Exit priest.*)

TREVIÑO: Before we bring out our special guest, let me give you a slight background. He is a very hardworking young man in the community. He is an outstanding citizen and an excellent business-man. Why, in fact, he's probably the only used car salesman that I trust. Marcos Cortez! (FATHER CRUZ *comes and whispers something to* TREVIÑO.) Excuse me, there's been a slight delay. (COR-TEZ *enters as in first scene.*)

CORTEZ: Hey, bring in a couple of those guards and close those doors! I want a couple of men down here in the first row and some-one to watch these exits. (*Addresses audience.*) My name is Marcos Cortez and I've come here tonight to speak on the truth behind the Chicano Movement. (*Freeze—drum roll—unfreeze.*) They should go back to Mexico where they come from. Wouldn't you agree, Mrs. González?

VIRGIE: No. I don't. (*Freeze—drum roll—unfreeze.*)

MRS. BECERRA: What do you know about Guadalupe? You live in Santa María. (*Freeze—drum roll—unfreeze.*)

CORTEZ: I'm a vendido?! When are you people going to stop mak-ing excuses for your laziness!? (*Freeze—drum roll—unfreeze.*)

SRA. MORENO: Mandamos a nuestros hijos para que los eduquen, no que los maltraten. (*Freeze—drum roll—unfreeze.*)

CORTEZ: Obviously you women in the Chicano Movement don't know your place. Why aren't you in the home taking care of your children where you belong?

VIRGIE: We are taking care of our children. What do you think we're doing here? (*Freeze—drum roll—unfreeze.*)

CORTEZ: The question is "Who is responsible for putting the par-ents up to such a thing?" I'll tell you who. It's groups such as MECHA, the Brown Berets and the United Farmworkers who are willfully deceiving and misinforming the community. (*Unfurls the flags—drum roll.*)

VIRGIE: This is not a political meeting! (*Drum roll.*)

SR. MORENO: ¡Es contra la ley usar una escuela pública para funciones políticas! ¡Usted está quebrando la ley!

SALVADOR: ¡Esta junta era para discutir los problemas de nuestros hijos!

SOMEONE IN AUDIENCE: You're a vendido!

SR. MORENO: Cálmese, señorita. Es un títere de los rancheros.

SOMEONE IN AUDIENCE: ¡Que viva la huelga! ¡Qué viva la causa! ¡Qué viva César Chávez!

EVERYBODY IN AUDIENCE: ¡Que viva César Chávez! ¡Que viva César Chávez! (*Freeze.* POLICEMAN *stands on stage left and reads report: Actors come up on stage as they are called by name.*)

POLICEMAN: Sheriff's Department, Santa Barbara County, Offense report. On March 16, 1972, this officer was on duty at the Guadalupe joint union school. I and other officers attended the meeting because we had reports that the UFWA, the Brown Berets and MECHA would attempt to disrupt the meeting at the school. The speaker, Mr. Marcos Cortez, has very opposite political views from those involved with the organizations previously mentioned. It became apparent that there were many persons at the meeting that were trying to keep Mr. Cortez from speaking. This officer saw and heard many persons stand up and shout in Spanish. The noise became so loud that Mr. Cortez was not able to continue and the meeting was stopped. Described below are the actions of listed suspects and witnessed by fellow officers and witnesses . . .

Suspect number one: VIRGINIA GONZALEZ. As the tempo of the disruption became worsened, suspect number one got up from her seat and approached the front of the building where Cortez was standing. She got in front of Mr. Cortez and began to yell at him and at the audience. Some of what suspect said was in Spanish, and this officer could not understand what she said. She appeared to be very worked up. After apparently getting a signal from another male Mexican, she again went to the front of the room and began yelling that the meeting was not political. Through investigation it was found that suspect number one is currently applying for citizenship and is very involved in the parents' committee in Guadalupe and also involved with the United Farmworkers. Sentence: Two years probation.

Suspect number two: MARIA MORENO. Suspect stood up numerous times and yelled at the speaker. The suspect is known to be involved in both the parents' committee and United Farmworkers. Sentence: Two years probation.

Suspect number three: MIGUEL FUENTES. During the meeting this officer observed suspect yelling and apparently directing Virginia González to the front of the room. During the meeting, suspect was seen conversing with a large crowd of Brown Berets. Suspect is active in many organizations, but is deeply involved with the United Farmworkers. Sentence: Ten days in county jail and three years probation.

Suspect number four: SALVADOR OCHOA. It was learned that suspect was one of the individuals making much of the disturbance. It was also found that suspect is not a citizen of this country. Suspect is deeply involved with the parents' committee and is a member of the United Farmworkers. Sentence: Five days in county jail and three years probation.

Suspect number five: RUBEN HERNANDEZ. Officer Martinez advised this officer that he had observed listed suspect making a disturbance at the meeting by yelling at the speaker. Suspect is a known member of the Brown Berets. Upon further investigation, it was learned that this suspect was not at the described meeting.

Suspect number six: ANTONIA BECERRA. Mr. Cortez and other witnesses related that they observed suspect sitting in the front of the room with another suspect. Both suspects were yelling and disturbing the meeting. Suspect is associated with the parents' committee and is also deeply involved in the United Farmworkers. Sentence: Suspended.

Suspect number seven: JUAN MORENO. This officer observed suspect stand and yell at the audience in Spanish. This officer did not understand what he said, but he appeared to be exremely excited. From all indications, this suspect was one of the leaders, and provoked the audience with his remarks. Suspect is head of the education committee and is not a citizen of the United States. Suspect is deeply involved with the United Farmworkers. Sentence: Forty-five days in county jail and three years probation.

VIRGIE: (VIRGIE *steps out in front and addresses everyone.*) Señoras y señores, venimos desde Guadalupe aquí a la cárcel de Santa Bárbara protestando el arresto de nuestros esposos y amigos. Han sido acusados de un delito, el que es habernos organizado para pedir que las escuelas den a nuestros hijos una mejor educación. We should not be ashamed of what we've done. On the contrary, we should be proud. Yes, of having been able to be recognized as men and women and children struggling for something that is nothing more than just. Porque no es justo que se nos humille por ser pobres y mexicanos. No es justo que abusen de nuestros hijos en las escuelas. No es justo que a nuestros hijos se les niegue la oportunidad de adquirir una educación que los saque de la cárcel de la pobreza. Cada vez que se pide justicia, hay que sacrificarse and our brothers have sacrificed themselves. Because we as human beings have a right to that justice. And if it's a crime to fight for the education of our children, si es un crimen el pelear por la educación de nuestros hijos, ¡entonces que nos echen a la cárcel a todos!

(*Guitar strum. Heads are lowered.* DEMONSTRATOR *sings.*)

DEMONSTRATOR: Señoras y señores, aquí termina
La historia del pueblito guadalupano
Y ahora con respeto les pediré
Que escuchen la canción de despedida.

Ustedes que ya escucharon
La historia que se contó
No sigan allí sentados
Pensando que ya pasó
No basta sólo el recuerdo
El canto no bastará
No basta sólo el lamento
Miremos la realidad.

La historia que han escuchado
No se les vaya a olvidar
Está pasando ahorita
No dejen que pase más
Amerindia es tan grande
Mil cosas pueden pasar
Si es que no nos preparamos
Dispuestos para luchar
Tenemos razones puras
Tenemos por qué pelear
Tenemos las manos duras
Tenemos por qué ganar.

Unámonos como hermanos
Que nadie nos vencerá
Si quieren esclavizarnos
Jamás lo podrán lograr
La tierra será de todos
También será nuestro el mar
Justicia sea para todos
Y abrace la libertad
Luchemos por los derechos
Que todos deben tener
Luchemos por lo que es nuestro

Que nadie nos vaya a vencer.

Unámonos como hermanos
Que nadie nos vencerá
Si quieren esclavizarnos
Jamás lo podrán lograr
Si quieren esclavizarnos
Jamás lo podrán lograr.

Money

Money was first produced as a workshop by the Ensemble Studio Theater in New York City in 1976 and was followed by another production at the Body Politic in Chicago in 1978. Of the New York production, critic Mel Gussow observed that Girón was " . . . asking tantalizing questions about matters of life support: Where does the money go? Where should it go? And what effect does it have?"[1] Noting that the Ensemble Studio Theatre production was a work-in-progress, Roderick Mason Faber commented, " . . . the four characters have a sharp vividness that makes one want to see the play again when it is a work more progressed than at present."[2] The text presented here represents the playwright's subsequent revisions; improvements that make the play ready for further productions. But the theme of this play is not without risk, indicating the fact that sometimes the necessary theater can be dangerous as well.

Proof of that danger is the fact that Girón was fired for having written *Money*. The incipient playwright had worked for two previous foundations, and it was while employed as a program officer in a third foundation that it occurred to him to write a play about the effects of money and power on the poor. In the playwright's words,

"Although there are almost 26,000 foundations in this country, there are virtually no plays about them. Once I had written *Money*, my wife, being a very moral person, advised me to tell the foundation people that I had written this play, but that it did not have to do with them. I then met with my supervisor and began to tell her this when, before I could finish my sentence, she said, 'Then you don't belong here.' "[3]

Dismissed on the spot, Girón left the foundation world to explore his potential as a writer.[4]

"If a foundation officer is contemptuous of his co-workers and supplicants seeking financial aid, particularly women, he is not fit to dispense charity," the playwright commented in discussing this play and the role of women in our society. Some of the material in the play is based on true incidents and real people. "The story about Clark is actually true," Girón relates. "A friend of mine married the heir to a vast fortune and she described her wedding night as the most horrible experience of her life. Her husband had only had sex with prostitutes. As a young man—like the fictitious Prudden—her husband's father had told him, 'Don't marry it, buy it!' "

"The foundations were co-opting people during the seventies," the playwright continued, "in foundation parlance they called it 'enlightened self-interest.' " Having witnessed the corporate foundation world from within, Girón was able to expose actual events and emotions that influenced his decision to write this play. Girón's mother's comment about his becoming a "stoneface" obviously affected the characterizations in *Money*, for that is what Prudden represents, those stonefaces of the corporate foundation world who give out monies for self-aggrandizement with no passion whatsoever. Prudden is passionless and his life is meaningless. He is also above the law, because " . . . our tax laws grant the very rich the right to decide how their tax dollars will be spent."[5]

In the playwrights words, "*Money* is a poetic metaphor, not an exposé." As such, this play should not be perceived as a "naturalistic" play, although the setting is described to look like real foundation headquarters. If the setting is a recreation of an actual office, this "reality" is sharply contrasted with the allegorical-like characters. Actually, this play is a modern morality play in which Prudden and Floyd are the allegorical figures representing the corruption that can be caused by powerful men and their lackeys, contrasted with the apparent victims of their greed in Magda and Antonio. Magda's very name, taken from Magdalena, cannot escape notice, as she has become the archetypical prostitute, selling herself for money.

Magda has come to the foundation with a double agenda. At first, the audience does not know her ulterior motive, thinking that she is only looking for funding for her clinic. We know that Antonio and Magda are in some kind of relationship, but we can sense that this woman will use whatever means necessary to achieve her goals. She seems, in fact, to be using Antonio, just as she is destined to use the foundation itself. Her coolness, her determination, are at once compelling and distracting. "Who is this woman?" we ask, sensing that her reasons for being here are far from ordinary.

All the while the characters do not seem to speak to one another, but to themselves. Early in the play Antonio is telling Warren about Magda's life: "She's had it rough." He continues, "Had to put a fellow she married in a box when she was just a kid." Antonio is actually describing Warren when he says, "The family arranged for a man who worked for them" to get her husband's body and escort it back to them. Neither we nor Antonio, realize that he is describing Warren, nor that Warren knows that he is the man in question. When Antonio then says that the "escort sexually attacked Magda," Warren quickly changes the subject by referring to the temperature of the room, seeming to ignore Antonio out of disinterest.

259

When Warren changes the topic of conversation, the discussion then goes from the general (we do not yet know Magda, so she is an abstraction) to the specific: this room is cold. Girón's technique of having his characters talk around a subject leads to a fascinating play on words, ideas and emotions that develops as the play's action unfolds. In the playwright's words, "There is an emotional subtext throughout the play," and this subtext seethes under the facade of corporate respectability.

"Prudden pisses ice water," Warren tells Antonio, in another reminder of the indifferent frigidity of these people and their surroundings. The medieval morality plays frightened their audiences into Christian submission with visions of Hell's mouth, complete with flames reaching out and devils with firecrackers on their tails taunting the audience as they threw "sinners" into the fire. In Girón's morality play, however, this hell is cold. But the people that matter are hot.

Magda's story about the dog at China Lake fighting to liberate itself from the rich young man's car is certainly a metaphor for her own struggle as a poor person. When she utters the name Clark Prudden, however, her story becomes more than an anecdote about some stranger. This was Prudden's son, we learn, and Magda enjoys telling Warren and Antonio who she really is: "He wanted to buy me . . . a new dress. He wanted to buy me. He wanted to show me the world from way up in his airplane. And I let him. (*Pause.*) You people have a lot to pay for." The playwright closes the first act with Prudden's entrance immediately following this discovery. Prudden's appearance, an entrance anticipated throughout the first act, leaves us in delicious suspense when the curtain closes on his seemingly naive question: "What have you brought us today, Anthony?"

But the question is not innocent. Prudden does not ask "Who have you brought us today?" but "what?" Magda is an object to Prudden, a potential recipient or another name for the rejection file. He also calls Antonio "Anthony," leaving no doubt about his ability to manipulate his people and anybody around him. By calling him "Anthony," Prudden takes away Antonio's cultural identity and we are left to wonder if this token Hispanic realizes how he is being used.

Act Two further reveals the relationship between the giver and the receiver. Although both Antonio and Warren are in the room, when Magda asks to be alone with Prudden he responds, "You are alone . . . You've got the privacy of the confessional here. I'm your neighborhood priest." "And I'm a poor sinner," she responds, continuing, "I know that. But are all poor men automaticaly sinful because they're poor?" Prudden's immediate answer is "They pray a lot," leaving Magda's reply to complete the thought: "To you."

All the while, the other two men do not exist in either Prudden's or

Magda's minds. In this foundation you can have a "private" conversation in the presence of lesser employees, as if the other two were invisible servants. When Antonio finally interjects supporting remarks about Magda, Prudden quickly retorts, "Are you taking notes! Get back to your knitting! Pencil in one hand, pad in the other, mouth shut, eyes down, ears open!"

The passion that drives Magda and Antonio is always apparent, contrasted with the indifference of their would-be benefactor. In an uncharacteristic show of emotion, however, Prudden himself makes the ultimate declaration of why he and others like him give their money away: "From the beginning of time the rich helped the poor—not to fill a few rotting bellies—but for the good of their own selfish, immortal souls!" Prudden remains cool and detached during his interview of Magda until she reaches into her purse, looking for something. Prudden lunges for her and grabs her wrist. The other two men think that she is reaching for a weapon, but when Warren shouts, "Careful—she's dangerous!", Prudden answers, "Quiet! I'm counting. You've got a fever, I think. . . . You're burning up." And she is. The question then becomes, "Will Magda get what she wants—and what is that?"

As the second act progresses, the playwright sets us up for one thing and reverses our expectations, creating more questions that will soon be answered. Did Mr. Curraciolo really leave a bomb behind Prudden's chair? Why does Magda know Luis, the Mexican who delivers coffee? Is this Luis a member of a possible conspiracy created by Magda to bomb the foundation? Does Antonio really love Magda? Will Antonio betray her?

If the characters vacillate from one objective to another, creating a sense of non-reality, that is the playwright's vision of what this world is really like: a world in which people do not connect with one another except on a superficial level. By the conclusion of the play, however, all these questions have been answered but two: "Will Antonio return and will Magda overcome the foundation's propensity for co-optation?"

The hope is that Antonio can really get out of it, that he will save himself and do well outside the corporate foundation structure. In the playwright's eyes, if Antonio escapes the foundation world, he will become a real person. In contrast, Magda will get her revenge by infiltrating the foundation or "ripping it off," to use a street phrase from the period in question. Magda's first act of retaliation is to get Warren dismissed, which is on her personal agenda. Magda has infiltrated this bastion of wealth and power and, by playing Latin music on her radio, she is making this space her own, ready to bring about positive changes for her community. Antonio, however, had lost touch with that community and represents some hope for social change and justice working on the outside.

Like Charley Bacon, the protagonist in Girón's later play, *Charley Bacon and His Family*, Antonio must leave the corporate world to find his true self. The two characters are very much alike, in fact, because both discover through the course of their odyssey that what they thought of as success was only what they believed society wanted them to be. Charley must dance to free himself from that world without emotion, as he successfully performs the Yaqui Deer Dance on the corporate plaza. Antonio is not going to literally dance, perhaps, but he is going to seek his truth elsewhere, using the mambo as his symbol of liberation. Significantly, his dance will be to a Latino rhythm.

[1]Mel Gussow, "Dempster's Ensemble Studio Invests in Plays and People," *New York Times*, 14 May 1976, n.p.

[2]Roderick Mason Faber, "Money," *The Village Voice*, 17 May 1976, n.p.

[3]Unless otherwise indicated, this and all subsequent quotes by the playwright are from telephone interviews, August 1988. In fact, Girón notes that S.N. Behrman wrote a light comedy about a man who works at a foundation titled *But For Whom, Charlie?* (out-of-print; available in ms. form from Samuel French, Los Angeles and New York, 1964), but there are no other plays that question the foundation world.

[4]Significantly, a very important Off-Broadway producer wanted to produce this play and cast the following actors in a workshop production: Raúl Juliá as Antonio, Jane Alexander as Magda, Douglass Watson as Prudden and Terry Kaiser as Warren. But a fully mounted production was never realized because the producer was advised against it by his development staff who feared contention from major corporate donors. However, Girón is quick to advise potential producers that, in fact, the Ensemble Studio Theater actually increased its corporate support after its production of *Money*.

[5]David Johnston, " "Deciding How Your Tax Money Will Be Spent," *Los Angeles Times Book Review*, 3 January, 1988, p. 8.

Arthur Girón

Arthur Girón was born in New York City in 1937, the son of a Guatemalan dentist who was then serving his government as the Guatemalan Consul in New York. While he was still a child, Girón's family moved to Hollywood, California, where his father was a dentist to the stars at MGM Studios. When Girón was thirteen years old his father passed away and his mother returned with Arthur and his brother to Guatemala. After the somewhat idyllic world of Hollywood (he used to swim every week in Carmen Miranda's pool), Girón began to discover his Latin American heritage, acting in Spanish classics in Guatemalan villages. "Guatemala has a rich theatrical heritage of ritual and drama," Girón reminds us, enthusiastic about his country's place in the development of a theatre in the Americas that pre-dates the arrival of Columbus by several centuries.[1]

While living in Guatemala, Girón could think of nothing but the theater. He had seen the Russian actress Eugenie Leontovich and Charles Laughton in *The Cherry Orchard* in Los Angeles and he could not get that picture out of his mind for the four years he was in his parents' homeland. He then returned to Los Angeles and begged Ms. Leontovich, who had studied with Stanislavski, to teach him to act. Girón studied with the Russian actress for four years and also completed a degree in Theater at UCLA. But with a mother and brother to support, Girón had to give up acting and enter the "respectable" world of banking and foundations. After a few years of this career he decided to return to Guatemala once again, where he married Mariluz Asensio. He and Mariluz then moved to New York.

For several years Girón had been thinking of a play about Edith Stein, the Jewish philosopher who became a Carmelite nun and died in a concentration camp at Aushwitz in 1942. Edith Stein's dramatic life posed many questions for Girón, themes that would recur in his writings: "Is it possible to change one's life in middle age? Can one be two persons at once? Why won't the world accept us as we are?" While working in the corporate world, Girón pursued a Master of Fine Arts degree in playwriting in the evenings, leading to his first play to address these themes, *Edith Stein*.[2] Once completed, *Edith Stein* was immediately optioned and first produced at the Arena Stage in Washington, D.C., under the direction of Zelda Fichandler in 1969.[3]

The initial interest in *Edith Stein* essentially launched Girón's future career as a playwright, forcing him to confront the very issues his first play questioned, to take a critical look at his own life and current occupation. In the words of John Glore, "his efforts to become a 'normal,' respectable man had turned him into what his mother used to call a 'stoneface'—a man out of touch with his heart."[4] He then decided to "commit to that which inspired him," and he successfully pursued the playwright's craft. To Girón's credit, each of his subsequent plays has been produced professionally, including *Money* (1976),[5] *Dirty Jokes* (1976), *Innocent Pleasures* (1978), *Becoming Memories* (1981)[6] and *Charley Bacon and His Family* (1985).[7]

After writing *Money*, Girón did not investigate an overtly Hispanic theme until he wrote *Charley Bacon and His Family*, an autobiographical exploration of the questions raised in *Edith Stein*. With a renewed interest in Hispanic themes, Girón welcomed a commission from Joesph Papp to write a play about the relationship between the U.S. and Central America. Tentatively titled *A Dream of Wealth*, this new play employs the metaphor of the United Fruit Company in Guatemala to dramatize the consequences of conquest among Mayan women, their Spanish lords and a band of high-spirited banana cowboys.[8]

A Dream of Wealth is the first play in a trilogy dealing with aspects of "Manifest Destiny." The other two plays examine the Mexican-American War and William Walker's attempt to conquer Nicaragua. "The Mexican-American War was this country's first Vietnam," the author states, "and nobody ever talks about it." Walker's intrusion into the lives of Nicaraguans also demonstrates a North American propensity to treat Latin Americans like innocent, naive "little brothers" who do not know what is best for them.

Girón began teaching playwriting at Carnegie-Mellon University in 1981 and is currently the Head of the Graduate Playwriting Program at this prestigious institution. He divides his time between New York City and Pittsburgh. The Girón's have one son, Felipe, who graduated from Boston College in 1987 with a degree in Philosophy and who now works in New York City.

Along with his activities as a playwright and teacher, Mr. Girón has been very instrumental in the development of several Hispanic arts and theater organizations in New York. He has served on the board of directors of such organizations as TOLA (Theater of Latin America), Museo del Barrio and the Institute of Contemporary Hispanic Art. He also helped establish AHA, (Association of Hispanic Arts) and Theater for the Forgotten, which is a theater that tours to prisons. Girón is a founding member of Ensemble Studio Theater in New York City and is a member of the Dramatists Guild and the Writers Guild of America. Needless to say, directors and producers alike look forward to more plays from this intelligent and sensitive writer.

¹This and all subsequent statements by Mr. Girón are from a series of telephone interviews with the playwright in August and September of 1988. The only extant pre-Columbian play is the *Rabinal Achi* (The Warrior of Rabinal), performed by the Maya-Quiche peoples in Guatemala for centuries. This play was published in the following editions: *Rabinal Achi*, translated by Richard Leinaweaver, *Latin American Theatre Review*, 1 (Spring 1969): 3–53 and *Rabinal Achi; Teatro indígena pre-hispánico*, Francisco Monterde, ed. (Mexico: Ediciones de la Universidad Autónoma, 1955).

²In what might be termed an ironic twist, given the theme of the play published in this anthology, Mr. Girón notes that he was able to complete *Edith Stein* with a fellowship from the Ford Foundation, which allowed him a residency at the Arena Stage.

³*Edith Stein* was produced by the Zephyr Theatre in Los Angeles, directed by Lee Sankowich in 1979. In 1988 Mr. Sankowich directed *Edith Stein* for the following companies: Pittsburgh Public Theater; GeVa Theater, Rochester, New York; and the Pilgrim Project, New York.

⁴From the program notes by John Glore for *Charlie Bacon and His Family*, produced at the South Coast Repertory Theatre, Costa Mesa, California, in 1987. *Dirty Jokes* was produced by the Academy Festival Theatre in Lake Forest, Illinois, directed by Lee Sankowich and starring Michael Moriarty. *Innocent Pleasures* was produced by the Ensemble Studio Theatre in New York City, directed by Harold Stone.

⁵*Money* was Girón's M.F.A. thesis play for Hunter College of the City University of New York.

⁶First seen at the Illusion Theatre in Chicago, *Becoming Memories* is Girón's most produced play, with subsequent productions at the South Street Theater, New York City, 1983; South Coast Repertory Theater, Costa Mesa, California, 1984; Pittsburgh Public Theater, 1985; NYU Undergraduate students at Tisch School of the Arts, 1985 and 1986; Cornell University, 1986, and the Juillard School, 1988. Other productions in 1988 include: The Renegade Theater, Hoboken, New Jersey, and Hofstra University, directed by Carol Coustendieck. *Becoming Memories* is published by Samuel French, Inc., New York, 1987.

⁷*Charlie Bacon and His Family* was first produced in 1985 by the Ark Theatre Company in New York City. This play was also produced in 1988 by the John Drew Theater in Easthampton, New York.

⁸*A Dream of Wealth* is in draft form, as yet unproduced or published.

Money

By Arthur Girón

CHARACTERS

Antonio
Warren P. Floyd
Magda Webb
Leslie Prudden
Luis
Sr. Carrasco

ACT ONE

On top of the world, the 59th floor tower offices of a corporate foundation in San Francisco, California. The conference room before us represents the zenith of exhilirating modern design. Functional, elegant, cold, its lines and textures conspire to carry away the visitor with gleaming authority, and evident wealth. A home for the business nobility.

The space is marked by a blazing white, luxuriant rug. Above it, a chandelier lighting unit. Below it, a large, polished, marble-top conference table and three straight-back chairs. The one with arms belongs to WARREN, *the two armless chairs are reserved for* ANTONIO *and the visitor of the day.*

On the table is a telephone. Next to it is a carafe with glasses, a small stack of file folders, secretarial pads and newly-sharpened pencils. There are also the remains of a messy paper-bag lunch. Beneath the table is a wastepaper basket.

A well-polished brass spitoon rests in front of an imposing wing chair belonging to MR. PRUDDEN. *Nearby is a free-standing ashtray.*

The large hulk of WARREN P. FLOYD *lies curled-up on the rug.* WARREN *is* MR. PRUDDEN's *assistant. He is sixty, wears a crumpled jacket that does not match his trousers, light-colored socks, and a tie that only reaches mid-belly. His pockets are always stuffed with folded newspapers, half-smoked cigars and junk.*

Once a powerfully built bodyguard, WARREN*'s body is largely flab—though it can still muster the momentum of a steamroller.*

ANTONIO *walks onto the rug carrying his paper-bag lunch. He is* WARREN*'s assistant and in his 20's. Though he was meant to roam wild, he has managed to put on corporate coloration: a new business suit, a clean white shirt, handsome tie, polished shoes. He is well-combed, and has a mustache and glasses.*

ANTONIO: Hey, Pop. Mr. Floyd? (*Pause.*) Old man. (*Pause.*) Warren. (ANTONIO *gives a piercing whistle.*) You dead?

WARREN: Not yet. (*He doesn't move.*) Come back when you've learned how to wake a man up. Spic bastard.

ANTONIO: How about a kick in the ribs, sir?

WARREN: (*Indicating his ass.*) How about a kiss on this here cheek? A sweet kiss.

ANTONIO: What are you trying to pull? (ANTONIO *moves to the table and starts eating his lunch.*)

WARREN: Beats the rug in my office.

ANTONIO: Tired, huh?

WARREN: Cold.

ANTONIO: Why don't you sack out in Mr. Prudden's office? Use the plush sofa in there. Just get on all fours and head down the hall. You want me to pick the lock? Take off, why don't you!

WARREN: Never missed a day of work in my life! (WARREN *suddenly smiles and stretches with satisfaction.*) Had me a real nice hot dream. Only it ain't no dream. I had it happen to me. It happened, so nobody can say it didn't. High point of my life. And nobody can take it from me. On my own two feet, I was. Really shooting through that desert. Hot wind tearing at me. Jacket, tie, shirt, every which way—and there she was, sure enough. Shivering and waiting. Looking like she'd stolen her mama's black slip. She was wet.

ANTONIO: Cried a lot?

WARREN: Wet. (*Pause.*) Biggest thing that ever happened to me. (*Pause.*)

ANTONIO: A guy called. Said he was going to blow this foundation off the face of the map.

WARREN: She coming today? Your lady?

ANTONIO: Yes.

WARREN: Think you'll get some money for her?

ANTONIO: Yes.

WARREN: I don't. She a friend of yours?

ANTONIO: Yes.

WARREN: Can't be too important.

ANTONIO: She deserves it.

WARREN: What's that got to do with the price of beans? (*He lifts a leg and farts. He takes a bottle out of the wastebasket, takes a swig, and puts it back in hiding.*)

ANTONIO: She's had it rough. Been through the fire. Had to put a fellow she married in a box when she was just a kid. An Air Force man. His family wouldn't let her bury him. They wanted to get his body back. Wanted her to ship him north by train. The family arranged for a man who worked for them to get down there. She said he just appeared out of nowhere and took over. (*Pause.*) Said he hardly said a word. Two hours out he attacked her.

WARREN: It's colder than a polar bear's nose! Wasn't like this when I started. No air-conditioning then. Had to wear our jackets all the time, even in summer. I started out as a messenger boy forty years ago, you know. Running all over the place. Out of breath all the time. Looking for the inside track. Saw my chance to get on board pretty quick. Yes, sir! A big chance came right my way—it could happen to you. Had to take a message to top management. The man was lunching at his club. Hottest day of the year it was. Hung my jacket on a peg, rolled up my sleeves, and covered those eight blocks in five minutes. I found my man, handed him the note—he, he didn't take it. Nope. Just stared at me. Said, "Go back and put on your jacket." (*Pause.*) So, I went all the way back. Put on my jacket. Went back to the club and gave him the note. (WARREN *shivers.*)

ANTONIO: Why suffer? Call someone. Tell them to turn up the temperature. Call premises.

WARREN: Can't. Haven't the authority. (*Pause.*) What's it feel like, working near the best people on earth? Giving out millions of dollars a year? You're on the right side of the fence, kid.

ANTONIO: On the right side of the fence, with a boot up my ass.

WARREN: They don't pay much. (*Pause.*) You think folks would want to bomb us if we weren't important? Don't pay attention, though, when they call all hot and bothered. Ha! Ha! Had a spade call me last week. Burning mad. Phone got red hot with his talk—"You fat cat, mak'n us beg for yo bread, mak'n us crawl. Rapp'n to de press and TV cameras about how yo chang'n things, make'n 'em better.

Yo just mak'n sure things stay the way they's always been—YOU ON TOP AND US ON DE BOTTOM!" Ha! Ha! Phoney baloney. Said this bomb was going to rip us wide open. Don't pay no mind to that crap. I've had thirty-five of those on the line. But I'll give you some advice, free of charge. When you get a school teacher voice at the other end of the line, saying short and sweet to vacate the premises in thirty minutes so no one should get hurt—run! And let me know. It's colder than a witch's tit! God-damned climate control. They're killing me off.

ANTONIO: Who?

WARREN: Management.

ANTONIO: Who's management?

WARREN: I don't know.

ANTONIO: You're management.

WARREN: Who? Me? Nobody's told me that before.

ANTONIO: I'm telling you.

WARREN: Who are you? Some spic dropout prick management picked out of some trash can to show how liberal we are. Got any Kleenex? I'm out of toilet paper. (ANTONIO *gives him a paper napkin.*) God. Sixty years old and still blowing my nose with paper napkins.

ANTONIO: Ever hear of handkerchiefs?

WARREN: Yeah. I heard of them. Heard of slimy spic bastards, too. Doesn't mean I have to buy 'em. (WARREN *gives an explosive sneeze.*)

ANTONIO: God bless you.

WARREN: Thanks, mate. I'll warm up. I'll just close my eyes and serve up my hot dream. I'll be sweating all over in no time.

ANTONIO: Premises will cut the cold air in no time. Call them. Then you won't need your hot dream on company time.

WARREN: I need it more every day. Company gave it to me, anyhow.

ANTONIO: Go on. Call.

WARREN: Can't.

ANTONIO: Go on.

WARREN: Nurtz.

ANTONIO: You've got a right, Mr. Floyd. You've been here forty years. Give the order.

WARREN: (*Picking up some letters.*) Christ! You writing turn-down letters to all these people with today's date? You crazy? We just got these requests in. Here, type 'em over, put a date next month on them, then send them out. You want people to think we aren't giving their requests serious consideration? (ANTONIO *has picked up the telephone*.) You put that down. (ANTONIO *starts dialing*.) Wait up! Don't . . .

ANTONIO: Calma, calma, señor Floyd.

WARREN: You want to put my tit in the wringer? (ANTONIO *extends the phone to* WARREN *who is paralyzed.* ANTONIO *speaks into the telephone*.)

ANTONIO: Hello? Is this the premises division? I'm calling from the fifty-ninth floor. The company's foundation. Community relations. Yes. We're freezing here. The air-conditioning seems to be broken. We can't control it from here, and it's on too strong.

WARREN: I'm not taking the blame.

ANTONIO: I'm calling for our supervisor, Mr. Prudden. No, he's not here. He couldn't stand the cold. Look, we'd like you to put the temperature up a few notches. Let me speak to your supervisor.

WARREN: God . . .

ANTONIO: (*Imitating* PRUDDEN*'s voice*.) Hello, hello, Leslie Prudden here. Listen, we are very uncomfortable and we would appreciate your doing a better job of controlling the air on fifty-nine. I can't afford to have any more people on sick leave. Very well. I want it done right away. (ANTONIO *puts the phone down*.)

WARREN: You're a good liar. You'll do all right here. (WARREN *takes the bottle out of the wastebasket, takes a swig and puts it back*.) Used to be just father and me for years. Prudden pisses ice water. You don't. You're different. It's good having someone else close by. I panic, sometimes. (*Pause*.) Thanks, kid. (*Pause*.) For a while there I thought you were going to put a switchblade in my back and walk away with the gold in my teeth—God, I hate poor people! They're all over the place. Pushing and shoving, knifing each other, trying to get at the dough before the next fellow, hands stretched out. "Sorry, can't help you," I say, "not funding your type of program this year." "I'll change my program to fit your program," they say. "I'll do anything, just give me the money!" When's she coming? When's your lady friend coming? (ANTONIO *begins to clear the table of paperbags, etc., making sure that the table shines once again, and reviews the room to see that everything is spotless. He uses his own handkerchief to polish things*.)

ANTONIO: Just about now. (WARREN *takes out his bottle again, takes a swig, puts it back and lights a cigar*.)

WARREN: A real lady's man, huh?

ANTONIO: We're close.

WARREN: Meet her down in China Lake?

ANTONIO: China Lake?

WARREN: You said she was at the base down there when . . .

ANTONIO: No, I didn't.

WARREN: What kind of woman tells a man she's been molested? How'd she tell you? You just don't go around telling people about a thing like that. How come she told you? You're pretty innocent, you know that? People come up here all the time telling all kinds of wild stories, hoping to get a bigger slice of the pie. What she want?

ANTONIO: Justice.

WARREN: Don't start that fancy-pants talk if you want me to understand you. What she want?

ANTONIO: Money.

WARREN: 'Cause some man put his hand on her?

ANTONIO: Seed-money to start up a free clinic.

WARREN: I'll put her in her place. I know how to handle her. Leave her to me.

ANTONIO: (*Quick tempered.*) She's mine! This is my client. She's going to put me on the map around here.

WARREN: Mustn't let a woman do that, get in your thoughts that way. Taking you over. She's been working on you trying to get a buck. And a low-down way of doing it, too. Getting you all hot and bothered. God, women are raped all the time. I'll bet they're better for it, too. Who's going to believe her, anyway? She tell the cops down there? They got a record?

ANTONIO: No. She just got off at the next stop. In a kind of daze, I guess.

WARREN: Just unloaded the boy's body, huh? Abandoned the place.

ANTONIO: This flunky really wanted his body, not hers. She knew that. They didn't want her to come back.

WARREN: That what she thinks?

ANTONIO: That was his assignment. To humiliate her. That's how they operate. They had a very low regard for her.

WARREN: She was poor, huh?

ANTONIO: Started living again in the fields. Working with migrants, wetbacks.

WARREN: Can't get lower than that.

ANTONIO: After a while, Magda started helping them. Saved her life.

WARREN: Maggie? Maggie? Maggie? You sure that's her name?

ANTONIO: Go home, old man. (WARREN *curls up on the rug again.*)

WARREN: I have no home.

ANTONIO: I'll take you home. In a little while.

WARREN: This is my home. (ANTONIO *touches* WARREN's *forehead to see if he has a fever.*) You're a pretty one, not tough at all—pretty cocky though. I knew a pretty Latin chick like you. Most beautiful people on earth, I'll say that. Warm and pretty. Warm and pretty. You know what you do to people, don't you?

ANTONIO: I know. I'm very sure of myself.

WARREN: Didn't have to work your way up, huh? The ladies in personnel just took one look at you and started falling all over themselves.

ANTONIO: It was easy. You see, sir, you people are just low-class animals. Me, I've got manners, traditions. I sucked it from my mother's breast—breeding, taste, pride. What you suck from your mother's breast, mister? (WARREN *thinks about it.*) You think about it. See, it doesn't matter if I haven't got a dime, because I am what I am and no one is going to take that from me. I've been told I'm somebody all my life—I sucked it. All your life you've been told you're nobody—that you should be grateful to the company for allowing you to work for them. Well, I feel just the opposite. The company is lucky to have me. Me. I don't need no diploma, no personnel types, to let me know who I am. I'm the new American race, did you know that? The new American race—I've got the blood of Spanish kings in my veins mixed with the best blood of Indian princes. I've got the best of both worlds!

WARREN: (*Impressed.*) I didn't know that.

ANTONIO: Look it up in my personnel file, if you don't believe me. There it is, the whole story. My family's older than Mr. Prudden's, for God's sake.

WARREN: Prudden know that?

ANTONIO: I don't tell him everything. I go back . . . to 520.

WARREN: 520 what?

ANTONIO: 520 A.D., animal. To Clovis!

WARREN: Clovis?

ANTONIO: You know General Clovis. About how one day he was sitting on his throne on a mountainside facing a million barbarian—mongoloids. There was Uncle Clovis on one side of this river and Genghis Kahn on the other. Uncle Clovis only had a handful of knights on his side. And there were the mongoloids ready to sweep over Europe. What was he going to do? The savages started making their wild sounds . . . (ANTONIO *starts whooping it up*) . . . and ringing their cymbals and bell and charging across the river at Uncle Clovi's team. And Clovi's wife, Clothilda, pulling at his sleeves, telling him to retreat his forces and run! (ANTONIO *makes more*

wild sounds.)
WARREN: Yeah? Then?
ANTONIO: Clovis didn't budge. He was waiting for a sign.
WARREN: A sign?
ANTONIO: And the black Arabian horses were charging up the hill, practically on top of him when Uncle Clovis looked up and there, in the sky, was a burning cross. A burning cross in the sky. And he said . . .
WARREN: Yeah . . . ?
ANTONIO: Charge! And Genghis Kahn looked up and his mouth fell open 'cause then he knew God wasn't on his side. And he drops his scimitar and high-tails it out of there 'cross the river and out of Europe never to be heard from again.
WARREN: Where'd you get that story?
ANTONIO: From my mother's breast. She didn't have to tell me anything. I sucked it. See, I'm on the side of the civilized people and you're on the savage side.
WARREN: What do you mean? I'm a good Catholic.
ANTONIO: You ever suck a story like that? I come from the best people. This Clovis, you know who he was? Charlemagne's great grandfather. He had all of Europe for his backyard. Carlomagno did, my relative. Carlomagno—that's Spanish for Charlemagne. He had lots of kids. And you know what happens when fortunes get divided up. Cousin Hernán Cortez didn't have a penny, so he had to come over here and pioneer for his fortune. He came from a good family, as I have demonstrated, and his generals and soldiers, too. But the folks back home wouldn't allow them to bring over young women from good families. So here he was with his generals without women. So, they made a name for themselves over here and all the big Indian chiefs gave their daughters to them as war prizes. My great, great grandmother was one of these princesses. Her name was Califa. Sat on a throne of gold. Califa! California was named for her. So you see . . .
WARREN: That's a lot of bull.
ANTONIO: I'll prove it to you.
WARREN: Prove it!
ANTONIO: You blind? Can't you tell I was born to be a king or something? Look at these teeth. (ANTONIO *opens wide.*) Terrible.
WARREN: Bad teeth—that's good?
ANTONIO: Of course, that's good. Everyone knows the bluer your blood, the more you're falling apart. Like the plaster inside old

palaces. Everyone knows peasants have good teeth. Look at yours. Like a crocodile.

WARREN: I go to the dentist, damn it!

ANTONIO: You open beer bottles with your teeth. I've got bad eyes.

WARREN: My eyes are bad.

ANTONIO: My eyes are terrible! Comes from generations of people reading books without pictures, man. I read the whole American Encyclopedia. See these glasses. You think everybody on my block's got glasses? Just a couple. I got the worst eyes on the street! Ask personnel, they know all this.

WARREN: So that's why they give you the run of the place. Because of your background.

ANTONIO: They know I've got leadership qualities. See this mustache? That's my Spanish blood. Full-blooded Indians don't have too much hair on their faces.

WARREN: Where'd you get your red lips? Where'd that kisser come from?

ANTONIO: You know what, Mr. Floyd? I feel sorry for you. That's why I tell you these things. To brighten your day.

WARREN: Yeah. We talk good together. We have some great bullshit sessions. Just like in the service. Pals. Young, crazy talk. I had a lot of fun in the service. Didn't give a shit about anything then. You don't give a shit about anything now, do you? I admire your guts. Don't even wear a T-shirt.

ANTONIO: Huh?

WARREN: Don't have the decency to cover up those knobs, those hard tits of yours everyone can see through those two-for-a-dollar shirts you wear.

ANTONIO: You've gotten off the track, old man.

WARREN: Off the track. Yeah, I've gotten off the track. And I want to get on again. (*Pause.*) I want to have some fun! Some fun! (*After a moment, he gets the idea to play "telephone" and goes through the motions of dialing.*) Ring. Riiing! I'm calling you, bastard, pick up the phone. Answer it! (ANTONIO *picks up an imaginary receiver.*) Hello? Antonio? This is your old buddy, Warren. Ha! Ha! Well, I'm calling with some good news, yeah, with an announcement. Well, you remember how serious and business-like I always am, well I'm calling to tell you that I've worked hard enough and long enough and that I'm available for—for some socializing, a little dancing, a little playing around. Know of any parties? (*Pause.*) Know of any parties? (*Pause.*) Know of any good parties?

ANTONIO: Yes.

WARREN: Where?

ANTONIO: My place.

WARREN: What's the celebration? I can hear the racket all the way over here.

ANTONIO: My . . . my wedding. (WARREN *is stunned.*)

WARREN: I'll be right over. (*They slowly put their phones down.*) Congratulations, kid. Congratulations.

ANTONIO: Thanks.

WARREN: Who's the bride? Not your lady friend who's coming today. Right?

ANTONIO: I always dreamed about a woman like that liking me. She's the queen of the world. A real empress. (WARREN *slowly advances toward* ANTONIO, *who starts backing away from him around the table.* WARREN *seems to have grown a few inches.*)

WARREN: Congratulations . . .

ANTONIO: Did I tell you the story of my birth?

WARREN: I don't want to hear any more.

ANTONIO: (*Getting desperate.*) It was a snowy night. Big snowstorm. There were no more rooms anywhere in the hospital . . .

WARREN: You're making me feel bad.

ANTONIO: . . . except one! Reserved for the Princess of Siam. (WARREN*'s ape-like arms slowly rise over* ANTONIO*'s head, brush down the young man's back and pin his arms.*) Well, the Princess didn't show and when my father told them who they were, they let my mother use it. (ANTONIO *is caught in a vise.* WARREN *now takes* ANTONIO*'s hands and locks them behind his back, in the style of a French apache dancer.*) So, I was born in the bed of the heir to the Siamese throne. (*They are motionless.*) I don't want to hurt you old man.

WARREN: I want to dance with you.

ANTONIO: I paid a lot of money for this suit! (*But* WARREN *is already transported into a world of crepe paper decorations and rag-time music. He remembers a song from his younger days, Pinky Tomlin's "Curbstone Cutey."* ANTONIO *is swept into a grotesque, funny, sad, one-step by the sheer bulk of the man.*)

WARREN: (*Sings.*)

> "He's just a curbstone cutey,
> His mother's pride and beauty,
> They call him Jelly Bean.

"He parts his hair in the middle,
  And presses it down—
And spreads his little Jelly Bean
  All around town. (*He begins coughing, but continues having a good time cutting a rug.*) My, my grandma, she knew what life was all about, said to me, "Warren, if you're taking a gal out tonight, blow your nose, clean your ears, and wash under your arms!" Ha! Ha! (*Sings.*)
"The girls they all love him,
  They think he's a riot,
    If you know what I mean.

"He never drinks beverages,
  Beers or light wines,
He orders ice cream sodas
  Every time.

"He's just a curbstone cutey,
  His mother's pride and beauty,
    They call him Jelly Bean—
I mean
    They call him Jelly Bean!"
WARREN *is seized by a serious fit of coughing, and breaks away from* ANTONIO *who stands paralyzed, mute. When the coughing stops,* WARREN *is panting, spent, getting ahold of himself again.*) Ah, me . . . ah, me . . . I get carried away, sorry, had a lot of fun, though. I stepped on your toes a lot, didn't I? I'm sorry I stepped on your . . . I don't have someone to play with too often, you know what I mean, Jelly Bean. Ha! Ha! Cracks me up. You know what I am? A serious business man. That's what I am. Prudden's armpit. The best! Ha! Ha! Ooops! Got to take a piss. (WARREN *starts to go.*) Got to see a man about a . . . if anybody wants me, tell 'em Mr. Floyd is on important beeswax! (*He is gone. Trembling, leaning against the table,* ANTONIO *does not move. He is paralyzed with loathing and disgust. Pause.* MAGDA WEBB *quietly enters. In her mid 30's, she wears a suede coat with a red lining. She drinks in the luxury of the room, as she removes her sun glasses. There are areas of quiet despair that lie beneath her smooth arrogance and the ease with which she uses her lovely body. Her sensibility springs from a Latin source. Under pressure, her instinctive weapons for survival are on the side of humour, impulse, attempts at intimacy, even outra-*

geousness, rather than the more typical responses of the woman in a business environment who tries to hold her own with men on a mental, pragmatic level. She has polished her salesmanship over the years to a refined degree. MAGDA *is a professional beggar.*)

ANTONIO: Stay out! Stay out! Don't look at me! (ANTONIO *still does not move.*) The kill's coming out and I can't stop it. I've got to kill someone, cut somebody up, make things right again or I'll go crazy. Why do you have to be here right now, this minute, to see me like this? God, you're cruel—don't look at me, I'm sweaty, slimy. I feel things in this place I've never felt before. Things I don't like. It's all sour. And I'm not sour. This place gives me bad breath.

MAGDA: What happened?

ANTONIO: I don't know what happened. (MAGDA *puts her arms around him.*)

MAGDA: I'll sew you up. I'll make you well. Hold on. Hold on.

ANTONIO: I stink real bad, don't I?

MAGDA: No, no, no, no. Hold on. (*He holds tightly to her.*) Nobody smells like you.

ANTONIO: What does that mean?

MAGDA: When are you going to stop being so touchy, so sensitive? You simply smell like Antonio. You smelled like this the first time I met you.

ANTONIO: Don't say that. I've tried to change. I look pretty much like everybody else down here, don't I?

MAGDA: It's a good smell, baby. It cures me every time. (*He kisses her neck with gusto several times.*) That's it. That's it. I don't care. Mark me up. Up and down and around. Just hold on. Don't let them get you down. You're better than any of them. You're the best there is. They can't come close. They can't humiliate us. You and me, we're family. The biggest, most loving family. We belong on this earth. They want to spit us out, right off the face of the map. But we'll hold on for dear life. My sweet, sour, smelly, dearest, dearest baby. (*Once she has assured herself that she has been able to cure him,* MAGDA *pulls away. They look, smiling, at each other.*)

ANTONIO: More?

MAGDA: Not now. Later.

ANTONIO: Do me a favor?

MAGDA: Later.

ANTONIO: Don't call me smelly. Please.

MAGDA: How come you didn't do what I said? Why did you leave your business suit at home? There it was on its hanger in the closet this morning. I had to lug it all the way down here.

ANTONIO: What do you mean? This is the best suit I've got. (MAGDA *shakes her head no.*)

MAGDA: Your hippopotamus suit, baby. Didn't I tell you that when you go out into the business world you have to put on your hippopotamus skin every morning and zip it up all the way to your chin? Now, you've got to stand by me today, so you better put it on. Come, come. (*She holds out the heavy, imaginary suit and he steps into it. First one foot, then the other.*)

ANTONIO: You know what? These people are crazy. (*He sticks in one arm, then the other.*)

MAGDA: Don't worry. We're much crazier. (*Using her thumb "hitchhike" style, she inserts it into his crotch and zips it up his front all the way to his chin.*) Now, nobody can hurt you. (ANTONIO *has now fully recovered.*)

ANTONIO: Someday these weak bastards are going to make one mistake too many and this man is going to take a walk on a couple of heads. I've had to stop being what I really am for too long around here, just so I could put father's pay check in my pocket.

MAGDA: Don't call him that. Prudden's not your father.

ANTONIO: He likes to think he is. Everybody calls him that. I told you he got me a credit card?

MAGDA: He did?

ANTONIO: Look. It came in the mail this morning.

MAGDA: It's beautiful, baby.

ANTONIO: Nobody'd give me a credit card before I came here. I'm a solid citizen in the eyes of the world.

MAGDA: That's nice. I envy you.

ANTONIO: But to my way of thinking, I was really a solid citizen before I came here. Not now. I don't like what this job is doing to me.

MAGDA: You're doing fine. I'm proud of you.

ANTONIO: Well, if I weren't around, I guess the money would only go to people who didn't really need it too much. Grants would never go to people like you. If it weren't for me, you wouldn't be here today.

MAGDA: I know. I'm grateful.

ANTONIO: You shouldn't have come.

MAGDA: What are you scared about, darlin'?

ANTONIO: They don't understand somebody like you.

MAGDA: I don't want to get you into trouble.

ANTONIO: Maybe you should leave right now.

MAGDA: You could lose your job? Antonio? (ANTONIO *turns away.*)

You like this luxury, don't you? (*She brushes her hand over the table and casually sweeps a desk clock into her large purse.*)

ANTONIO: It's clean.

MAGDA: You're really an aristocrat at heart.

ANTONIO: Nothing like you has ever walked in the door. If Prudden supported a free clinic he might even walk off with another humanitarian award because of me. But now that you're here suddenly . . . well, I'm taking a big chance.

MAGDA: I need the money.

ANTONIO: I know, but . . .

MAGDA: I need the money right away. I'm tired of that crumby neighborhood! I'm tired of all those dirty-looking people holding on to me . . . they're pulling me down. I'm drowning, baby. If I don't move out of there now, right now . . . oh, you will do your best! (ANTONIO *turns to her.*)

ANTONIO: I don't want to hurt you. See, I . . . I've got to tell you something about myself.

MAGDA: (*Explodes.*) About how the night you were born snow was falling and there was no room at the Inn! About your Uncle Clovis and Aunt Clothilda! About your bad teeth, fallen arches and lousy vision!

ANTONIO: See, you think I'm pretty important around here. And, well, I am important, but I'm not that important. Sometimes I can't stop them from . . . I've tried before. They, they don't care too much about people's feelings.

MAGDA: Who can resist giving money for a free clinic? It's the going thing. I've got a great story about a poor kid who gets run over by a truck. And if things get rough, I've got the one about the guy who vomited all over my steps. What always gets them is the one about kids suffering from malnutrition . . . bloated bellies, flaking skin, hair falling out. (*She laughs trimphantly.*) My hungry angels! (*Pause.*)

ANTONIO: They will say no.

MAGDA: They will love me! Oh, how they will love me! (*She violently tears open her coat under her left arm.*) Yes. (*Pause.* WARREN *enters. Hair combed, tie straight, refreshed. He does not approach, but looks them over from a distance.*)

WARREN: Hi, mate.

ANTONIO: (*To* MAGDA.) Este es un loco. Como Quasimodo, el gordo feo en "The Hunchback of Notre Dame" . . . en uno de los Classic Comics that you let me read.

MAGDA: (*To* ANTONIO.) (Dónde está el señor Prudden?

WARREN: Mr. Prudden is lunching at his club.

MAGDA: (*To* ANTONIO.) I look forward to meeting him.

ANTONIO: He always disappears for a couple of hours when there's a bomb scare.

MAGDA: You had a bomb scare?

ANTONIO: Yes. But we're used to it.

MAGDA: And Mr. Prudden isn't.

ANTONIO: Luckily. It's very peaceful when he's not around. (MAGDA, *careful to stay clear of* WARREN, *begins to move about.*)

MAGDA: (*To* ANTONIO.) You are so removed from everything up here. How can you stand it? It's so clean and quiet and well protected. A big guard stopped me downstairs and searched me. A big, sweet guy. Kind of dumb. He apologized, though. I told him he had a lousy job and he just smiled. I said he could do better and he's going to call me. Was that all right?

ANTONIO: Mr. Floyd, this is Mrs. . . .

WARREN: I know who she is. Here. Put this on the burner and give me seventy-five copies. (*He hands* ANTONIO *a blank sheet of paper.* ANTONIO *doesn't take it.* MAGDA *takes out a portable radio and turns the dial until she finds some smooth Latin music.*)

ANTONIO: I don't go near that machine.

WARREN: Scram. Here's the key to the Xerox room.

ANTONIO: It's the flashing light. It sterilizes you.

WARREN: Put the cover on.

ANTONIO: The hinge broke off again. They took the cover away to be fixed.

WARREN: Close your eyes when the light flashes on.

ANTONIO: You don't have babies with your eyes! (MAGDA *has taken a cigarette from her purse and is waiting for someone to light it.*)

WARREN: Hey! Better not light that. Mr. Prudden won't like it. There's no smoking and no drinking and no music on the premises! (ANTONIO *lights* MAGDA*'s cigarette.*) I'm still standing here with a piece of paper in my hand.

MAGDA: There's a beggar down in your lobby, did you know that? Playing an accordion. He looked so lost in that cold place, wearing an old tuxedo in the middle of the day, playing rhumbas and ice-skating music. He had a little girl with him. A darling little thing, keeping time to the music, moving her hips and shoulders. Nobody applauded. I gave the little girl some money and he smiled.

WARREN: That's Mr. Carrasco . He's part of our cultural enrichment program.

MAGDA: That's sad.

WARREN: What's sad about it? He's cleaning up. He's got two jobs. For twenty years he was just about the only shoeshine man allowed up here. Then we gave him his big break and now he shines shoes and gets a few bucks for playing in the lobby. You know how many people would like to do that?

MAGDA: I don't like to see a man bending down wiping another man's shoes.

WARREN: It's good, honest work.

MAGDA: Will I be searched going out, too? Or is one searched only when one comes in?

WARREN: Depends.

MAGDA: On whether I take something from you? Or rather, if you think I've taken something from you. You think I want to take something from you, don't you? If I wanted protection, would your company guards protect me? What if you had taken something from me? Could I call your security office? Give me the telephone number of your security office.

WARREN: (*To* ANTONIO.) Women really go for me, do you know that? The beautiful, pin-up style, I mean. Stick with me. I'll set you up in no time. A couple of weeks ago I was just driving along the freeway after church, giving some kids a good time, when this beautiful dame drives alongside me in a powder blue convertible, turns to me and smiles. She presses her foot on the gas, gets ahead of me. But I catch up, swing right alongside her. I smile. She smiles. We play that again and again up the road until I shoot way ahead of her, pull over and park. I wait. She drives up, pulls over and parks. I say to the kids, "Wait a minute," I get out, walk back to her car, take off my hat and say, "Thanks for playing with me on the road." She smiles and pulls away. Well, I got her license number, of course. And when I get home I call a friend of mine who was the police chief in San Jose in those days and I say to him, "I just saw an old school buddy of mine on the road that I haven't seen in twenty years. I got his license number and I'd like to get in touch with him." He says, "I'll call you back." Ha! Ha! Thirty minutes later he calls back with the telephone number. It's in Sausalito. I pick up the phone and this sofa-bed voice answers. I say, "Hello. I'm the fellow on the freeway who . . . " And she says, "I thought you'd never call!" Ha!

ANTONIO: (*To* MAGDA.) What did you have for lunch? (MAGDA

searches through her purse for another cigarette. She finds an empty pack, crumples it into a ball and tosses it on the floor.)

MAGDA: This place is too clean. I'd like to mess it up a bit. Give me a cigarette. (ANTONIO *gives her a cigarette and lights it. MAGDA inhales deeply and exhales with deep satisfaction.*) An ice-cream sandwich.

ANTONIO: You don't take care of yourself.

MAGDA: It was delicious. I love ice-cream sandwiches.

ANTONIO: You look a little pale.

WARREN: An older woman, big in politics, says to me, "Have a drink with me at the St. Francis." So I say, "Okay." Sitting at the next table is this old guy with one of the most beautiful young chicks I've ever seen. They seemed to be having some sort of argument. She was crying, looking down at the table. She never looked up at me. They kept arguing, and she kept crying and then they got up an went out. The Maitre D' comes over to talk to my lady friend and I say to him, "The couple who just left seemed to be having some trouble?" And he says, "Oh, that's Mr. and Mrs. so and so." Well, I get home and there's the name in the phone book. I call and a woman says, "Oh, you probably want the new Mrs. so and so." and gives me a Sausalito phone number. I call and this creamy voice answers. I say, "I was at the table next to yours at the St. Francis yesterday and I . . ." And she says, "I thought you'd never call!"

ANTONIO: Didn't you have enough money?

MAGDA: Enough money?

ANTONIO: To get something more than an ice-cream sandwich.

MAGDA: Actually, I had two.

ANTONIO: Oh, it wasn't the money, then.

MAGDA: Yes. It was. It's always "the money," isn't it? (*She gives a sudden laugh.*) I stole them, actually, and they started to melt in my bag.

WARREN: You want to go out with me?

MAGDA: When?

WARREN: Right now.

MAGDA: What for?

WARREN: Kicks.

MAGDA: No.

WARREN: Let's go.

MAGDA: How much will it cost me? I mean, what will you pay?

WARREN: How much do you want?

MAGDA: Plenty. (*A sudden, amused laugh.*) I haven't been free and easy for some time.

WARREN: (*To* ANTONIO.) What did I tell you?

MAGDA: I want some sort of payment.

WARREN: (*Worried*.) So?

MAGDA: I've come for it.

WARREN: Some sort of payment, huh?

MAGDA: Some sort of satisfaction. Of recognition.

WARREN: Yeah. A little cold cash in the old bread basket.

MAGDA: If that's the only sort of satisfaction you people can give, it will do. Money moves you, I know.

WARREN: You miss a meal or two and you people start bellyaching to beat the band. Come whining and wagging your tails and wanting to get your chompers on the titty. (*He lights a cigar*.) You people think you deserve it all.

MAGDA: Yes. I am hungry.

WARREN: (*To* ANTONIO.) She wants a slice of the pie.

MAGDA: I want the pie.

WARREN: Your appeal doesn't stand a chance around here, lady. Let's save ourselves a lot of grief, before it's too late. Come on, I'll take you down. (MAGDA *does not move*.) Shop's closed. Gone to lunch.

MAGDA: (*To* ANTONIO.) How long did you say before I get the money?

WARREN: Get off, lady. You're dead here. Warm up to some other foundation. And here's some advice, free of charge, before you start knocking on doors. The first word you say is "Please." And the second word you say is "Please," and the third word you say is "Please." Now let's go.

ANTONIO: (*To* MAGDA.) It takes a while.

MAGDA: Who decides?

ANTONIO: Management.

MAGDA: And nothing gets to management if it doesn't pass Leslie Prudden.

WARREN: And nothing gets to Mr. Prudden if it doesn't pass me. I'm cancelling this appointment. (*He flips off the radio*.) You show Mrs. Prudden out.

MAGDA: Mrs. Webb.

ANTONIO: We've been preparing for this meeting for some time.

WARREN: Goddamn you, get her out of here. (*Slight pause*.) I'm calling security.

ANTONIO: You haven't got the authority.

MAGDA: Yes. Call them. The number is 6772.

WARREN: (*To* ANTONIO.) You just burned yourself, kid. You're out of the family for all time. You ain't got no power to protect you now, no how. Why'd you open the door for her?

MAGDA: I want some of Mr. Prudden's seed-money. An injection of hard cash now is what I need. $75,000 for the first year. You have many different types of grants, but there is one special grant that I read about in the papers every year, "The Prudden Family Award for Community Service." $75,000. I deserve it. I dream about it. Antonio, please find Mr. Prudden. Please, darlin'. I won't embarrass you. He'll like me. You'll see. And we'll celebrate afterwards, my baby.

ANTONIO: Prudden will eat her up! (*He leaves.*)

WARREN: I won't take the blame. I won't take the blame.

MAGDA: If the elevators stopped running, how long would it take me to get down the stairs?

WARREN: It'd take you forever and a day to get down and it'd wear your legs down to the knees. You've got pretty good legs, though, I guess.

MAGDA: It frightens me to be so high up. I like it too much. (*She looks in her purse for a cigarette but doesn't have one.*) Sonia, my mother, always used to carry a little piece of garlic in a coin purse she had. Poor thing, she believed that if you carried a little garlic, you'd always have some money . . . even a little. I envy you, your place, your home here. Why don't you feel safe, my dear?

WARREN: You nuts? Everybody I know thinks I'm the luckiest guy alive. Want to shake my hand? Know this hand's been shook by the best in the country. Prudden's are first-rate people, everybody knows that. Got more dough than I can count. I know I'm nothing. It's no secret. But they have me close just the same. (*Pause.*) Guess they know they can count on me. Yes, Ma'am. I've got a good record, a lifetime of finding ways to keep bad news from coming through that door. Keep them safe. Tell them what they want to hear, never tell them what they don't. Mr. Warren P. Floyd is keeping them pure, lady. (MAGDA *smiles to herself, then turns away.*) Don't believe me, huh? I know I'm a lucky guy. I'm in the center of the catalyst. When it comes down to the crunch, call Warren P. Floyd. Counted on me to bring Clark back, remember Clark Prudden, the boss's boy? Gave me the assignment. Hard to believe a big, brave kid like Clarkie being in a coffin . . . Rode with him all the way up from China Lake . . . in charge of the whole operation. "Thank you for bringing my son back to me," Prudden said. Shook my hand at the station. Rode in the limo right next to him that day. First time. We were close. He asked me into the house. Gave me a drink. Gave his bodyguard a drink.

MAGDA: I want this rug. For me.

WARREN: Yeah. It was a big day.

MAGDA: (*Caressing the rug.*) It's like a field.

WARREN: Lots of dollars woven into that rug. Had to break a wall down to get it in.

MAGDA: Lock the door.

WARREN: Huh?

MAGDA: I want to take off my stockings.

WARREN: I've got a cold.

MAGDA: I want to feel it with my bare feet.

WARREN: You probably talk loud in crowded buses; laugh at funerals . . . (*In silence*, MAGDA *rolls her stockings down her beautiful legs.*) We don't raise our voices around here! Now, calm down. I love it here and I won't stand around and be party to any wild, crazy stuff. You ain't messing up a hair of that rug! I love it here and I don't want anybody disturbing a thing! God, why'd you have to come here? Haven't been able to sleep a wink all week 'cause of your crazies. Had somebody break into one of the offices downstairs last week. Didn't take much, but you know what the disrespectful damn fool went and did? Went into the board room, propped himself on top of the marble table and left his calling card! Left a turd there this big! Most horrible thing I ever heard of. (*Almost in tears.*) God, I come in here every morning in fear, yes, FEAR that on this table, or on the . . .! I can't take too much more . . . (MAGDA *is enjoying the luxurious depths of the rug.*)

MAGDA: It's like a milk bath or a private garden. Could be somebody's fur. (WARREN *covers his face with his hands, rubbing his forehead and his eyes.*)

WARREN: Got to get some glasses. Glare in here is making me blind. This new lighting's no good. Bad as the climate control. Got to get some shut eye.

MAGDA: My program has all the necessary parts. All I need is the proper seed-money to come my way. The public relations possibilities for the company are phenomenal. My program will carry the Prudden name. You could point that out to him.

WARREN: Sell. Go on, sell. It's a free country.

MAGDA: Seventy-five thousand. What's seventy . . .

WARREN: Got your garlic in your bag? Some of your Mama's garlic? A great big piece? A real good piece? You're asking for a mighty potent sum, you know. You better clear out now. I don't want to have a mighty unsatisfied lady on my hands.

MAGDA: Don't. Please, don't dismiss me like that. Nowadays, even Sonia has stopped telling me I'm beautiful. Used to tell me all the time. Made me feel good. Kept me going. Washed the dust from my face and told me I was the most beautiful thing. Gave me some rotten grapes and told me to play out of the sun. I'd hang myself if I had to go through all of it again. But I miss . . . I miss the way people looked at me. Those nice warm waves I walked through. All the time, everywhere.

WARREN: (*Quietly.*) Wonderful thing it was. High point of my life. (*Pause.*) Did I dream it? (*Pause.*) We got along.

MAGDA: You're a funny guy. A dumb guy. (*They sit quietly for a time. Then MAGDA breathes a deep sigh, rises with renewed strength and resolve. She stands straight and silent for a moment, then whirls from WARREN and reaches for her stockings.*)

WARREN: Oh! Let me put them on you. The way I'll bet married folks do. Sometimes. (*They face each other.*) You going to hurt me, huh? (MAGDA *turns her back and without fuss, puts on her stockings.*)

MAGDA: You're a good servant, aren't you?

WARREN: I have the run of the house.

MAGDA: Poor Antonio.

WARREN: Pimp.

MAGDA: Convince Mr. Prudden that I am worth $75,000.

WARREN: It ain't the money, huh? What are you here for?

MAGDA: I saw a horrible thing one summer in China lake, in the blazing sun, right there on the main street of the town. I was walking along when I saw my dream car standing there. The doors were locked and someone had left this magnificent, big dog inside with all the windows rolled up. Whoever it was had gone away and just forgotten about the big dog . . . hadn't left him even a half-inch of air. The poor animal had probably been barking his lungs out for an hour and people walking by and doing nothing and the owner hadn't come back. The inside of the car was ripped apart. The dog tried to push and shove the windshield open, kept banging himself against the glass until he smashed it. He was so desperate to get his head out of that hell that he pushed his way through the jagged edges, worming his nose out, then his whole head out. He'd gotten stuck and struggled whipping his neck and body around . . . but that only made it worse. And the broken glass just jabbed deeper into his throat. Before I could find the owner, open the door, do anything, he bled to death. His blood was all over me. This handsome young fella finally shows up. The owner. Clark. Cool as you please in his Air Force blues. Clark Prudden. A real rich man's kid, contempt written all over him. For the dog, for me half out of my mind. He took out his wallet. He wanted to buy me . . . a new dress. He wanted to buy me. He wanted to show me the world from way up in his airplane. And I let him. (*Pause.*) You people have a lot to pay for. (LESLIE PRUDDEN *authoritatively enters followed by* ANTONIO. PRUDDEN *is an elegant, aggressive, handsome man. In his presence* WARREN *and* ANTONIO *try to behave like obedient cadets.*)

PRUDDEN: Hello, hello. Sit down. Sit down. (MAGDA *remains standing.* PRUDDEN *turns to* ANTONIO.) What have you brought us today, Anthony? (*He quickly turns his gaze toward* MAGDA, *pleased, intrigued by her presence. Slowly, the lights fade.*)

ACT TWO

All as before.

PRUDDEN: (*To* MAGDA.) Sit down.

ANTONIO: Magda Webb. (MAGDA *doesn't sit.*)

PRUDDEN: (*To* ANTONIO.) Is there a Mr. Webb?

MAGDA: There is a Mrs. Webb. (*Slight pause.*) Painted by Gainsborough or Reynolds, I think. Very tall and thin, with a beautiful long neck and blueish-white hands. (*Extending her hand, she moves slowly toward* PRUDDEN.) Wearing a rich satin gown and . . . (PRUDDEN *takes her hand and holds it.*) serenely studying her own sunset, isolated from the cares of the world.

PRUDDEN: She sounds worth hanging in our collection.

ANTONIO: (*To* MAGDA.) Sir, Mrs. Webb won't take much of your time.

WARREN: Boss.

MAGDA: (*Interrupting, fixed on* PRUDDEN.) You have lovely paintings in your ladies' bathroom. But you have no ladies here.

PRUDDEN: I thought I recognized the fragrance, the smell of the soap we keep in our ladies room. The smell of musk roses really comes home to me. I'm glad you used it.

MAGDA: No. I didn't use your soap. (*She drops her hand.*) You have no ladies here.

PRUDDEN: No.

MAGDA: Why?

PRUDDEN: Why what? Pardon me?

MAGDA: You don't have any women on this floor.

PRUDDEN: No. We have to tackle important, sometimes awesome as-signments here. Confidential work . . . have a seat.

MAGDA: I don't like to see men having to do secretarial work.

PRUDDEN: Before the war, we only had male secretaries in the whole building. Yes, sir. Then, when women started coming, they began objecting loud and clear about the spitoons in all the offices. When Warren here, Mr. Floyd, put on a uniform, we put our spitoon in the closet. When he came back, we took the spitoon out of the closet and showed our secretary the door. Mr. Floyd can't function without it.

WARREN: Boss, I gotta talk to you . . .

PRUDDEN: Can't you see I'm busy? (*To* MAGDA.) Have a chair, any chair.

MAGDA: I become aroused, you see, when I sit for long spells. Expen-sive furniture makes me particularly impatient.

ANTONIO: Mrs. Webb is worthy of attention.

PRUDDEN: Mrs. Webb or Mrs. Webb's program? (*He sits in the winged chair.*)

ANTONIO: They're one and the same.

PRUDDEN: But what if Mrs. Webb were to die, or be arrested, marry, give birth, move on to other things? What guarantee do we have that the program will continue? We can't invest our money in something that hasn't the chance of a long life.

ANTONIO: Our money will insure the life of the program.

MAGDA: (*To* PRUDDEN.) Is it true that you have never waited for a bus on a street corner? (MAGDA *takes one of the straight chairs and moves it to a position of combat opposite* PRUDDEN. *She sits from time to time,* MAGDA *crosses and uncrosses her legs.*)

ANTONIO: Mrs. Webb is a widow.

MAGDA: (*To* PRUDDEN, *business-like.*) I would like to be alone with you.

PRUDDEN: We are alone.

ANTONIO: She's done big things.

PRUDDEN: You've got the privacy of the confessional here. I'm your neighborhood priest.

MAGDA: And I'm a poor sinner. I know that. But are all poor men automatically sinful because they're poor?

PRUDDEN: They pray a lot.

MAGDA: To you.

PRUDDEN: I learn a surprising amount about this town. Where the sensitive areas are, the illnesses. Right from this chair. We cannot function as a healthy corporation if the community isn't healthy, too. So we apply an injection here, a booster shot there. We've got to be healthy for the good of all. The corporation is the most highly evolved system for human development yet known to man. It . . .

MAGDA: (*She breaks in.*) Oh, your face, your throat, are doing the most fascinating things! I taught two deaf-mute girls once. I learned to read lips, but the movement of the muscles here (*Touches her cheek.*) . . . and here . . . (*Touches her forehead.*) . . . and here . . . (*Touches her throat.*) Tell me more. I meant it when I said I wanted to speak with you alone. Without any distractions. (*Smiles.*) I'm putting my life on the line, you know. It cost me a lot to get here.

PRUDDEN: We have an established process. It wouldn't be fair if I interviewed you alone. Everyone who comes for money is interviewed like this. If you want to relate to us, it will have to be in the prescribed manner. We don't make exceptions. You're no different from anyone else.

MAGDA: I am.

PRUDDEN: Everyone feels that way. Just this morning a hysterical nun called. Said she was a bandleader. Said she was calling from a booth in a gas station near her school. The members of her drum and bugle corps had soaked themselves with gasoline and were threatening to light a match if I didn't give them the money to buy uniforms.

MAGDA: What did you say?

PRUDDEN: That we don't contribute to religious organizations. I open my mail. A Hindu gentleman writes that he has a drippy nose and bad teeth. Could I get him a wife? If I don't get him a wife in three weeks, he'll drown himself in the Ganges.

MAGDA: What are you going to do?

PRUDDEN: The letter was postmarked 1968. I go down to the lobby on my way to lunch. A desperate character grabs my arm and says he's got to have $300,000 to put a curtain across the Grand Canyon.

MAGDA: Don't make fun of me.

PRUDDEN: You think I'm lying? Okay. What big thing have you done?

MAGDA: On the hottest day of the year, I walked into the biggest, the classiest motel in China Lake, went right out to the pool and dove in. A servant came over to the side of the pool to ask me if I belonged, and before he could open his mouth I said, "Bring me a towel." And he did.

ANTONIO: She's a teacher. (*Pause.*) She's not so hot academically, but that's not the important thing, if you know what I mean. The people in her neck of the woods are eating out of her hand. She does things for them.

PRUDDEN: Are you taking notes! Get back to your knitting! Pencil in one hand, pad in the other, mouth shut, eyes down, ears open! (*To MAGDA, perfunctorily, trying to collect his thoughts.*) Yes. Well, if you asked me to bring you a towel, I guess I would.

MAGDA: If I snuck into your pool and you found me, you'd offer me the run of the place? Would you? And then you'd go inside and call the cops. You money guys are a real tease, aren't you?

PRUDDEN: We're slow and careful.

MAGDA: My God, there are people all over the country in rooms like this, wanting something, all keyed up.

PRUDDEN: We give them more than enough time to settle down.

MAGDA: And open up.

PRUDDEN: Yes.

MAGDA: And how long before the money comes?

PRUDDEN: Putting money into a person's program is a very delicate operation. In my life . . . well, when you give yourself like that, put your name on it, the company's name on it for all the world to see . . . that's mighty important in my view. It's no different than a marriage really. Once cash begins to flow into a worthy organization . . . well, it's happened, the cork's off for all time. And you hope to God the bride doesn't get drunk and make a fool of herself with all your money pouring into her. But it's usually a grand thing. I make sure it is. (*Pause.*) It's got to be love, honor and obey.

MAGDA: Wow, all this time I've been wondering what part of this big time body you really are. And now I know. You're not the head, you're the cork.

PRUDDEN: No. The conscience.

MAGDA: That's sweet. (*She chuckles.*) Someone, oh, very close to you, once said that you have a dollar sign tattooed on your left buttock.

PRUDDEN: What do you mean sitting on expensive furniture makes you impatient?

ANTONIO: She's exhausted.

PRUDDEN: (*To ANTONIO.*) Cut it. (*To MAGDA.*) I'm pretty naive about certain things and I like to know what people are talking about.

MAGDA: Someone you knew told me you have a mind as precise as a dentist's drill.

PRUDDEN: You don't mind my asking?

MAGDA: Not at all. I rather enjoy going to the dentist.

PRUDDEN: You do?

MAGDA: Yes. I love to just lie back, a captive there. Besides, I have marvelous teeth. And all he ever does is poke me around the gums, which I think is a lot of fun.

PRUDDEN: You expect me to supply you with some sort of sensation?

MAGDA: I have a long, established process . . . a prescribed manner, too, for interviewing anyone. It would be unfair if I interviewed you differently. My way of judging a person is quite simple. I trust what my body tells me. I will try to be more precise. I had a friend, as beautiful as a movie star. She was a deaf-mute. She loved to dance. (*Unconsciously*, MAGDA *moves her hands in sign language*.) I asked her how she could do that without hearing the band playing. And she said she guided herself by the vibrations she felt coming up through the floor, up the soles of her feet and up her legs, her waist, her back. You might say I'm a deaf-mute in a sense. I'm guided by . . . (*She stands, trying to keep her balance*.) Wait. (*There is a sound of strained creaking, as if we were on the deck of an old wooden sailing ship and the mast felt a tugging wind on a rolling sea. The chandelier begins swinging gently*.) We're moving, the building. (*Some pencils roll off the table. A howling wind rattles windows throughout the floor. It subsides. The creaking stops*.)

PRUDDEN: The building is designed to sway in the wind. If it didn't, it would crack or topple over, wouldn't it? It stopped now. Don't worry.

MAGDA: (*To* ANTONIO.) You didn't tell me about the wind, about the building swaying in the wind!

PRUDDEN: Now, what would the fellows who put up this building say if they saw you all rattled like this? They'd say you didn't trust them.

MAGDA: I don't. (PRUDDEN *gets the basket from under the table and fishes out* WARREN*'s bottle*.)

PRUDDEN: Why don't you have a drink? Warren always keeps a bottle hidden in the garbage can.

MAGDA: Wastebasket.

PRUDDEN: Sorry. Wastebasket. It's just that so much of our mail is garbage. (*He pours a drink into a glass. She doesn't accept it*.)

MAGDA: And what do you do with your gifts from possible grantees?

PRUDDEN: Did you send the cigars? Warren is supposed to tell me about these things. That was a mighty fancy humidor. Thank you.

MAGDA: No. I didn't send you cigars.

PRUDDEN: I know. That awful LP. The inspirational hymns. Only you could have sent inspirational hymns. What then?

MAGDA: A telephone pole. You have so much time on your hands, I thought it'd be the answer to a whittler's dream. I really wanted to give you that, but I knew the guards downstairs would think it was some kind of weapon. So I settled for something a lot smaller. Beautifully made, delicate, with a timing mechanism and detonating device you wouldn't notice in a doll's house.

PRUDDEN: (*Sardonically.*) You're an expert in "explosive devices."

MAGDA: In garbage. (PRUDDEN *saunters over to her.*) It's not on my person, but you may not search me in any case. I'm having your gift delivered by a messenger. If I don't get what I want, the messenger will leave it. And I will activate it. If I do, well, the messenger will know and take it away.

PRUDDEN: You just made that up, didn't you? To throw me off balance.

MAGDA: You don't like my gift?

PRUDDEN: What do you want?

MAGDA: I want to move your furniture around. That's what I want.

ANTONIO: Being on the go all the time without even enough bread to pay for a bus sometimes can make your head spin off in all kinds of ways. The people in her program are very generous. They give her what they can. But Magda never has enough.

PRUDDEN: That's an expensive coat.

MAGDA: It's the most important thing I've got.

PRUDDEN: Must have cost you quite a bit.

MAGDA: I needed it.

PRUDDEN: You paid for it, I mean, you bought it? You were lucky to find such a nice hide second-hand.

MAGDA: Nobody had worn it out of the store when I put it on.

PRUDDEN: But there's a mean cut there, under your arm. (MAGDA *puts her hand on it.*)

MAGDA: (*Proudly.*) It hurt.

PRUDDEN: Why didn't you do something about it?

MAGDA: It still hurts.

PRUDDEN: Something can be done about it. Can't it?

MAGDA: It just happened.

PRUDDEN: Just happened?

MAGDA: Downstairs.

PRUDDEN: Here?

MAGDA: One of your guards. When I came into your lobby I felt immediately that I was being observed, that I could be stopped, questioned, attacked at any moment. I knew Antonio had given my name to the guard department, had set up the appointment, that everything was straight. But I didn't want to stop. I just kept walking through the lobby toward the elevators and one of the men kept yelling, "Show me your identification. Hold on there! Give me your name!" at the top of his lungs, everybody staring. He didn't care. Another guard grabbed my arm and more guards rushed over. One of them opened my purse and I don't like being held that way. I don't like men prying my purse open, intruding their fingers. I tried to free myself and get my bag back. I tore it away from him and everything spilled all over the floor. When I was trying to push them off me . . . the coat split open.

WARREN: (*To* MAGDA.) What the hell are you talking about? We don't owe you nothing! What have we got to do with you now? If you hadn't worked your magic on the boy, you wouldn't be here at all. You think we let every crackpot in the door? What have we got to do with you?

PRUDDEN: We don't raise our voices here.

WARREN: (*To* PRUDDEN.) A dog near suffocates in a hot car and gets all cut up. What's that to do with us? So he stuck his head through the windshield of that damn Pontiac. Clark didn't tell him to! (*To* MAGDA.) Don't come soaking up this rug with your red stuff. Just don't go splashing any around here, trying to mess things up! We're the top and we don't owe nothing to nobody. We work for our money and spend it where we like. It's ours! Ours, you hear? Ours. You've got no right. The dough we give out is one whole percent of earnings! Profits! You hear that EARN-INGS!

ANTONIO: Mr. Floyd.

WARREN: (*To* MAGDA.) Every motherfucker in this here corporate family . . .

ANTONIO: (*To* MAGDA.) What did you say to him?

WARREN: . . . works all year to make this company go and go big. And every year we go bigger and every year that one percent gets fatter. And all that money, every damn cent of it, comes out of the pockets of Mr. And Mrs. Stockholder. It belongs to them. It's their property, their profits. And if they didn't want to give a penny, they wouldn't have to. We're not like some of those crazy, fancy-pants private family foundations that have money to burn and no one to answer to.

Sure as there's a God in heaven, when that annual meeting rolls around, we've got to answer to every stockholder and if one of them doesn't like where we're putting their money, we've got hell to pay. (*To himself.*) Every man, woman and child in town is breathing down our necks, wanting to get fat on our tax-deductible sweat. Half of them no good phonies. Collecting sympathy grants right and left, telling the world they're helping the little guy and filling their pockets all the while. No good phonies . . . (*To* MAGDA.) . . . phonies. Ever hear of the poverty industry? Guess you know all about it, huh?

MAGDA: (*Quietly.*) What do you know about poverty?

WARREN: We're the best in the business.

MAGDA: Helping the poor is a business?

PRUDDEN: Your bedtime reading obviously isn't history. From the beginning of time the rich helped the poor—not to fill a few rotting bellies, but for the good of their own selfish, immortal souls! Why, I remember my grandmother weighed down with huge baskets of food going into the snow to visit her poor. She was bound and determined to have an afterlife befitting her wordly status. We lost her after a particular cold spell. Our concerns are more earthly these days, but the aim's the same. By helping others we help ourselves.

MAGDA: The papers say you are a great humanitarian.

PRUDDEN: You do read then?

MAGDA: But not in bed. I suppose I shall. When I'm old. But I can't picture it. (LUIS, *a young man in a white coat, carries in an elaborate silver tray with coffee and cookies. There are only two cups.* PRUDDEN *does not acknowledge his presence in any way.*)

PRUDDEN: It was my son's idea to establish a foundation. He provided me—provided us—with a mechanism to preserve and extend ourselves throughout the city.

MAGDA: Buy off the discontented and they will not destroy you? Or rather, destroy the discontented by buying them.

PRUDDEN: We hope they will buy us. We put some pennies in their pockets so that they'll buy our products. But the poor are a very minor part of our portfolio, you might say. There's very little profit in it.

MAGDA: Your great, great, great grandfather was a famous pirate, wasn't he?

PRUDDEN: No. That's another company.

MAGDA: Sorry. (LUIS *has completed setting up the coffee—an operation as intricate as the preparation of a Japanese floral arrangement.*)

PRUDDEN: Do you take cream and sugar?

MAGDA: Luis knows how I like it. (PRUDDEN *notices* LUIS *and* MAGDA *smiling at each other with familiarity. He is taken aback.*)

PRUDDEN: How is that possible? (LUIS *serves* MAGDA, *then* PRUDDEN.)

ANTONIO: She's done her homework.

MAGDA: Gracias, Luis. And please bring two more cups.

PRUDDEN: This isn't the clerk's cafeteria. They know where they can go for coffee if they want some. We can't afford to give coffee to every Tom, Dick, and Harry in the place. They understand that. (MAGDA *stands and puts her cup on the tray without drinking it.*)

MAGDA: (*To* LUIS.) Take it away.

PRUDDEN: Leave it. I might want some more.

MAGDA: I have been to other foundations. You are not the best in the business. (LUIS *leaves.*)

PRUDDEN: My way of judging a request is pretty simple, no matter what comes down the pike. Urgency of need. A basic need.

ANTONIO: Her needs are critical.

PRUDDEN: Her needs?

ANTONIO: The needs of those she assists.

PRUDDEN: Who are?

MAGDA: They come to me.

ANTONIO: They haven't any place to go. Nobody pays any attention to them. They're just farmworkers, maybe some on welfare, you know, humble people. Not dumb, but not too educated. With little stores, beat-up old cars, you know, humble people. They go to church.

MAGDA: They were afraid of me. Coming all the way, to this place, to see you. Three hours on the road is almost like going to another planet for some of them. They're afraid that maybe something will happen to me. That I won't come back. That you will hurt me. I explained that you gave money away for worthwhile projects. That only frightened some of them more. They think what you do here is unnatural. What sort of man spends his days giving away thousands of dollars? What sort of a devil? Three of the older men didn't mind losing a day's pay to come up with me. They hadn't said a word to me about it, but there they were early this morning at the depot in their hats and funeral suits. But I told them I wanted to come alone. And they obeyed me.

ANTONIO: A lot of babies named after her.

MAGDA: I teach them things. The children in the daytime, the parents in the nighttime.

ANTONIO: Like if some wasp bastard won't rent to some family, she tells them how to fill out an application. You know, what you should tell the landlord, what you shouldn't. Put another name.

PRUDDEN: Lie?

ANTONIO: They get in, that's the important thing. They're pretty desperate.

MAGDA: You probably read about us in the paper. (*She hands* PRUDDEN *a clipping.*) Keep it. It's my personal copy. I'm very proud of that. That character owns buildings up and down the coast. We filed suit against him. And we won. It's a historic decision. He has to post all openings now. Anyone who can pay the rent can apply now.

WARREN: I'll take that.

MAGDA: No! (WARREN *and* MAGDA *reach for the clipping. It rips apart.* MAGDA *gives a cry of pain. She picks up the pieces and puts them in her bag.*) ¡Desgraciado!

PRUDDEN: The man you embarrassed. The gentleman you sued, the owner of those buildings. That gentleman is a friend of ours.

MAGDA: He's no gentleman.

PRUDDEN: We only do business with gentlemen. He'd have every right in the world to be angry with us, wouldn't he, if he found out that we supported you? You didn't know what you were doing just now, did you?

MAGDA: I knew.

PRUDDEN: Why did you offer me that clipping?

MAGDA: I wanted you to know that I am good. At what I do.

PRUDDEN: But that's not all you want.

WARREN: Mr. Prudden can't give you any more of his time. I'll take you down.

MAGDA: I think about you all the time. Out there in the middle of nowhere. Out in the colonies. Dreaming and dreaming and never owning anything. Yes, I think about you all the time. I can't help it. Your company has branches all over the place. Even three hours away. Those cold fingers of yours reach into my purse all that distance. Isn't that a laugh? We have a financial relationship. We buy and buy and all that dough gets shipped up here and very little is left behind. We don't see it. Now all that giving, coming from just one side, makes for a pretty lousy relationship. I want you to give me a seed money grant to set up a free clinic. The only hospital around is a big, private place that won't take people like us. It's run by Irish nuns. They were poor once, too, and now they've got a good thing going for themselves. I guess I don't blame them. They'll burn in hell anyway. (*She glances at* ANTONIO.) Last week a little boy was run over by a farm truck in front of my school. I picked him up and took him up the hill to the hospital. The head nun there wouldn't let anybody do anything for him. Kept saying crazy things like, "Does the family have medical insurance?" And me standing there with this bloody body in my arms. "Take him to the general hospital!" the old witch kept screaming. "But it's thirty miles away!" I kept saying. And nobody was doing anything, just standing around. Staring at me and me screaming for someone to do something, for someone to please help me!

PRUDDEN: Are you a tax-exempt organization?

MAGDA: (*Swept away, enjoying the drama.*) What? What? The child was unconscious.

PRUDDEN: Tax-exempt?

MAGDA: I thought he was dead!

PRUDDEN: Are you a tax-exempt organization?

MAGDA: Wha . . .

ANTONIO: Yes, yes . . .

MAGDA: Yes, I am what you said. I have the papers. (*She tries searching in her bag.*)

PRUDDEN: What are you getting in there? (*He suddenly lunges from his chair toward* MAGDA. *With expert directness, he takes her wrist.*)

WARREN: Watch it!

ANTONIO: Don't!

WARREN: Careful—she's dangerous—boss! (PRUDDEN *holds her fast. He looks at his watch.*)

PRUDDEN: Quiet! I'm counting. You've got a fever, I think.

MAGDA: What are you counting.

PRUDDEN: The tempo of your heart. Sixty, seventy beats a minute, that's normal. You're not. You're burning up.

ANTONIO: She doesn't listen to me. I've told her. I've tried to stop her doing so much. She's organized marches, pray-ins up to that hospital, trying to get it to open up. In the rain even, they were all praying in front of the hospital. She's even got the bishop into it!

PRUDDEN: How desperate are you?

MAGDA: I am very happy. I am completely happy. I have everything I want.

PRUDDEN: Are you sure you didn't use some of that soap?

MAGDA: Yes.

PRUDDEN: Did the boy die?

MAGDA: What boy?

PRUDDEN: You're trembling. Does your body tremble when you tell lies? Your face, the perspiration on your face. Why, you're radiant. You're dreaming now, aren't you? Why have you fastened on to me? You're dreaming something about me. It's been pouring out of you. From the moment I came in. Something, what? You want to blow my head off. You want to harm me and my family . . . my employees.

ANTONIO: Leave her alone!

PRUDDEN: Your body is steaming. That's what you desire, isn't it? You're wet with it! Your heart is ticking away a mile a minute. You could explode in my face, couldn't you? Couldn't you? (*Pause. PRUDDEN turns to the men.*) We have a limited amount of money to give. We wouldn't be doing our job if we gave it to small groups, to people no one has ever heard of, when we can easily give it to established organizations of greater scope . . . where our dollars would affect larger numbers of people. We don't want our assistance to be invisible!

WARREN: Don't give her any ammunition.

PRUDDEN: Don't you know a "non-person" when you see one! (*ANTONIO lunges toward PRUDDEN. WARREN grabs him and holds him.*)

ANTONIO: Goddamn you! Don't say that! She's not just anybody! She's . . .

PRUDDEN: She's no different than the boot black or the coffee boy! What's the coffee boy look like, Warren? He brings us coffee every morning of his life. What's he look like? What's his name?

ANTONIO: Goofy's got . . .

PRUDDEN: Goofy?

ANTONIO: Magda . . .

PRUDDEN: Goofy? Goofy?

ANTONIO: That's, that's a name I call her. (*PRUDDEN laughs. Then WARREN joins in.*) She's got these eight-by-ten cards, see. Full of facts. Names of personnel directors, politicians, real estate people, midwives. A couple of years ago she just had a couple in a shoebox. Now she's got a whole roomful of shoeboxes. (*PRUDDEN and WARREN's laughter increases.*) And filing cabinets! (*More laughter.*) A mimeograph machine! (*More laughter.*)

PRUDDEN: And a Board of Directors.

ANTONIO: Sure. They meet on her front porch. (*More laughter.*) She's been coming quiet-like, putting her finger on what's rotten and then going for it. Bam! It's like an army of ants hit the place. Chewing all the way to the bone. Magda's beautiful!

PRUDDEN: She's a lovely thing, but no gentleman.

ANTONIO: It's good for the company to have somebody like her on our side . . .

PRUDDEN: Who is she? Has anybody ever heard of her? Warren, have you? Who has ever heard of her?

ANTONIO: I have. I HAVE!

PRUDDEN: Warren, he hasn't heard a word I've said.

ANTONIO: You want a fire-bomb in your soup, don't you? You're begging for it! (*Silently,* SR. CARRASCO *enters carrying his shoeshine box. A small, old gentleman, he still wears the ancient tuxedo he dons to give accordion concerts in the lobby.* PRUDDEN *automatically moves to his chair for his daily shine.* MAGDA *and* SR. CARRASCO *meet behind his back. The old man bends over* MAGDA*'s hand and kisses it with familiarity and affection. She touches his box and* SR. CARRASCO *nods "yes." Since—in* PRUDDEN*'s view— the shoeshine man is a "non-person," he proceeds as though* SR. CARRASCO *were not even in the room.* SR. CARRASCO *kneels before* MR. PRUDDEN *and carefully places* PRUDDEN*'s foot on the box.* SR. CARRASCO *does not open the box, take out his equipment or clean* PRUDDEN*'s shoes. Artfully, without* PRUDDEN *noticing,* SR. CARRASCO *waves his magician's hands over the shoes as if he were really cleaning them.*)

PRUDDEN: Christ All Mighty! What's got into you? Warren, can you feature anyone wanting to harm us? Why, the damn newspapers are always reporting the good we are doing.

ANTONIO: Stop! Just stop!

PRUDDEN: We don't raise our voice here, do we, Warren? I thought he had become one of us. I thought he had stopped being irrational, emotional. I thought that cluck-cluck, girlie stuff was a thing of the past. God, we've got a little sister in the family.

ANTONIO: I . . . I can't take the double-think that goes on around here.

PRUDDEN: You're just becoming a businessman, Anthony, that's all. Growing pains. Don't you think, Warren?

ANTONIO: But I'm paid to . . . I . . . I thought I was doing the right thing.

PRUDDEN: He "thought." He "thought!" You are not paid to think, sir, but to do what your superiors tell you. I ought to have Mr. Floyd here take down these trousers of yours and go to work with his belt. A few licks right here and now'll snap your caboose back on the track. What's happening? Where'd the cool air go? It's suffocating in this place. Cooling system must have broken down. This whole place is put together with spit and chewing gum. Damn engineers ought to be in jail. Why is this woman here? I've never had such a person in my house. What do you mean allowing a person like that? I wouldn't go to the corner to buy a newspaper with a person like that. And I wouldn't allow you to go to the corner with a person like that. Probably steal your shoes before you got back. What has she done for you? Company didn't want me to hire you. Know that? Told them I needed you to deal with people—people your own kind. They said "No. Go." I told them I'd pay for you out of my own pocket. They didn't want you. Personnel didn't think you were much. Go and check the files. So they said if I coughed up some dollars every two weeks—at my own risk—I could have me a sub-standard, unemployable to train. You know that? Don't tell me I don't help the poor. (SR. CARRASCO *has finished. He rises, bows to* PRUDDEN. *Without giving him a glance*, PRUDDEN *hands him some small change.*) She going home tonight, or is she going to spend the night with you? What has she done for you? I don't care to know.

ANTONIO: I . . . I like it here, if you know what I mean. I can wear a suit, a tie, it's clean. (SR. CARRASCO *steps behind* PRUDDEN's *chair, puts down his box and kisses* MAGDA's *hand.*)

MAGDA: Sir, you play the accordion beautifully. (SR. CARRASCO *departs empty-handed.*)

PRUDDEN: It's suffocating, I said. What about getting some cold air in here!

WARREN: I'll call premises.

PRUDDEN: Good. You're a good servant, Warren. When you behave and don't think too much.

WARREN: It wasn't my fault. Antonio thought it was too cold. He called premises and said you wanted the cold off.

PRUDDEN: (*To* ANTONIO.) You used my name?

ANTONIO: Yes. I did. (ANTONIO *looks over at* WARREN.)

PRUDDEN: If you don't approve of the climate here, I think you should make arrangements to find work elsewhere. Pronto. Who would take you, I don't know. The only thing you're good for is giving away other people's money.

ANTONIO: I know you don't mean that. I know you like me.

PRUDDEN: Listen to me—learn this: you don't go into an office expecting to be liked or to be loved!

MAGDA: You don't know how to deal with me, do you? (*Pause.*) The first time a stranger clawed his way up my front stairs, vomiting every step of the way, I didn't know what to do either. Except I knew he was in trouble. And it was keep'n him or letting him mess himself up in the street or in some jail cell. He picked the right street, the right door, the right lady, all right. Guess someone told him I'd, well, spent a long time in nothing land, too. He just wanted to be a child for a little while and have someone wipe his mouth, clean him up and send him on his way with a name and an address on a piece of paper. You might say he was my first client. Okay, a guy comes and vomits on my doorstep and I eat it. Well I've been eating that sort of vomit for years! All that thick kind that builds up until it's got to come out or kill you. And having it on the menu every day doesn't make it any easier to swallow. Yes, I take it in, but it's just as disgusting as the first time. But you know what? By some sort of magic all that diet has been vitamins A, B, C, D and E for me! I've got muscles now you'll never have in a million years carrying money bags to the bank! You give according to need, you said. You pick your grant winners according to "urgency of need." Pick, pick, like an old vulture sitting in your chair, picking away, sampling all the tasty needs before you. Well, I bring you a banquet! A feast to delight any foundation. Pain galore! You've got a whole community standing right in front of you. Feed. Feed. If you want to save your life. Feed. If you want to save your soul. Feed, you phoney, you need me! Get some calories into this morgue. This poor man's excuse for a foundation! Foundation? Mediocre incompetents all of you! Lording it over housing projects when you live in palaces. What do you know? What do you know? Nothing. You're going to put money into my program and it's going to spread through my community like wildfire! There's going to be a glow in this place like you've never known. We have to have a clinic for young mothers, kids, old people. God, they still have witchdoctors, healers they go to. Drug stores are their clinics. These druggists are getting rich! Nutritionists we need. Kids going around with bloated bellies, their hair falling out, their skin full of sores because they don't eat right. I want to set up special training programs so that if someone wants to paint, he doesn't have to walk out of a store with tubes of paint under his sweater. I want books, medicine. I want space. I want doors to open! You're going to put money into my program, you are going to put your name on it, and at least this foundation is going to have something to point to with pride. I'm going to feed you. And I don't care if you choke on me, but, by God, you're not going to spit me out again! (*Pause.* PRUDDEN *turns from* MAGDA. *He covers his eyes.*)

PRUDDEN: There's blood on your dress.

MAGDA: No, there isn't.

PRUDDEN: That's how he saw her the first time. With blood all down her front from that damn dog of his. All fired up, ready to cut his heart out. (*He smiles to himself.*) My God, the poor kid said that one look and all his blood rushed between his legs. That if he didn't dump his load he was going to blow to smithereens! (*He turns to MAGDA.*) That was Clark's first letter about her.

ANTONIO: What's he saying? I don't understand . . . está loco.

MAGDA: Yes. There's blood on my dress. All over me. You bastard! You rich bastard! (MAGDA *bursts into tears.*)

WARREN: (*With derision.*) He says he's going to marry her.

MAGDA: You want to marry me?

WARREN: That's what he told me, Mr. Prudden.

ANTONIO: That's a lie.

MAGDA: You think I'm good. You think I'm kind.

ANTONIO: You're crazy.

MAGDA: A saint.

ANTONIO: Everybody in her neighborhood thinks she's a crackpot. Anybody can get anything they want off her. Cigarettes, car fare, anything. Anything . . . she . . . she . . . the guards downstairs didn't . . . they didn't mess up her coat, that's a lie.

MAGDA: You really love it here. Don't you, darlin'? You'd kill for it.

ANTONIO: I'm sorry. Mr. Prudden, I'm sorry.

MAGDA: You're doing fine, baby. Protect what's yours. Hold on like mad.

ANTONIO: I'm sorry. I'm sorry.

MAGDA: I'm proud of you, baby.

ANTONIO: Shut up!

MAGDA: Save yourself.

ANTONIO: You're right, Mr. Prudden. We should never allow people like this up here.

MAGDA: People like you.

ANTONIO: Me? I'm nothing like you. You never do anything the way everyone else does. You turn the night into day. Everybody who's decent is fast asleep and you're up, clipping newspapers. You complain about not having enough money, but you keep your lights on all night. You've got the biggest electric bill within a radius of a thousand miles! Do you eat three meals a day? No. You never eat and you're fainting all the time, but you eat eighteen times a day!

Pure junk! You say you haven't money even for buses, but you walk
a couple of miles a day and have to buy new shoes all the time! You
won't take vitamins. You won't wear that wristwatch I gave you. You
keep the house full of smelly stray dogs. You refuse to spell when I
know you can when you want to. You're smarter than anyone I know
and you've sat still through a thousand college lectures, but will you
get a degree you can hang up on the wall? Never! You won't take
any advice. You're not humble . . . that's your problem. Face it.
Face it. We're second rate. Admit it.

MAGDA: You don't belong here.

ANTONIO: I do. I'm not like you. If I could be out there, starting up
programs, fighting on my own, I would. But I can't yet. So, don't
talk to me. I don't know you.

MAGDA: Do you remember the boy who died dancing the mambo?
(*Laughter bubbles up in her.*) No, I guess you wouldn't. You're
much too young. It was just a small item in the paper. I clipped it
out. The headline said, "Boy Dies Dancing Mambo." It was just a
couple of sentences. The paper said a boy went mad for the mambo.
He loved it so much . . . (*She's really laughing now.*) . . . that he
couldn't stop doing it day and night until he dropped dead! I tried it,
too. But it didn't work. Oh, Antonio, I wish I had known you in my
mambo days.

ANTONIO: I'm sorry about this, Mr. Prudden.

MAGDA: A girl doesn't get a proposal of marriage every day . . .

ANTONIO: (*To* PRUDDEN.) I've really got the best interests of the company at heart. I'll prove it. You want me to sign a piece of paper?
You've got me for life!

MAGDA: (*Breaks in.*) Deep feelings are sacred, I know, but I've got to
tell you so you won't torture yourself. The only way I could get past
those guards was through you. I used you, baby. That's all. I used
you. So, don't feel bad, I mean about betraying me.

ANTONIO: Listen! Will you stop being nice to me!

MAGDA: I'm grateful. But I don't need you anymore.

ANTONIO: Just, just don't tear yourself down on my account. You think
anybody is going to believe you? You're, you're so nuts about me,
it's embarrassing. But, I'm used to it. A lot of women feel the way
you do about me.

MAGDA: I had to get in. At any cost.

ANTONIO: (*He pulls out a coin purse wrapped with several rubber
bands. It takes some doing to get the purse unwrapped and opened.
Inside are coins and neatly folded bills. He unfolds them and emp-*

ties the coin purse into his hand and offers this money to MAGDA.)
I don't want you to go back and face that bunch empty-handed. Stick
out your hand. I'm going to give you everything I've got on me. You
came for money and I'm going to give it to you. Now, open that
hand of yours. Come on. Take it. Take it and, and just take your
bus . . . you, you dirty bitch! (MAGDA *has been advancing slowly
toward him. She passes through his outstretched hands filled with
money and takes him in her arms. She presses him to her and kisses
him. Arms outstretched,* ANTONIO *tries not to respond. But it is
impossible not to respond to* MAGDA, *and slowly we see his arms
encircle her back. His fingers begin to spread and caress her and
the coins and bills seem to melt from his hands and rain down*
MAGDA'*s body to the rug.*)

WARREN: Think about baseball, kid, and you won't get a hard on. That's
what a priest told me and he ought to know. Think about baseball!
(*But* ANTONIO *and* MAGDA *are oblivious to him and continue
their embrace.* WARREN *continues quietly now, almost to himself.*)
They shouldn't do that. Management wouldn't like that. This is
embarrassing as all hell. They should stop. What's going to happen
if they don't stop? (*To* ANTONIO *and* MAGDA.) Hold on there.
Hold on now! Respect! Respect! God, all hell is going to break
loose. They're smashing the place up! You better get out of here,
Mr. Prudden. They're letting go . . . they're really letting go. Don't
look straight into it. (MAGDA *and* ANTONIO *are hardly moving.*)
Lord, Lord, Lord, will you look at that. Hot and sweet as honey. I
want some too, I want some . . . (WARREN *is drawn to the couple, but before he reaches them,* MAGDA *ends the embrace, looks
at* ANTONIO *for a moment, then turns from him. With satisfaction,
purpose and strength,* MAGDA'*s hand skims up her middle and
rests on the top button of her coat, she unfastens it. Then the second, the third, and so on down. Her eye catches* ANTONIO'*s
money lying at her feet. She sinks to her knees and begins collecting
the bills and coins, carefully placing them back into* ANTONIO'*s
coin purse.*)

PRUDDEN: Clark Prudden, my son, met and married a woman in China
Lake. He said the first time his clothes came off, money flew out of
his pockets and that his bride threw herself on the rug . . . and
played with it. (MAGDA *finishes filling* ANTONIO'*s coin purse,
gets up and drops it into one of* ANTONIO'*s pockets. She takes off
her coat and hands it to* WARREN *without a glance on her way to a
chair. She sits, back straight, alert.*)

ANTONIO: (*To* PRUDDEN.) I have to have her . . . if you know what I mean. Mr. Prudden. I can't live without her. She makes me a little insane, father. I have to have her all the time. Please . . . I want to marry her. I beg you.

PRUDDEN: Young men are selfish bastards. My son didn't want me near his bride. He wanted her all to himself. But at night, oh, yes, I could lie back and the pictures would come. I could imagine the two he had said so much about. His letters, his letters were filled . . . it became cruel after a while . . . to keep me from . . . any man who read his letters would . . . I couldn't have my secretary see them. Warren, but Clark wouldn't mark them "personal"—I begged him to—he would just send them. It amused him. He said, money couldn't buy her, that she was a natural. "She's a natural, father!" Babbling, begging, reminding me of the animals we keep on our ranch, of the warm seasonal fluid the females emit that brings the bulls to them, a uteran furor, an intense physical heat she produced not at certain times, but filled his nostrils at all times and was irresistible to him! BUY IT! DON'T MARRY IT! (PRUDDEN *stuffs bills into* ANTONIO's *hands*.) Warren will give you the names and addresses of safe women, women who will be no danger to you, my boy. Women you don't have to marry, women you don't have to love. All the rest want your money, Clark. You're too young, too innocent, Clark. They all want your money. Warren will fix you up. He'll take care of you. He'll protect you.

MAGDA: Sonia, my mother, wanted to protect me, too. She used to hang a bag of camphor down between my breasts and pray the strong odor would keep the boys from taking me from her. But one did. And I let him. He was crazy and so was I. Lifted me to him and I saw it all—no pain, protection, luxury, love for all my life, forever! How he grasped for it! Blind, annihilating me, grinding me to nothing. And not knowing it. Because that's what he thought love was, I discovered. Some sort of self-gratification. He'd only been with whores and didn't know the difference. He didn't know how to treat a bride. Didn't know how not to humiliate me. That's what his papa taught him it was all about.

PRUDDEN: The kid was satisfied. He was doing all right.

MAGDA: He never gave me a thing. Clark Prudden never could give a woman anything. You saw to that. What did you think, that he'd never discover that his sport was a sort of torture for me? That I wouldn't tell him he was carving me up for good, to stop, that he wouldn't care? He cared.

PRUDDEN: I don't want to hear about it.

MAGDA: He cared.

PRUDDEN: It was some kind of mechanical failure. I have the telegram.

MAGDA: He cared. I guess he was still young enough. Still desperate enough. But not old enough to wait.

PRUDDEN: I'm not to blame for that.

MAGDA: I did force my mind back to that first feeling for him so that I could help him, be charitable. Oh, I concentrated all my strength to regain, but he thought I'd closed myself to him. And I had. Me, I was too young, too. I couldn't stop him going out and taking his anger up and up into the sky and driving straight into the earth. But, oh, yes, he learned one thing before, before . . . THAT MAKING A WOMAN HAPPY IS THE MOST IMPORTANT JOB A MAN HAS ON THIS EARTH!

PRUDDEN: There is nothing wrong with me.

MAGDA: How could there be? You're not human. Up here apart from the cares of the world. Powerful, protected, not feeling a thing. Just waiting for us to come bend our knees before the throne. Just like Clark. You are too attractive in your cloth of gold, too desirable. Dazzling. You cost too much.

PRUDDEN: There was nothing wrong with Clark.

MAGDA: The Indians didn't think the conquerors were human either. They thought those dazzling men were gods, too. But when those gods began to misuse them, the Indians tried an experiment. One day, while they were helping the Spaniards to build a bridge, they took one of the captains and held his head under the waters to see if he would die.

PRUDDEN: Clark was drinking too much, that's all. I know. I heard him. He called me. I didn't want to take it, so Warren took it on the extension in his office. They didn't know I was still on. Clark told Warren to tell me . . . You know, he was talking and he was practically dead already. I didn't know. I thought he was drunk, wild vomit talk, out of his head words about me, can you imagine? About my life, that we were maimed for life. To tell me.

MAGDA: Didn't you call him back?

PRUDDEN: (*In great pain.*) Oh, but . . . no . . . we can't, you see we've never known how to, to deal with certain . .. the, the irrational part of life in our family. Embarrassing feelings. Way back, my father, he came west to make his fortune in cattle, see. The day he left home, my grandfather took him to the railway station. Somehow, the old man knew he'd never see his son again. When my father boarded the train, the old man burst into tears. My father didn't know what to do. He suddenly leaned out of the train, stretched out his arm toward my grandfather and tweaked his nose! (*He chuckles suddenly, then stops.*) When my father died, the shock was so great for my mother that she showed nothing, of course, but her body went to sleep, too. Years later, she told me that the shock had been so great that her periodic discharge, her monthly flow of blood dried up forever. Nothing has flowed from me since Clark stopped living.

MAGDA: It's terrible to be impotent. What's worse, no tienes música.

PRUDDEN: Speak in English!

MAGDA: What I said was, "You have no music." There's no melody in you.

WARREN: (*To* PRUDDEN.) I knew you wouldn't want her near Clark again, but she just followed that coffin right onto the train and I . . . well, I couldn't keep her off. She just stood with her pretty arm on the coffin.

PRUDDEN: I can still hear Clark laughing at me. Letting me know I couldn't have any. Never had any like it! When I saw him dead, well, I didn't want "any" anymore. (*Turning to* MAGDA.) Now I do.

WARREN: She knew I'd be coming for her, but she didn't move. She just stood there, one hand on the coffin and I let my hand swim up her skirt. God, I never had it so big in my whole life.

MAGDA: (*To* PRUDDEN.) Each time I got a woman a better job—that was a victory for me against you. Each bastard foreman fired was a victory against you. Every farm kid who reads better, every father I help write his name better . . .

ANTONIO: (*Breaks in.*) Why didn't you tell me? Why did you do it? They touched you. They got into you. You were one of them all the time. You did set me up. You did set me up. All that time.

WARREN: You want some names? I've got 'em. Best money can buy.

ANTONIO: All that time.

WARREN: You wanna stay on father's payroll, kid?

ANTONIO: Why didn't you trust me?

WARREN: Stay out of this! (ANTONIO *whirls on* WARREN, *jumps him, pummels him, but* WARREN *is too strong for* ANTONIO. MAGDA *and* PRUDDEN *remain distant, not moving or interfering.*)

ANTONIO: Infidel animal Anglo barbarian bastard! Coward! Inhuman coward! Criminal clerk-jerk! Unimportant slob! Illiterate uncivilized unfeeling peon prick! ¡Puerco desgraciado! ¡Cobarde! Slave! I believed . . . I believed . . . (WARREN *throws* ANTONIO *off.*)

WARREN: Schmuck.

ANTONIO: I believed . . .

MAGDA: (*With scorn.*) What did you believe, my prince? That it was "good" for the company to have someone like me on their side? Or that I was good for you? What did you believe? (*Pause. The wind starts up again. The chandelier sways and the lights flash briefly on and off. No one pays much attention to this.*)

ANTONIO: I don't know. I think I'm going crazy in this place. I've never known anyone like you, Goofy. Never felt so good. Sure, I used you. It was perfect. I really thought you'd help me score a few points here. I mean, if somebody complained that we weren't doing enough for the little guy, we could point to you. I wanted father to like you. Wanted you to warm him up. Get him to loosen up. It's up to people like us to stick our hands way down inside their throats and pull them inside out—for their own good. Because we've been privileged. We know it's a big deal if we get through the day all right. They don't. If they did, they wouldn't do what they do. You think it's normal that we spend more money on consultants than we give out in grants?

WARREN: Shut up about that.

ANTONIO: See, just like kids. They like to keep secrets. How much is it, Warren, that you get for each proposal you send over to the experts? A couple of bucks?

WARREN: I don't know what you're talking about.

ANTONIO: So he encourages all sorts of people to submit propsals, and they're sitting at home eating their hearts out waiting for an answer. Most of them get nothing and big Warren gets fringe benefits.

WARREN: Well, if we didn't get proposals we couldn't very well justify our existence, could we? I'm not dumb. Want people to think we're twiddling our thumbs. Haven't you always said, Mr. Prudden—"Act busy."

ANTONIO: Why can't we really be busy!Once a week you let in a beggar up here so you can have your kicks and feel superior. God, we could do so much. I thought, I really believed I could get you to see things differently if you could get within touching distance of the street, but all you do is spend all day telling each other how "good" you are, how busy you are, you're "snowed," snowed, snowed under.

PRUDDEN: I thought you liked me. You want a raise, is that it? (ANTONIO *becomes sick. He reels toward the spittoon and vomits into it.* PRUDDEN *turns to* MAGDA.) Help him.

MAGDA: I'm not your servant.

PRUDDEN: Help him out!

MAGDA: I'm no nurse!

PRUDDEN: Hold his head.

MAGDA: I can't. (PRUDDEN *takes her by the arm and forces her to move toward* ANTONIO, *who is lying on the rug, his head over the spittoon.*) I don't want his stuff on my stockings! It's spilling on the rug. (*She breaks away from* PRUDDEN *and turns way in disgust.*)

PRUDDEN: (*To* WARREN.) Clean him up. (WARREN *tears some pages out of* MAGDA*'s proposal and starts mopping up the rug.*)

MAGDA: Hey! Don't use that! That's my proposal. It cost money to get one of those things together.

PRUDDEN: The boy, not the rug!

WARREN: I don't have a handkerchief. (PRUDDEN *takes out his breast-pocket handkerchief and tosses it to* WARREN.)

MAGDA: Seventy-five thousand for the first year. A seed-money grant to start up a free clinic. I think that's a reasonable amount. (*Suddenly, the lights go out entirely. The group is silhouetted in the waning afternoon light.*) With a grant from you I could raise more. With you as bell cow in my fund-raising campaign, other corporate donors would follow your example. You have one grant that is particularly suitable for my operation. Your annual "Prudden Family Award for Community Service." Seventy-five thousand. Pay attention to me. Pay attention to me for once! (*The lights come on full.* WARREN *is on the floor with* ANTONIO*'s head on his lap. He is wiping* ANTONIO*'s mouth.* ANTONIO *is still clutching the bills* PRUDDEN *stuffed into his hands.* PRUDDEN *crouches near him.*) Seventy-five thousand.

PRUDDEN: He's a hero-worshipper from way back, isn't he, Warren? (*To* ANTONIO.) Look, I don't want you to go out of here thinking badly of me. I'm not your enemy. Not me. So, don't go telling your friends otherwise. I'm a triumph, a success, and that's what you love about me and you know it—so smile your famous smile for me. (ANTONIO *doesn't.*) Get the kid some water. (WARREN *pours a glass of water from the carafe.* PRUDDEN *takes it from him and drinks it down.*) Thanks. People always get a kick out of it when I tell them how I discovered Anthony one night at the wheel of a cab. Or rather how he discovered me. (*To* WARREN.) Get some towels from the john. (WARREN *transfers* ANTONIO *from his lap to* PRUDDEN*'s and goes.* PRUDDEN *unbuttons* ANTONIO*'s collar and ministers him with tenderness.*) At first, when I couldn't sleep, I'd stretch my legs an hour or two. But then I started walking farther and farther, all night, every night. Looking for Clark, I suppose. (WARREN *returns with moist paper towels and hands them to his boss.*) Warren's told me I shouldn't wander around through dark places. But I must. That night, after I was notified, I was a dead man, too, just about. Sometimes, the dogs would bark if someone came near the house. The safety lights down in the park came up through the trees. Shadows were moving all over my ceiling. I tried to talk to them. They were alive. I called up Clark. Some nights, lying on my bed I'd look up and imagine . . . (*To* MAGDA.) Him together with you. So I went out, looking for more reflections, more shadows until . . . (ANTONIO *sits up.* PRUDDEN *stands up.* MAGDA *slowly comes to* ANTONIO *and kneels on the floor before him.*) Anthony picked me up in his good cab, God knows where. Stuck his head out of the window and startled the hell out of me. Insisted I'd be robbed or worse if I didn't get in. Said I was being followed. He drove me home. Talked a wild streak that night and I expected I did, too. And by the time I was on my doorstep, I'd offered him a place. Here. With me. He doesn't think I've maimed his life. He's doing fine.

ANTONIO: I really loved you, Goofy. You know that?

MAGDA: You're not second rate, baby. I am.

ANTONIO: I could work something out. Forgive you, maybe.

MAGDA: I wish . . . who needs this grief! See what I get for messing around with kids.

ANTONIO: Goofy, marry me. (*She gets up and moves away from him.*)

MAGDA: It's their country, baby. They run it.

PRUDDEN: Warren will take you around to see a couple of girls. You'll feel as good as new.

ANTONIO: (ANTONIO *slowly gets up, whips off his tie. Through the following speech he slowly divests himself of his corporate identity: takes out a key ring and removes his office keys and tosses them on the marble table; takes off his company pen and pencil and tosses them, too; a note pad; his credit card, etc.*) Promised me the Foundation would be mine someday, remember? 'Cause Mr. Floyd was too stupid. Guess that was a phoney, too, huh?

MAGDA: Shut up!

ANTONIO: You all know the story about the monkey who wanted to make love to a skunk? Well, he did. And when it was over, he said, "I didn't get as much as I wanted. But I got as much as I could stand!" You know what I'm going to do? I'm going to find a hardware store and buy me one of those big brushes for cleaning floors. With the hard bristles. And I'm going to go home and take a shower and put a lot of soap on it and scrub and scrub until I get off all that dirt from this place! I want to thank you. Thank you both. For making me feel good. I don't feel bad. I feel great. This place is all yours. You're welcomed to it, both of you. And you can tear each other apart all you want—until there's blood all over the place. My life doesn't have to be that way. I say it doesn't. You, you need protection. I don't. From now on you need protection from me! Because I know there's got to be more people like me out there than people like you. And I'm going to find 'em. And we'll be outside. Free—riding our chargers, founding new cities, new towns—we'll be the new nobility—por Dios! And when the new age comes, people will look and wonder and say, (*Pointing at* WARREN .) "He was an unnatural man who gave up his life for a company. Although he knew he was so disrespected by his fellow businessmen that they placed him in a tower as far away from them as possible. And ordered him to do a phoney day's work. Man's work." (*Indicating* PRUDDEN .) "And he spent his days with an idiot to serve him and clean up after him and for a time . . . " (*Indicating himself.*) " . . . a fool ate out of his hand. But worse of all, he gave charity a bad name. And she . . . she could have been Queen of the World." My mambo days aren't over. I don't care if I die dancing it, I'm going to dance it. On your damn board room tables. (*He sweeps files from the tables, tosses paper in the air.*) Your offices, and I'm going to laugh about you for the rest of my life. And I'm going to feel good, and nobody, but nobody is going to make this man feel this bad, ever again! (ANTONIO *goes.*)

PRUDDEN: Doesn't understand A-1 about how progress works. So open-minded his brains dropped out. (*To* MAGDA.) You really put him through the wringer today, didn't you? But he loves me, all right. He'll be back. He admires me. He'll be back. Sure he will. He's loyal. I've got him for life. And cheap, at that. (*To* WARREN.) If anyone asks where Antonio is, say he's out with the flu. And tell the Guard Department not to let my son in the building. He can apologize in writing. You'll have to do his work now.

WARREN: But I've got too much work to do as it is. I'm snowed! (MAGDA *has been studying herself in a compact mirror, mopping the perspiration and dabbing at herself with powder.*)

MAGDA: (*To* PRUDDEN.) You want some?

PRUDDEN: No. I'll call premises. (*He moves to the telephone and dials.*)

MAGDA: You look as if you could use some.

PRUDDEN: I have to do everything around here.

MAGDA: (*Facetiously.*) I know what you mean. If you really want something done, you have to do it yourself.

PRUDDEN: Can't depend on anybody nowadays.

MAGDA: You said it.

PRUDDEN: Thousands of dollars paid out in salaries for what?

MAGDA: Waste, waste, waste.

PRUDDEN: (*Into phone.*) Why in God's name don't you pick up your telephone! This is Leslie Prudden. Leslie Prudden. Is this the premises division? What's going on with the climate control on Fifty-nine? Fifty-nine, the company's foundation. Foundation! What's the matter, are you new here? Foundation! Philanthropy, grants, giving, good will! Well, you'd better learn and learn fast because this is the heart and soul of the company—get your supervisor—GET HIM! Her?!

WARREN: (*To* MAGDA.) You didn't really want the kid, did you? I'm a pretty important guy around here. We could listen to the radio at night together. I bet the company'd chip in a little for a weekend honeymoon, just so I could keep you off the streets. Prudden knows I'd watch you like a hawk.

PRUDDEN: This is Leslie Prudden on Fifty-nine. We're burning up here. That was . . . I'm sorry, I made a mistake earlier. It was an error. We're burning up, we can't breathe. We can't function. We have some valuable art up here. Paintings. The climate is set at a precise level, if it changes it could harm them. They could crack! (*He puts the phone down, agitated, excited. He takes off his jacket.*)

MAGDA: You'll feel a lot better after you've given me a grant.

PRUDDEN: (*Attacking with all guns.*) I have no intention of giving you a grant. We normally take months to review a grant request, but I can tell you that today I've had ample opportunity to look you over and, frankly, I don't think you're good enough.

MAGDA: Good enough!

PRUDDEN: We wouldn't be doing our job, would we, if we helped someone truly incapable of helping others? It wouldn't be fair to the many good people who have pending requests. We only have a limited amount of money available and . . .

MAGDA: What are you talking about? What the hell are you talking about?

WARREN: I'll take her off your hands. Don't sweat it. I'll make sure she doesn't make trouble for you.

PRUDDEN: As Warren told you, I'm the best in the business.

WARREN: A real beaut, huh? (*To* MAGDA.) You're a beautiful thing, you know that?

PRUDDEN: She's uncommonly attractive.

WARREN: A prize.

PRUDDEN: Yes, she is.

WARREN: I don't blame the kid. Drove him right up the wall.

PRUDDEN: Yes.

WARREN: (*To* MAGDA.) I think you'd better give the soap back.

MAGDA: (*To* PRUDDEN.) You owe me.

PRUDDEN: You are good, you are kind, you are a saint! MAGDA: I know what I am.

PRUDDEN: Yes. (MAGDA *takes out a pair of sunglasses from her bag and puts them on.*) Yes.

MAGDA: I haven't had anything to eat for hours. My head . . . (PRUDDEN *slowly takes out a gold cigarette case, taps a cigarette on it, and puts the cigarette to his mouth. He waits.* WARREN *lights it.*) I'm exhausted. (PRUDDEN *calmly removes her sunglasses.*)

PRUDDEN: Too exhausted to hold a boy's head while he was emptying his life into a spittoon?

MAGDA: The glare in here! Don't you know I haven't slept for a hundred years! I'm . . .

PRUDDEN: You're burned out.

MAGDA: Burned out! I have feelings enough to keep this building warm all winter!

PRUDDEN: But not charitable ones, I'm happy to say. (*He steps toward her. He puts the sunglasses back on her face.*) Goodness always gums up the works. (*Looking steadily at her, hardly moving, his hand travels up her leg under her skirt and stays there. She doesn't move a muscle. He removes his hand. Staying close to her he begins to circle her slowly, breathing her in. She does not move. He is in back of her.*) Take Anthony's position.

MAGDA: You thought Mr. Floyd would put me in my place. Diminish me.

WARREN: You put me on that train with her and . . .

MAGDA: (*Not moving.*) Rammed that power and prestige of yours into me for life.

WARREN: (*Quietly, savoring it.*) She, she was kind of quiet. Kind of in shock. Didn't say a word. Did everything I said. Kissed her tears. Stayed in my arms, just me and her. Alone, riding together. Miles from nowhere. You really missed something.

PRUDDEN: (*Soothingly.*) A blunder like that, what can it mean over the space of a lifetime? Things like that happen every day.

MAGDA: (*Not moving.*) I don't want to see the old man's face around here ever again.

PRUDDEN: Warren? (*Pause. He turns to* WARREN.) Mr. Floyd.

WARREN: Now wait a minute! Wait a minute! (MAGDA *turns on her portable radio. Faintly we begin to hear a Latin beat. Slowly, it increases in volume and intensity.* WARREN *begins to pace, searches in his pockets, pulls out a cigar stump and lights it.*) I'm not taking early retirement! Not me. I want every cent that's coming to me.

PRUDDEN: (*Quietly.*) I've warned you time and time again to improve your appearance, Mr. Floyd.

WARREN: She's a troublemaker. She's a troublemaker that one.

PRUDDEN: You persist in reading newspapers at staff meetings and smoking those God-awful cigars.

WARREN: Think if you hire her, that's going to keep her from stirring up trouble?

PRUDDEN: I've run out of excuses for your tardiness.

WARREN: God, all my life I've stuck by the rules, done everything I've been told . . .

PRUDDEN: (*Yanking cigar from* WARREN*'s mouth.*) Put out that cigar! You leave the men's room reeking and I get complaints. You leave newspapers tossed all over the floor in the john. What must management think of me that I allow it? You embarrass me, Mr. Floyd.

WARREN: You're supposed to protect me, me, not some wetback.

PRUDDEN: How do you get liquor in the building?

WARREN: Always kept trouble from coming in that door. Kept you clean. Kept Clark in line. Followed your orders. Made him respect everything his old man stood for. Drove him to and from school. Drove him around weekends, nights . . .

PRUDDEN: The liquor bottles in your office—all jammed in the wastebasket with the dozens of unanswered letters. You know we pride ourselves in answering every piece of paper that comes into this office.

WARREN: Taught Antonio to leave his balls at the door. On my own time. Made a model employee out of him. Taught him to forget all his fancy pants dignity crap. Kept him in line for you. Told him the streets are crawling with dignified, unemployable people. "Who's working?" I asked him. "People who can take it," I told him. "The humiliations, the put downs, all the deballing crap. I told him, patience, endurance, stepping in line, not feeling a thing—that's what puts money in the bank."

PRUDDEN: No, sir. We can't have it. Management will not stand for your sloppiness any longer. I'm afraid you'll have to find something else. I need the space. (*Pause. MAGDA picks up* SR. CARRAS-CO*'s shoeshine box and hands it to* WARREN.)

MAGDA: Sr. Carrasco forgot this. Please return it to him. (*She turns and helps her new boss to put on his jacket*.)

WARREN: I guess you want her for yourself, huh? I don't blame you. SOMEBODY OUGHT TO BOMB THIS PLACE!!!

PRUDDEN: Who would do such a thing?

MAGDA: Why, just think of the good that we do.

PRUDDEN: Yes. Just think. (MAGDA *extends her arm and tweaks his nose. The Latin music continues to grow as the curtain falls*.)

El Teatro de la Esperanza

As indicated in the introduction to and commentary following *Guadalupe*, that docu-drama placed El Teatro de la Esperanza firmly on the map of the Chicano theater Movement. *Guadalupe* was the proving ground for the young troupe and, following the successful tour of Mexico in the summer of 1974, it was clear that the Teatro was ready to spread its wings and fly alone. The director and his wife bid the group Godspeed as the core members committed themselves to a full-time theater company, unhindered by school or other distractions such as a job in the "real world." Teatro de la Esperanza was ready to become a professional teatro.

Working collectively, without a single director, the Teatro members continued to refine and perform *Guadalupe* for a second year and then turned their attention to creating their next production. *Guadalupe* was inspired by actual events and was created through research and documentation. Because the Teatro members had chosen to dramatize a recent and still unfolding issue, they could not deviate too far from the truth. They wanted their audiences to appreciate the fact that what they were seeing was no exaggeration but a re-enactment of actual and current events. With audience and critical response to *Guadalupe* fresh in their minds, the Teatro members decided to develop the docu-drama form even further and looked for a historical event to dramatize.[1]

When attempting to reveal the history of the Chicano and Mexicano in the United States one is confronted with a legacy of either misinformation or complete neglect. Thus, any theatricalization of the Chicano's historical presence in the U.S. often becomes a sort of exposé rather than a dramatization of well-known facts. Since few in the audience have prior knowledge of the events portrayed and many may even have preconceived arguments against a statement that forces them to question the status quo, the Chicano dramatist is confronted with the task of creating a play that not only questions history but contradicts traditionally accepted misconceptions.

During the mid-1970's the U.S. government stepped-up its deportations of undocumented workers, blaming them for the ecomonic recession effectively creating yet another misconception about the Mexican in this country. This current problem motivated the Teatro to investigate the immigration history. Research revealed the fact that the U.S. government had deported hundreds of thousands of Mexicans whenever the economy was in crisis, blaming the Mexicans for the scarcity of jobs. Here were actual historical events of which few people were aware.

The Teatro members knew that they must address this important issue, drawing attention to the present situation by exposing historical precedents. If the schools were going to ignore the Chicanos' existence, the Teatro accepted the responsibility of educating its public. The process of creating *Guadalupe* prepared the group to tackle this larger issue. While *Guadalupe* demonstrated the effectiveness of a docu-drama based on recent events, the Teatro members now elected to combine fact with fiction within a historical context.

Using the mass deportations of Mexicans both in the past and in the present as a historical framework, the Teatro members juxtaposed factual incidents with the fictional life of Amparo Villa. They chose the device of a two-track plot line which follows Amparo's life and also traces the story of her son, Samuel. Samuel and Amparo are the *víctimas* in this difficult drama made all the more effective because we know them both so well. Samuel's rejection of his mother represents the ultimate repudiation of his history as a Mexican, a denial of who and what he really is.

After several months of research, development and rehearsal, the Teatro premiered *La víctima* on Cinco de Mayo of 1976 at the University of California at San Diego. Any conjectures that the group might fall apart without a single director were banished that night as the audience watched this engrossing drama unfold. The audience was moved by every gesture, touched by every line of dialog. Provoked to laughter and tears, the crowd affirmed the Teatro's hopes that it had created a piece even better than the previous docu-drama. It was one of those rare moments in the theater for this observer when all of the elements came together perfectly. *La víctima* proved that the Teatro was a professional theater, a collective capable of creating necessary theater.

With another successful production to offer, Teatro de la Esperanza continued to build a touring network. The auditorium in La Casa de la Raza was not large enough to sustain a theater company through modestly priced ticket sales; therefore, the Teatro earned the income necessary to employ people on a full-time basis by touring nationally. *La víctima* proved a very successful production wherever it was presented and the Teatro earned a national and international reputation for being one of the best *teatros* in the country. In 1978 the Teatro became the second Chicano theater group to cross the Atlantic, when the troupe was invited to perform *La víctima* in Poland, Yugoslavia and Sweden.[2]

In 1979, the Teatro created its third major play: *Hijos: Once A Family*, about a Mexican/Chicano family struggling to make ends meet, but eventually falling apart. Unlike the previous two docu-dramas, this play is totally fictional. The central figure is an alcoholic Mexican father whose children reflect the extremes often found in immigrant families: the daughter totally rejects the Mexican culture and marries an Anglo; one son is a street gang member and the third is alone in his quest for a unity that is impossible to achieve. Significantly, all of the action revolves around a strike at the factory in which most of the family members are employed.

Like Jesus Pelado Rasquachi in the Teatro Campesino's *La gran carpa de la familia Rasquachi*, the father in *Hijos* cannot sustain the heartbreak of a disintegrated family and he dies a broken man. Unlike the *Carpa*, however, this play does not employ the broad, comical style of Valdez's creation. *Hijos* is more concerned with the details of everyday family life and problems, performed in a realistic acting style. All of the action takes place in a barrio cantina and six or seven actors portray a number of roles through flashbacks and transformations of setting indicated by simple prop or costume alterations executed on stage. *Hijos* was hailed for its realistic portrayal of people from the barrio as well as for its sympathetic attitude towards their problems.

After a two-year period of unsuccessful collaborations, the Teatro revived *Hijos* and *La víctima* in 1982, presenting the two plays in repertory on tour. In 1983, while still producing these two plays, the group began creating *Y la muerte viene cantando*, a performance about the Latin American woman presented through *corridos*, dance and narrative. In this production the characters are all skeletons, echoing the Teatro Campesino's use of *calaveras* in the style of the Mexican illustrator, José Guadalupe Posada. This production toured to Nicaragua in 1984 and was very well received. The Teatro is the only Chicano theater group to perform in Nicaragua and Cuba; indeed, no other Teatro has ventured south of Mexico.

By 1984 the group began touring another new creation, *Lotería de pasiones* ending the year with a touring repertory of both *Lotería de pasiones* and *Y la muerte viene cantando*. The next year the troupe adapted Dario Fo's farce, *We Can't Pay; We Wont Pay!* into *¡No se paga; no se paga!* placing the action in the barrio. This production was very successful and toured nationally and was performed to great acclaim at the TENAZ festival in Cuernavaca, Mexico.

The year 1986 marked an important turning point for the Teatro, for the group made the decision to relocate to San Francisco, California. The members of the Teatro had discussed the possibility of moving to a larger urban center for years and San Francisco seemed capable of sustaining a resident Chicano theater company. Adding to the attraction of the move was an invitation to be the resident theater company in the Mission Cultural Center, in the heart of San Francisco's Latino community. After a year of settling into their new community, the Teatro produced a very successful revival of *Hijos: Once a Family* in 1987.

In 1988 the Teatro produced a new work written by one of the group's members, Lalo Cervantes, titled *Teodolo's Final Spin*. They produced this play in their theater and on tour, once again proving that the Teatro could sustain a professionalism that served as a role model for other groups across the country. The Teatro had previously produced individually written plays, but this production was the most successful attempt at exploring beyond the collective process. Under the direction of José Guadalupe Saucedo and Anita Matos, two other members of the troupe, *Teodolo* explored the fate of a Chicano garbage collector who joins the Army only to find himself assisting the Contras in Central America. The production showed influences of the farcical *¡No se paga; no se paga!* and was performed in the fast-paced commedia dell'arte style ideally suited to this kind of play.

The productions of *Hijos* and *Teodolo's Final Spin* assured the Teatro a respectable place in the San Francisco theater community. Curiously, this city had never had a resident professional Hispanic theater and Teatro de la Esperanza has filled a great need. However, the Teatro is no longer a collective, but like the Teatro Campesino, hires actors for specific productions. A small administrative staff runs the daily business and the artistic leadership is headed by Rodrigo Duarte-Clark and Rubén Castro Ilizaliturri. Duarte-Clark joined the group in 1973 and Castro began working with the Teatro in 1978.

Plans for 1989 include a dramatized production of the Chilean folk cantata, "Santa María de Iquiqui." The touring production will have live music, dance and dramatizations of the more theatrical scenes. The group also plans another revival.

El Teatro de la Esperanza continues to grow and evolve, adapting to a new home and ever changing conditions. As the only full-time Chicano theater troupe that regularly tours beyond its own region, this teatro has a major responsibility to a growing public. The TENAZ Manifesto of 1973 declared, "Si el pueblo no va al teatro, el teatro tiene que ir al pueblo." The Teatro is doing just that, employing theater artists and taking its theater to the people.

[1]The original creators of *La víctima* were Estela Campos, Michael Cordero, Nilda Cordero, Rodrigo Duarte-Clark, Marta Hernández, Romelia Morales, San-

tiago Rangel and José Guadalupe Saucedo. All but Mrs. Cordero had been involved in the creation of Guadalupe in 1974.

[2]See the "Commentary" following this play for the reactions of the European critics.

La Víctima

La víctima has been performed by the Teatro de la Esperanza from California to New York and in parts of Europe, always to audience acclaim. After referring to the audience's thunderous applause following the Teatro's performance of *La víctima* at the 1977 TENAZ festival in San Diego, Raúl Ruiz wrote, "Only one other time have I ever seen this type of reaction at a festival performance . . . this same teatro group electrified [the audience] with their fantastic rendition of *Guadalupe*, without a doubt one of the finest expressions of Chicano creativity in the field of drama."[1]

In the fall of 1978 the Teatro performed at INTAR's theater in New York City before crossing the Atlantic to perform at the Kalambur Festival of Theatre and Open Air in Wroclaw, Poland, and at the BITEF festival in Belgrade, Yugoslavia, as well as in Stockholm, Sweden. A Yugoslav critic commented, "Obviously 'La víctima' represents not only a high artistic achievement, but an important social document as well."[2] Tadeusz Buski observed of the performance in Poland, "It was the evening during which I was really moved. I was taken by their noble simplicity, and even more by their passion and commitment."[3]

The play has also been produced by other teatros, mostly community-based troupes, with great success.[4] The Guadalupe Cultural Arts Center in San Antonio, Texas, produced *La víctima* in 1984. This production benefitted greatly from the participation of Jorge Piña and Ruby Nelda Pérez, who had previously performed the play as members the Teatro de la Esperanza. Piña directed and his wife Ruby revived the role of Amparo which she had eloquently performed with the Esperanza troupe. One local critic commended Piña "for mounting what is clearly the best piece of dramatic work yet staged in the renovated Guadalupe Theater."[5]

In 1986 *La víctima* was directed by another former member of the Teatro de la Esperanza, José Luis Valenzuela. Produced by the Los Angeles Theater Center, the play remained as potent in 1987 as when it was first produced. This professional production was greeted favorably by the Los Angeles critics and enthusiastically by the Mexican and Chicano audiences in particular. A long time observer of Chicano theater, Sylvie Drake described this production of *La víctima* as a "self-assertive piece that drives home its points with strong humor and a subtext fraught with warnings."[6] Ms. Drake further observed, "Most astonishing of all is how invigorating it is to rediscover in 'La víctima' some of the political ardor that dominated the theater of the early 70's . . . "[7]

Like the people in the audience who had no knowledge of the mass deportations of Mexicans, the critics were left somewhat stunned by the revelation. Michael Lassell summed-up the sentiment with the following observation: "For many non-Latins, it is a shocking lesson in what has gone on in this century; to Latins, already familiar with the litany of degradation, it is a call for solidarity to force change. For everyone, it is a statement that the morality of democracy has its limits, and they are at the Rio Grande. . . . "[8]

While the Teatro de la Esperanza's productions of this play had been produced very modestly in order to tour, Valenzuela's version had to be adapted to a totally different venue and an audience with distinct expectations. Therefore, this was a fully mounted production designed for one space. The docu-drama was embellished with massive backdrops, projections and sliding panels that became trains—many of the luxuries seldom associated with Chicano theater. Also, the cast was made up of Latino actors, who had been brought together for this specific production, rather than a seasoned ensemble. Furthermore, most of the Spanish dialog had to be translated into English in order to reach the theater's English-speaking audiences.

Despite the changes in the Los Angeles Theatre Center's production of *La víctima*, it worked because it remained true to the play and its message. Although Mr. Valenzuela had not been one of the original creators of *La víctima*, he had been a vital member of the Teatro de la Esperanza's creative team for several years and understood the group process. The actors could certainly relate to the problems illustrated in the text; they had only to walk out of the door of the theater in downtown Los Angeles to experience the issues, for the language on the streets and in the businesses is Spanish.

La víctima has been hailed as a milestone in the development of Chicano theater, praised for its dramatic structure and for the fact that it presents theatrical documentation of significant events in the history of the Mexican in the U.S. Most importantly, *La víctima* proves that good theater can be written by a collective. Like many Chicano plays, *La víctima* presents us with a family in crisis, but unlike any other Chicano play to date, this story is couched in a Brechtian style that, like *Guadalupe*, makes us continually think about the events being portrayed.

As in *Guadalupe*, the actors in *La víctima* sit at the sidelines, reminding the audience that this is a play. They watch the action unfold as if they, too, were the audience. This "distancing," as Brecht would call it, keeps the audience from sinking into subjectivity during important moments of social commentary. Like a Greek chorus, continually watching and commenting upon the enfolding action, the actors represent the audience itself, even as they discreetly change a hat, shirt or scarf in preparation for the next character and the next entrance.

The placards which introduce each scene, along with the spoken quotations, provide historical references from which to better understand the issues, and the musical narrative makes additional comments upon the action as it unfolds. The use of music in this drama is crucial to the whole, both as narrative and as counterpoint to the action, employing familiar *corrido* melodies altered to tell another story. This is another Brechtian device, as mentioned in the commentary following *Guadalupe* in this collection.

Because this play was created by the adults who would be portraying the characters involved, the Teatro made a conscious choice to have the same actor portray Sam as a boy, a teenager and a mature father. Curiously, this convention of having an adult play a child works quite well in a Brechtian docu-drama, since the audience members are never asked to "willingly suspend their disbelief," as in a realistic play. All of the other characters are played by the same core of actors, again asking the audience to accept this convention—and they do, quite naturally. Again, there is no denying that this is a performance, these are performers and they have a story to tell. But these Brechtian devices do not restrict emotional responses.

The scenes in this play are carefully crafted to allow a certain mixture of subjectivity and objectivity. While the above-mentioned devices attempt to keep the audience thinking, other moments encourage the audience to feel emotions. The moment in which the young Samuel and Amparo are separated at the train station is chilling and heartbreaking at once. The final tableaux showing Amparo as she appears to Sam, re-telling him the words to the song she sang to him as a child, is meant to be very touching and it is. This scene also forces us to think.

Once again we are presented with another Chicano/Mexico family in crisis. The family has always been at the center of Chicano theater, for it has represented the link with the past through the Mexican parents and grandparents and the bridge to the future through their Chicano offspring. Amparo and her family provide the audience with very recognizable symbols: the Mexican parents, proud of their heritage, juxtaposed with their children who are neither Mexican nor Anglo-American, searching for their place in the society. As in most Chicano dramas, the threats to the stability of the family are based on financial problems, but this play also explores the theme of deportation.

The threat of deportation, in the past and in the present, gives *La víctima* an urgency seldom found in most plays. One of the play's most compelling scenes is when Antonia attempts to smuggle her mother back into the United States as the audience holds its collective breath hoping for their success. When they get past the official and into the U.S., audiences generally cheer this blatant disregard for unjust laws that would separate families. The Teatro carefully created this moment of suspense to heighten the point about how families can be kept apart. The Teatro members also knew that many Chicanos and Mexicans would have experienced the often humiliating ordeal of crossing the border and being treated differently because of the color of their skin. When Amparo successfully gets across, it is a victory for all Mexicans and Chicanos.

A new immigration law went into effect on Cinco de Mayo of 1987, allowing amnesty to longtime residents and new sanctions against employers who hire undocumented workers. Even as skeptics were denouncing the bill, its proponents were hailing it as the long-needed solution to a national dilemma. *La víctima* could lose its potency if the threat of deportation were to cease, but few observers believe this will happen, for there will always be people coming to the U.S. in search of a better life and there will always be employers looking for cheap labor. With that in mind, it is safe to say that *La víctima* will continue to be an example of the necessary theater: a document that educates as it entertains; illuminating the history of a people while questioning a system that would deliberately exclude them.

[1]Raúl Ruiz, "Teatro de la Esperanza y 'La víctima'," *La Raza Quarterly*, Summer, 1977, p. 19.

[2]From the Teatro's press packet; no bibliographic information is given other than: "Oslobodjeni, Belgrade, Yugoslavia, 14 September 1978."

[3]Press packet: Wroclaw, Poland, 8 October 1978.

[4]Community and university productions of this play include: Teatro Latino de Minnesota, directed by Rodrigo Duarte-Clark in 1984; Sacramento State University's Teatro Espejo, directed by Manuel Pickett in 1986; and productions by Teatro Chicano de Tucson, Arizona, and the Zachary Scott Theater, in Austin, Texas.

[5]Ed Conroy, " 'La víctima' Full of Emotion," *Express-News*, 17 December 1984, p. 4-D.

[6]Sylvie Drake, "Political Ardor Revamped in 'La víctima,' " *Los Angeles Times*, February 14, 1987, Part VI, p. 1+.

[7]Ibid, p. 7.

[8]See Janice Arkatov, "Stage Week: A Wealth of New One-Acts at the Colony," *Los Angeles Times*, March 1, 1987, Calendar Section, p. 47.

La víctima

by El Teatro de la Esperanza

PROLOGUE

NARRATOR: The Chicano is a victim of a subtle and complex form of oppresion which differs from traditional forms, yet results in the same end: The exploitation of one group for the benefit of another.

Rosita Alvírez Corrido Tune

Les voy a contar la historia
De lo que les pasa a los pobres
Buscando en este mundo
Como remediar sus dolores
Como remediar sus dolores.

Soy pobre y muy mexicano
Y ya me dan en la torre
Hundidos en la pobreza
La Revolución ya nos corre
La Revolución ya nos corre.

En 1913
Muchas familias se fueron
En busca de mejor vida
De la matanza corrieron
De los balazos huyeron.

SCENE ONE

PLACARD: Northern Mexico late night 1915. The mass migration.

MAMA: ¿Ya pronto llega?

PAPA: Ojalá.

MAMA: Andale, siéntate, ¿pa' qué te cansas?

PAPA: (*Ignoring her.*) Ya antes de la madrugada debe llegar. Pero quién sabe. (*To son.*) ¡Andale tú! Pon la oreja a las vías.

HIJO: ¿Mande?

PAPA: Que pongas la cabeza contra las vías para ver si viene el tren.

HIJO: No oigo nada.

PAPA: (*Perturbed.*) Ay muchacho, mira así.

MAMA: Tiene miedo José. Mira qué negrá está la noche.

PAPA: Collón, vaya a ver por allá. (Son exits.) ¿Comó está la niña?

MAMA: Ya está dormida, mírala.

PAPA: Se le ven los ojos hinchados.

MAMA: Estaba llorando allá en la casa. (PAPA *moves away in reaction.*) Es que le duele dejar el rancho.

PAPA: ¿No le dijiste que vamos a volver?

MAMA: Sí, le dije (*Softer.*) pero no sabía cuándo.

PAPA: (*Beginning to get upset.*) ¿Qué?

MAMA: Pues se me hace que no volvemos pronto. No le quería decir nada.

PAPA: Mira, nomás vamos un rato hasta que se calmen las cosas en estas partes.

MAMA: ¿Hasta que se termine la Revolución?

PAPA: ¡Sí! Y ya pronto se acaba.

MAMA: Eso es lo que dicen, pero nunca se termina; siempre sigue la destrucción, la matanza, el peligro pa' nosotros.

PAPA: Mujer, tú no sabes nada. (*Getting excited.*) Las cosas van a cambiar. (*Child begins to wake up.*)

MAMA: La niña, la despiertas. (*He backs off as she makes sure the child is asleep. Trying to break the tension.*) Ni sabes lo que me preguntaba esta mañana. Me preguntaba si tenían chicle allá en los Estados Unidos. (*Laughing to herself.*) Pos, como no le dije . . . Uh, y muchas cosas más, juguetes y cosas bonitas y modernas. Hasta dicen que hay máquinas que vuelan. Fíjate nomás, qué país tan más avanzado ¿verdad?

PAPA: Así dicen. A lo menos allá no hay guerra, y no hay nadie que te quite la tortilla de la boca.

MAMA: (*Trying to change the subject.*) La niña está mejor. Cuando primero supo, se puso muy triste y lloraba mucho. Ayer la vi con su caballito, parecía platicar con ese animal.

PAPA: Sí, le habla, me fijé un día, le habla como si fuera gente.

MAMA: Esta vez, parecía despedirse de él. (*Son enters.*)

HIJO: ¡Apá! ¡Apá! el tren, el tren ya viene, se pueden ver las luces por allá abajo!

PAPA: (*Nervously and hurriedly.*) ¡Levántense, pues! (*Picks up lantern.*)

MAMA: ¡Andale, Amparito, levántate, mijita, apúrate, que ya llegó la hora! (*As they get their bags together the child is folding her blanket. The other three stand apart getting ready for the train. She turns to cast a last look at her land. Waives, turns and takes three steps, music starts.*)

SONG: A las ciudades llegaron
    Trabajo por ahí encontraron
    Los niños se crearon aquí
    Pronto los años pasaron
    Volverse algún día pensaron
    Al fin se quedaron aquí.

    Amparo para mujer iba
    Lista para empezar su vida
    Dentro del amor ella cae
    Al fin se le llega su día
    Con un hombre mentado Villa
    A ver qué fortuna le trae.

SCENE TWO

NARRATOR: Los Angeles 1922. During the 1921 economic crisis the Mexican national became a scapegoat for the failures of the American economy. Mexican workers bore the burden through deportations, establishing a pattern which continues to the present.

PLACARD: The first deportations.

AMPARO: (*Running out.*) Lupita, Lupita, hurry, hurry!

LUPITA: ¿Qué Amparo, what happened?

AMPARO: No'mbre, nomás quería que me vieras.

LUPITA: What?

AMPARO: Es que me quiero ver bien gut, pa' cuando venga you know who.

LUPITA: Ga Li, acabas de salir del bathroom.

AMPARO: ¿Cómo me veo? Mi cabello, mi vestido, mi lipstick . . .

LUPITA: In my opinion, es que todo en su right place.

AMPARO: ¿No me veo muy tight, aquí por la cadera?

LUPITA: No'mbre, entre más tight, mejor; o sólo que te quieras quedar para vestir santos.

AMPARO: No! No! Hurry up! Vámonos que mi papá está looking. (*They both go over to father.*) Ay papá, aquí estamos.

PAPA: ¡Sí! Qué tanto hacían allá. Ya mero te traía de las orejas. ¡No te digo Amparo, nomás te dejo sola y te vuelves pinga! (*Music.*) Andale, ésta me la prometiste a mí.

AMPARO: Sí, Papá.

PAPA: Con permiso, Lupita.

LUPITA: Pasen. (LUPITA and AMPARO *exchange looks.*)

AMPARO: Qué bien baila Papá. (JULIAN and ROBERTO *enter.*)

PAPA: ¡Es más lo que me duelen los callos!

AMPARO: (*Points finger to* ROBERTO *and* JULIAN, *so* LUPITA *can notice, but father catches on.*) Si quiere, nos sentamos.

PAPA: No, se me hace que voy a querer bailar todas contigo.

AMPARO: ¡Ay, qué bien! (*Scene switches to guys and* LUPITA *running over to them.*)

LUPITA: Roberto, I come in case you no see me.

JULIAN: Buenas noches, Lupita.

ROBERTO: ¿Veniste con Amparo?

LUPITA: Sí. Está dancing con su Apá.

JULIAN: La he visto. Es bonita. ¿Es muy amiga tuya?

LUPITA: ¡Sí! Yo y Amparo somos like this. (*Shows with closed fingers.*)

JULIAN: A ver si me la presentas. Ella es de las que me recetó el doctor.

LUPITA: ¡Claro que sí!

JULIAN: ¿No se enoja su Papá?

LUPITA: ¡Oh, no! Estamos en los United States. Aquí no son tan old fashioned como en México. (*Scene switches back to* AMPARO *y* PAPA.)

PAPA: Ya hija, vamos a sentarnos tantito antes de que me pegue un ataque.

AMPARO: Sí Papá, a sentarnos se ha dicho.

LUPITA: (*Runs over to them after they sit.*) Baila perfectamente.

PAPA: Gracias, Lupita. (LUPITA *pulls* AMPARO *up stage.*)

LUPITA: Viste a Roberto, he come.

AMPARO: Sure! Y también a su friend.

PAPA: Y yo también los vi . . . muchachitas, estoy viejo pero no ciego. No veo lo que no me conviene. (*Music.*) Esta es para Amparito. Andale, vamos a bailar. (LUPITA *interrupts.*)

LUPITA: ¡Ah, no! (LUPITA *grabs* PAPA *and brings him out to dance.*) Está es mía. Qué callos ni qué callos.

PAPA: Que Lupita, vamos pues a sacarle brillo al piso.

LUPITA: Es okay. (LUPITA *and* PAPA *freeze.* ROBERTO *and* JULIAN: *go over to where Amparo is.*)

ROBERTO: Buenas noches, Amparo.

AMPARO: Buenas noches, Roberto.

ROBERTO: Aquí te presento a un amigo.

JULIAN: Julián Villa, mucho gusto.

AMPARO: Mucho gusto, creo que lo he visto. ¿Es de aquí?

JULIAN: No. Soy de Michoacán.

AMPARO: Y ¿qué hace por aquí?

JULIAN: Ando buscando trabajo.

AMPARO: Pues, ojalá encuentre, porque dice mi papá que es más lo que desocupan que lo que ocupan.

JULIAN: Eso sí. Antes trabajaba con la compañía de Santa Fe, pero como usted lo ha dicho, fui uno de los miles que desocuparon.

AMPARO: Bueno, Roberto, no le pudieras conseguir trabajo en la South Pacific?

ROBERTO: Eso es lo que vamos a ver. Hasta pa' mí fue difícil, pero como ya conozco al señor Olivas de la tienda del Supply, claro que él me ayudó.

JULIAN: Bueno ya, ya. Hay que pasar la noche platicando de cosas más interesantes. ¿Gusta bailar, Amparo?

AMPARO: Sí. Sí . . . Bueno creo que debo esperar que mi papá regrese. Ya mero se termina la pieza.

JULIAN: Sí, claro. (*Begins to walk away. She pulls him.*)

AMPARO: Pero si gusta, puede esperarse aquí.

JULIAN: Claro, aquí me espero, con todo gusto. (*Scene switches to* LUPITA *and* PAPA. *Some are leaving as they return from dance floor.*)

PAPA: (*Looking at* JULIAN.) Mira nomás qué causalidad. (*Everyone sits.*) Buenas noches, Roberto.

ROBERTO: Buenas noches, mire aquí le presento a un amigo.

JULIAN: Julián Villa a sus órdenes.

PAPA: Mucho gusto. Usted es nuevo por aquí ¿verdad? No le he visto en mi cuadrilla.

JULIAN: No señor. Ahorita no tengo trabajo.

PAPA: Huy, en estos tiempos está muy pelón hallar trabajo.

JULIAN: Pues, como dicen, necesitamos otra guerra para que haya más trabajos. (*Music.*)

ROBERTO: Andale, Lupita, esta pieza es de nosotros. (*They both excuse themselves.*)

JULIAN: Señor, ¿me permite bailar con su hija?

PAPA: Pues si ella quiere. Ni modo de que la amarre. ¿Quieres bailar, Amparo?

AMPARO: ¡Sí, Papá!

PAPA: Andale pues.

JULIAN: Con su permiso, señor.

PAPA: Pasen. (AMPARO *and* JULIAN *go to dance*; PAPA *always watching.*)

JULIAN: La vi desde que entró.

AMPARO: Ay, ¿por qué no nos tuteamos.

JULIAN: Parecía que tu papá te tenía pegada.

AMPARO: Es que soy su única hija, y no quiere creer que su hijita se está haciendo una mujer.

JULIAN: Ah, comprendo.

AMPARO: ¿Dijiste que eras de Michoacán?

JULIAN: Sí. Mi papá tiene un ranchito.

AMPARO: Y ¿piensas quedarte aquí?

JULIAN: Bueno, eso depende.

AMPARO: Oh.

JULIAN: Si hay trabajo y . . .

AMPARO: ¿Y qué?

JULIAN: Bueno, es que ya tengo veinte y seis años y . . .

AMPARO: Y ¿todavía no te casas?

JULIAN: No, pero . . .

AMPARO: No te has encontrado tu pareja.

JULIAN: No sé, soy un hombre muy movido. Me encanta bailar. (*He trips over* AMPARO's *feet*.)

AMPARO: ¡De veras! A mí también.

JULIAN: Cantar, ¡mucho más!

AMPARO: Yo canto cada domingo en la iglesia.

JULIAN: Y los tamales me enloquecen.

AMPARO: Tamales, qué coincidencia. Es mi platito favorito.

JULIAN: Tenemos mucho en común, ¿verdad?

AMPARO: Sí, parece que sí. (*Music stops.*) Bueno aquí se acabó esta tanda. (*Everyone is disappointed: Ah, ah, ah . . .* AMPARO *and* JULIAN *go back to chair laughing.*)

AMPARO: ¡Ah, Papá! Yo y Julián tenemos los mismos gustos. Le gusta bailar, le gusta cantar . . .

PAPA: Ah, qué bien. ¿Y también le gusta trabajar?

JULIAN: ¡Seguro que sí! (LUPITA *cutting the conversation, begins to fan herself.*)

LUPITA: ¡Ay! ¡Ay! ¡Qué calor! Está bien hot. ¿Amparo?

AMPARO: Hot? ¡Ah, sí! ¡Uy, uy! Me estoy asando.

LUPITA: Te ves bien red. ¿Por qué no salimos a tomar aire los cuatro?

JULIAN: Bueno, Lupita, eso depende si don José le da permiso a Amparo.

AMPARO: Papá, me da permiso . . .

PAPA: No, señorita. No des fiesta nomás porque estás en bola. Acabas de bailar. Sales, te pega un aire y te quedas hecha chicharrón.

AMPARO: Pero Papá . . .

PAPA: Qué papá, ni qué papá. Espérese unos minutos y luego los cinco salimos a tomar aire.

AMPARO: Ay, Papá, creo que ya se me está bajando el calor. Fue nomás unos segundos que me quedé atarantada.

LUPITA: Pues, me van a perdonar, pero yo sí tengo que tomar aire. ¿No, Roberto? Excuse me. (*They exit.*)

JULIAN: Yo me quedo.

PAPA: Qué Lupita, ¡Chiquita pero picosa! (*Looks over to* JULIAN *and begins to interrogate him.*) Y tu papá, qué hace Julián?

JULIAN: Mi papá.

AMPARO: Es dueño de un rancho.

PAPA: Ah, qué bueno.

JULIAN: Bueno, no es exactamente un rancho. Es más un . . . ranchito . .

AMPARO: Ah, y tan humilde de pilón.

PAPA: Y ¿buscas trabajo?

JULIAN: Bueno, si el . . .

AMPARO: ¿Que no me dijiste que empezabas el lunes?

JULIAN: Pues, Roberto dice que va a tratar de . . .

AMPARO: Ay, Julián, dilo como es. Tú sabes que . . .

PAPA: Bueno, a quién le estoy hablando, ¡¿a ti o a Julián!?

AMPARO: No, Papá, pero . . . (LUPITA *runs in hysterically.*)

LUPITA: ¡Amparo, Julián, agarraron a Roberto!

JULIAN: ¿Cómo? ¿Quién?

LUPITA: Se me hace que fue la policía. Le pusieron las handcuffs y lo pucharon a un car.

AMPARO: Pues ¿qué hicieron?

LUPITA: ¡Nada! ¡No hicimos nada! (*Police come running in.*)

POLICEMAN #1: All right stop the music. We want to see some proof of identification.

LUPITA: ¿Qué? No entendemos, qué es lo que quieren.

POLICEMAN #1: We want papeles . . . uh, papeles.

AMPARO: Quieren identificación.

LUPITA: Roberto no tenía y se lo llevaron.

POLICEMAN #2: If you don't show us something, we'll be forced to take you in.

PAPA: Más vale que les enseñemos algo. (*All freeze except* POLICEMAN *who come upstage.*)

POLICEMAN #2: Hey Mac, what's good for identification.

POLICEMAN #1: I don't know, but I think they get some kind of receipt when they cross the border.

POLICEMAN #2: Okay. Ask them for their border crossing receipts.

POLICEMAN #1: Okay, fine. (*All unfreeze.*) We need your border crossing receipts, señores.

LUPITA: Recibos, recibos de la frontera, no los traemos.

POLICEMAN #1: Hey Mac, they don't have any.

POLICEMAN #2: Well, why don't you go check the one in the car.

POLICEMAN #1: Okay. (*He exits.*)

POLICEMAN #2: Next time you'd better carry some form of identification or we're going to have to take you in. Let's close this dance, come on, let's move! (*All freeze.*)

SONG: La migra no los ha echado
Por un pelo se han escapado
En este país se quedó
Casada y feliz ella estaba
No sabía lo que le esperaba
La migra temor le dejó.

SCENE THREE

PLACARD: Los Angeles, Amparo's home.

NARRATOR: At the height of the Depression the American labor force suffered a 25% unemployment rate. For the Chicano worker, the unemployment rate rose to a staggering 80%. The Depression, 1930's.

AMPARO: (*Singing.*) "No, no, no, no señor, yo no me casaré." Pero ¿qué estoy cantando? Casada, con un hijo, otro que viene en camino . . . (SAMMY *enters.*) Y tú, hijo ¿qué tienes? ¿Qué? Te dieron tus 1, 2, 3.

SAMMY: No Amá, nobody hit me.

AMPARO: Entonces, ¿por qué esa carota de sargento mal pagado?

SAMMY: Ama, you know what?

AMPARO: No, I don't know what?

SAMMY: Ahora no jugué con Ramiro.

AMPARO: Pues déjalo, hijo. Maybe he didn't want to play.

SAMMY: No, Amá!

AMPARO: Que está enfermo.

SAMMY: No, he's not sick, es que he not here no more!

AMPARO: ¿Cómo que no está?

SAMMY: Yeah, Amá. Ramiro, his mother, su apá y su brother, everybody went to México.

AMPARO: ¡Válgame Dios!

SAMMY: Antonio told me that they took away el trabajo del apá de Ramiro.

AMPARO: Esto es injusto, y también al señor Barragas, y al señor López y quién sabe a cuántos más.

SAMMY: ¿Qué, Amá?

AMPARO: No, nada, hijo. Ven siéntate aquí tantito. Tú estás todavía chiquito, pero eres muy vivo.

SAMMY: Ga', Amá, I know!

AMPARO: Anda, tú. Mira, hijo, ahorita no hay trabajos para muchos padres and when a father doesn't have a job, his family doesn't eat. ¿Verdad?

SAMMY: Ga', amá, ¡yo sé!

AMPARO: Bueno entonces, tú tienes que entender que todos se tienen que ir pa' México.

SAMMY: Ga', amá, que feo.

AMPARO: Sí, hijo, y ojalá nunca nos pase eso a nosotros.

SAMMY: Pero, I na' gonna see my friend Ramiro no more.

AMPARO: Yo sé que lo vas a extrañar, pero dale gracias a Dios que tu papá todavía tiene su trabajo.

SAMMY: Mamá, maybe Ramiro come back?

AMPARO: Lo dudo, hijo.

SAMMY: Nunca, ga', yo ya no voy a tener a nobody.

AMPARO: No te pongas triste. Mira, hijo, I remember when I first came here y dejé a mi caballito en México. Estaba así chiquita como tú. I was sad too, pero luego para consolarme mi mamá me cantaba una canción, y yo luego luego me ponía feliz. ¿Quieres que te la diga? (SAMMY *nods*.)

AMPARO: Cuando lejos te encuentres de mí
      Cuando quieras que yo esté contigo
      Piensa en todo el amor que te di
      Y verás que estaré yo contigo.

SAMMY: ¡No entiendo, Mamá! Oh, Ramiro no está, but you'll always be there, huh, Amá!?

AMPARO: Sure m'ijo, si yo nomás te lo digo para que no estés tan triste. Ya mero viene tu papá de trabajar, y llega con un hambre que si no . . .

SAMMY: Amá, verdad que cuando el baby nazca le vas a poner el Samuelito Número 2 just like me.

AMPARO: Cómo no. Sólo eso me faltaba. Dos cortados con la misma tijera. Andale, vete. No hijito, ésta va a ser niña porque me está dando unas pataditas muy chistositas. Y le vamos a poner Antonia. (SAMMY *exits and* JULIAN *enters*.) Ah, ya llegaste.

JULIAN: No, esto que ves es un mono pintado.

AMPARO: ¿Tienes hambre?

JULIAN: No.

AMPARO: Mira, un taquito con frijoles y chile.

JULIAN: Te digo que no tengo hambre.

AMPARO: Oye, Julián. Fíjate que ahora me estaba contando Samuelito que al papá de Ramiro le quitaron el trabajo.

JULIAN: A él también, eh.

AMPARO: ¿Qué está pasando aquí, Julián? ¿Por qué siempre nos usan?

JULIAN: ¡Porque nos usan para sus convenencias!

AMPARO: ¿Qué?

JULIAN: No nada. Oye, Amparo, ven para acá. Siéntate, mi amor. Amparo, ¿te acuerdas que hace poco que te estaba platicando, que en México el presidente Cárdenas está repartiendo tierras?

AMPARO: Otra vez con la misma cosa. Y tú te crees. ¿Qué quieres, regresarte a aquella miseria? Pues, muchas gracias porque yo no, ni me digas, porque se me enchina el cuero.

JULIAN: Hombre, Amparo, pudiéramos regresarnos a nuestra tierra, a México. I've always wanted to go back. Es un sueño que siempre he tenido.

AMPARO: ¿Pero de qué estás hablando? Qué andas en las nubes ¿o qué? Yo te hablo de una cosa y tú me sales con otra.

JULIAN: Y fíjate, Amparo. Este gobierno is going to pay our way for free, imagínate, Amparo, gratis.

AMPARO: Ni gratis, ni como sea me quiero ir. Y ahora menos. We're going to have a baby. Como piensas que nos vamos a ir. Chihuahua, ponte a pensar.

JULIAN: Amparo, por Dios . . .

AMPARO: Qué Amparo, ni que tu abuela. ¿Tu crees que sea justo que nos echen nomás porque les da la gana?

JULIAN: Amparo, ¿qué no entiendes que nos tenemos que ir?

AMPARO: No nos tenemos que ir, tú tienes tu trabajo.

JULIAN: ¡Me quitaron el trabajo! ¿Que no oíste? Me echaron como a muchos otros.

AMPARO: Pero, ¿Por qué te corrieron?

JULIAN: Porque no hay trabajos.

AMPARO: Te buscarás otro. Yo tengo fe en ti.

JULIAN: ¿Que no entiendes que estamos en una depresión? Aunque busque y busque, no hay. No hay trabajo para nadie, mucho menos para el mexicano.

AMPARO: Pero ya estamos acomodados aquí. Samuel es feliz y tiene sus amiguitos.

JULIAN: ¿Y qué quieres que haga yo? Yo sin trabajo, ¿cómo diablos los voy a mantener? Chihuahua, hombre, hay que aprovechar los pasajes gratis y las tierras que está repartiendo Cárdenas.

AMPARO: Entonces, ¿qué, Julián? ¿Irnos así nomás, sin dinero, sin nada?

JULIAN: Con una fregada, ¿qué quieres? ¿Dime? ¿Qué vamos a hacer?

AMPARO: Yo no sé, Julián. El niño por nacer, y si me enfermo en el camino, ¿y adónde vamos a llegar? Ni casa ni nada tenemos allá.

JULIAN: Ya pues, Amparo. Ya pues. Mira, tú te quedas aquí hasta que nazca el niño, y yo me voy primero para tener todo listo pa' cuando llegues tú. Pero ya, lo que no quiero es que por un coraje vayas a perder al niño.

AMPARO: Mira, Julián, lo que no quería es desapartar a la familia, pero creo que tienes razón.

JULIAN: Sí, hombre. Aquí nomás nos necesitan y somos burros para trabajar. Pero nomás no hay y somos lo primeros que estorbamos.

AMPARO: Ya no tienes que decir más. I'll go tell Samuel, pero no sé cómo se va a poner. (*Freeze. Scene is broken with the sound of the train.*)

SCENE FOUR

NARRATOR: Train station, Los Angles. In 1932 during his election campaign, incumbent President Hoover promises to rid the country of Mexicans.

PLACARD: The Repatriation 1935.

AMPARO: (*With child in her arms.*) Andale hijo, apúrate.

SAMMY: Ga', Amá. I'm already tired. What's that place called?

AMPARO: Durango, hijo. Tu papá va a ver a Antonia por primera vez.

TRAIN ATTENDANT: All aboard!

AMPARO: (*Playing with baby in arms.*) ¡Qué Pasó, mi niña!

TRAIN ATTENDANT: Come on everybody! (*Whistle.*) Come on, lady, let's hurry up. Hey, lady!

AMPARO: Andale, hijo, vámonos. (*She begins to walk away, looks back.*) Andale. (*Everyone freezes.* SAMMY *gets lost in the crowd on the platform in slow motion. Freeze is broken by a yell.* AMPARO *moves on into train and plays with child.*)

TRAIN ATTENDANT: Let her rip! (*All freeze. Swishing of train begins.* AMPARO *looks for* SAMMY.)

AMPARO: ¡Hijo!

SAMMY: ¡Mamá! (*The last sounds of a distant train can be heard. Pause of four beats is given and scene is broken with song.*)

SONG: Se dice que el tiempo cura
Las penas que hay en la vida
Pasaron más de quince años
Y a Amparo no se le olvida
Y a Amparo no se le olvida.

Mendoza fue la familia
Y al hijo lo recogieron
El niño se hizo hombre
Amor de padres le dieron
Amor de padres le dieron.

SCENE FIVE

NARRATOR: Los Angeles, Clara's family porch. Emerging from World War II as one of the most decorated of ethnic groups, the Mexican-American mistakenly considered himself to be a full-fledged American. Consequently, young Chicanos enlisted for the Korean War believing it to be a way out of the barrio, and an avenue for social mobility.

PLACARD: The first Mexican-Americans.

SAMMY: (*Guitars play chords to "Crei," setting a romantic mood. SAMMY and CLARA come out when the bar is played again. Both sit and freeze at the same time. Music stops.*) Wacha all the stars.

CLARA: (*Walks up to him.*) Uh huh. Sammy? Don't you think it's kind of funny that I've known you for practically all of my life, but not really until six months ago? That's when we fell in love.

SAMMY: Yeah. It just kind of happened, just like when lightening strikes. ¡Palo! I mean, I saw you practically every day. We played sometimes. God, I lived so close. Let's see . . . first, when the Mendoza's adopted me. It was the old house on the corner. (*Pause.*) After the train left . . .

CLARA: (*Sympathetically.*) Don't think about that. (*She kisses him.*)

SAMMY: (*Somewhat comforted.*) Okay, okay. Then we moved into the blue house next door. (*Pause.*) You know, I can't believe it's been fifteen years already . . . then the old house, then by your house. Just like that!

MOTHER: Clara!

CLARA: (*Without turning.*) Yeah?

SAMMY: Go on, she's calling you.

MOTHER: Clara, te metes o te meto!

CLARA: Okay! Okay! I'm coming. (*She kisses SAMMY on cheek and exits.*)

SAMMY: Chingao, man, mañana me voy y los vatos are already calling me El Veterano. Ese veterano, where's your uniform? "Shut-up, stupid." I really wish Uncle Sam would have drafted them, too. We could have some good times getting pedo all the time. That would be crazy to have a whole regimento to ourselves. (*Pause.*) But what if you don't come back or what if you come back in a box. Simón, you're coming back. You gotta make it back, Sammy. You owe it to yourself, and especially to your familia. Hijo, man, Clara's right. They really helped you in everything. Aunque ni fueron tus verdaderos padres, te dieron el amor de padres. It's gonna be hard to say goodbye to them tomorrow. I feel like I'll never see them again. (CLARA *sneaks out behind him.*)

CLARA: Boo! (*She laughs hysterically.*)

SAMMY: (*Kind of angry kiddingly.*) You crazy or something? You scared me.

CLARA: Oh, Sammy!

SAMMY: (*Perturbed.*) What did your Mom want anyway?

CLARA: (*Hesitant.*) What did she want?

SAMMY: Yeah, what did she want?

CLARA: Oh, she wanted to tell me that it's getting late. It's nearly 11:30. (*Hinting.*) I have to go in a little while. They already went to bed. They said to say goodnight and good luck . . . ah . . . she didn't want to interrupt anything.

SAMMY: What do you mean?

CLARA: Oh nothing! It's just that she thought she might . . .

SAMMY: (*Perturbed.*) Might what?

CLARA: Oh, she thought she might walk out when you were asking me . . . that is . . . if you want to . . . I mean if you were going to ask me if . . .

SAMMY: (*Thinks for a second.*) Don't you think I know what you're up to. Ya te conozco mosco. (*As she stands there coily, finger in mouth, child-like but very controlled, he turns away from her, pulls out a comb and combs his hair. Clears his throat, turns to CLARA who already has her hand out. He takes it, looks her in the eyes and kneels.*) Clara? (*Clears throat again.*) Clara, ¿te aranas conmigo?

CLARA: What?

SAMMY: ¿Que si te casas conmigo? Will you marry me?

CLARA: (*In ecstasy.*) Yes! You know I will (*Smothers him with kisses.*) ¿Mañana?

SAMMY: No. I have to go tomorrow!

CLARA: Oh, Sammy! I'll wait till you come back. We're going to have ten couples, two padrinos, two madrinas, one ring-bearer, two flower girls, a big reception, a four-tier cake and a $500 dollar ring!!!

SAMMY: Wait, we haven't made any plans yet!

CLARA: I'll be right back! I'm going to tell my mother!!! (*Exits, running with joy. SAMMY stands there wondering if he made the right decision. Just then his friend PACO passes by.*)

PACO: Ese veterano. ¡Chingao! You still here?

SAMMY: No! This is the Statue of Liberty.

PACO: Ese heartbreaker, how come Clara ran inside the house screaming? No la hagas chillar, ese.

SAMMY: No, ese! She ran in to tell her parents that we're getting married.

PACO: ¿Simón, ese? Really? Ya era tiempo. Hey, let's go get some birrias. I got them out in the carrucha, come on man!

SAMMY: Wait a minute, man! (CLARA *runs out. Doesn't notice* PACO.)

CLARA: Oh, Sammy, she's so happy . . . Paco, Paco, did he tell you? We're getting married! We have it all planned out. We're going to have ten couples, two padrinos, two madrinas, one ring-bearer, two flower girls!

SAMMY: Clara?

CLARA: (*Ignoring him.*) Everybody will be dressed in pink, except me in white. We're going to have a big reception, a five-tier cake and a $500 dollar ring, huh Sammy?

PACO: (*Semi-doubting, but makes play on the pressure.*) Really, Sammy?

SAMMY: Ah . . . ah . . . yeah? (*All freeze.*)

SCENE SIX

PLACARD: Los Angeles/Korea.

NARRATOR: Chicanos and other national minorities constitute a disproportionate percentage of the armed forces. In the most recent war, Chicanos comprised nearly 20% of the casualties, while making up only 5% of the national population. The indoctrination 1951–1953.

MAILMAN: Got another letter for you, Clara. Smells like it's from the army.

CLARA: Oh thank you, Charlie. (*Reading letter.*) Dear Clara, boot camp is really crazy and ese sergeant está loco. He is a real F. You remember that cross on my hand? (*Soldiers standing in line, sergeant walking back and forth.*)

OFFICER: Mendoza, what is the meaning of that cross on your hand?

SAMMY: It's a cross, sir!

OFFICER: A cross? For what? To single you out as different?

SAMMY: No sir, it's . . .

OFFICER: (*Yelling.*) Well, you're not different. Do you hear that? We are all soldiers and we are all the same. You are a soldier too, Mendoza. Do you hear that? (SAMMY *is silent.*) Repeat it Mendoza, say "no sir, I am not different."

SAMMY: No sir, I am not different! (*Yelling.*)

CLARA: (*Reading letter.*) I really miss you, Clarita. It's hard here. I really get mad at that sergeant. Sometimes I feel like punching him across his fat mouth. (*Turning page.*) Honey, these days we have been going to classes to learn how to fight the enemy. I always liked school and learning, but I don't understand these sergeants. (*Switch to* SAMMY *in classroom.*)

OFFICER: Men, we will be fighting in Korea. Jones, what are we fighting against. Right! Communism. If it's in your back yard or across the ocean, we fight against it.

SAMMY: Sir, why don't we let the Koreans fight for themselves?

OFFICER: (*Disgusted.*) Mendoza, if someone was beating up your little brother, would you just stand there and watch?

SAMMY: No, sir!

OFFICER: What would you do?

SAMMY: I'd help him, sir!

OFFICER: That's exactly what we are doing in Korea, helping them Mendoza, helping them. Do you understand that?

SAMMY: (*Embarrassed.*) Yes, sir! (*They both freeze.*)

CLARA: (*Reading letter.*) You know that sergeant he knows a lot of things. Honey, the classes aren't so bad anymore. I'm learning a lot. I understand why I'm over here, baby. I'm fighting for you, Clara. For everybody back home, for our country. (*Changing pages.*) Darling, we arrived in Korea on the 20th of this month. It's pretty bad here, and scary too, especially when we go out into the village. I can't wait to leave this place and see you again, honey.

OFFICER: Okay, men. Attacking a village is no different from the regular combat we've been having with these gooks. Everyone is the enemy. Men, women, children, they are all communists.

SAMMY: Does that mean we shoot civilians, too?

OFFICER: We shoot communists, Mendoza, not civilians, communists! (*Yelling.*) Now move!

SAMMY: Yes, sir! (*Both freeze.*)

CLARA: We had our first taste of war, honey. Today I learned how tough it is to be a good soldier. But it is worth it to stop the communists from taking over Korea. (SAMMY *as if walking through the jungle. Sargeant signals* SAMMY *to come forward.*)

OFFICER: Shoot, Mendoza, they're up ahead!

SAMMY: They're women and children . . .

OFFICER: (*Interrupts.*) Shoot . . . kill the communists, you fool, before they kill you. Kill the communists!

SAMMY: (*Lifting his rifle.*) Kill the communists! (*Getting louder.*) Kill the communists!

OFFICER: That's an order, Mendoza!

SAMMY: (*Getting louder until he shoots.*) Kill the communists! Kill the communists! (SAMMY *shoots. Freeze.*)

CLARA: Darling, I can't believe I'm going home in two weeks. You know, if it hadn't been for that sergeant, I would have never made it home again. I kind of feel sorry I had to leave his platoon. I love you, darling. I can't wait to be with you. I'll be home soon. Love, Sammy! (*Freeze. From off stage the army sounds can be heard. Then music starts.*)

SONG: En México nos hallamos
　　　Con la familia de Amparo
　　　De su hijo no se ha olvidado
　　　Aunque tiempo había pasado
　　　Aunque el tiempo había pasado.

　　　Se encuentran en su ranchito
　　　Muy duro lo han trabajado
　　　Tratando de mantenerse
　　　Las deudas los traen endrogados
　　　Todo lo que tienen es fiado.

SCENE SEVEN

PLACARD: Durango, Mexico.

NARRATOR: Amparo's home: the porch. It is no coincidence that 80% of all Mexicans who cross the border illegally come from the six poorest states in Mexico. They come believing that a better life awaits them. The better life.

MEÑO: Chihuahua, Apá, qué suave vivir en los Estados Unidos. Antonia me dice que hay de todo. ¿Qué se acuerda usted de allá? Mi hermano, ¿cómo se llamaba?

JULIAN: Tu hermano se llamaba Samuel, ¿que no te acuerdas? Tú sabes que lo perdimos. Hicimos todo por encontrarlo: escribimos cartas, hasta nos regresamos, pero de nada sirvió. Y tu madre . . . jijo, ni le digas de ese país, porque se enchila.

MEÑO: Pues, entonces Antonia me vio la cara de menso.

JULIAN: No, Meño, en aquellos tiempos había cosas bien bonitas, unos edificios altos y bien grandotes.

MEÑO: Apoco, Apá. ¿Más grandes que el banco nacional?

JULIAN: Uf . . . Meño, en esos edificios pudieras meter la plaza de la esquina, unas cien chivas y hasta la vaca vieja que tenemos ahi afuera.

MEÑO: ¡Caramba, Apá!

JULIAN: Y ahora, pues, me imagino que los Estados Unidos ya tiene unos edificios que le pegan a la luna.

MEÑO: ¿A usted no le gustaría volver?

JULIAN: No, Meño, si me voy, me quedo tieso en el camino. Ves que estoy apenas. Y tu madre, como te digo, ni le acuerdes.

MEÑO: Pos, yo sí. Tantas cosas bonitas. Yo quisiera conocer otros lugares, otras partes, otras caras . . .

JULIAN: Ba . . . pues ya te cansaste de la mía.

MEÑO: (*Still in a daze.*) ¡Sí!

JULIAN: (*Hitting him on the head.*) ¡Ah, sí!

MEÑO: Digo, ¡no! Pero, ¿aquí qué tenemos? . . . Dice Antonia que allá podemos ganar dinero . . . y le apuesto que si yo me fuera, le pudiera mandar a Apá pa' que se cure.

JULIAN: Pa' que me cure . . . Meño, ningún doctor me quita lo que Dios ya puso. Y tú, ¿dónde me saliste tan trabajador? Aquí no te da la gana ni de ordeñar la vaca.

MEÑO: Esa vaca vieja, no le sale ni agua.

JULIAN: Ya, cállese. Oye, que Antonia fue la que te alborotó a irse pa' allá?

MEÑO: No, Apá!

JULIAN: ¿No? Ahorita que venga de despedirse de sus amigos, vamos a ver . . . hum . . . si lo que tengo de viejo, lo tengo de chango.

MEÑO: Pues, ¿qué piensa, que yo no puedo pensar solo?

JULIAN: No, quién dijo eso, si tú eres tan inteligente, si a todo le tiras pero a nada le pegas. (AMPARO *and* ANTONIA *enter.*) Andale, ve, ayúdale a tu madre. ¿Cómo les fue, Amparo?

AMPARO: Bien, bien.

JULIAN: ¿Te despediste de tus amigos, Antonia?

ANTONIA: Sí, Papá, les dije que mañana salgo para los Estados Unidos.

JULIAN: Ah, qué bueno. Oye, Antonia, te quiero preguntar algo.

AMPARO: Y yo te quiero preguntar algo a ti.

JULIAN: Vaya, ¿ya veniste de mal humor?

AMPARO: Pues, como no voy a venir de mal humor, si me acabo de encontrar con el Doctor Barrera.

JULIAN: ¿Me lo saludaste?

AMPARO: No te hagas payaso. ¿Por qué no me dijiste que necesitabas una operación?

JULIAN: Porque las operaciones son para los que tienen remedio y dinero.

AMPARO: Pero, quién sabe, la operación fuera tu remedio.

JULIAN: No, señora. ¿Ya te volviste loca o qué? No hay dinero pa' comprar la semilla, mucho menos pa' una operación que de nada me sirve. Trague y trague píldoras, y creo que me pongo peor.

AMPARO: Julián, tú tienes que . . .

JULIAN: 'Ora sí. Tú, entre más vieja, más sorda. ¿Que no oíste? No hay, no hay y no hay.

AMPARO: Ya, pues.

ANTONIA: Mira, Mamá, yo he estado pensando . . . yo sé que usted le tiene rencor a los Estados Unidos, pero ¿por qué no nos . . .

AMPARO: Oyeme, Antonia, tú ya vas por un caminito que a mí no me está gustando.

ANTONIA: Vámonos pa'l norte. Allí mi papá se puede curar, hay doctores buenos.

AMPARO: Cállate, hija, no quiero recordar eso.

ANTONIA: ¡Papá!

JULIAN: Qué Papá ni que nada. Como piensas que voy a dejar a mi ranchito . . . La tierra que yo trabajé, la que nos dio de comer.

ANTONIA: Antes, Papá, pero ahora no tienen ni pa' la siembra. El banco no les dio el préstamo y les va a quitar su ranchito si no les pagan las deudas. Y no crea, Papá, aunque no estoy aquí, me doy cuenta de lo que pasa.

JULIAN: Qué bonito, Amparo.

AMPARO: Ella es nuestra hija y tenía que saber que estabas enfermo.

JULIAN: No, Antonia. Mira, todo lo que ves aquí es parte de mi vida: las montañas reverdes, el río que corre, aunque de vez en cuando se seca, mi maíz que veo crecer con tanto orgullo y hasta mis animales viejos. No, hija, ¿cómo crees que voy a dejar a mi ranchito?

AMPARO: ¡Tu padre tiene razón!

ANTONIA: Pero, Mamá, aquí ya no tienen ningún futuro. Siempre trabaje y trabaje y nunca tienen nada. Por última vez . . .

AMPARO: Y por última vez te digo que no pongo ni un solo pie en ese país. ¿Qué piensas, que es tan fácil olvidar lo que me pasó allá?

ANTONIA: No, Mamá, pero las cosas han cambiado.

AMPARO: No, hija, eso nunca cambia.

JULIAN: Ya pues, Amparo, si no nos vamos a ir.

ANTONIA: Está bien, Mamá, pero por lo menos dejen que . . .

MEÑO: Sí, yo puedo trabajar y mandarles mucho dinero.

AMPARO: Oye, Meño, ¿qué piensas que es fácil? ¿Y aquí? El trabajo del rancho, ¿quién lo va a hacer?

ANTONIA: Que los vecinos le den una manita.

AMPARO: Y la siembra, ¿quién . . .?

ANTONIA: ¿Cuál siembra, Mamasita? Si no hay dinero pa' la semilla. Ya tienen más de un año atrasados con los pagos, y el banco les dio el último plazo para que paguen las deudas.

MEÑO: Yo no tengo obligaciones, no estoy casado, y fíjese, Apá, les pudiéramos mandar dos cheques.

AMPARO: Ya sabemos que estamos bien jodidos, pero ustedes no son padres y no saben cómo se siente.

ANTONIA: ¡Ya sé, Mamá! Pero mi papá ya no puede trabajar. ¿Cómo le van a hacer?

JULIAN: Y este burro ¿en qué va a trabajar?

MEÑO: En lo que sea.

AMPARO: Y ¿cómo lo van a cruzar?

ANTONIA: Es fácil, Mamá. Con un coyote. Luego yo mismo le consigo trabajo allá en la fábrica. Tenga fe, Mamá.

MEÑO: Voy, ¿Mamá, Papá?

AMPARO: Bueno, ya casi están allá. Sea por Dios.

JULIAN: Acuérdate que vas a ir a trabajar.

MEÑO: ¡Ajúa! Ya me voy pa' los Estados Unidos. (*Exits.*)

AMPARO: Mira, hija, nomás cuídense mucho, y nos escriben en cuanto lleguen.

ANTONIA: No se preocupen. Todo se va a arreglar.

AMPARO: Que Dios los ayude. (*Freeze. Broken by music.*)

SONG: Antonia y su hermano
  A California llegan
  Los dos están trabajando
  Aunque mexicanos
  Su vida van cambiando
  Costumbres de aquí van agarrando.

SCENE EIGHT

PLACARD: Los Angeles. An apartment.

ROSITA: (*Already looking for* Meño.) Oh, pretty good. ¿Dónde está Meño?

ANTONIA: (*Somewhat perturbed.*) Ahi está en el cuarto.

ROSITA: Did you tell him Antonia?

ANTONIA: Sí, le dije.

ROSITA: Pues, ándale, tell me what he said. Is he going?

ANTONIA: Ah, no. Me dijo que no puede porque tiene que, ah . . . salir con unos amigos.

ROSITA: Well, let me talk to him. (*Walks over to the bedroom, in a sweet voice.*) Meño, Meño. I know you're in there. Me lo dijo tu hermana. (*Pause. Not so sweetly.*) Meño, abre la puerta or I'm coming in. (*No response.*) Okay, Meño, entonces entro.

MEÑO: No, no entres.

ROSITA: Andale, Meño, I just want to talk to you.

MEÑO: No, no estoy vestido.

ROSITA: Pues, ponte la ropa, porque voy a entrar, I'm coming in. (*She raises foot up as if to break the door down.*) Where are you, Meño? Oh, I know where you are.

MEÑO: No, estoy dormido. ¿Que no ves que estoy dormido?

ROSITA: Pues, quítate los zapatos.

MEÑO: (*Busted. He angrily tears covers off.*) Ya, déjame solo, tengo mucho que hacer.

ROSITA: ¿Por qué de tanto apuro?

MEÑO: Voy a salir y ya salte de aquí antes de que te corra.

ROSITA: Que pronto te levantas. ¿Que vas a ver a la Cherry?

MEÑO: (*Angrily yelling to* ANTONIA.) Antonia, Antonia, sácala.

ROSITA: Ya, ya me voy, al cabo que no me gustan los usados.

MEÑO: Salte este momento.

ROSITA: Ahora que andas con esa gabacha, piel de masa, you think you're it, don't you? (*She leaves bedroom.*) Antonia, I'm leaving. I didn't come here pa' que me insulte.

ANTONIA: Espérate un momento, Rosita, y nos vamos juntas.

ROSITA: No, en esta casa no me estoy ni un momento más.

ANTONIA: Entonces nos vemos en el baile, okay?

ROSITA: Bueno. Okay. Pero no te traigas a ese animal. (*She exits.*)

ANTONIA: Ay, cómo eres malo, Meño.

MEÑO: ¿Pa' qué la dejaste entrar al cuarto?

ANTONIA: Ella se metió.

MEÑO: Hm . . .

ANTONIA: Oye, Meño, ¿no se te olvidó mandar el money order?

MEÑO: ¡No!

ANTONIA: ¿Mandaste los cien?

MEÑO: ¡Cincuenta!

ANTONIA: ¡Cincuenta! ¿Por qué cincuenta?

MEÑO: ¡No me alcanzó!

ANTONIA: ¡Ah! ¡No te alcanza pa' tus padres, pero si te alcanza pa' tus viejas!

MEÑO: ¡Ya no chingues!

ANTONIA: (*Mimicking* CHERRY.) Esa cabrona de Cherry con su "buy me this and buy me that."(*There is a knock at the door.* ANTONIA *goes to answer it.*)

MESSENGER: Western Union, could you sign here, please? Thank you. (ANTONIA *closes door.*)

ANTONIA: Es un telegrama.

MEÑO: ¡Déjame ver! (*He takes it from her and reads it. He sits sadly as he hands it to* ANTONIA. ANTONIA *reads it, pauses.*)

ANTONIA: ¡¡¡Apá!!! (MEÑO *goes to embrace her. Both freeze.*)

SONG: La pobre de Amparo
      Viuda se ha quedado
      Y ahora no le queda otra
      Dejar a su ranchito
      Venirse con sus hijos
      Cruzar la frontera se ha dicho.

SCENE NINE

NARRATOR: U.S./Mexico border. Former Commissioner Chapman of the Immigration and Naturalization Service states: Desperate Mexican Nationals stream toward the United States and hope to get in by any means possible. PLACARD: The border crossing.

ANTONIA: (ANTONIA *and* COYOTE *are seated on* AMPARO *as if she were hiding under the seat of the vehicle.*) Mamá, no tenga miedo, ¿eh?

AMPARO: Miedo, ¿cuál miedo?

ANTONIA: Nomás acuérdese de lo que le dije.

AMPARO: Sí, ya sé, keep low. Chihuahua, ojalá no nos salga cola.

COYOTE: Cálmense, hombre. Si ahorita tiemblan, ¡al cruzar les va a dar chorro!

ANTONIA: Ya, ya vamos llegando.

COYOTE: Apriétese el caboose, seño. No sea que por un soplado sola se vaya a entregar.

ANTONIA: Sús, ahi vamos (*Blesses herself.*) Ayúdanos, Dios mío.

BORDER PATROL: Good afternoon. U.S. citizens?

COYOTE: Yes, sir! Is a nice day, eh? (BORDER PATROL *does not acknowledge him.*)

BORDER PATROL: Can I see your papers? (*Both show papers.*) Okay, fine. Let's check the back of the truck.

COYOTE: Yes, sir.

BORDER PATROL: You carry animals, plants, vegetables, fruits, liquor, or illegal drugs?

COYOTE: No, sir! None of that.

BORDER PATROL: Yeah. That's what they all say. (BORDER PATROL *and* COYOTE *freeze.*)

ANTONIA: (*Whispers.*) Amá, no se mueva.

AMPARO: Estoy apretada.

BORDER PATROL: Okay, let's see the front.

COYOTE: Sure, no problem. (BORDER PATROL *looks inside truck, stares at* ANTONIA.)

BORDER PATROL: So, you're from Los Angeles, huh? (ANTONIA *nods.*) You work there?

ANTONIA: Yes, in a factory.

BORDER PATROL: Why did you come to Mexico?

ANTONIA: My mother's very sick. I came on an emergency.

BORDER PATROL: I see! (*Looks around almost as if inspection is complete, then looks back at* ANTONIA *again. Begins to rattle the seat.*) Does this seat come off?

ANTONIA: I don't think . . .

COYOTE: No, but I can try. Let me get a screwdriver. (*Checks glove compartment.*) Sorry, sir, I don't think I have one. (*Mother relieved.*)

BORDER PATROL: That's all right. We do. (*Mother panics.*)

VOICE: (*From offstage.*) Hey, Mac, we caught a bunch of them. Need your help!

BORDER PATROL: (*Yells.*) Okay! (*To* COYOTE *and* ANTONIA.) All right, you're clear. (*Starts to walk away.*)

AMPARO: (*Whispers.*) ¿Ya se fue?

BORDER PATROL: (*Hears her and returns to truck.*) Did you say something?

ANTONIA: No!

SCENE TEN

NARRATOR: Los Angeles. An apartment. There are over three million Mexican workers illegally in the southwest alone. Although their labor is necessary to maintain a stable economy, they are for all practical purposes without rights.

PLACARD: The strike.

AMPARO: (*Jokingly.*) ¿Qué, no tienes hambre?

MEÑO: Not too much.

AMPARO: ¿Qué no te gustan mis tamales?

MEÑO: Es que me duele la panza.

AMPARO: (*Examining him motherly.*) Yo te he visto muy preocupado. Es el trabajo, ¿verdad?

MEÑO: (*Lying.*) Todo está bien.

AMPARO: ¿Estás seguro?

MEÑO: ¡Yo no me quejo! Si quieres oír quejas, pregúntale a Antonia.

AMPARO: Oye, y todo esto, ¿dónde está ésta?

MEÑO: Allá con sus juntas.

AMPARO: Ah sí, ya me acuerdo. Si me dijo que había una junta de los trabajadores allá en la fábrica.

MEÑO: Sí, allá anda de marimacha metiéndose en líos.

AMPARO: Cómo, hijo, ¡explícame!

MEÑO: Es que están haciendo mucho barullo allá en la fábrica, que quieren mejores sueldos y que se van a poner en huelga.

AMPARO: ¿Huelga?

MEÑO: Nomás dicen.

AMPARO: Y Antonia ¿también está en esto?

MEÑO: Uh, pos se cree la mera jefa. Vale más que le hables antes de que pierda el trabajo. Ya corrieron al Nacho que también andaba en la misma cosa.

AMPARO: Y ¿por qué lo corrieron?

MEÑO: Pues, que era su culpa. Andaba de organizador, que nos pusiéramos en huelga, y así buscando el pedo, y afuera.

AMPARO: Pero no se te hace mal que lo corrieron. Tiene hijos.

MEÑO: Bueno, el que mete la mano en la lumbre . . . (ANTONIA *enters. He glances up at her and then turns away. She is upset, but greets her mother, then she turns to* MEÑO.)

ANTONIA: ¿Por qué no fuiste a la junta? Te dije que era muy importante.

MEÑO: Is none of my business.

ANTONIA: Ahora corrieron a Ramiro y a Don Arturo.

MEÑO: Pues, ni modo.

ANTONIA: Y qué si me corren a mí, Meño, ¿no te importa?

MEÑO: Pues, ¿pa' qué fregados te metes?

ANTONIA: Meño, ya tengo dos años trabajando, y tu casi uno, y todavía nos pagan el mismo desgraciado sueldo . . .

MEÑO: (*Refuting.*) Yo oí que la unión nos iba a ayudar a subir el pago.

ANTONIA: (*Semi-pleading.*) Son mentiras, Meño. Así lo hicieron el año pasado nomás para callarnos, pero por fin no nos dieron nada. (MEÑO *doesn't respond.*) Meño, ahora en la junta nos decidimos ponernos en huelga.

MEÑO: ¡Huelga!

ANTONIA: ¡Comenzando mañana!

MEÑO: ¡Ahora sí la fregaron!

ANTONIA: ¿Y tú, Meño?

MEÑO: No, señora, yo no me meto.

ANTONIA: Y mañana, ¿cruzas nuestra picket line?

AMPARO: Antonia, ¿qué tantos se pusieron en huelga?

ANTONIA: Casi todos. (*To* MEÑO.) Sólo unos que no se han decidido.

AMPARO: Pero, hija, ¿que la compañía no quiso negociar?

ANTONIA: Ni nos quieren ver, Mamá.

MEÑO: Mira, Antonia, a lo menos tenían trabajo, ahora no tienen nada.

ANTONIA: No teníamos nada, Meño.

MEÑO: Váyanse pa' México si creen que lo tienen tan mal.

AMPARO: Mira, hijo, aunque estén más pobres en México, a ustedes también apenas les alcanza. Imagínate una familia con niños.

MEÑO: Se hubieran esperado.

ANTONIA: ¿Esperar qué, Meño? ¿Que corran a los demás?

MEÑO: ¡Hasta que la unión nos diera el apoyo!

ANTONIA: El patrón y la unión no te da nada. Si tú quieres algo, se lo tienes que sacar a fuerzas.

MEÑO: Mira, Antonia, si me salgo, ¿cómo pagamos la renta y los biles y qué va a comer mi mamá? . . . ¿o ya se te olvidó de madre?

ANTONIA: Por eso estoy en huelga. Pa' que mi madre, y otras madres como ella, coman mejor, y sus hijos no tengan que sufrir como nosotros.

MEÑO: Está muy peligroso, ¿que no entiendes?

ANTONIA: Sí, pero para ganar hay que arriesgar.

MEÑO: ¡Ya déjame en paz!

ANTONIA: Te pones en huelga ¿sí o no?

MEÑO: (*To* AMPARO.) Amá, esta burra no entiende nada.

ANTONIA: ¡Lo que tienes es que eres un cobarde!

MEÑO: No puedo.

ANTONIA: Cobarde.

MEÑO: No tengo papeles.

ANTONIA: Cobarde.

AMPARO: Cállense los dos. Sobre todo son hermanos, y no se deben estar peleando como perros y gatos. Miren, hijos, yo soy vieja y he visto mucho de estas cosas. Su Apá antes me decía, "Oye, Amparo, será que a Dios le gustan mucho los pobres, pues mira nomás qué tantos puso aquí en la tierra." Hay muchos pobres sobre la tierra y unos cuantos ricos. A ver díganme, ¿cómo puede ser eso? Es que los pobres están así, separados, y no así, juntos. (*Freeze. Music.*)

SONG: Samuel, el hijo perdido
  Ya una familia él tiene
  Veremos cómo ha vivido
  Hace lo que le conviene
  Hace lo que le conviene.

SCENE ELEVEN

NARRATOR: Los Angeles. Immigration Detention Center. Those in power offer social and economic rewards to some individuals who are willing to aid in the suppression of their own kind.

PLACARD: The job promotion.

SAMMY: What's your name?

VICENTE: Vicente Fernández.

SAMMY: How old are you?

VICENTE: Veinte y ocho.

SAMMY: ¿Entiendes inglés? ¿Has estado en los Estados Unidos otras veces?

VICENTE: No.

SAMMY: ¿Estás seguro? ¿Que no te recuerdan nada los nombres Juan García y Ricardo Montez?

VICENTE: ¡No!

SAMMY: ¿Qué crees, que somos tontos? Nosotros tenemos tus huellas digitales. (*Angrily.*) Ya van tres veces que te deportamos. Y a mí nunca se me olvida una cara. (*Looking at suspect.*) ¿Dónde trabajas esta vez?

VICENTE: En la Fitzgerald Company en la Calle Ocho.

SAMMY: ¿Conoces a otros trabajadores ilegales allí?

VICENTE: No sé sus nombres.

SAMMY: ¿Pero si hay otros illegales allí?

VICENTE: ¡No sé!

SAMMY: ¿Cómo que no sabes? Me acabas de decir que no sabías los nombres de ellos. ¿Los podrías reconocer?

VICENTE: Creo que no.

SAMMY: ¿Con quién vives?

VICENTE: Vivo solo.

SAMMY: Y tu familia, ¿dónde está?

VICENTE: En México. Yo estoy aquí solo.

SAMMY: Y ¿por qué no te quedas en México con tu familia? ¿Que no entienden ustedes que es ilegal cruzar la frontera sin documentos?

VICENTE: Entonces ¿por qué nos dan trabajo si no nos quieren aquí?

SAMMY: I'll deal with you later. (SAMMY *enters boss's office.*) Mr. Mills, I got your note this morning, but I've been very busy.

MILLS: Yes, I know. Mitchell is bringing in those illegal aliens just a little faster than we can process them.

SAMMY: Yes, he is doing quite a job.

MILLS: (*Gettin up from his desk.*) Sit down, Sam.

SAMMY: On your desk?

MILLS: Sure! Why not? You've been here for over fifteen years, haven't you?

SAMMY: Twenty, sir.

MILLS: Oh sure, twenty. You know, I've heard good things about you. (*Pats* SAM's *back.*) You've been doing a fine job. I'm sure your wife and daughter are just as proud of you as we are.

SAMMY: Thank you, Mr. Mills.

MILLS: Sam, how is your daughter? How is she doing in college?

SAMMY: Well, fine.

MILLS: Notice how tuition is going up these days? Sam, this is your chance to really prove yourself. I know you can do it.

SAMMY: Mr. Mills, somehow this is different . . .

MILLS: It's not different Mendoza! It is like any other job. There are always requirements, and if you want the job badly enough, then you work hard at it. You understand, Mendoza?

SAMMY: Yes, sir, Mr. Mills. It's a great opportunity.

MILLS: We can't think of anyone else to fill the position, not unless we give the job to Gutiérrez.

SAMMY: Oh no, Mr. Mills. I mean, that's if you think he should do the job . . .

MILLS: Mendoza, it's people like you that make this outfit so successful. We have a responsibility to our citizens. Those aliens, those aliens are taking jobs away from American workers, and now they have the nerve to go out on strike. Do you understand the seriousness of this problem, Mendoza?

SAMMY: Yes, sir, I do! It's a big responsibility. (MILLS *holds* SAM's *arm in a reassuring manner. Freeze.*)

SCENE TWELVE

NARRATOR: Los Angeles. Mendoza's living room. The attainment of the American Dream at any cost results in a variety of feelings, ranging from shame to self-hate, thus creating a need to justify the actions taken to achieve it.

PLACARD: The justification.

CLARA: (CLARA *is in the kitchen as* SAM *walks in, troubled.*) Is that you, Sam? Oh, Sam, how'd it go today?

SAMMY: All right.

CLARA: Le me fix you a drink.

SAMMY: No, I don't want one.

CLARA: Well, Sam, what happened? Did you talk to Mr. Mills?

SAMMY: Yes.

CLARA: What did he say?

SAMMY: We just talked.

CLARA: Did you get the promotion?

SAMMY: Yeah, I mean they offered it to me.

CLARA: Oh, Sam, that's wonderful. I even cooked you a special dinner to celebrate.

SAMMY: I said they offered it to me.

CLARA: What? I don't understand the difference.

SAMMY: It's not the assignment I wanted.

CLARA: But you got the promotion, right?

SAMMY: Yes, but I'm not sure I want it.

CLARA: Why, Sam? It's a promotion.

SAMMY: Davidson got the Internal Affairs slot and they want me to be out in the field for six months.

CLARA: Six months.

SAMMY: Directing raids.

CLARA: That's not too long.

SAMMY: I'm thinking of just waiting.

CLARA: But, Sam, you can have the promotion now, why wait six months? You should jump at the opportunity, they might think you don't want it.

SAMMY: I don't really want that assignment.

CLARA: Sam, I don't understand you. We've been waiting . . .

SAMMY: I don't want to be out in the field.

CLARA: Sam, it's only six months.

SAMMY: I never did like it.

CLARA: Don't be so selfish, Sam. Think of your family.

SAMMY: You don't understand, do you?

CLARA: It's important . . .

SAMMY: It's not exactly nice being out in the field.

CLARA: But, Sam . . .

SAMMY: It's not exactly nice having to pull people out of their homes, they start screaming and crying, Clara!

CLARA: The promotion . . .

SAMMY: All the pushing and shoving, it's like herding cattle. It makes me sick.

CLARA: Well, it makes me sick to hear you talk like that. That promotion means a lot to us, Sam. To me, to Janie. We've worked for it all these years. When you first got the job they hardly paid you anything. I've always had to worry about money lasting; we went through some hard times to get here. And, Sam, you promised, you promised that someday we wouldn't have to worry about money. And now, the property taxes are going up and Janie's college tuition is making things tight for us. With the promotion, Sammy, we don't have to worry. This is our chance.

SAMMY: So where's Janie?

CLARA: She drove down to the store to get olives for the salad. She should be back any minute.

SAMMY: How long is she staying?

CLARA: She has to go back Sunday, her classes start the next day.

SAMMY: Oh, I was hoping she could stay a little longer this time.

CLARA: Her classes start the next day.

SAMMY: Well, at least she's getting her education.

CLARA: You know, Sam, I'm a little worried about her education.

SAMMY: Why's that?

CLARA: She's taking these wierd classes about Mexican-American history. I didn't even know they taught them at college.

SAMMY: They have them at some of the colleges now.

CLARA: And you know what, Sam, this is kind of silly, but she put one of those Chavez stickers on her car, one of those black eagle things, you know?

SAMMY: She did?

CLARA: She's picking up those ideas at college. I think she joined one of those Chicano Power groups at college and they're putting ideas into her head.

SAMMY: Well, Janie's an intelligent girl.

CLARA: Janie's young and naive.

SAMMY: She's twenty years old, Clara.

CLARA: Well, I think you should tell her to take that stupid sticker off her car.

SAMMY: We'll talk about it. (JANIE *walks in.*)

JANIE: Hi, Dad. You home early?

SAMMY: No, I'm just not late this time.

JANIE: Oh, Mom, they didn't have the kind you wanted, so I got these.

CLARA: Uh, that's all right, let me go put them in the salad. (CLARA *exits.*)

JANIE: Is something the matter with Mom?

SAMMY: Oh no, it's nothing. She's a little worried.

JANIE: About what?

SAMMY: It's that sticker you got on your car.

JANIE: Oh, yeah, she told me this morning.

SAMMY: Actually, I kind of wanted to know why you had it on there too?

JANIE: Well, I believe in what it stands for and I support the farmworkers union.

SAMMY: But you know there are two sides to every issue and I've read some very negative things in the papers about Chavez . . .

JANIE: I've read them too.

SAMMY: Well then, young lady, I guess you know what you're doing.

JANIE: Yes, Dad, I've given it a lot of thought.

SAMMY: So you're mother tells me you've got to go on Sunday. (CLARA *enters, she's regained her composure.*)

CLARA: Well, dinner's almost ready.

SAMMY: Good.

CLARA: Oh, Janie, did your father give you the good news?

SAMMY: Clara, can't it wait?

CLARA: Why? She should know right now.

SAMMY: Not yet.

CLARA: Well, if you won't tell her, then I will. Janie dear, your father, your father has been offered a promotion.

JANIE: Oh!

CLARA: And it includes a big raise.

JANIE: That's nice.

CLARA: Aren't you proud of your father?

JANIE: I guess so. Congratulations, Dad.

CLARA: This promotion means bigger responsibilities for your father.

JANIE: Oh, what do you have to do?

SAMMY: Well, I'll be out in the field now coordinating searches and apprehensions.

JANIE: You mean you'll be dragging the people in and arresting them?

SAMMY: Actually, Janie, I'll be more involved in directing large scale apprehensions at large employment facilities.

JANIE: You'll be in charge of immigration raids?

SAMMY: Yeah, sort of . . . (JANIE *gets up and begins to walk away.*)

CLARA: What's wrong, Janie? Does it bother you to see your father get ahead in his field?

JANIE: No, but . . .

SAMMY: But what?

CLARA: Janie, what's the matter with you?

JANIE: I'm sorry, but a lot of my feelings have changed.

CLARA: Including respect for your parents.

JANIE: I've been away, I'm not the same.

SAMMY: So what's changed?

CLARA: You still have a nice house and lots of nice things, just look, look!

JANIE: But they don't make me happy!

SAMMY: Janie, tell me this. What is it that's really bothering you?

JANIE: Dad, it's your job.

SAMMY: What about my job?

JANIE: I don't like what you do!

CLARA: For heaven's sake, Janie . . .

SAMMY: You never complained about it before.

JANIE: Dad, please listen.

SAMMY: Janie, it bought you the food you ate and the clothes you wear . . .

JANIE: Yes, but . . .

SAMMY: And this house.

JANIE: Yes, but . . .

SAMMY: And this house, and isn't it paying for your education?

JANIE: Yes . . .

SAMMY: But now you have the nerve to tell me you don't like what I do.

JANIE: Dad, you're deporting Mexicans!

SAMMY: I deport illegal aliens. I don't care if they're Colombians or Mexicans!

JANIE: We're Mexican!

SAMMY: We're American citizens and don't you forget that!

JANIE: Why do you deport them?

SAMMY: Because it's my job, that's what they pay me for!

JANIE: How can you deport your own people, Father?

SAMMY: I do it so that we can eat, so we can live.

JANIE: You, Father . . .

SAMMY: So you can live . . .

JANIE: You of all people . . .

SAMMY: So you can eat . . .

JANIE: You should hate what you do!

SAMMY: I'm proud of my job!

JANIE: Who separated you from your mother?

SAMMY: Shut up! (SAMMY *slaps* JANIE.)

JANIE: You just don't understand! (*She exits.*)

CLARA: Sammy!

SONG: El Sammy mortificado
       No sabe lo que debe hacer
       Le van a subir el sueldo

Este hombre no puede entender
Que su alma él iba a perder

Cuarenta años han pasado
Que Amparo a su hijo no ve.
Quien iba a creer que un día
Los dos se irían a ver
Los dos se irían a ver.

SCENE THIRTEEN

NARRATOR: Los Angeles, 1972. When the Mexican national goes on strike, not only is he confronted with the basic struggle for workers'r rights, but he must also face the additional threat of deportation.

PLACARD: The raid.

STRIKER: (*Scene opens with strike in process, one of the strikers is telling the others instructions and encouraging them to be calm and non-violent. They break into loud chants. One of the strikers spots the strikebreakers approaching and yells.*) Here come the scabs! (*At this point the strikers freeze and the scene at the home begins.*)

ANTONIA: Meño, vámonos. Ya van a ser las twelve o'clock.

MEÑO: Yo fui ayer todo el día.

ANTONIA: Pos, yo también, pero is our turn today again.

MEÑO: Ya me cansé de esa mentada picket line.

ANTONIA: Andale.

MEÑO: Mira, hace tres semanas y no estamos ganando nada.

ANTONIA: ¿Cómo que no?

MEÑO: Pos, sí, mira, tres semanas sin work. Tres semanas sin dinero.

ANTONIA: Sí, pero pronto nos ayudan otros sindicatos.

MEÑO: Y pa' acabarle de fregar, nos echan los esquiroles, los escabs . . .

ANTONIA: Eso quiere decir que estamos ganando.

MEÑO: ¿Cómo que estamos ganando? ¡Estás loca!

ANTONIA: Cuando nos echan los strikebreakers quiere decir que los patrones ya no se aguantan. (*Freeze, beat, unfreeze. Scene returns to the strike. Strikebreakers approach, first one, then another. Strikers yell "scab" etc. to make it clear to audience. A second scab passes by yelling at the strikers. A strikers tries to talk to him, but the scab pushes him instead. They grab each other and freeze. Focus changes to the home, ANTONIA and AMPARO are in the kitchen.*)

AMPARO: ¿Dónde está tu hermano?

ANTONIA: Allí en el cuarto, ahorita nos vamos a la picket line.

AMPARO: Mira, Antonia, tengan cuidado.

ANTONIA: Sí, Mamá.

AMPARO: Ya me dijieron de los rompehuelgas.

ANTONIA: No se preocupe, Mamá. Todo va a estar bien.

AMPARO: Así es como sucede la violencia.

ANTONIA: Todo está calmado, los trabajadores no quieren pleito.

AMPARO: Sí, pero hay peligro.

ANTONIA: No va a pasar nada, verás.

AMPARO: Ojalá, y acuérdate, muchacha, que tu hermano no tiene papeles.

ANTONIA: Yo sé.

AMPARO: Y si hay pleito, pues llega la policía . . . (*Freeze. Focus returns to the strike. The striker and scab continue their scuffle as the scab strikes the striker and follows him to the ground. The other strikers pull the scabb off. One of the strikers helps striker up to a sitting position.*)

STRIKER: Señor López, are you all right? (*Freeze and return to the home. ANTONIA is alone as MEÑO enters.*)

MEÑO: Antonia, Antonia, quieren que vayas a la picket line!

ANTONIA: ¿Quién te dijo?

MEÑO: El señor Frausto telefonió y dice que te apures.

ANTONIA: ¿Por qué? ¿Qué pasó?

MEÑO: Que hubo un pleito y que golpiaron al señor López.

ANTONIA: ¿Señor López?

MEÑO: Sí, le pegó uno de los escabs. (*AMPARO enters the kitchen hastily.*)

AMPARO: ¿Qué pasó?

MEÑO: Nada.

ANTONIA: Me necesitan en la picket line.

AMPARO: ¿Por qué?

ANTONIA: Es que ya mero son las doce, nos tenemos que ir.

AMPARO: Espérate, muchacha. Meño, a ver, dime ¿qué pasó?

MEÑO: Es que golpiaron a uno de los trabajadores.

AMPARO: ¿Qué?

ANTONIA: Golpiaron al señor López.

AMPARO: (*Ordering.*) No se me vayan.

ANTONIA: Tenemos que, Mamá.

AMPARO: ¿Por qué?

ANTONIA: Porque ahorita es cuando más se necesita el apoyo de todos.

AMPARO: Entonces me voy con ustedes.

MEÑO: No, Mamá.

ANTONIA: Tú te estás aquí.

AMPARO: ¿Pa' preocuparme de lo que no veo?

MEÑO: Más al rato te llamo por teléfono.

AMPARO: No, señor.

ANTONIA: No seas terca, Mamá. Estate aquí.

AMPARO: Pues me quedo. (*Focus returns to the strike. Señor López is taken off stage. They talk about what to do.* ANTONIA *and* MEÑO *show up.*)

STRIKER: Antonia, golpiaron al señor López. We took him to the hospital.

MEÑO: Y ¿cómo está?

STRIKER: He had a bad cut, pero está mejor.

ANTONIA: Pero ¿cuándo llegó la policía?

STRIKER: Almost immediately. Llegaron como unos diez carros. They didn't even warn us. They just all came at us at once. Just like that they took five people . . .

STRIKER: Pero creo que las cosas ya se calmaron. Voy a ir a reportarle al señor Bracamontes lo que pasó. El está allá en el west gate. (STRIKER *exits and a few seconds later* AMPARO *comes in hysterical, looking for her children.*)

AMPARO: Antonia, Antonia, dónde . . . ¿Dónde está tu hermano? (*She sees him.*)

MEÑO: Mamá, ¿qué haces aquí?

AMPARO: Meño, hijo, ¿no te golpearon? (*She's relieved to see that he's all right.*) ¡Qué susto me diste!

ANTONIA: ¿Por qué está tan nerviosa, Mamá? ¿Qué tiene?

AMPARO: Pues oí en las noticias que hace poco golpearon a un hombre, que lo mandaron al hospital, pero no dijeron quién.

MEÑO: Era el señor López, Amá.

AMPARO: Hasta a los viejos les pegan.

ANTONIA: Amá, no debe estar usted por aquí.

AMPARO: Yo no podía estarme en la casa sin saber cómo estaban ustedes.

MEÑO: Ya todo está bien, Amá, ándale, ya váyase.

AMPARO: No, hijos, yo tengo que estar donde y cuando me necesiten mis hijos. (*The sounds of the migra can be heard and the violence begins.*)

STRIKER: ¡Ahi viene la migra! (*Chaos, confusion and screams.* MEÑO *attempts to escape but is prevented by the Migra. He runs towards the middle but he is captured. He is dragged away by the Migra.* SAMMY *directs the raid. All the other people escape to the right hand side of the stage.* MEÑO *is grouped along with all the rest. The Migra officer turns towards* SAMMY.)

MIGRA: There's one that says she's a citizen.

SAMMY: That's okay, take them all in. We'll sort them out later.

MIGRA: What about the old lady?

SAMMY: What old lady?

MIGRA: (*Pulls her out.*) This one! (*Both* AMPARO *and* MEÑO *stare at each other.*)

SAMMY: (*Somewhat uncomfortable.*) Uh, take her in too. (*Freeze.*)

SCENE FOURTEEN

NARRATOR: Immigration interrogation room. Los Angeles. The immigration laws become stringent or lenient depending upon the fluctuations in the United States economic system. Because of this, during times of recession, thousands of Mexican families continue to suffer deportations and are denied the fundamental human right of working for a decent living either here or in Mexico.

PLACARD: The rejection.

MILLS: Very good, Mendoza. Excellent execution. (*Flipping through pad.*) I see you brought in twenty seven and fifteen of them were illegals. Fine job.

SAMMY: I figured the better strategy would be to bring them all in.

MILLS: That's the way we like to hear you think. Well done. (*Flips through pad.*) Female in her sixties. What was an old lady doing on a picket line?

SAMMY: The old lady.

MILLS: What's wrong, Sam?

SAMMY: You ever get the feeling you've seen someone before, but you can't place them?

MILLS: Well, with these aliens you can't tell one from the other. Gutierrez will be interrogating them, but if it's bothering you, check it out. (SAMMY *goes in to interrogate her.*)

SAMMY: Do you have your immigration papers? ¿Sus papeles? ¿Su mica?

AMPARO: No.

SAMMY: ¿Qué tanto tiempo tiene usted en los Estados Unidos?

AMPARO: Un año.

SAMMY: ¿Es de México?

AMPARO: Sí.

SAMMY: ¿De qué parte?

AMPARO: Durango.

SAMMY: ¿Durango?

AMPARO: Sí.

SAMMY: ¿Que no sabe usted que lo que hace es ilegal?

AMPARO: ¡No!

SAMMY: ¿Cómo que no? ¿No tiene papeles? ¿No ha estado en los Estados Unidos antes de esta vez?

AMPARO: Sí, cuando era niña hasta . . .

SAMMY: ¿Y cuál otra vez?

AMPARO: ¡No hubo otra vez! Nos fuimos en enero de 1935.

SAMMY: Ahora ¿por qué regresó?

AMPARO: Mi esposo murió. Me vine a vivir con mis hijos.

SAMMY: Oiga, y usted ¿que hacía en esa huelga?

AMPARO: Les estaba ayudando a mis hijos.

SAMMY: Oh, a sus hijos ¿eh? ¿Cómo se llama usted?

AMPARO: Amparo Villa.

SAMMY: La mujer, la que se llamaba Antonia, ¿era su hija?

AMPARO: ¡Sí!

SAMMY: Y el muchacho, ¿también era su hijo?

AMPARO: Uno de mis hijos.

SAMMY: Mire, señora, usted y sus hijos los tenemos que regresar a México.

AMPARO: ¿Por qué? ¿Qué hemos hecho?

SAMMY: Son ilegales. Están aquí contra la ley.

AMPARO: No hemos hecho nada mal. Me quedé viuda. ¿Cree usted que hice mal . . . ?

SAMMY: Es mi obligación . . .

AMPARO: ¿Cree usted que hice mal . . . ? (*They look at each other.*)

SAMMY: Yo no estoy para juzgar esos asuntos de familias. Yo hago lo que me dicen y lo que es justo. Usted tiene que entender que los tengo que mandar pa' atrás.

AMPARO: ¿Otra vez?

SAMMY: ¿Qué dice?

AMPARO: Como en 1935. Cuando echaron a mi esposo de su trabajo.

SAMMY: ¡Yo no sé nada de eso!

AMPARO: ¡No! A pesar de ser tan vivo, estabas muy chico para recordar. ¡Déjame recordarte! Era en los tiempos que echaron a miles de familias a México porque ya no había trabajo.

SAMMY: ¿Qué? Mire, señora . . .

AMPARO: Porque soy vieja, ¡óigame esta última vez!

SAMMY: Señora, tengo, tenemos que . . .

AMPARO: Nos echaron en el tren, todos en bola, apretados, nos gritaban y nos aventaban como si fuéramos animales.

SAMMY: Pero . . .

AMPARO: Lo único que me alegraba era que por primera vez mi esposo iba a ver a nuestra niña. Cuando la vio se puso feliz, pero su felicidad no duró porque por desgracia . . .

SAMMY: ¡Cállese!

AMPARO: ¿Es mexicano?

SAMMY: ¡Eso no importa!

AMPARO: ¡A mí, sí! ¿Cómo se llama?

SAMMY: ¡Mendoza! ¡Mendoza!

AMPARO: ¿Su primer nombre?

SAMMY: ¿Qué?

AMPARO: Dime tu primer nombre.

SAMMY: Samuel, pero eso ¿qué tiene que ver conmigo?

AMPARO: Quiero saber. Dime, ¿por qué haces lo que haces?

SAMMY: ¿Por qué hago qué?

AMPARO: ¡Esto!

SAMMY: Es mi trabajo.

AMPARO: Es su trabajo corretear y empujar a gente como si fuéramos animales.

SAMMY: ¡Ya no!

AMPARO: Ustedes son fríos y sin compasión de nadie.

SAMMY: Es mi trabajo, señora. ¡Es mi trabajo!

AMPARO: ¿Es su trabajo separar familias?

SAMMY: ¡No!

AMPARO: ¿Cómo le gustaría ser separado de su madre?

SAMMY: ¡Afuera! ¡Sáquenla! ¡Sáquenla! (*Freeze.*)

SCENE FIFTEEN

NARRATOR: Mendoza's home. Los Angeles. The individual who chooses to take part in the process of dehumanizing others inevitably begins the process of his own dehumanization.
PLACARD: The victim.

CLARA: (SAMUEL *and* CLARA *are in bed stage right.* SAMMY *wakes up screaming, falls off the edge of the bed.*)
Honey, what's the matter. Are you all right? (SAM *still screaming.*) Sweetheart, you've just had a bad dream, that's all.
SAMMY: I didn't want to do it . . . I had to . . .
CLARA: Do what, dear? You're not making sense.
SAMMY: I know who she was.
CLARA: Who darling? Who? What's this all about?
SAMMY: Today . . . an old woman . . . she was an illegal. I had to . . . I had to deport her.
CLARA: Honey, I don't understand. Isn't that your job? It's never bothered you before. It's probably just that raid. Maybe we should take that vacation, just the two of us . . . huh?
SAMMY: No . . . her name was Villa. Amparo Villa. (CLARA *gasps for a second, realizing that it is his mother.*)
CLARA: Oh, honey, are you sure? There must be some mistake. She must've made up that name.
SAMMY: You don't understand. She had a daughter named Antonia. That's my little sister.
CLARA: That can't be true.
SAMMY: But it is. She even asked me. How would you like to be separated from your mother? I couldn't stand it!
CLARA: Honey, that lady was not your mother. A real mother would have looked everywhere until she found you. Did she say she was your mother?
SAMMY: No . . . and I didn't say I was her son. I wanted to hold her. She got on the bus, sat down. She never once looked back. My dream tonight, back at the train station. I was a little boy again, and it was just her and I . . . (SAMMY *gets up and begins to walk slowly towards dream.*) She was on the train near the window. It started to move . . . slowly . . . (*He yells.*) ¡Mamá! (*He begins to cry!*)

CLARA: Sweetheart, please stop torturing yourself! It's only a nightmare. Just think of all the love the Mendoza's gave you. That woman didn't deserve to be your mother. She left you out in the cold . . .

SAMMY: I didn't want to . . .

CLARA: Dear, there are a lot of things in this world we don't want to do, but we have to. You know that. She was an illegal and a law breaker. Don't you understand? You did the right thing. You were just doing your job, and you did it well. Just think of her as another routine case. She's not your mother.

SAMMY: She's not my mother?

CLARA: That's right. She's not your mother. Oh honey, just think about our happiness. Our entire future is at stake. All our lives of sacrifice. Now we can move into a nicer home . . . Our dream house . . . like we always wanted. And honey, our Janie will soon realize her mistakes.

SAMMY: (*Convincing himself.*) She's not my mother.

CLARA: That's right, dear. She's not your mother.

SAMMY: She's not my mother. (SAMMY *repeats this with growing intensity. Music starts with* AMPARO *reciting "Cuando lejos." He begins to tremble and loses control. He turns toward his dream and shouts.*) I hate you! I hate you! (*Then more pleading to* CLARA.) Clara. (*He curls to the ground.* CLARA *comes over to comfort him. Freeze. The scene breaks with the strumming of the guitar, all come into place for the singing of the last song.*)

SONG: Señores, ya aquí se termino
      La historia de un alma que murió
      Hay que mirar la ciega decisión
      Que mata al ser, la mente, el corazón
      Y no permite ver lo que es la realidad
      Es tiempo que miremos la verdad.

      Es hora ya de nuestra libertad
      Hay que formar la nueva sociedad
      Renacer el hombre y la mujer
      Para vivir como es nuestro deber
      Juntos marchar, cantar, unirnos y gritar
      El grito de la hora de luchar.

      De pie cantar que vamos a triunfar
      Avanzan ya banderas de unidad
      Y tú vendrás marchando junto a mí

Y así verás tu canto y tu bandera,
Florecer la luz de un nuevo amanecer
Anuncia ya la vida que vendrá
Y ahora el pueblo que se alza en la lucha
Con voz de gigante, gritando adelante.

De pie cantar que vamos a triunfar
Avanzan ya banderas de unidad.
Y tu vendrás marchando junto a mí,
Y así verás tu canto y tu bandera
florecer la luz de un nuevo amanecer
Anuncia ya la vida que vendrá.

Bibliography

Austin, Mary. "Folkplays of the Southwest." *Theatre Arts Monthly* (August, 1933): 599–606.

Bagby, Beth. "El Teatro Campesino: Interviews with Luis Valdez." *Tulane Drama Review* 11 (1967): 70–80.

Booth, Willard C. "Dramatic Aspects of Aztec Rituals." *Educational Theatre Journal* 18 (1966): 421–428.

Brokaw, John. "A Mexican-American Acting Company, 1849–1942." *Educational Theatre Journal* 17 (1975): 23–39.

————. "The Repertory of a Mexican-American Theatrical Troupe: 1849–1924." *Latin American Theatre Review* 8 (1974): 25–35.

Bruce-Novoa, Juan. "El Teatro Campesino de Luis Valdez." *Teatro Crítico* 4 (1978): 65–75.

————. and Valentín, David. "Revolutionizing the Popular Image: Essay on Chicano Theatre." *Latin American Literary Review* (1977): 42–50.

Campa, A. L. "Religious Spanish Folk-Drama in New Mexico." *New Mexico Quarterly* 1 (1931): 3–13.

————. *Spanish Religious Folk Theatre of the Southwest*. Albuquerque: University of New Mexico, 1934.

Diamond, Betty. "Brown-Eyed Children of the Sun." *The Cultural Politics of El Teatro Campesino*. Ann Arbor: University Microfilms, 1977.

Drake, Sylvia. "El Teatro Campesino: Keeping the Revolution on Stage." *Performing Arts Magazine* (September 1970): 56–62.

Goldsmith, Barclay. "Brecht and Chicano Theatre," in Joseph Sommers and Tomás Ybarra-Frausto (eds.) *Modern Chicano Writers*. Englewood Cliffs, NJ: Prentice-Hall, Inc., 1979, pp. 167–75.

Harrop, John and Huerta, Jorge A. "The Agitprop Pilgrimmage of Luis Valdez and the Teatro Campesino." *Theatre Quarterly* 5 (1975): 30–39.

Huerta, Jorge A. "Chicano Agit-Prop: The Early Actos of El Teatro Campesino." *Latin American Theatre Review* 11 (1977): 45–58.

————. "El Teatro de la Esperanza: Keeping in Touch With the People." *The Drama Review* 21 (1977): 37–46.

————. *The Evolution of Chicano Theatre*. Unpublished doctoral dissertation, University of California at Santa Barbara, 1974.

Johnson, Winifred. "Early Theatre in the Spanish Borderlands." *Mid-America* 13 (1930): 121–131.

Kanellos, Nicolás (ed.) *Mexican American Theatre: Then and Now*. Houston: Arte Publico Press, 1983.

_____ . "Sexto Festival de los Teatros Chicanos." *Latin American Theatre Review* (Fall 1975): 81.

_____ . *Mexican American Theatre: Legacy and Reality*. Pittsburgh: Latin American Literary Review Press, 1987.

Klein, Maxine. "Theatre of the Ancient Maya." *Educational Theatre Journal* 23 (1971): 269–276.

Kourilski, Francoise. "Approaching Quetzalcoatl: The Evolution of El Teatro Campesino." *Performance* (1973): 37–46.

Lesnick, Henry (ed.) *Guerilla Street Theatre* New York: Avon Books, 1973.

Malpede Taylor, Karen (ed.) *People's Theatre in Amerika*. New York: Drama Book Specialists, 1972.

McCracken, Ellen. "Guadalupe." *Educational Theatre Journal* (1975): 554.

Morton, Carlos. "I am recreating our own reality: A Nuestro Interview with Luis Valdez." *Nuestro* (November 1977): 30–37.

_____ . "The Teatro Campesino." *The Drama Review* 18 (1974): 71–76.

Pottlitzer, Joanne. *Hispanic Theatre in the United States and Puerto Rico*. New York: The Ford Foundation, 1988.

Ramírez, Elizabeth Cantú. "The Annals of Chicano Theatre: 1965–1973." M.A. Thesis, Theatre Arts, University of California, Los Angeles, 1974.

Rosenberg, Joe. "La Compañía de Teatro Bilingüe." *Educational Theatre Journal* 30 (1978): 240–252.

_____ . "Rehearsal Problems in Bilingual Theatre." *Latin American Theatre Review* 11 (1978): 81–90.

Savran, David. "Border Tactics; Luis Valdez Distills the Chicano Experience on Stage and Film." *American Theatre* (January, 1988): 15–21; 56–57.

Shank, Theodore. "A Return to Aztec and Maya Roots." *The Drama Review* 18 (1974): 56–70.

Steiner, Stan and Valdez, Luis (eds.) *Aztlán*. New York: Vintage Books, 1972.

Taylor, Karen Malpede. *People's Theatre in Amerika*. New York: Drama Book Specialists, 1972.

Valdez, Luis. "El Teatro Campesino." *Ramparts* (July 1966): 55–56.

Weisman, John (ed.) *Guerilla Theatre*. Garden City: Anchor Press/Doubleday, 1973.

Yarbo-Bejarano, Yvonne. "From 'acto' to 'mito,' A Critical Appraisal of the Teatro Campesino." In *Modern Chicano Writers*, op. cit., pp. 176–185.

Plays and Anthologies

García, Anthony J. *The Westside Trilogy: Three Actos About Denver*. Denver: Su Teatro, 1982.

Garza, Roberto J. (ed.) *Contemporary Chicano Theatre* Notre Dame: University of Notre Dame Press, 1976.

Girón, Arthur. *Becoming Memories*. New York: Samuel French, 1987.

Huerta, Jorge A. *El Teatro de la Esperanza: An Anthology of Chicano Drama*. Santa Barbara: El Teatro de la Esperanza, 1973.

Kanellos, Nicolás and Jorge Huerta (eds.) *Nuevos Pasos: Chicano and Puerto Rican Drama*. Houston: Arte Publico Press, 1989.

Moraga, Cherrie. *Giving Up the Ghost*. Los Angeles: West End Press, 1986.

Morton, Carlos. "El Cuento de Pancho Diablo." *Grito del Sol* 1 (1976): 39–85.

———. "El Jardín." *El Grito* 7 (1974): 7–37.

———. *The Many Deaths of Danny Rosales and Other Plays*. Houston: Arte Publico Press, 1985.

Osborn, M. Elizabeth. *On New Ground: Contemporary Hispanic American Plays*. New York: Theatre Communications Group, 1987.

Portillo Trambley, Estela. *Sor Juana and Other Plays*. Tempe: Bilingual Review Press, 1985.

Sánchez-Scott, Milcha. *The Cuban Swimmer and Dog Lady*. New York: TCG Plays in Process, 1984; and New York: Dramatists Play Service, 1989.

Valdez, Luis. *Actos*. Houston: Arte Publico Press, 1989.

———. *Bernabé*.In Roberto Garza, *Contemporary Chicano Theatre*. Notre Dame: University of Notre Dame Press, 1976, pp. 30–58; and *West Coast Plays* 19/20 (1986): 21–51.

———. *Dark Root of a Scream*. In Lilian Faderman and Omar Salinas, (ed.) *From the Barrio*. San Francisco: Canfield Press, 1973, pp. 79–98; and *West Coast Plays* 19/20 (1986): 1–20.

———. *Pensamiento Serpentino*. San Juan Bautista, Ca.: Cucaracha Publication, 1973; and in Arte Publico Press's reissue of *Actos*, op. cit.

———. *The Shrunken Head of Pancho Villa*. In *West Coast Plays* 11/12 (1982): 1–61.